Cycling in Europe

Nicholas Crane

The Oxford Illustrated Press

Printed in England by J.H. Haynes & Co Limited

ISBN 0 902280 77 5

Line illustrations by John Gilbert Rankin
The Oxford Illustrated Press, Sparkford, Yeovil, Somerset, BA22 7JJ

CONTENTS

Acknowledgements

For fun and laughter through the backroads of Europe, special thanks to Elaine Russell-Wilks, Mark Hampson, Peter Inglis and Doug Whyte; for the original inspiration I hold responsible my father Hol Crane, who in the late forties cycled across the continent more than once, and for moral support and unquenchable wanderlust I am deeply grateful to my mother Naomi and grandmother Dr Ruth Dingley. Many kind people gave their time, and opinions, and helped to fill in the blanks on my cycling map of Europe, notably Liz and Tony Allott, Fiona and Phil Johnson, Vivienne Drake, Christa Gausden, John Gilchrist, Martin Goodchild, John Haigh, Arne Lindgren, Janet Meurling, Gill Pound, Dr Michael Spencer and Jeanette Walker, while Rob Walker provided the space for this book to get off the ground. Cousins Richard, Adrian and Christopher Crane contributed companionship, spirit and lent a bike in Spain, while Patricia Dawson (McCarta Ltd), Terry Denny (Blackwell's Booksellers), J. Dubois (Institut Géographique National), Lucas Hilgen (Esselte Kartcentrum), F.J.M. de Kok (Koninklijke Nederlandse Toeristenbond) and Margaret Manning (Stanfords International Map Centre) were helpful beyond the normal call of duty.

For Elaine

INTRODUCTION

Bike Magic

A huge leather beret plastered with bird-droppings shaded a pair of twinkling eyes and a stubbly chin. Jacques Courtois was the thinnest Frenchman I had ever seen, and he was shouting at us. We freewheeled, then stopped. Jacques stopped too; the revs of his moped died away and peace was restored to the D11. Friends had told him in L'Ile Jourdain that two foreign cyclists were passing through, and now he was asking if we would like to come back to his farm for lunch.

With uncle, grandmother, Jacques and Mme Courtois, and two daughters around a twelve-foot-long wooden table, proceedings began with three bottles of farm-brewed cider. Then came the aperitif: bowls of cool red wine with sugar and lumps of bread and ice bobbing in it. Wine ran down our cheeks; mouths were wiped on sleeves. We ate straight off the table, with a single dagger-like knife each. From a doorway somewhere in the room's dark recesses Mme Courtois ran a shuttle-service till a long row of irresistible platters and bowls had accumulated. In no particular order omelette, gherkins, vinegared beans, cockles and mussels, ham, crabs, tomatoes, lettuce, bread, cheeses and jam were assaulted, and swilled with an inexhaustible supply of rough red wine. By the time cognac was poured, the table was a gastromonic graveyard, strewn with rejected rinds, pips, crusts, shells and other inedible debris. From politics and the problems of the small French farm the conversation had mellowed into life histories and wine-making techniques.

Late in the afternoon, we stepped out into the bright light, took photos of our hosts, ourselves, the bikes, a cow, our hosts again, promised to send postcards and wobbled off along the farm track towards the D11. Back on tarmac, between the bulging hedgerows of butterflies and blackberries, we pedalled gently southwards with heads full of balmy summer scents, intoxicated with the day – wondrously grateful to the stranger on the moped.

Unexpected opportunities are one of the many joys of bike touring. Nearly anything can happen. Out in the open, moving at speeds closer to walking than driving, you are a lot more receptive to surroundings than a motorist can ever be; *all* your senses can run riot. You can feel the heat on your forehead and rain on your shoulders, feel each pothole and runnel, smell the farms and hear the streams. Touch the grasses as you ride by. You can become part of the landscape, merging harmoniously into its natural momentum. A car by contrast stays outside, an alien object designed and driven to belittle the countryside.

You do not have to be super-fit to enjoy riding a bicycle in Europe: you can have as much fun with a pair of creaky old legs and a shopping bike as you can with quivering quadruceps and a ten-speed. The art is to be adventurous; travel rewards the adventurous spirit. Anything is possible. Talk to people, try strange foods and cycle up tiny mysterious roads; you can never stop discovering. The bike itself is one of your most helpful assets; people are interested in visiting cyclists, and underneath may be flattered that you think it worth all the effort to pedal a pile of metal around *their* neck of the woods. The bike is often an instant conversation starter: 'Where have you come from? How many kilometres a day do you cycle? How many gears do you have? The bike is a great leveller, for people can see you have nothing to hide; you do not fill their street with noise, dust and fumes – you are not intimidating. Every time you jump onto the saddle and head for foreign shores you are making a commitment to the environment; if it all gets too much there will not be a door to slam and radio to turn on in order to escape (though there might be a café just down the road!). Cycling makes one humble and that is the greatest virtue any traveller could wish for.

Which brings us to Europe, and why it should be such a good place for visiting by bicycle. It has a tremendous variety of scenery, on a scale which makes it possible to see and feel changes with every day's cycling. Monotonous scenery is rare. Europe has been called the 'peninsula of peninsulas', for its shores are incredibly devious and total something like 32,000 kilometres. There are mountains and ice caps, near deserts and broad rivers. But the most cycled is that charming unpretentious mix of chequered fields and woods divided by narrow winding backroads, bubbling streams and little villages. It is a cultural treasure chest too, and you do not have to ride far before finding a medieval church or castle; the cities are full of museums and great architectural works.

My choice of countries to include in this book is somewhat arbitrary, the main criterion being that they are what I feel are the most popular 16 options for cycle-touring. It was tempting to include parts of

Eastern Europe, but with Morocco as close to the UK as Bulgaria, how could I have ignored the dramatic touring areas of North Africa too. I had to draw the line somewhere; I hope you enjoy this version of 'Europe' as much as I have done.

Tour Planning

Advance Information

A good variety of general information can be obtained from the national tourist organisations, whose addresses appear at the end of each of the Chapters. These offices can usually supply free (small scale) maps, calendars of events, public transport information and regional tourist literature which describes the accepted 'sights'. Nowadays most national tourist organisations expect you to send them stamps, postal orders or international reply coupons to cover the cost of post and packing. It may also be worth writing in advance to the local or regional tourist offices of the area you plan to visit; these small bureaux are often more in touch with local affairs and amenities, and can send specialised information on particular activities and more detailed accommodation lists than the national tourist offices.

Most public libraries have comprehensive travel sections, though there is usually a run on the most popular books from spring onwards; so do your reading early in the year.

Where To Go

There can be few things more exciting than to travel by whim, plucking from the air some romantic destination and pedalling off with a minimum of fuss. Watching your friends' faces when you tell them you have just decided to go for a cycling holiday in the Lofoten Islands, is a moment worth savouring; there is a pleasure in absurdity. But while the impulsive traveller thrives on the unplanned and unexpected, there are those for whom detailed preparation and an analysis of all the possible destinations are a major part of the fun. This chapter is for the maker of plans.

For most of us there are four main questions to resolve before we can decide where to go!

Terrain If the sight of upward sloping tarmac makes your spirits and energy drop through your bottom bracket then there is not a lot of point in planning a holiday round the Norwegian fjords or Massif Central – you should instead be looking at the flatter areas of Austria, France and Germany, or more traditionally, Denmark, Belgium, Netherlands. On the other hand, if you are one of those lucky people who do not mind hills, or even enjoy them (yes, these people really exist), then Europe is your oyster. No slope can deter you. Of course, if you are not sure how you will cope with hills, you can always mix a flat area with adjacent hillier terrain, giving you the option to try one or the other (or both) once you reach the country: Flanders and the Ardennes (Belgium); Fünen and Zealand (Denmark); the Loire and Massif Central (France) are examples.

Consult the Ride Guide Chart on page 7 and fill in the column on Terrain. This will give you a selection of alternatives from which to choose.

Scenery This is by nature tied in with whether or not you mind hilly roads and what your enthusiasms are; if you like mountain scenery it follows that the roads will go upwards for some of the time! It is also true that the more spectacular the scenery (generally) the less historic and cultural interest there is to hand. In most parts of Europe however it is possible to take in a bit of several types of scenery, say mixing coast with mountains, (Corsica, Northern Spain, Yugoslavia, Greece, Norway) or great river valleys with pleasantly undulating farmland (the Loire or Danube). Forests and hills seem to come together, as do those vast arable farms and the flat areas. Real wilderness areas like the unpopulated expanses of northern Scandinavia, southern Spain and the rugged heights of the many mountain areas have a special beauty of their own, but have infrequent cultural diversions.

Consult the Ride Guide Chart on page 7 and fill in the column on Scenery. Already you will now begin to see your options of where to go changing.

Interests Few travellers will not admit to enjoying the odd castle or cathedral, museum or medieval town; but some areas have more interest than others: central Italy has a wealth of historic towns and religious architecture; Greece has its classical sites; Germany its rustic rural buildings and preserved medieval settlements; Spain its glorious cities and Scandinavia its charming wooden fishing villages. And France has its cafés and bars! Or you may want to combine a biking holiday with some other interest such as hill-walking, bird-watching, canoeing or gastronomy, in which case you have probably already got a good idea of where you want to go.

For those who haven't however, turn to the Ride Guide Chart and fill in the Interest column. Having now filled in these columns you will possibly begin to see a pattern emerging so that those touring areas with just one tick by them are becoming less likely as an option whilst any with three are looking a strong possibility.

Weather There is a theory that you either like hot, sunny weather and so head towards the Mediterranean for cycling holidays, or prefer cooler, temperate weather so stay in England or gravitate towards northern Europe and Scandinavia. How do you get on in hot weather, and does the prospect of rainy days on holiday fill you with loathing?

Europe has enough different climatic areas to suit all tastes, and by working in with the touring seasons (see page 6) you should be able to come to a comfortable compromise. Anyone who dislikes intense heat should avoid Corsica, the Pyrénées, Greece, most of Italy, Portugal and most of Spain and Yugoslavia, whilst those who are prepared to put up with hot spells might like Austria for example, and those who like 'the devil they know' and prefer a British-type climate can choose from a number of countries including Norway, Sweden, Denmark and parts of France.

Turn to the Ride Guide Chart and fill in the column on Weather.

Accessibility The cost of travelling to an area, how long it takes, and how complicated is the journey, may well have a bearing on your decision of where to go. A short cheap journey (such as a Channel ferry crossing) may turn you in favour of France, Belgium and the Netherlands, or the chance of a really low cost charter flight may push you towards one of the package-tourist centres like Corfu, Crete or Portugal. If you want to spend the minimum time travelling out in order to maximise your time spent there, then it is obviously not worth looking at involved ferry/train combinations to places like southern Italy or northern Norway. On the other hand, travelling out to your touring area may be a part of the fun.

Again, turn to the Ride Guide Chart and fill in the last column. You should now have a good idea of which places are totally unsuitable for you (those with zero ticks), those which you may like to consider (3/4 ticks) and those which should be ideal for you (5 ticks).

Having done that you may now wish to add in a number of other factors which can swing the balance towards or away from an area. If you can speak the language or have friends and relations you can call on during the tour, that is a big plus. If you hate flying, that cuts out many possibilities. And what type of bike do you have? If it is a heavy roadster then the Alps would be ambitious. Islands have a lot in their favour because they present a clearly defined area that can be fairly thoroughly explored in a week or two of riding; there is a satisfying sense of completeness in having 'circumpedalled' say Corsica, one of the Danish islands, Crete or Sicily.

Physical epics and outrageous adventures are easier to find in far away mountain ranges than they are among the bungalows of Belgium, while interesting food is more commonly found on the tables of France or Denmark than on those of Lapland. And how does the available accommodation fit in with your proposed area? – if your budget or preference dictates youth-hostelling then central Yugoslavia is out. Finally, by studying the rates of exchange and relative costs of living you may find some options opening; others closing – Sweden is for example a lot more expensive than Portugal.

The Ride Guide Chart

As a little bit of light entertainment which may help get your handlebars turned in roughly the right direction, this chart can be used for picking out the touring areas most suited to your ability and interests.

From each of the five groups of factors listed below, pick the one consideration that is most appropriate to you and mark a tick in the corresponding boxes on the chart. For example, if you want to cycle somewhere with mixed terrain, tick all the empty boxes in column 'b' under the heading Terrain. The crossed-through boxes cannot of course be used. When you have worked through all five groups, add up the number of ticks you have on each line. The line with the highest total corresponds (in theory) with the area most suited to you. (All the areas listed can be found described in the 'Ride Guide' sections of this book.) And if the chart tells you to go to Galicia, when you are really keener on Crete, please do not write in.

	Key	*Terrain*
a	flat	level riding (but may be windy)
b	mixed	a mixture of level and hills; undulating
c	hilly	predominantly hilly; quite exerting
d	mountainous	very long exerting climbs; low gears necessary

		Scenery
e	spectacular scenery	outstanding views; high drama
f	good scenery	very attractive, charming, picturesque
g	passable scenery	pleasant without being especially notable

		Interest
h	high interest	lots of history and culture; other diversions
j	medium interest	you will not get bored
k	low interest	area of low population, maybe a desolate wilderness

		Weather
l	hot summers	the hottest parts of Europe; searing middays
m	warm summers	predictably pleasant; hot spells
n	warm and damp summers	generally pleasant but might rain
o	temperate	no warmer or drier than Britain

		Accessibility
p	easy to reach	a short cheap journey
q	not bad to reach	within reach of a 2 or 3 hour plane flight, or simple ferry journey
r	hard to reach	involves different forms of transport and up to 2 days to reach

	Terrain				Scenery			Interest			Weather				Accessibility			
	flat	mixed	hilly	mountainous	spectacular scenery	good scenery	passable scenery	high interest	medium interest	low interest	hot summers	warm summers	warm and damp summers	temperate summers	easy to reach	fairly easy to reach	hard to reach	Totals
	a	b	c	d	e	f	g	h	i	j	k	l	m	n	o	p	q	r
Austria Vorarlberg & Tyrol	X	X	X			X	X	X			X	X		X	X	X		
High & Low Tauern	X	X	X			X	X	X			X			X	X	X		
Danube & Vienna		X	X	X	X		X			X	X	X		X	X	X		
Salzkammergut	X		X	X		X	X	X			X	X		X	X	X		
Carinthian Lake District	X		X	X	X			X	X			X	X		X	X	X	
Belgium Flanders		X	X	X	X	X		X			X	X	X	X			X	X
Ardennes	X	X			X	X		X	X			X	X	X	X			X
Denmark Jutland		X	X	X	X	X		X			X	X	X	X	X			
Fünen		X	X	X	X		X			X	X	X	X	X		X		
Zealand	X		X	X	X		X			X	X	X	X	X		X		
Bornholm	X	X			X	X		X			X	X	X	X		X	X	
Finland Eastern Lakes		X	X	X	X	X			X	X		X	X	X		X	X	
Lapland	X		X	X	X		X	X	X			X	X	X		X	X	
France Lower Normandy	X		X	X	X		X			X	X	X	X	X			X	X
Brittany	X	X			X	X		X	X			X	X	X	X			X
Loire Valley		X	X	X	X	X			X	X	X	X	X			X	X	
Massif Central	X	X			X	X		X	X			X	X	X		X	X	
Vosges	X	X			X	X		X	X			X	X	X		X	X	
Alps & Provence	X	X	X			X	X	X			X	X		X	X	X		
Corsica	X	X	X			X	X	X	X			X	X	X		X	X	
Pyrénées	X	X	X			X	X	X	X			X	X	X		X	X	
Germany Schleswig Holstein		X	X	X	X	X		X			X	X	X	X		X		
Central Uplands	X		X	X	X		X			X	X	X	X		X	X		
Eifel & Hunsrück	X	X			X	X		X	X			X	X	X		X	X	
Eastern Forests	X	X			X	X		X	X			X	X		X	X	X	X
Schwäbische Alb	X	X			X	X		X		X	X		X	X	X	X		X
Romantic Road	X		X	X	X		X			X	X	X		X	X	X		X
Black Forest	X	X			X	X		X	X			X	X		X	X	X	X
Bavarian Alps	X	X	X			X	X	X			X	X		X	X	X		X
Greece Peloponnese	X	X	X			X	X		X	X		X	X	X	X	X		
Epirus & Pindus	X	X			X	X		X	X		X	X	X	X	X	X		
Aegean Islands	X	X		X		X	X	X			X	X	X	X	X	X		
Crete	X	X	X			X	X		X	X		X	X	X	X			X
Italy Dolomites	X	X	X			X	X	X	X	X		X		X	X	X		X
Italian Lakes	X	X		X		X	X	X		X	X		X	X	X			X
Central Italy	X	X		X	X		X		X	X		X	X	X	X			X
Abruzzi	X	X	X			X	X	X	X	X		X	X	X	X	X		
Southern Italy	X	X		X	X		X	X		X	X	X	X	X	X			
Sicily	X	X	X			X	X	X		X	X	X	X	X				
Sardinia	X	X	X		X		X	X	X		X	X	X	X				
Luxembourg The Oesling	X		X	X	X		X	X			X	X	X		X	X		X
Bon Pays & Little Switzerland	X	X		X	X		X	X			X	X	X		X	X		X
Netherlands North & South Holland		X	X	X	X	X		X	X	X	X	X				X	X	
Veluwe		X	X	X	X	X		X		X	X	X	X		X			X
Zeeland, North Brabant & Limburg	X	X	X	X	X		X		X	X	X	X			X	X		
Friesland, Groningen & Drenthe	X	X	X	X	X		X		X	X	X	X		X			X	
Norway Sörlandet & Telemark	X	X		X	X		X	X	X		X	X	X		X			X
Western Fjords	X	X	X			X	X	X	X		X	X	X			X	X	
Northern Norway	X	X		X		X	X	X	X		X	X	X		X	X		
Portugal The North	X	X		X	X	X		X	X		X	X	X	X				X
Estremadura	X	X		X	X	X		X	X		X	X	X	X				X
Algarve	X		X	X	X	X		X	X		X	X	X	X				X
Spain Cantabria & Galicia	X	X			X	X	X	X		X	X	X	X					X
Castile & Central Sierras	X	X		X	X		X	X		X	X	X	X	X				X
Andalusia	X	X		X		X	X		X	X	X	X	X	X				X
Balearic Islands	X	X		X	X		X	X		X	X	X	X	X				X

	Terrain				Scenery			Interest			Weather					Accessibility			
	flat	mixed	hilly	mountainous	spectacular scenery	good scenery	passable scenery	high interest	medium interest	low interest	hot summers	warm summers	warm summers	warm and damp summers	temperate summers	easy to reach	fairly easy to reach	hard to reach	Totals
	a	**b**	**c**	**d**	**e**	**f**	**g**	**h**	**j**	**k**	**l**	**m**	**n**	**o**	**p**	**q**	**r**		
Sweden Bohuslän Coast	X		X	X			X	X		X	X	X	X		X		X		
The South	X		X	X	X		X		X	X	X	X		X		X			
The Large Lakes	X		X	X			X	X		X	X	X	X		X		X		
Värmland & Dalarna	X	X		X	X		X	X	X		X	X	X		X	X			
Jämtland	X	X		X	X		X	X	X		X	X	X		X	X			
Lapland	X	X		X	X		X	X	X		X	X	X		X	X			
Switzerland The Jura	X	X	X			X	X	X	X		X		X	X	X		X		
Mittelland	X		X	X	X		X	X		X	X		X	X	X		X		
Swiss Alps	X	X	X			X	X	X	X		X		X	X	X		X		
Yugoslavia Alpine Yugoslavia	X	X	X			X	X	X		X	X		X	X	X		X		
Istrian Peninsula	X		X	X	X		X	X		X		X	X	X	X		X		
Dalmatian Coast	X		X		X		X	X		X		X	X	X	X		X		
Montenegro	X	X	X			X	X	X		X		X	X	X	X		X		

When To Go

There are three tourist seasons: high season from mid May to mid-September; off-season from December to mid-March and the 'shoulder seasons' which occupy the intervening months. Prices tend to be lower in the off-season, when there are discounts at accommodation, cheap charter flights are available, and the cross-Channel fares are lower too. But probably the most significant factor governing when to go is the weather; a factor which can make or break a holiday. In the previous chapter we looked at the weather in different countries; here we consider how it varies at different times of year. Look carefully at the Average Daily Maximum Temperature charts given in each chapter, and compare these figures with those for your own country (the figures for Kew, London, are provided below to serve as a ready comparison). In professional travel circles it is widely agreed that 27°C is the ideal air temperature; a kind of Mediterranean-in-June paradise. Be wary of temperature and rainfall figures in tourist literature, as these are usually slanted to make the country look as appealing as possible.

Other factors which vary through the year are the sea temperatures, which may be important if you are planning a seaside/swimming holiday (the sea lags about $1\frac{1}{2}$ months behind the land in warming and cooling), and the dates of local and national festivals which you may want to tie in with.

Average Daily Maximum Temperatures (Centigrade)

	alt. in metres	J	F	M	A	M	J	J	A	S	O	N	D
Kew	(5)	6	7	10	13	17	20	22	21	18	14	10	7

The Biking Seasons

November – February The closed season for cycling holidays, though along the very southern fringes of Europe the weather may be kind enough for quick forays. The least cool places are southern Portugal, (and the southern Spanish coast), southern Sardinia, Sicily, the Balearics and the toe and heel of Italy. Overall it is cold and wet, with snow on high ground in the south, and down to sea level in the north.

March – April A chancy option, sandwiched between winter and spring, with the possibilities of both types of weather. Snow can still fall and temperatures can plummet, particularly at night. But a Mediterranean tour is possible, especially towards the end of April.

May – June Spring, a time when cyclists and the countryside are at last encouraged into action by the warming weather. For many, these two months are the best of the year, with foliage fresh and green and the landscape (and roads) as yet untrammelled by the hordes soon to follow. In most countries June is a good bit warmer than May. Scandinavia will be cool with snow still lying (though May and June are Norway's driest months), but the Mediterranean will be bursting with light and life. Check to see when and where the blossoms can be enjoyed. May is also a month when low-cost charter flights are available.

July - August Everywhere in Europe this is the warmest (or hottest) season for touring, temperatures normally being roughly the same in both months. The hottest places are southern and central Spain, Italy south of Rome, south-west Yugoslavia and Greece. The coolest areas are the high lands of central Europe such as the Alps and Pyrénées, and Norway – which is also the most damp. For the benefit of the extra warmth, this is probably the best time to tour Scandinavia. July and August are also the months when Europeans take their annual holiday, so main roads will be at their busiest and least pleasant.

September - October If you could not make the spring then this is the time of year to get out and enjoy the autumn tints of Europe's forests and woods. The first two weeks in September are frequently as hot as August (though it has been known to snow in Switzerland at this time) and overall September is a little warmer than May in all countries except Scandinavia where the two months have similar temperatures. By October temperatures have dropped sharply, though in places October is slightly warmer than April, except in Scandinavia, Austria and Switzerland, where the temperatures are about the same. October is the wettest month of the year in France, Italy, Spain and Switzerland.

How To Get There

Plane A quick and impressively easy method of reaching your chosen touring area with a bike. Nearly all airlines will carry your bicycle free provided it does not raise your total baggage allowance above the permitted 20kg, or provided it is one of the two pieces of baggage allowed. You pay excess baggage for every kg over the 20kg you exceed (a typical lightweight unloaded touring bike weighs 13kg). Tandems and tricycles can also be carried, though you should always ask the agent or airline in advance if there are any special conditions of carriage that have to be fulfilled. Flying a bike can be made easy by following these points:

1. Before buying your ticket always find out from the travel agent *and* the airline or charter-flight operator what conditions apply to the carriage of bicycles on their flights. Get their response in writing, so that you have an extra insurance should you come up against an obstructive check-in clerk (though I have never had any difficulty here).

2. It is often possible to have your bike transported exactly as it is, with no dismantling or adjusting, though it is a wise precaution to remove the pedals so that they do not damage other luggage or the baggage handlers' shins; always cultivate a sympathy with officials charged with handling your bike. Some transatlantic airlines provide protective boxes for bikes (which can be used for stowing other parts of your luggage too) or huge bags (which protect other luggage more than they protect the bike). You may be asked to turn the handlebars through 90°. If you are told to remove the wheels this should be politely resisted as it leaves delicate parts of the machine vulnerable to damage. It also makes it harder for the baggage handlers to move your machine about. Some airlines may ask you to deflate the tyres, though this is strictly speaking unnecessary as aircraft holds are pressurised nowadays. If you do deflate them, leave enough air for the bike to be wheeled without running on the rims.

3. To keep on the right side of everyone clean your bike up before you fly and do not smother the chain in fresh oil till after the flight! Protect your paintwork by taping strips of cardboard to the frame, and make sure all the removable accessories such as pumps, lights and water bottles are not left on the bike. If it looks as if you are going to exceed the baggage allowance, put compact heavy items such as tool kits, spares and food in your hand luggage, and if desperate wear all your clothes at once! Cameras should not be placed on the floors of aircraft cabins as the high-frequency vibrations can shake loose the tiny parts.

4. Always check-in with plenty of time in hand, just in case there is an unexpected hitch with the bike. Once the bike has been labelled at the check-in desk, a baggage handler will normally be called to wheel it away; wait till he or she arrives before leaving your bike. At your destination keep an eye open for your bike arriving other than on the baggage reclaim; normally someone wheels it separately into the hall.

5. If you have to change planes during your journey, find out in

advance whether as a 'passenger in transit' you have to reclaim then re-check-in your bike (and any other luggage) at the stopover airport. Not realising this I once 'lost' my bike at Zagreb.

6. If the bike is damaged in transit, the airline should normally accept liability (find out about this during your preliminary enquiry). Make your claim for compensation before you leave the airport; it may be that the eventual compensation will not be equivalent to the cost of repairing the damage, so it is a wise precaution to cover the bike beforehand on a general or travel insurance policy.

7. Many airports are delightfully easy to escape from on a bike; you simply pedal out of the exit and on to local roads – especially if, as is often the case, the airport is well clear of the city it serves. But at the vast international airports you may have to find a special cycle-track which feeds you clear of the complex. At Heathrow a cycle-path runs between the terminals and the Newport Road roundabout (on Newport Road which is just off the A4 halfway along the northern side of the airport). At New York's John F. Kennedy airport a cycle-path follows the Van Wyck Expressway out northwards to 134th Street in the South Ozone Park district. At Lisbon and Los Angeles you pedal straight out into a maelstrom of city traffic; at Arlanda (Stockholm) and Dubrovnik (Yugoslavia) the countryside starts beyond the airport gates.

8. If you have made a really long flight take the first day easy because cycling and jet lag are not comfortable companions. Budget accommodation can be exceedingly difficult to find around airports, so check what time of day your flight arrives; if it is late it may be worth booking accommodation in advance, or resting at the airport till morning.

Train 'France is for the traveller a civilised country as compared with England. Here we have to fight for our luggage on the platform at a journey's end; there we hand up a ticket to the hotel-porter and it appears. Here we have to pay exorbitant charges for the carriage of a bicycle; there it costs only a penny (for registration) from one end of France to the other, and the machine is neither lost nor damaged.'

Percy Dearmer, *Highways and Byways in Normandy*, 1901

Well, since the days when Percy sallied forth from Victorian England to pedal the continent the costs of long distance bicycle transportation have changed a little – as has the co-operation of the railway officials. But even so, Europe has the most dense railway network in the world and once you know a few ground rules it can still be an ideal way of moving yourself and bike across the continent. After all the bicycle and the train do have two things in common: both are energy efficient and neither are socially destructive. The only snag is, that with a couple of exceptions, most national railway companies do very little to provide information on carriage of bikes on trains and furthermore the rules and costs of transportation seem to be changed all too frequently; the situation as it stands in 1983 is described in each of the country chapters of this book, *but please double check* by asking at your station of departure for the latest rules – and even better contact the appropriate railway authority before leaving home. Paradoxically it is the richest countries with the most sophisticated rail systems which seem least co-operative regarding bikes.

Whether you are accompanying your bike on a train, or sending it unaccompanied as freight, there are a number of elementary precautions you can take which will reduce the chances of the two of you finishing up at different ends of Europe.

1. Make sure your name and address are clearly and immovably fixed to your bike; taped, tied or painted to a frame tube.

2. Remove all luggage and detachable items such as pump, lights, water-bottles.

3. Make sure your bike is labelled with its destination; in some countries (such as France and Portugal) you have to register the bike as luggage before getting on the train, in which case a station official will label the bike's destination for you. If you suffer from train neurosis as I do, surreptitiously check their luggage label is securely fixed to the bike; if it drops off, the bike may end its days rusting in a Budapest railway siding.

4. On internal journeys where you will be accompanying the bike, arrive at the railway station at least 20 minutes before the train is due to depart; see specific chapters later in this book for further details. Ask before buying your ticket whether it is possible to make the journey on the same train as your bike.

5. If the bike is travelling as accompanied luggage ask whether a station official will load the bike or whether you do it yourself. If the latter (which is preferable), then ask where on the platform the luggage waggon will stop so that you can wait at the appropriate spot and avoid a 100-metre sprint when the train arrives.

6. It is good for public relations not to delay the train while loading your bicycle; note that some European trains (for example some of the Dutch and Norwegian ones) have doors which are operated electrically by push-buttons from the outside.

7. On journeys where you are accompanying the bike, and which involve changes of train, it is often quicker and safer to register the bike to the change station and effect the transfers yourself. If it is left to the railway staff the bike may get delayed at a change and follow on a later (inconvenient) train. For example, on train journeys via Paris, it is better to register to the station of arrival, reclaim the bike, ride across the city and re-register it to your final destination.

8. On journeys which cross borders and on long internal ones, which involve changes of train, the bike may travel in a different train to yourself, and depending on the length of journey and number of changes, may arrive several days after you. If you want it to arrive at the same time, take it to the station say three days in advance and send it as unaccompanied luggage. Railway staff will handle the bike for the entire journey. Always tie all unaccompanied luggage into one bundle to avoid individual pieces getting separated or lost in transit.

9. If your bike is to travel unaccompanied, on a freight train, find out precisely which train it will travel on, and when it is due at its destination.

10. Each country has a different system of charges for bicycles (just occasionally they travel free); some charge according to distance, others a flat rate. If the latter, remember that you will be paying over the odds if your journey is a short one.

11. Bikes being sent from one country to another can normally only be registered from stations which have customs facilities – usually those in larger towns. Some of these customs offices are closed on Sundays.

12. If you are lucky enough to be able to load the bicycle into the luggage waggon yourself, put it out of the way and if possible fix it to the wall of the waggon so it cannot topple over during the journey. Elastic straps are good for this – but do not use your lock and chain because the guard may need to move it en route.

13. Neurotics can sit in the carriage adjacent to the luggage waggon, to check the bike does not get unloaded at the wrong station by mistake.

14. If, by cruel chance, you arrive at your destination but your bike does not, demand to see the highest authority and do not budge until genuine steps are taken to recover your machine. Most stations can telex other stations along the line and ask them to look for missing luggage. Finally, there is always a chance your bike might get mangled, so if you are planning train journeys, take out insurance cover before leaving home.

Lest this collection of cautions frightens you from going anywhere near a foreign railway station, let me add that of the many journeys I have made in such diverse countries as Norway, Portugal and Greece, I have never had my machine lost, stolen, damaged or sent to Budapest. But I have heard some dreadful tales ...

The only way around the cost and palaver of registration and documentation is to take your bicycle in the carriage as hand-luggage. You can only get away with this if you are on a small folding bike which will collapse into an inconspicuous package, or if you have a bike-transporter-bag into which you can fit a dismantled full-size bike. These bags are about the same dimensions as a very large suitcase; their main disadvantage is that you are lumbered with a big bag once you start cycling. But it could be deposited in a left-luggage store, or you could mail it on *Poste Restante* to a post office near your eventual destination. Note that the left-luggage stores at railway stations can be convenient for dumping panniers and so on, allowing you to explore a city or town on an unladen bike.

Ferry If trains are the most complicated way of transporting a bike, then a ferry is the easiest; you simply ride the bike straight on, having bought a ticket for the bike at the same time as purchasing your passenger one. On smaller local ferries – across rivers for example – bikes sometimes travel free; on most passages across seas there is a modest charge. The bicycle fares on Channel crossings vary according to season, and on some lines bikes go free. On sea crossings, always secure your bike to a handy stanchion to prevent it falling over; if one of the staff offers to lash your delicate double-butted 531 tubed bike with hefty nylon hauser, politely decline his assistance and use an elastic strap which will be less likely to buckle the bike in two.

Bus Although I once travelled across Europe from London to Athens on a bus with two companions and three bikes it is not an experience I would care to repeat; the bikes had to be fully boxed before departure, and at every break of journey (ferries and changes of vehicle) we had to actively prevent the drivers from abandoning them. Long-distance buses are however cheap, though it is imperative to clear with the operator in advance that it is acceptable to take bicycles as part of your luggage; again, get their response in writing so that you can wave it at disgruntled drivers and handlers in times of difficulty.

Motor car Continental bike enthusiasts often put their bikes on their car roofs to combine the two sorts of holiday. The best method of carrying them is a purpose-built bike rack. These are designed for the bike to be carried upside down, or the right way up but with the front wheel removed. Always bind the bike and wheels to the roof-rack with extra toe-straps or rope in case any fittings work loose. If you leave the car unattended, lock the bikes to the rack – and remember, if you drive into a garage or onto a car deck on a ferry, that you are one metre higher than usual!

In some countries there are regulations concerning the carriage of bikes on cars. In the Netherlands, for example, the bike must not protrude more than 20 centimetres on either side of the car, and the distance between the hindmost part of the bike and the rear axle must not exceed two-thirds of the wheel base and must never be more than 5 metres. Number plates and lights should not be obscured.

Still Draws The Night: Accommodation

It does seem that the more you spend on accommodation, the less interesting it becomes; at one end of the range you have a free night beneath the stars with the thrilling orchestrations of night noises and dawn chorus and at the other extreme you have the sterile sound-proofed, air-conditioned, all mod-cons five-star hotel. And in between these two are a whole variety of possibilities. What type of accommodation you choose is fundamental to planning a bike tour; it affects your route, and it affects how much luggage you have to carry. If you are camping, then your panniers have to carry in addition to their normal load, a tent, sleeping bag and cooking gear – in themselves relatively bulky and heavy. If you plan on 'indoor' accommodation such as hotels, guest houses or youth hostels, you can very often fit all your luggage into a single bag. Below, in order of cost, is a brief review of the options.

Hotels and Pensions For the rich biker hotels offer a wide variety of prices and facilities, with a standardised star-grading system being introduced throughout Europe. Pensions are somewhat cheaper and more friendly. It is best to look at the rooms available before parting company with any money, and make sure you have been told the complete costs (including local taxes and so on) before you agree to take the room. During the high season it is risky to rely on finding un-booked accommodation, particularly in prime holiday places like Switzerland. Local tourist offices are usually able to help with finding rooms, and there is often a room-finding service at the main railway station; here you may be offered places to stay by 'accommodation touts', but be wary of accepting late at night. The national tourist offices (see 'Information Sources' sections for addresses) usually publish abbreviated hotel and pension listings and supply them free.

Hotel proprietors have mixed reactions to storing bicycles; normally I have found them to be only too helpful in finding a safe overnight parking place, sometimes under cover – though in Athens I was threatened with eviction for daring to suggest my bicycle could come inside.

Rooms in Private Houses can be rented on a nightly basis in most countries. Very often these are good value for money, being cheaper than hotels and pensions, and characterised by a family atmosphere and good food. Breakfast is usually included in the price, and there is sometimes an optional evening meal. It is a fun way of meeting local people in their own houses, but, with no standardised facilities, it can be a hit and miss arrangement.

The addresses of these establishments can often be found at the local tourist office, or you can simply spot them by the roadside – usually advertised by a small sign in a front window, or by the verge. Unless you have found a published list of rooms for rent, it is not possible to book in advance, so they are mainly useful for the rider who does not mind looking for accommodation 'on the night', or for the camper wanting to sleep indoors for a change.

Youth Hostels Among cyclists these have probably proved to be the most favoured of the 'indoor' types of accommodation: low-cost, friendly and communal, with an outdoor travelling ethic that also finds sympathies with backpackers, hitch-hikers and other budget travellers. Unfortunately the latter category nowadays includes motorists looking for a cheap deal, and during high season it is not unlikely that you will get turned away from the more accessible hostels unless you have booked. If you are basing your tour solely on hostels and are visiting in July or August (or staying in major cities at any time of year) then you should book in advance – see the *International Handbook* for details. Three months is usually sufficient time for advance booking.

Hostels vary from country to country, but all have simple facilities, with men and women accommodated in separate 4 - 20 person dormitories, usually in bunk-beds which can range from deliciously comfortable Scandinavian-style beds to a lumpy palliasse sagging from one of those rickety assemblies of cast-iron tubes that threaten to collapse if the sleeper on the upper deck turns over too fast. Toilet and washing facilities are usually clean and basic, and there is often a members' kitchen where you can cook your own food over the stoves provided; utensils, but not always cutlery, are supplied. At many hostels the wardens can supply cooked meals at low cost. There is always a 'common room' where you can mix and meet with other hostellers, and hostels can be cheery social places where it is easy to find companionship; a friendship struck up over spaghetti bolognese in the members' kitchen can lead to a riding partner for the next leg of your journey.

There is generally no age limit for hostelling, though in Bavaria (Germany) there is a maximum age of 27. In some countries, family rooms are available. In return for the low costs you are expected to keep to hostel rules, which include being in by a certain hour, and sometimes helping with simple tasks such as washing up and sweeping. You make your own beds and must use sheet sleeping bags of the regulation design (bring your own, or hire one).

If you plan to use hostels exclusively then your route has to fit their locations rather than fit particular bits of scenery or towns you might have wanted to visit, so hostels can restrict your tour. In some areas they are close enough to each other to reach every night; in other parts you would have to supplement them with other forms of accommodation. If you are camping, then a youth-hostel card in your pocket gives you the option of the odd night in civilised surroundings!

Each country has its own youth hostels association. By international agreement the youth-hostel card of your own country (in Britain it is the YHA) is accepted in youth hostels of other countries, and you do not have to become a member of their association. When hostelling outside your own country, your membership card must bear your photograph. If you left home without a hostel card, you can buy a guest card from the association of the country you are visiting, or at one of its major hostels. In the UK, youth-hostel membership cards can be bought from the YHA Head Office, Trevelyan House, St. Albans, Herts, and also from the YHA Adventure Shops.

Together with a membership card you need a hostel handbook. The *International Youth Hostel Handbook Volume 1* (from YHA shops) lists and details in English every internationally-approved hostel in Europe; alternatively you can buy the more detailed national hostel handbook for the country you are visitng − normally they have explanations in English, and they sometimes list 'alternative hostels' not listed in the international handbook; addresses of where these national handbooks can be bought are listed in the IYH handbook, or obtainable from the YHA National Office and IYHF (see Appendices).

Camping In 1610 that ardent cycle-camper William Shakespeare wrote: 'Weariness / Can snore upon the flint when resty sloth / Finds the down pillow hard'; that lovely dreamy inertia which comes at the end of a day's pedalling does much to smooth the lumps of a French field! Sleeping out comes much easier than you could imagine in the comfort of your home; sleeping outside, the night breezes, the rustles and calls of tiny animals, dawn chorus and sounds of people up and about before the dew has dried, are a languorous lullaby. To spend your day cycling in the open country is a statement of affection, but that complete intimacy only comes when you sleep on its earth. If you have to go indoors, to a bed in a building following a glorious spell outdoors, it is rather like walking out of a terrific film before it has finished. On the other hand of course, if it is raining, windy and freezing then I'll admit that buildings do have their uses!

Camping offers you more freedom and flexibility than any other type of accommodation. You are free to choose where to put your bedroom and which direction it faces: point the entrance eastwards and you get the early morning sun, point the entrance towards the best view and you can enjoy the scenery from the cocoon of your sleeping bag.

Camping also gives you the freedom to cook and eat what and when you like; either making the meals yourself on a small camping stove, or leaving the tent for the evening and sampling the local fare. It allows unique flexibility of tour planning. You are not tied to whichever town or village has the next hostel or pension, and can design your cycling route solely around the places you actually want to visit. You are self-sufficient and self-contained, with your home on the bike; reliant on nobody. Camping is also the cheapest type of accommodation.

The only disadvantage of camping is that the equipment needed, can increase in a dramatic way, the load you have to carry. Tent-camping works better with two or more cyclists because you can split the weight of the tent etc between you; you can also share the effort of erecting the tent, cooking and so on. The quality (and thus weight and bulk) if your camping equipment can be a big factor in your enjoyment and comfort.

You can either camp on official sites, or camp 'wild'. Camp sites are found all over Europe, with concentrations in the tourist areas. The bigger more expensive sites often have amenities like hot showers, clothes-washing facilities, small shops and some even have cafeterias. At the other end of the scale there are the sites which are little more than a farmer's field with a toilet block at one end. Some youth hostels have their own camp-sites adjacent to the building, and these can be a good compromise since you are allowed to use the hostel members' kitchen and washrooms. Camp-sites in the cities are usually big and noisy and security is more of a problem.

Proof of identity is normally required, and many site managers ask for your passport as a deposit; resist this at all costs (it may get stolen whilst out of your possession). Offer instead, an International Camping Carnet which most sites will accept in lieu of a passport. The carnet also acts as a membership card to several European camping associations, allowing you to use their sites; it also gains you price reductions at some sites and covers you for third party insurance. At a limited number of sites – in the French national forests, in Denmark and Portugal – you will not be allowed to stay without a carnet. Application forms (and the carnets themselves) can be obtained from the Cyclists' Touring Club (supplied to members of the CTC only) and from the Camping Club of Great Britain (11 Lower Grosvenor Place, London SW1). Also worth obtaining in advance is a list of camp sites for the country you are visiting. The national tourist offices normally supply free an abbreviated listing and there are several commercially produced guides available from most large UK book shops. Once on tour you can pick up the local lists from local tourist offices; these often include the smaller (less expensive, often quieter and more fun) sites which the national guides have not discovered. It is very unlikely that you will ever be turned away from a camp-site, and even if you are told it is full, be persuasive and point out an unused corner 'just the right size for your tiny tent'.

Camping 'wild' away from designated sites, on rough open land or unused farmland, mountainsides and forests can be great fun. It requires a fair degree of prudence and discretion, with a knack for spotting possible places to sleep. It costs nothing, and can provide vivid experiences, giving you the chance to camp in spectacular locations, and in secluded corners. In most countries 'wild' camping is officially frowned upon, but in over 300 nights of camping *au sauvage* I have not once been turned off a piece of land nor (to my knowledge) offended any locals. Always try and obtain permission from the landowner before putting up a tent. Picking a good site is something of an art form. You have to start looking, say, an hour before you want to stop, keeping your eyes peeled as you ride for a likely looking field or wood, or friendly looking farmhouse. Un-made tracks (if no gate) very often lead to ideal sites. Never sleep in a planted field. Woods are good because they are sheltered and drier if it rains, but they can be eerie; hill-tops and cols are blowy and exposed; beaches are comfortable but very visible. You will find that the main pre-occupation of farmers concerning itinerant campers is the risk of fire (especially in hot, dry or forested countries like Greece or Norway), so be cautious with stoves and very wary of lighting open fires. Pick a spot away from anything burnable, and find some rocks or bricks on which to balance the pots (make sure they balance safely before filling them up). Dead wood still on the tree is usually drier than that on the ground. Paper and dry kindling will get the fire started and strong blowing – cyclists' lungs are especially good at this – will spark any dull fire into life. Afterwards return the rocks to where you found them, blackened side down, and douse and scuff the cinders. Never leave any hot embers which might later be caught by the wind and start a fire. If you are wild camping you do not have washrooms and water-taps to hand, so you need to have the capacity for carrying extra water; it is not difficult to get through a couple of litres per person between evening and morning. Stream water can sometimes be used but always needs boiling or purifying, or you may be near a farm which can supply your needs. If you are planning on much wild camping, take several water bottles or one of those plastic collapsible water containers. Whilst wild camping can be a marvellous way of spending the night, let me cover myself by adding that it is the least 'safe' of all the options, yourself and possessions being less secure than at an official camp-site. Be careful where you stop!

Planning The Route

Once you know which country you are going to and when, and have decided what type of accommodation to use, you can plan the actual cycling route. Whether you start pedalling with just a vague notion of where you are going, or whether you begin the tour with a detailed daily itinerary is up to you; some like to know exactly where they will be two days hence; others prefer the unpredictability that comes with making up the route as you go along. The route you end up taking is usually governed by availability of accommodation, how many kilometres a day you feel like cycling, what points of interest you want to visit along the way, and whether you intend a circular, 'linear' or fixed-centre tour. Elsewhere in the book you will find a tour suggested for each country; each tour is of course just one of many possibilities and is only intended as a helpful suggestion.

If you have chosen to stay in youth-hostels, or in selected camp-sites or hotels, then route-planning is rather like one of those childrens' 'joining-up-the-dots' pictures: your overnight stops are fixed and you simply have to make a route between them. If you are using un-booked accommodation then your route has to take account of the possibility that the first town or village you try might not provide rooms for the night – so plan to end the day at a place which looks as if it offers several alternative accommodation possibilities. Cycle-campers have the greatest route-planning freedom, because even if a camp-site does not materialise it is nearly always possible to find somewhere to put up a tent.

It helps with route-planning if you know in advance how far you enjoy pedalling in one day; if unsure, take a loaded bike out for a weekend ride from home. The golden rule is to plan daily distances a little less than you know you can *comfortably* achieve. This leaves a margin of time for the unexpected: friendly locals, punctures, alluring cafés, headwinds and so on. It is always the last 5 kilometres that are the hardest! (It sometimes helps to divide the day's ride up into a series of 'targets': a café in Nogent-le-Roi for elevenses, lunch by the château at Maintenon, mid-afternoon at the viewpoint in Rambouillet Forest. An easy way of avoiding over-committing yourself is to design a daily route which zig-zags rather than goes in a straight line – this gives you the opportunity of cutting off some of the corners if you look like running out of time and energy later in the day. As a very rough guide you can expect the following maximum daily distances:

non-athletic novice	15-30 kilometres
quite fit, but want to dawdle	50-60 kilometres
very fit; keen on covering distance	100-120 kilometres
supremely fit; pedalling all day	160-180 kilometres

Bear in mind that in southern Europe during high summer you have to fit your daily cycling around the intense midday heat. The hottest time is usually between 12 noon and 3pm (extended an hour at each end in the far south) and it is wise to do as the locals by taking a long *siesta*. In hot countries the most pleasant times for cycling are the early morning and evening.

Something else that can affect daily distances is the road surface; rough ground can halve your speed, and it is one of life's grossest ironies that descending a roughly-surfaced hill can be no quicker or easier than riding up it.

Prevailing winds in Europe are seldom predictable enough to be taken into account at the route-planning stage. The European landscape is so varied and rolling that with a couple of exceptions such as the *mistral* and Atlantic westerlies, the 2 metres of air closest to the ground cannot be reckoned to move in any one pre-determined direction. So you just have to hope that luck is with you! With ingenuity you can however make use of local winds; in coastal areas the different rates at which the sea and land warm and cool relative to each other can cause strong afternoon winds.

Fitting the route in with various points of interest is great fun; selecting your choice of small towns and villages, viewpoints, castles and museums, and rooting out the places most tourists do not visit is like picking up the clues on a treasure trail. Information on the whereabouts of 'sights' can be gleaned from tourist information and guide books; to get the most from a country it is well worth reading up on the area you intend to visit before making a detailed route. Most countries have nation-wide networks of local tourist information bureaux, and these are useful for adapting routes once the tour has started.

The overall 'shape' of your tour can take several forms. Circular tours, where you start and finish at the same place (say the airport, town or port which you arrived at from home) have the advantage that you get to know one particular area fairly well. On a 'linear' tour you start and finish at different places, for example cycling down through France to Santander in northern Spain, returning to the UK on the ferry to Plymouth. Linear tours can sometimes be trickier to arrange because you have to buy single tickets at each end. Another alternative is the 'fixed-centre' tour, where you base yourself at a town, camp-site, *gîte de France* or whatever, making day-rides without the encumbrance of lots of luggage. These are good if you want to explore an area in detail or if you are unsure about your ability to keep going day after day along a pre-planned itinerary. With a fixed centre you always have the option of ignoring the bike for a day or two. A variant of this is to plan a circular or linear tour, but aim to pause now and again, taking two or three days in one place for some fixed-centre riding. A final consideration is whether you might like to mix the cycling with some other activity. Biking through the Cévennes you could take some days off for hiring canoes and paddling down the Ardèche; or in northern Spain, swap the bike for some boots and go hiking in the Picos de Europa. There are myriads of possibilities: walking along way-marked paths, pony-trekking, sailing, bird-watching can all be fitted in with bike touring.

Maps The key to route-planning! As a teenager devoted to learning by mistakes I spent half my time doing things the wrong way, so when I set off for my first foreign biking trip I had only a very small-scale map of France which showed the country to have a total of about twelve roads. Neither did it help that the tour actually started in Holland. Saving money by not buying the best maps is a false economy.

While you are still at home, it can be useful to study a fairly small-scale map (say 1:1,000,000 or 1:500,000) of the country you are visiting. Such 'general planning maps' are handy for providing an overview of that corner of Europe, and the better ones have hill-shading which identifies the areas of harder biking! They can also be useful for planning train journeys, and some have sufficient detail for cyclists who may want to cross a country quickly using medium-size roads. Note that many national tourist offices supply free small-scale maps.

Maps for cycling are generally on scales of 1:250,000, 1:200,000 or 1:100,000. In places like Scandinavia, where there are relatively few choices of road, a scale as small as 1:400,000 is suitable, while riders wanting to do detailed local exploring will find the large scale 1:50,000 maps ideal. These large scales generally show all minor roads (and some of the bigger tracks too), with helpful details about hills. These will be marked with height-shading or contours, or (less satisfactorily) occasional spot-heights. Some of the better maps also have gradient 'arrows' on the steepest roads, and have a wealth of additional information such as tourist features, scenic roads outlined in green (note that such maps omit thousands of kilometres of unidentified scenic roads), antiquities, ferry details and so on. In short, there is enough on these large scale maps to get right off the beaten track – and to find your way back on to it again!

For rough-stuff cycling it is safest to use the scale of maps normally used by walkers. These are commonly 1:50,000, sometimes 1:25,000, and mark all tracks, with contours indicating gradients as well as showing details like individual buildings and small streams. In some countries the high quality of their 1:50,000 maps makes them superb for cycling, but because each sheet covers a relatively small area they can work out expensively unless you are planning to make several rides in one area.

The maps recommended for each country are listed further on in this book, and some specialist map suppliers are mentioned in the Appendices. Note that for maps published abroad it is usually less expensive to buy them in their country of origin.

Map Interpretation Use your map to its full, and it will guide you along the easiest, quietest, and most scenic roads. Where roads are marked along riversides they will be relatively level, while those going at right-angles to rivers and streams are likely to be hilly; roads running along the crests of ridges often stay high and level for many kilometres. A straight road running between two towns (or large villages) will carry fast traffic, and any major route between towns is guaranteed to be busy. Scenic roads are challenging to spot; roads over hill-tops often provide wide views and those narrow winding byways that follow every curve of a river are nearly always pretty. Hesitate before using long straight roads over flat agricultural country. Some maps identify 'scenic roads' with a green outline, and on the better editions (such as Michelin and IGN) these are a useful aid to route planning; these maps also mark viewpoints.

Good Company

Whether you enjoy travelling on your own, or with company, is something only you can decide; and if one thing is certain it is that strife will surely follow if you have a change of heart half way through a tour. If you aim to ride alone you need to be independently-minded and self-reliant, able to fend for yourself and to see through the highs and lows of a trip without a sharing fellow soul. Riding with company means making sure that you know your friend (or relation) well enough to last the two or three weeks of touring. Both options have their own benefits.

On your own you can indulge in your every whim without having to consider the needs and interests of your companion: choosing when and where to stop, how many kilometres to ride in a day, what to eat, who to talk to and so on. And very often the lone traveller is at an advantage when meeting locals; a Norwegian farmer is more likely to invite a single cyclist for supper than a group. The problem most likely to afflict the solo cyclist is isolation; unlike hitch-hiking, bus or train travel, it is rare to be able to talk with fellow travellers while actually moving, so you end up spending considerable periods each day absolutely on your own.

Biking in company means having a friend to share all the incidents and experiences along the way. It means having someone to talk to in your own language, someone to help when things get hard, someone to share decisions with – and to blame when things go wrong! Riding as a pair can be one of the most satisfying possibilities: you have the benefits of shared experience, can share the luggage carrying, yet are still a small enough group to be flexible. Providing you have fairly similar interests it should not be difficult to come to commonly acceptable decisions. Once you increase the number beyond two, my experience is that the life of the group can become as important as the travelling – moods are as likely to be set by the ambience of your companions as by the landscape through which you are cycling. Three always seems a bad number as it is easy for one person to get left out (unless you are all of very complementary characters).

Above three, you *can* have some great fun; I've enjoyed some of my most hilarious foreign touring with groups of 4 - 6, where the chemistry of the various personalities made sure there was always someone to laugh with – though I must admit I scarcely noticed the countryside, and to this day I am not sure quite where in France I spent those two weeks. As part of a group you can have the best of both worlds, riding on your own when you feel like it, yet having the benefit of travelling companions at other times. Daily arrangements can be flexible, where you agree to meet up at a pre-arranged place for elevenses or lunch, or more regimented, where you ride constantly as one large group – an option which at times can be unwieldy.

There are now many companies selling organised cycling tours to various parts of Europe (addresses in appendices), and these packaged holidays can be a good way of meeting new friends and of seeing a country by bike without the effort of making your own travel arrangements. The packages vary, the most comprehensive including travel out to the country, full accommodation, a tour leader and even a motorised 'sag-waggon' to carry the luggage each day. Groups are usually 10 - 20 people in size. Accommodation may be in youth-hostels, camp-sites or fully-appointed hotels, and on some tours even the bicycles are provided. Companies arranging such tours can be found advertising in the cycling Press, or can be contacted through the National Tourist Offices of the country concerned or (if you are a member) through the Cyclists' Touring Club. The national cycle-touring organisations like the CTC and Fédération Française de Cyclotourisme also have annual touring weeks, where you take various day rides of lengths to suit your abilities, with social events in the evenings. The most international of these is the annual AIT Rally, held in a different country each year and attracting hundreds of riders from all over Europe (details from the CTC). On a much more modest scale, the local tourist offices in a few countries (such as the Netherlands) offer route packages consisting of daily itineraries and an accommodation booking service; you choose what time of year to ride, and with whom you like.

From the North Cape of Norway southwards, overt interest in the opposite sex increases with each line of latitude crossed, peaking in the Mediterranean countries, where the interest shown by local men towards the woman traveller can be nothing short of harassment. The most vulnerable to pestering is the woman on her own, and unless you are confident of successfully fending off pushy males it is safer to travel with a companion. If it looks as if you are cycling under the 'protection' of a male companion the problem can often evaporate altogether. On your own it is unwise to leave accommodation-finding till after dark, and it is unsafe in many cities and towns to walk alone beyond dusk. This can be a real handicap if you want to enjoy night-time atmosphere. Avoiding eye-contact with possible sources of harassment, and not dressing provocatively (a simple enough requirement if you are wearing cycling clothing!) are a couple of precautions, and overall you have to rely on caution and perception, steering clear of any situation which may become annoyingly complicated.

Children can be taken on foreign cycling holidays, though the choice of area and time of year is obviously important; good weather and a relaxed and varied terrain are necessary. Places like Normandy, the Loire Valley, coastal Brittany, the Netherlands, Denmark and southern Sweden all have reasonably mild landscapes, with lots of quiet back roads and beaches (except the Loire). A fixed-centre tour is the easiest option, setting up a base in a farmhouse, camp-site or guest house, and making day rides into the surrounding countryside.

How to carry children on bikes depends on their age. The smallest can be carried in a special child-seat mounted behind the saddle. There are several types of these, the best being made from moulded high-impact plastic, with arm rests, a high back-rest (which also protects the back of the head) and special guards to prevent legs and feet hitting the spokes. Some seats also have a safety belt. Needless to say, the seat should be very securely bolted to the bicycle, and other luggage should be mounted in such a way that the bike's balance is not upset. The type of child's seat which bolts directly to the top-tube of the bike is not satisfactory for anything but very short rides. The other place that a small child can travel is in a trailer, facing backwards. These are fairly rare in the UK (more common in the US) and are a lot more cumbersome to ride with, as well as making it harder for the rider to keep a check on the passenger's welfare.

Older children, who want to sit on a bike 'properly', but who are not yet old enough to ride their own, can use 'kiddy-cranks' fitted to a tandem. These bolt to the tandem frame below the rear saddle, providing an extra set of miniature pedals within reach of a child's short legs. An additional chain links the kiddy cranks to the tandem's rear bottom bracket; the child can sit like a grown-up and twiddle the pedals making at least a moral contribution to the tandem's pace. These cranks can frequently be obtained second-hand from families who have outgrown them; look in cycling magazine small ads or ask around at your local cycling club. Older children can either ride on the back of a tandem powered by an adult, or on a small bike of their own. Protective cycling helmets for children are now readily available.

Bike and Equipment

Travelling light

Saint-Exupéry wrote 'He who would travel happily must travel light', and this is a maxim that should be ringing in your ears as you scurry about collecting all those items you are thinking of taking 'just in case'.

It is very easy to take too much luggage and very hard to carry it. Be ruthless: try laying out on the living room floor all the luggage you *think* you will need, then force yourself to discard half of it. A good tip is to make a detailed list of everything you take, then when you return from the tour, cross off everything you didn't use or you think you could have done without (and insert those you forgot). Then, next time you go away, you will have a better idea of what is useful and what is an unnecessary burden on those poor old legs! After all, part of the fun of bike touring is leaving behind the clutter and paraphernalia of everyday life.

In practice the amount of luggage you need does not increase with the length of tour (except for items like spare tyres), so you need as much for a week abroad as you do for a few months. If you are travelling as a pair or in a group, make sure you are not duplicating equipment and share out the task of carrying communal items like the tent, cooking gear, food and spares for the bikes. And you can test your ingenuity to the full by seeing how many grams you can shave off the various items of equipment you are taking – there is a whole range of sensible (and less sensible) ploys tried over the years by cycle tourists. These include taking aluminium cutlery not steel, cutting the handles off toothbrushes, guillotining the margins off books, tearing the pages out of paperbacks once you have read them, cutting your toenails etc. There really is no limit!

Below are some rough weight targets you should be aiming at not exceeding; add about 2 kg for touring in northern Europe or in late autumn/early spring, when you will need extra clothes:

Indoor accommodation (youth hostels, hotels, pensions etc) tour 12 kg
Camping tour (with tents, sleeping-bag and cooking gear)   17 kg

The following sections contain general hints about types of equipment. Check lists can be found in the Appendices.

Clothing

1. Washing powder is a lot lighter than the extra garments you might have considered stuffing into the panniers instead.
2. Stiff-soled shoes – the stiffer the better – reduce pedal pressure on the underneath of your foot, and are much more efficient than bendy-soled plimsolls for example.
3. A jacket is essential; it keeps you warm in the evenings and in bad weather, and also prevents chill when descending passes where the sweat from the ascent would otherwise quickly cool you down (racing cyclists stuff a newspaper inside the front of their jersey for descents). On really long ascents it is worth remembering that the actual air temperature falls about $1.7°C$ for every 300 metres climbed. The jacket should ideally be windproof and showerproof and also 'breathe'; allowing you to pedal without getting damp on the inside from trapped perspiration. Fine-

weave cotton-mix fabrics and the Goretex materials are excellent. If you are going to a wet country you need a fully waterproof top layer; either a Goretex jacket, cape (not too good because it flaps wildly in the wind) or a cagoule (not breathable so tends to get as wet on the inside as outside if worn for long). Avoid if possible baggy jackets, which catch the wind and make cycling harder.

4. Trousers and shorts should not have thick seams you have to sit on, and ideally be of natural fibres, or a mix. Purpose-made cycling shorts often have a towelling or chamois insert which makes life a little more cushy. If you plan to ride in trousers, take a pair which are not loose and flappy, and which have enough 'give' in the material to allow the knee unrestricted movement. Jeans are not generally comfortable for long rides. For spring and autumn riding in wettish areas, take a pair of waterproof overtrousers.

5. A hat is useful when it rains, for keeping the sun out of your eyes in Mediterranean countries, and for preventing headlight dazzle when night-riding. But it has to be the sort of hat which cannot blow away; berets are quite good.

6. Gloves are essential for autumn, spring and winter touring, though in emergency a pair of socks works well.

7. Several thin layers of clothing (such as T-shirt, shirt, thin jumper, jacket) allow you better temperature control than a couple of really thick layers. Garments that open down the front also allow adjustable ventilation, and they should be long enough at the back so that a chilly gap cannot open up as you lean forward to the handlebars.

8. Thermal underwear is excellent for winter touring and for exerting riding in cool countries (eg Scandinavia). It allows the perspiration to 'wick' away from the skin so avoiding damp patches which can cause chills.

9. A warm jumper is handy for those cool evenings and nights if you are camping; even the Mediterranean can be chilly after dusk.

10. Lightweight walking shoes or boots are useful if you plan to mix biking with hiking. Try and find some footwear which suit both purposes as shoes are a heavy and bulky item to carry.

Miscellaneous Equipment

1. A compass is essential if you plan any hiking in remote or mountain regions, and it can be a handy aid while biking if you get totally lost and need to take a bearing from a cross-roads.

2. Sunglasses can be a comfort in clear bright conditions, especially when riding on white dusty Mediterranean roads where the glare can be blinding. The sort with curly wire arms are less likely to fly off if you turn your head suddenly when riding quickly.

3. Paperback books are useful for rainy days and early evenings. Only

take one or two as they can be swapped with other travellers at youth-hostels, camp-sites, railway stations, or with bored hitch-hikers waiting on slip-roads.

4. A small frameless rucksack which can be folded into a compact bundle is useful for pedestrian expeditions around cities and for hiking. Alternatively a handlebar-bag or pannier can be modified for shoulder carrying.

5. Elastic straps with wire hooks are useful for tying on luggage and loaves.

6. Plastic bags are handy for keeping the contents of your panniers dry during wet weather, for separating clean and dirty clothes, and for storing food. And if you are unexpectedly caught out in cold or wet weather, a pair of plastic bags fixed over the feet are remarkably effective at keeping your toes warm; do not forget to take them off if you go into a cafe!

7. Silk scarves, a tie, jewellery, a thin dress are lightweight concessions to good taste should you want to mix in high places.

8. A camera (and lenses) should be carried surrounded by something soft to protect it from road vibration; a handlebar bag can be adapted and compartmentalized to form a cushioned camera bag which is also very accessible for those quick shots.

Bike Tools and Spares

The points noted below are directed at riders who intend to be mechanically self-sufficient; those that know how to (and do not mind) fixing breakdowns.

1. Before you leave home check over the bike and make sure that you have a tool for every adjustment and component. Some tools, such as an adjustable spanner, do several jobs.

2. A freewheel removing tool can be invaluable if you break a spoke on the block side, but do not take a long wrench for the tool; you can always borrow one from a garage or truck-driver.

3. Oil and grease can very often be obtained free at petrol stations since the amounts needed to keep a bicycle moving are so modest; so it is not really worth carrying your own supply.

4. A file is useful for taking down spoke-heads, and if you have one with a triangular cross-section, you can also use it for cutting metal.

5. Spare spokes can be carried by taping them to a frame tube or rear pannier.

6. A spare tyre is necessary if you are going to tour on rough roads for any length of time; carry it by folding it into three. This requires a simple but cunning contortion impossible to explain in words. Ask your local bike shop to demonstrate.

7. Spare lamp batteries should be carried in a water-tight plastic bag.

8. A length of galvanised wire is useful for emergency repairs such as fixing a loose mudguard or broken pannier mount. It should be of a gauge thin enough to work with the pliers in your tool-kit, and can be carried inside a handlebar tube.

9. Spare bulbs for lamps can be carried wrapped in tissue and gently wedged in a handlebar tube; alternatively some types of handlebar end-plug have integral bulb-holders.

Camping Equipment

1. Sleeping bags with artificial fillings such as Hollofil and Thinsulate tend to be bulky though they have the big advantage of maintaining their insulation when wet. Duck-down fillings are warmer (and more expensive), can be compacted into a smaller space and lose their insulation in the wet. If you are thinking of travelling very light, without a tent, the new generation of bivouac bags, with a Goretex outer, are worth looking at.

2. A sheet sleeping bag used inside your main bag is much easier and cheaper to clean than a quality sleeping bag. In hot countries this duality gives you the option of sleeping in just the sheet.

3. A sheet of polythene from a hardware store is a thrifty compromise for bankrupt bikers with no tent or money. This can be used to make a shelter, or as a groundsheet for sleeping under the stars.

4. A closed cell foam sleeping mat is an optional extra and can make a difference when sleeping on stony or hard ground. But they are bulky to carry; the best place is along the top of a pannier rack (front or rear).

Cooking/Eating Equipment

Be careful! It is easy to over-equip in this department.

1. One lightweight aluminium billy-can can suffice, even for two people – though it does require ingenuity and juggling. The lid should convert into a frying pan or plate. If you want more cooking containers, invest in a nest of billy-cans which fit neatly inside each other.

2. Big mugs with parallel sides hold more and are less likely to fall over than tall tapered mugs. Use plastic for lightness; enamel ones are heavier and can chip.

3. An aluminium spoon and knife is light and effective; a fork is not really necessary (the Army even sharpen one side of their spoon handle and use that as a knife!).

4. Extra water-bottles are needed if you are thinking of camping wild: the options are to carry several of the pint-size bottles, mounted on the bike frame if possible, or a large collapsible plastic water container. In hot countries you need a minimum of two water-bottles (two pints) and in remote hot parts a capacity of up to four pints per person.

5. Camping stoves come in several varieties. Traditionalists favour the

Primus or Optimus type – a compact and powerful design which burns pressurised paraffin (kerosene in America). These are ignited by burning a small reservoir of methylated spirits (though broken up bits of solid fuel will do, and are less messy to carry). Paraffin is available in Europe but it can often take some time and effort to find. Cleaner and easier to use (but more expensive on fuel) are the butane stoves ('Camping Gaz'/C206). Their main snag is that the butane cylinders do not last long and they are bulky to carry. So if you are using one regularly you have to find a stockist every other day, or carry a number of spare cylinders. A less efficient alternative is a simple meths-burning or solid fuel stove – these sometimes come in small kits together with pans. American 'white gas' is generally unavailable.

Documents

1. For UK riders a valid passport or British Visitors Passport is necessary; application forms for both are available from main post offices (see Appendices). At the time of writing British citizens do not need visas to visit any of the countries described in this book.
2. Vital documents such as your passport, cheque cards, money etc should never be left unattended on your bike. Carry them in a money belt, in a 'secret' pocket sown to the inside of your shorts, or in a wallet hung round your neck.

The Bicycle

Whole books have been written about setting up and maintaining a bicycle (see Appendices) so we are not going to delve into the world of ball-bearings, oil and spindles but look briefly at what you can and cannot get away with when it comes to sorting out a suitable machine for carrying you about the continent.

The first thing is that it does not necessarily follow that the more you spend on a bicycle the more you appreciate the country through which you are travelling. But up to a point, the more you spend the more comfortably and faster you will be able to travel. The bike on which I made my first foray abroad was an approximate assembly of second-hand parts which cost less than half the passenger fare across the Channel; a close friend made her first foreign biking trip – a journey across France – on a single-speed sit-up-and beg. To a degree it's a question of 'horses for courses'. If, as you cycle through the British countryside, you are largely unaware of the machine beneath you, then you are probably well suited and you will continue this state of unawareness when you get abroad. But if on the other hand a cricking pedal is driving you mad with worry each time you ride to the shops then *before* you set out is the time to buy a new pedal. Likewise, if every hill is a nightmare because you simply cannot heave your un-geared leviathan to the summit, it is time to get a new bike.

Which bike suits you depends on where and what type of cycling you are planning, and how far you want to cycle each day. So, if you are contemplating emptying your purse over the counter of your local bike shop, I have described below three imaginary grades of bicycle.

The Slow Roller

The most skeletal and under-nourished of the velocipede family, capable of carrying you slowly around flat places like Holland, Denmark, Flanders and the smoother parts of France. In other hillier areas you will end up pushing it, but then what is wrong with a gentle walk now and again? With beginners in mind a few basic points are included.

Frame Make sure the frame is not cracked or out of alignment. Preferably the frame should be a conventional 'diamond' or ladies' frame with 26 or 27-inch wheels – small-wheeled shopping bikes are not suitable for touring.

Wheels There should be two of them, both of which should be round, with no broken spokes.

Gears If your slow-roller has just a single speed, then you really are limited to the flat areas; strong winds and hills may mean dismounting. But a three-speed hub gear will get you over a surprising variety of terrain though it's best to try to avoid any Alpine assaults just yet.

Brakes You need one for each wheel, and they should be powerful enough to stop the bike quickly when it is fully loaded. Test before buying.

Saddle You cannot do without one.

Handlebars Unless completely destitute, fit them with handgrips or tape, and end-plugs.

Pedals One for each foot.

Carrier A solid rear carrier is necessary, and a handlebar-bag or basket useful.

The Comfy Cruiser

This bike can come in a wide range of designs and conditions, but it will have all the basic ingredients necessary to pedal anywhere in Europe; its specifications and comfort should carry you up the steepest longest hills and over the broadest plains. The Comfy Cruiser is also a good starting point for upgrading to a Super Tourer as the cash becomes available; it can also be bought second-hand as a 'sports bike' and converted without too much expense. I am assuming the owner of a Comfy Cruiser is familiar with the basic technicalities.

Frame The design should be a conventional 'diamond' pattern, or if preferred for ladies the 'mixt' style with two parallel tubes (twin laterals) running from the head-tube to the seat-tube or rear drop-outs. Tubing should be good quality such as Reynolds 531 plain-gauge, or even butted if you are thinking of upgrading the machine to Super Tourer status.

Wheels Steel hubs are heavier than aluminium ones, but are perfectly satisfactory. Nuts instead of quick-release skewers on the ends of the axles make the wheels harder to steal but slower to remove when you get a puncture. Solid spindles are reputedly less durable than quick-release spindles. Most Comfy Cruisers come with 36-spoked wheels but you might like to equip the bike with a 40-spoke rear wheel to cope with the extra weight of your luggage. Aluminium rims are lighter than steel ones but more likely to deform; steel rims provide very poor braking in the wet but are solid.

Gears As important as *how many* gears is the *range* of gear ratios they span (see Appendices for explanation of gear ratios). A touring bike ideally has gears that range from about 30 inches to 85 inches (95 inches if the rider is strong). These are sufficient to pedal over the Pyrenees and to make the most of strong tailwinds. The gaps between each ratio should be as evenly spaced as possible and not too large; big jumps in ratio are hard for the legs to adjust to. A 10-speed is therefore better than a 5-speed because it means smaller differences between each gear (though in practice you always tend to 'lose' 2 gears out of 10 through overlap of ratios).

Brakes Aluminium side-pull or centre-pull. The former are more powerful, lighter weight and have fewer parts (so need fewer spares), but are harder to adjust. Cheap side-pulls can be an infernal nuisance as they often rub irritatingly on one side of the rim. Centre-pulls on the other hand are adequate, they stay adjusted and can be neglected for longer periods of time.

Saddles Plastic-topped saddles are unyielding and sweaty over long rides. Solid leather saddles, like the Brooks range, need breaking in like shoes before they conform to your backside, thereafter they are very comfortable. Saddles with leather tops, a layer of foam padding and a moulded plastic base need no breaking in, and provided you find one that suits you well from the start they can be very comfortable. If you are looking at new saddles, try an anatomic model which has raised portions designed to take pressure off the crotch.

Handlebars Most Comfy Cruisers come with drop handlebars, which have the advantage of offering about four different hand positions, the lowest of which is useful for riding fast or into strong winds. Flat handlebars allow you to ride in a more upright position (good for peering over hedges and riding in traffic) with a straighter back, but provide a less efficient riding position than drops. In both cases, tape (or grips) and end-plugs should be fitted.

Pedals Toe-clips and straps are easy to fit and considerably increase pedalling efficiency.

Carrier A flimsy carrier loaded with luggage will sway unnervingly from side to side, and upset the balance of the bike. Since they are easy to fit, a good quality, rigid carrier is one of the simplest ways of increasing the safety and performance of the Comfy Cruiser. If you do buy one, make sure it can take panniers, and that it has two forward arms which attach to the seat-stays (thus making it a 'four-point' mounting) or that it is is triangulated (like the Blackburn models) to prevent sway.

The Super Tourer

The ultimate touring bike, built to last a lifetime and fitted with components to your choice.

Frame Either a diamond frame or ladies' twin lateral design, constructed from double-butted (or plain gauge) tubing for lightness and strength. Frames of this quality often come with a number of special brazed-on fixtures for routing brake and gear cables, mounting the rear derailleur, bottle cages, gear levers and so on. The ultimate is to have a frame custom-built to your own body measurements with design features personally selected, and your own choice of components and accessories. Head and seat tube angles are normally around 72° or 71° for smoothness of ride and clearance of the front mudguard from the toe-clip. Wheelbase is around 41 inches.

Wheels Top quality small-flange aluminium hubs, fitted with either quick-release skewers or solid spindles according to choice. Quality spokes, 36 front and (if you are planning heavy touring) 40 rear, with top quality aluminium rims. Wheels should be hand-built by an acknowledged expert wheel-builder. 'Unbreakable' plastic mudguards should be fitted.

Gears Gear ratios specially chosen to suit your own strength and style of riding; a safe choice is front chainrings of 46 and 30 teeth, and a freewheel fitted with 14-16-18-22-26 sprockets. A triple chainset increases further the scope for extending the overall range of gears and number of intermediate ratios. The derailleurs themselves should be good quality aluminium and steel with features like the open cage which facilitates easy chain removal. Gear levers could be mounted in the ends of the handlebars.

Brakes Top quality aluminium side-pulls provide the best per-formance, and these can be set up with free-running teflon-lined cables for super smooth control.

Saddle An all-leather model or a top anatomic model, both of which should have saddle-bag loops. If it still does not feel quite right, the Americans have designed water-filled anatomic saddles and a variety of saddle covers from sheep-skin to variable-density foam.

Handlebars Fit the bike with a pair of handlebars that are the same width as your shoulders, and with the popular 'randonneur' bend which provides an extra hand position on the 'elbows' of the bars. Either cover the bars in comfortable tape (cloth is good) or with foam cushioning; this comes in different thicknesses, thin foam being good for people with small hands, while the thickest variety provides maximum cushioning (at the expense of response). A rear-view mirror can be fitted to the bars; useful for riding in traffic.

Pedals Good quality, with reflectors, aluminium bodies and steel side-plates (for durability), steel toe-clips and tough straps. Toe clips come in three lengths, so fit the bike with a pair which suit your feet.

Carrier A four-point fixing or triangulated aluminium carrier, designed for panniers. For bulkier loads fit a lowloading front carrier which allows you to mount a front pannier centred on the wheel hub – this design has a less detrimental effect on the bike's steering than does the conventional front carrier with its platform level with the front brake.

Loading up

There are two main principles to remember when you load up a bicycle:
1. The luggage should be accommodated so that it upsets the bike's balance as little as possible.
2. Everything should be securely attached to the bike, yet still be accessible.
Reaching the first goal is helped if you have kept your luggage down to the bare essentials. The aim should be to centre the weight as close as possible to an imaginary point around the bike's centre of gravity (the chainset area) – so you do not put heavy items on the handlebars or towards the back of the rear carrier. Water bottles obviously fix to the main triangle of the bike while heavy things like tool kits should go say at the front of your rear panniers. Never carry bags on your back because it can make you unbalanced and it is better to let the bike take the load anyway.

How you attach the luggage to the bike, and where individual items get packed depends on how much luggage you have and what kind of bags and carriers you have. Either you can invest in purpose-designed panniers and bags or design your own. Several manufacturers now offer complete 'systems' of bicycle luggage, very often intended to fit with a particular brand of carrier. Such integral systems are expensive but are stable with good accessibility – normally with several pockets and dividers. Off the bike, some of these systems snap together to form convenient hand luggage. All bike bags need to be tough and waterproof, so before buying check the stitching and make sure the fabric is proofed. Most bags are nylon.

If you cannot afford a new set of panniers, handlebar bag and on, fashion your own models from ex-Army kit bags. Providing you have a stable carrier, and the bags do not interfere with the wheels you cannot go far wrong.

The various options for luggage carriage are as follows.

Rear Panniers

These attach to each side of the rear carrier, and like the saddlebag, form the basis of any luggage carrying system. Rear panniers can be used for carrying a tent, clothes or food – anything in fact – so are versatile. Sizes vary from compact models with a single main compartment closed by a drawstring, to sophisticated (and expensive) designs with a large capacity and up to five separate zipped compartments each. These multi-pocket models mean that you can separate items like tools from food, dirty clothes from clean ones, and so on, while making it easier to find specific items quickly. The only disadvantage of multi-pocket panniers is that they encourage you to fill each compartment with things you do not really need! The lower leading edge of rear panniers should always be sloped so that your heels do not foul the bag.

Methods of attaching panniers to carriers vary, but the standard suspension system consists of two top hooks and spring or elastic to pull the bottom of the pannier in tight to the carrier. The better quality panniers are designed to fit specific models of carrier, so make sure the two are compatible on your machine. Some panniers now have quick release plastic buckles, and these are a lot easier to use than the old method of threading a tape through a narrow metal buckle; difficult with cold fingers.

Saddlebags

The black duck-cloth saddlebag, frayed by decades of use and bleached by the sun, is a part of the British touring heritage; it attaches to saddlebag loops on the saddle (though sadly many modern saddles are not fitted with these loops) with an additional strap around the seat post. It is a convenient position for access, and the weight is carried nice and centrally. But capacity is limited and you have to be travelling light (say hostelling) to get away with a saddlebag as your only luggage. Most saddlebags have two handy outside pockets.

There are also now a number of small bags which can be fitted behind the saddle, just big enough for a cape and tools.

Top Bags/Stuff Sacks

Usually these are single compartment bags which can be strapped to the top of the rear carrier, useful for carrying bulky, light items like a sleeping bag.

Handlebar Bags

Extremely convenient for carrying items you want to keep to hand, such as a camera, sunglasses, gloves and so on. The better handlebar bags come with a steel frame which fits by a clamp or shock cord to the handlebars. It is important that the frame and bag are clear of your brake levers, and that they allow enough space for you to ride with your hands on the 'tops' of the bars. It is vital that the bag and frame be rigid; any sway will have disastrous effects on the bike's steering. Be careful too with the really large handlebar bags, because the tendency is to overload them with heavy items and this makes the bike cumbersome to handle. Most bags can be quickly removed and carried by a shoulder strap, so they are also a useful place for carrying valuables you do not want to leave unattended on the bike – of all the types of bike bag this is the only one that can safely be rummaged in whilst cycling (but do not do it on busy main roads!).

Front Panniers

These can make a good balanced partnership when used with a pair of medium sized rear panniers. The best sort are those which can be attached to the 'Blackburn Lowrider' type of carrier, which centres the weight of the pannier about the front wheel hub. Front panniers mounted higher on the conventional front carriers tend to make the steering heavy.

Frame Bags

Not often used or seen, but a sensible bag for spreading the weight of your luggage. Frame bags strap into the main frame triangle of the bicycle, allowing enough clearance for the pedals to turn. It is important the bag does not sag when filled. Most are surprisingly capacious, and their central position makes them a good place to carry heavy items like tool kits. Check they leave enough clearance for a water bottle and pump. An alternative to the frame bag is a home-made rigid structure of aluminium or plastic. My father once made a 'frame-case' which could carry up to 3 litres of water, 6 eggs and a camera! Bear in mind that when you fill in the main frame triangle, you are increasing the sideways wind-resistance of the bike, and in strong winds the handling can be slightly affected.

Riding Loaded

Provided you are not overloaded, and that your load is not wrongly distributed, you should have no problems balancing and riding your bike. But a bike with 15kg or so of luggage does *feel* completely different to its unladen state; if this is your first tour, take the bike out on local lanes and get the feel of riding with that extra weight before committing yourself to foreign highways. You will find the machine altogether more sluggish – you will not be able to burst forth from the traffic lights and dance nimbly up the hills. Gears are the key to saving effort; pull away in a low gear and work up the ratios.

Cornering should be as smooth and as easy as riding an unloaded bike once you have got the hang of it. In traffic remember that if you have panniers you are wider than normal and give cars and pedestrians that extra bit of leeway. If there is a couple of you, and you are confident and practised riders, then slipstreaming each other can be effortlessly pleasant: a loaded touring bike, with panniers sticking out sideways collects a lot of wind resistance. You can cheat this wind by riding close behind another cyclist, though be careful never to overlap front and back wheel. It requires concentration, with nasty consequences if you get it wrong!

On long hills try and maintain a steady even rhythm from bottom to top, changing gear with any changes of gradient, but aiming to keep your body at a constant output; any sudden bursts of effort will destroy your momentum. While we are on hills, remember that on those switchback hairpin climbs the easiest part of an upward bend is on the outside, where the gradient will be less steep because of the greater radius of curve. But watch the traffic. On especially steep sections you can ride out of the saddle, standing on the pedals for greater power. The British call this 'honking', presumably a reference to the flared nostrils, screwed-up eyes and strangled wheezing that accompany many of us on a stiff climb; in France it is elegantly termed riding 'en danseuse'. Coming down those hills a loaded bike takes more stopping than an unloaded one, so anticipate corners, potholes and other traffic well in advance.

Care and Calamity

Playing Safe

You have two things to protect when you go on a biking holiday: your possessions and yourself, the latter being rather harder to replace than the former. The least expensive form of insurance is called 'care', and this involves making sure that you do not fall off your bike, making sure you do not walk round Naples railway station with your wallet hanging out of a back pocket, and perhaps most important of all, making sure you do not run over an innocent pedestrian or ride into the back of a Ferrari while ogling at a *patisserie*-window full of cream cakes. Care can spare a lot of bother, but you also have to guard yourself against a colourful array of random misfortunes over which you have little or no control; crazy drivers, food poisoning and felons can put you in hospital or leave you penniless. So there are a number of sensible precautions you should take before leaving home.

Medical Precautions

If, prior to your holiday you have any kind of ailment or are under medical care, consult your doctor; similarly do not set off abroad with a tooth-ache which could turn nasty after a week or so. Also ask your doctor whether you need any extra immunisations to cover the countries in which you plan to ride; in particular make sure that your polio and tetanus immunisations are up to date, and if not, arrange a booster. Cholera, typhoid and hepatitis are rare in Europe, but have been known to break out in Mediterranean countries. Scrupulous attention to what you eat and drink is the best protection, though if in any doubt about the risks, see your local doctor.

The British Medical Association publish an excellent (and inexpensive) little booklet which tells you how to deal with everything from the DHSS to dysentery; *Health on Holiday* can be ordered from Family Doctor Publications, BMA House, Tavistock Square, London WC1H 9JP.

EEC Reciprocal Health Arrangement

Nationals of the UK (and of other EEC countries) who are currently insured are entitled to the reciprocal health arrangements between EEC countries. The details of these are described in the DHSS booklet SA30 called *Medical Costs Abroad*. The arrangement ensures that should you have the misfortune to require medical attention during a holiday in any EEC country (Belgium, Denmark, France, West Germany, Gibraltar, Greece, Irish Republic, Italy, Luxembourg, Netherlands) then you should be able to get urgent treatment free or at reduced cost on the same terms as its own insured people.

To qualify, you must obtain Form E111 (the Certificate of Entitlement) before leaving the UK; this takes just a few minutes down at your local DHSS office (if you are applying by post, allow at least one month), and at the time of writing the application form for Form E111 is included in booklet SA30. There is no cost involved. Form E111 is issued together with a leaflet giving detailed instructions on its use in the event of treatment being necessary.

Whether you enter a medical establishment under the umbrella of Form E111 or under a travel insurance policy (see next section) the normal procedure is that you pay on the spot for the treatment, and claim from the social services or insurance company later. So bear in mind that a doctor, dentist or hospital may demand substantial sums of cash at short notice – I have even heard of a doctor demanding money before treating a broken leg!

Travel Insurance

The medical treatment you can get in the EEC countries may be more complicated to obtain than in Britain, it will probably be less comprehensive and it will not cover the cost of bringing you home. So it is a wise precaution (recommended by the British Medical Association) to take out a travel insurance policy which includes cover for personal accident, medical and other expenses, and emergency repatriation by air ambulance. The same policy should cover contingencies such as baggage and personal money loss, journey cancellations, loss of deposits and third-party liability. And make sure that the small-print does not exclude cyclists (some outdoor activities are classed as 'hazardous sports'), and that your bike is included in the baggage cover. Alternatively, if your bike is insured for home use, you may find it better to extend your domestic insurance policy.

Money Matters

The European financial system is not designed for people who spend most of their time in the countryside, moving at 15 kilometres per hour. So when you set off abroad on a bicycle your money supply needs to be suited to your speed and location; a credit card is as much use to a Sardinian bar-tender as a pair of pedals to a polecat. What you need then is a pocketful of *lira;* too bad they would not change your travellers' cheque at that last town.

Before you leave home, work out how much money you will need (with some spare for emergencies); and in what form you will carry it. You can order from your bank *foreign currency* which can be useful for seeing you through the first couple of days' touring, especially if, like me, you need a while to work out what a foreign bank is called and what one looks like. Or if you arrive at a weekend. *Travel cheques* also have to be ordered before you leave. These can be supplied in your own currency or a foreign one and have the advantage that they can often be cashed at big hotels and shops, as well as banks. And they have a safety procedure whereby you can claim a refund if they are lost or stolen. There is always a charge made for changing each travel cheque, so it works out cheaper (but less flexible) to have a few large denomination cheques than many small ones. Many banks belong to the *Eurocheque scheme* which allows you to cash your own bank cheques at any foreign banks displaying the Eurocheque sign; you may need to obtain a special card from your bank before leaving home. Another alternative is the Girobank system of *Postcheques* which can be cashed at foreign post-offices; since these are often open for longer hours than banks it can be a flexible system. *Credit cards* can be used anywhere abroad that displays the appropriate sign – normally restricted to establishments in towns and cities. Finally it can be useful to take some of *your own currency* in note form, just in case all the cheques and cards fail to work.

What type of money you choose to carry depends on what banking arrangement you already have and are therefore used to, and on where you are going. If your tour visits towns frequently then you can play safe and keep the amount of loose cash in your pocket down by cashing cheques only when you need the money. On a tour in remote areas, postcheques and hard currency give you the greatest flexibility. In any event your bank or post office will be able to provide advice on their own facilities for foreign banking, and often publish their own handy travel guides for use by customers abroad.

A – Z of Horrors

A light-hearted look at some of the traumas that can face the unwary cyclist in Europe. Most problems can be avoided by common-sense and care, while the rest, such as headwinds and punctures, are a matter of luck. Which I am sure you will have!

A *Accidents.* Always leave a margin of safety when descending hills, overtaking parked vehicles (watch for car doors), and negotiating junctions and heavy traffic. If you are careful, the unbelievable should not happen. You should be carrying sufficient medical dressings to cope with grazes (the most common result of falling off a bike), and should have any wounds professionally attended to as soon as possible. If injuries are serious, and if you have banged your head (even if you feel OK at the time) flag down a passing motorist and ask for assistance.

B *Breakdowns.* Known to occur at the most inconvenient time and place: after dark, in the rain or 50 kilometres from the nearest town. Don't panic! There is nearly always an easy solution. Tackle the problem at a relaxed pace; if you cannot mend it, see if you can make a bodge repair which will get you to the nearest bike shop. Most bike shop owners are amenable to distressed foreign cyclists, particularly if you pander to their pride as technicians. Failing a bike shop, most farms and garages have workshop tools and proprietors for whom mechanical ingenuity (bodging) is second nature.

C *Cobbles.* Probably the worst road surface ever invented: if you ride over them fast the high-frequency vibrations shake your teeth loose, blur the vision and undo every nut and bolt on the bike. Ridden over slowly, cobbles have a rustic charm for the first 5 metres; thereafter they are a long-drawn out purgatory of aching forearms and pummelled backside. Continentals call cobbles *'pavé'*, a word that seems to be derived from *'pas vélo'!* Wet cobbles are unbelievably slippery.

D *Dogs.* You have seen that sport where greyhounds chase a mechanical hare around a track; well this is the one where dogs chase cyclists. Canine attackers have two tactics: The Ambush, where the dog has been eyeballing your slow advance for several hundred metres and suddenly flies from nowhere in a fury of crazed yapping, and The Pursuit, where an animal idling by the roadside watches you pedal past, acknowledges your greeting with an innocent glance then just as you relax it stands up and starts a furious chase. If you are a fit rider the recommended reaction is to ride as fast as possible, and the dog will soon get bored. If you feel yourself slowing down, just look over your shoulder at the dog. You'll go faster. Some books suggest beating off attacking animals with bicycle pumps and proprietary sprays, both of which can, in the excitement of the moment, make you fall off.

E *Exhaust.* Disgusting grey fumes breathed by motorists. The ultimate exhaust experience is to be riding up a very steep hill sucking in great lungfuls of clean mountain air when a juggernaut crawls past spewing diesel into your gaping mouth from one of those face-level side-pointing exhaust pipes the diameter of the Blackwall Tunnel.

F *Food Poisoning.* Caused by imbibing unclean food or drink and leading to 'gippy tummy' (ie travellers' diarrhoea). Do not eat in fly-infested restaurants with dirty lavatories; thoroughly wash all fruit and vegetables before eating them; be cautious about unwrapped cheeses, yoghurts and cakes in southern Europe; make sure all meat, poultry and fish is well cooked and never drink any doubtful-looking water. The British Medical Association say that tap water is generally safe to drink in all European countries except Austria, Yugoslavia, Spain, Portugal, southern France and the Greek Islands. If in doubt, boil thoroughly, or add water sterilisation tablets or drink bottled mineral water.

G *Gravel.* When found on sharp hairpin bends gravel is inclined to cause cyclists to slide along the road on their hips and elbows; brakes are dangerous to use. Roads which are wet, muddy or oil-logged have the same effect.

H *Headwinds.* A very tedious climatic condition known to reduce cyclists to tears. There is no point in fighting a headwind; drop to a lower gear and take it slowly. You may find the wind is only affecting a particular stretch of road and that things improve after a few kilometres. Or call it a day and hope for better weather tomorrow.

I *Insects.* Small black airborne objects flying at cyclists' face level which bounce off the roof of the mouth and get lodged in the throat to cause violent fits of coughing and swearing. Large insects like bees can smack into a forehead with the force of a small pebble and tiny insects have a habit of getting stuck on legs, in the hair and eyes.

J *Juggernauts.* The most dreaded of beasts on the road, usually confined to major routeways and known for showing little regard for cyclists. Juggernauts can hurtle past so fast that their slipstream sucks you in towards them, then blows you out towards the verge. Italian 'nauts have additional trailers which can cause a double suck-blow effect. Never get on the inside of a juggernaut on a bend because the trailers often cut the kerb by inches.

K *Knock.* Also known as 'bonk' and 'sag'; 'hunger knock' is bikers' vernacular for a fairly memorable symptom that strikes riders who are over-exerting themselves. If you are unused to lots of exercise, and try to cram in too many kilometres your blood-sugar level can start to fall and affect the central nervous system with 'hunger knock'. You feel shaky, go into a cold sweat, become unstable on the bike and yearn for something sweet to eat. Carbohydrate such as bread, sugar, dried fruit and so on will make you feel better. A similarly drastic condition is heat exhaustion. This can creep up on you without your being aware of its presence; with a breeze continually blowing over you, much of your sweat is instantly evaporated and you have little idea how much body moisture you are losing. To a motorist sitting inside a sweltering car in pools of perspiration the reminders of body-moisture loss are fairly apparent, but on a bike you can be perfectly dry on the outside yet chronically dehydrated inside. Heat exhaustion is thoroughly unpleasant and is usually accompanied by headaches and feelings of nausea; the remedy is to rest in a cool place with adequate fluids and salts. Prevent heat exhaustion by taking regular drinks from your water bottle as you ride and by avoiding over-exposure to the sun.

L *Lost or Stolen.* When your whole material world consists of a couple of bags and a bike, it is particularly distressing when even a small part of it goes missing. Avoid accidentally losing things by always packing items away in the same place so you are more likely to notice any absences. Avoid theft of the bike by always locking it (with the best lock you can afford) to an immovable object, preferably outside a public building where passers-by would notice anyone trying to break the lock. Keep a note of the bike's frame-number (one copy with you, one left at home) and make sure you know the identifiable features of the bike should you have to describe it to police. A bike which looks dirty and unattractive is less likely to draw attention than a sparkling clean model. Never leave valuables in a hotel room. Report any theft immediately to the local police.

M *Manhole Covers.* Planted by road engineers to buckle bicycle wheels, the worst specimens having raised lips or being deeply recessed in the tarmac. Drain gratings are similarly dangerous, with the added novelty that should their bars be oriented parallel with the road there is every chance half your front wheel will disappear underground. The ubiquitous pothole is a more traditional bane of cycling life, most lethal when it appears unexpectedly on a fast descent; some potholes have horribly sharp edges which can destroy wheel-rims and tyres. In cities, watch out for tramlines; always cross them as close to right-angles as possible, to avoid the risk of getting your wheels stuck in the slots ...

N *No Room at the Inn.* To arrive at your destination after a long day's pedalling and to find that the hostel, hotel or guest house is full, is one of the direst of nightmares. The moral is to finish your day's riding with plenty of time in hand for locating vacant accommodation, or to book in advance.

O *Other Road Users.* Most road users are considerate people, but always be prepared for the unthinking and manic. Pedestrians can step off a kerb without looking, cars overtake with just a few centimetres clearance – or they pull out of junctions into your path. Buses and trams do not appear to have facilities for deviating from their regular part of the road, no matter what is in their way. The safest attitude is to imagine that every road-user has the potential to knock you off.

P *Puncture.* Announced by a bang, a hiss or an inexorable softening; accompanied by a sinking of the heart. Best countered by carrying a spare inner tube which can then be fitted quickly and easily, leaving the punctured tube to be mended at leisure. Like breakdowns, punctures tend to occur at the least convenient moments.

Q *Quarrels.* Steer clear of them; they are worse than breakdowns and headwinds.

R *Rattles.* The bike's way of telling you that something is about to fall off. Common rattles are caused by mudguards and luggage carriers.

S *Stings and Bites.* Things that sting include bees, wasps and hornets, scorpions, hairy caterpillars and jelly fish. In Europe none of these stings are likely to be fatal but some (such as scorpions and bees) can be very painful. If camping in southern Europe, always shake out your shoes before putting them on. Snakes are common in some parts but will not attack unless frightened. Wear long boots when walking in snake areas, and watch carefully where you put each step. Most dangerous are animal bites: if you are bitten or scratched by any stray or wild animal wash the wound at once with soap or detergent and water, and flush thoroughly with clean water then seek medical advice locally. Animal rabies is prevalent in some parts of Europe (including France and Yugoslavia). More details can be found in the BMA's 'Health on Holiday' booklet.

T *Tunnels.* Nasty on a bicycle because in some countries there are some long, unlit and unventilated tunnels. Their blackness is accentuated by the sudden change from daylight to dark as you ride into the entrance; a good rear light is essential for safety, and a powerful front light will make forward vision easier, though it normally takes longer for the eyes to adjust to the lack of light than it does to ride through the tunnel. Watch out for rough-hewn walls and deep drainage gutters, and for potholes caused by water dripping from the ceilings. In some places such as the Alps and in Norway there are tunnels banned to cyclists.

U *Ultra-violet.* The sun, that rare and wan visitor to northern climes can be a brilliant, powerful force further south. On a bike you are particularly prone to sunburn, being out in the open all day and being lulled into thinking that it is cooler than it really is by the soothing breeze that wafts over your skin as you pedal. Burning is caused by ultra-violet light radiation, the UV being able to pass through clouds, though to some extent it is blocked by smoke and smog. Intensity of UV radiation increases with height, so you have to be careful when cycling in mountain regions – especially if you have fair hair and blue eyes, red hair or freckles. Avoid burning by gradual acclimatisation: shade yourself with clothing for all but half an hour on the first day, then double your ration of sun each day. Sunglasses and a hat with a brim, and of course suntan lotion are helpful accessories.

V *Vague Maps.* Some marks are so imprecise they are little more than cartographic doodles. Small roads and out-of-the-way villages are usually the most inaccurately marked, notably on map series covering Mediterranean countries. The map excuse "This map is so vague it is impossible to tell where we are" is an excellent ploy for using when a critical companion accuses you of losing the way.

W *Willing Helpers.* These come in many guises, but an example is the Portuguese railway official who painstakingly writes out a desti-nation label for your bicycle but accidentally sticks it to another package while you are offering him a beer for being so co-operative. Five hours later at Lisbon you collect a box of oranges from the baggage office and a hill-farmer in Galicia gets a ten-speed touring bike. A more common type of willing helper is the pedestrian who gives you very detailed instructions on how to find the wrong road out of town.

X *Xenophobic Customs Officials.* The sort that makes you unpack the entire contents of your panniers and tool kit so that he can see what he should take with him on his forthcoming cycle-tour.

Y *Yerk.* Any sudden unpleasant motion which upsets the smooth, dreamy rhythm of pedalling. Common causes of yerks are slipping gears which can dump you excruciatingly onto the cross-bar, and snatching brakes which can send you over the handlebars.

Z *Zebras.* If you see one of these you got on the wrong plane.

GREECE

If you are a dreamer and a romantic, and enjoy riding bikes by mountain and sea under clean scorching skies, you need look no further! Cycling in this, the most consistently beautiful of Mediterranean countries, has to be leisurely and unhurried for the distractions are many. It may be the cool of a café, a jumble of toppled temple columns, a swim from shelving sand or the intriguing alleys of some peeling coastal port. Or maybe it's a monastery roof glimpsed through a gap in the trees, or caves, or a hill to scramble up for a better view. Or a taxi-driver on holiday from Athens who wants to talk about his working youth spent in England. Breaks from the saddle are also encouraged by the ferocious heat during the summer, which can make biking in the middle of the day simply too gruelling; by the climbs which can often be very long, and the roads which are not always kind to the backside.

   Four-fifths of the country is mountain, with slopes dried for much of the year into a buff brown; just for a few weeks in spring does the new grass bring green to the landscape. Scrub, wild flowers, aromatic herbs and shrubs vie with the loose stone and rock, with olive trees, eucalyptus, cypress and pines providing the shade. Most of the rivers run dry in the summer. The few flat areas, like the Plain of Thessaly, are heavily cultivated, roastingly hot and airless in July and August; no place to ride a bike.

Such are the coast's convolutions that the furthest point from the sea is only 140 kilometres distant, at Lake Prespansko in the north. There are some 1,400 islands, nearly all of them mountainous, while inland many of the peaks top 2,000 metres in the wooded ranges of the Pindus. The coast is remarkably varied, ranging from sheer cliffs to long sandy strands, tiny secluded coves to long rocky peninsulas. What better therapy than to lie by the murmuring Mediterranean while a liquid sunset evaporates into the darkening horizon; watching for the shooting stars and satellites to cut the night in clean white lines then dropping to sleep as a quietening concerto of donkeys, cicadas, dogs, shepherds, goat-bells and birds make their final sounds of the day.

Apart from the bike traveller, there are two sorts of tourists in Greece: the hedonistic type who never strays more than a kilometre from the beach they've flown directly to from home, and the do-Greece-in-a-week type who rush blinded and sweating in coaches and cars between Athens, Mycenae, Delphi, Epidauros, Olympia *et al*. To avoid the hordes of camera-toting tourists (who contribute little to the mysticism of these sites) I strongly recommend visiting them early or late in the year – or spending the night as close as possible to the site, and making sure you're first through the gate in the morning. Just five minutes alone in Mycenae can set you up for years!

The tidal wave of tourism that has swept the accessible parts of Greece over the last 20 years has left its mark in the knick-knack stalls, hotels and beach developments. These are mostly in the east, where the country's biggest road links Greece's major cities: Salonika, Larissa, Volos and Athens. Elsewhere tourist development is centred on major ports (like Patras) the airports (Corfu, Kos, Rhodes, Mykonos etc), and archaeological sites.

Most Greeks seem to respond to bike travellers in a positive, heartwarming and often embarrassingly-generous manner – maybe because it's clear you are making more than the usual effort to feel their country. You can get pushed along streets by crowds of rascally enthusiastic small boys and introduced to complete strangers – soon friends – at café tables. Handing me his donkey, a young man once insisted on pushing my heavy bike up the cruelly-steep hill beyond his village; at the top he bade us wait beneath a tree and returned with a shirt full of deliciously ripe pears. Like all of us, the Greeks are charmed when you make an effort to speak in their own language, however clumsy it sounds. English is surprisingly widely spoken, and in many villages there's a teacher, seaman or ex-waiter willing to speak.

Country shops sometimes have limited supplies of food, though bread, yoghurt, *feta* (goat's milk) cheese, tinned squid and sardine, vegetables and fruit are abundant. In towns, at quayside restaurants you can eat salads, fresh fish and grilled, baked or casserolled meat; it's traditional to look in the kitchen and see what's cooking rather than to rely on the menu. Meals in *tavernas* are less expensive. Guaranteed to render biking impossible are *ouzo*, an explosive aniseed aperitif, and *retsina*, a resinated wine; cafés often sell several kinds of sticky cake, ideal for replacing lost calories, as well as ice-cold pop and beer *(Fix)*. A long siesta in the middle of the day is *de rigueur*, and in the evening there's commonly a community stroll *(volta)* when young and old dress up to talk, drink and take the cool evening air. The currency is the *drachma* (dr) divided into 100 *lepta* (l); virtually the whole population is Greek Orthodox. The Greek alphabet is used throughout the country and it is well worth getting acquainted with the Roman equivalents of the symbols.

Ride Guide

The Peloponnese

Legend, history and romance perfume the air which washes over this maple-leaf shaped 'island' loosely attached to mainland Greece at the Corinth Isthmus. And adventure too, for this rugged, surprising and intensely beautiful landscape is full of incident for the independent traveller. Not many foreigners have had the privilege of touching the Elysian splendour of this haunted land from such a sensitive and receptive vehicle as the bike.

Most tourists turn their backs on the Peloponnese in favour of the (paradoxically) more accessible islands of the Aegean; what tourist 'honeypots' there are, can be found around the coast – relatively few pause to explore the beautiful and fairly un-touched interior. The most commercialised part (and therefore the bit with the most traffic) is the peninsula of Argolis in the north-east; it's close enough to Athens for day-trippers whose normal circuit is the Corinth Canal ('My, isn't it *deep'),* Ancient Corinth, Epidauros (open-air theatre), Nauplia (fine castle and port), Tiryns (ramparts and Heracles' birthplace), Argos (another castle and reputedly Europe's oldest continuously-inhabited town) and of course Mycenae (Agamemnon's tomb, Lion Gate etc). Try and visit these places out of sequence with the coach parties! The fine beaches around Nauplia are well favoured by the package holiday industry.

One of the most lovely parts of inland Peloponnese is Arcadia, the central mountain region. Here you can pedal along broad valley bottoms

beneath tough-looking 2,000-metre peaks then spend several kilometres winding gradually upwards towards the bare rock of the ridges, passing the odd village. From high up, the clusters of white-painted houses look like starbursts against the verdant green haze of the valley floors. Some of the best roads have no tarmac, so it's best not to be in a hurry. Further south, the awesome Taygetos range stretches for over 100 kilometres from near Megalopolis (an unpleasant industrial town) to the tip of the Mani peninsula, steep-sided, snow-capped in winter and crossed at one point by a splendid 1,300-metre pass; on their eastern flank is the modern town of Sparta (the scanty remains of its famous predecessor lie on the outskirts), and a few minutes biking towards the mountains is the ruined Byzantine city of Mistras, perched on a Taygetos outcrop. Leave your bike at the bottom and scramble up through the alleys and briars, past the restored churches, palaces and roofless houses to the summit citadel – the views are immodest.

The Peloponnese coast is varied, with some of the least-spoilt, empty (and elusive) beaches in the Mediterranean. In places the coast is rocky and inaccessible, sometimes with small secluded sandy bays or on the north-western stretch from Patras round to Pylos, with long stretches of uninterrupted sand. Some of the big valleys get mosquito-infested near the coast. Near the west coast is Olympia, original site of the Olympic Games and further south-east is the remote and evocative temple of Bassae.

The three spiky peninsulas which reach out from the Peloponnese towards Crete are all worth exploring by bike. My own favourite is the central one, whose mountain spine is an extension of the Taygetos; stony, brown and barren hills tapering southwards to form a region whose remoteness and lack of succour have attracted a fiercely independent spirit. The best approach is from the lovely coastal town of Gythion through a castle-guarded gorge and over a high pass to Areopolis, gateway to the Mani – a land whose warlike inhabitants built square fortified tower houses with crenellated tops. Community relations were so bad that the inhabitants used to add a few feet to their towers overnight to prevent their neighbours across the alley from slinging rocks at them in the morning; some of the towers are several stories high, and the various 'strata' of building layers can clearly be seen. They still stand in forlorn and extraordinary groups across the hillsides. The whole area is very dry; the locals eat 'prickly pear' cacti and used to net flocks of small birds. A memorable ride can be taken most of the way to the tip of the peninsula – Cape Matapan. South of Vathia there are donkey-tracks and the going is very rough. The Cape itself is only a little short of being the most southerly point of mainland Europe.

The only really touristy part of the Mani peninsula is the cafe area around Pirgos Dirou. Of the other two southern peninsulas, the western one is wider and shorter, with Pylos, Methoni and Koroni (all attractive and historic ports) as its main towns. Riding over its hilly backbone in summer you'll find the air syrupy with the smell of grapes dehydrating on sheets in the sun, on their way to becoming currants. The eastern peninsula has Monemvasia as its crowning glory, once a great port, now a derelict town beneath an immense rock topped by the ruins of a Venetian fortress.

Epirus and Pindus

Not as varied as the Peloponnese, but a challenging area for the lover of mountain biking and wilderness. There are fewer archaeological sites here than south of the Gulf of Corinth, and the coastline is less exciting; there are very few towns of any size this side of the Pindus.

The least strenuous part for bike touring is the coast and islands, whose softer green hills and modest peaks are only half the height of the starker sharper ranges further inland. Igoumenitsa is very often the starting point for a tour of the north-west; it has ferry links with Corfu, Italy and Yugoslavia. Not far south of here is Parga, the main resort on this coast; from here southwards to Preveza there used to be an exhilarating 'ride' along rocky donkey tracks, through remote villages and past vast and deserted sandy beaches, but since I dragged and bumped my bike this way several years ago, new roads have been built and the area opened up to noisier traffic. At Nikopolis (just north of Preveza) are the sprawling remains of the mighty Roman city built by the Emperor Augustus to commemorate his victory over Antony and Cleopatra at the nearby Battle of Actium. There's a pleasant, easy ride along the north shore of Preveza's inland lagoon. Moving on south, Missolonghi sits by a swampy delta, where the poet Lord Byron died during the Greek War of Independence (the Park of Heroes is a lovely shady spot!).

The main route inland from the coast is along the well-surfaced road from Igoumenitsa, a spectacular ride through some of Greece's highest mountains – which continue to gain stature eastwards till they culminate in the wooded Pindus range (2,000 metres) which runs the length of central Greece, from Albania in the north to the Gulf of Corinth in the south. Just north of Klimatia (before you reach the pretty lakeside town of Ioannina) is the village of Zitza whose plunging waterfall and dizzy heights won Byron's affection, claiming them to 'shock yet please the soul'. But the most fantastic sight of all is on the other side of the mighty Metsovon Pass, at Meteora. On top of bare basalt columns that leap vertically for hundreds of feet above the road are several fourteenth-century monasteries so inaccessible that inhabitants had to be hauled up in rope baskets. It's in this central part of Greece that the Pindus mountains are at their most dramatic (though strangely, Greece's highest peak, Olympus, is not here but stands on its own over by the Aegean). Most of the narrow mountain roads in these parts are rough and uncompromising. Quieter and more remote than the Igoumenitsa-Metsovon route is the exciting mountain ride which crosses the Pindus from Agrinion, via Karpenision to Lamia, passing great reservoirs, huge forests and crossing a 1,250-metre pass. At the very southern tip of the Pindus range, where the mountains broaden and dip into the Gulf of Corinth is the most famous site in Greece, Delphi; rich in atmosphere and on a splendid location are many remains, among them the Temple of Apollo, site of the enigmatic oracle which influenced Mediterranean fate for 600 years.

Of the Ionian islands, three are big and interesting enough to warrant visiting with a bike. They are a lot greener and more tree clad and hospitable than those of the Aegean, though earthquakes have destroyed much of their architecture.

Corfu is very British, romanticised by Lawrence Durrell and overrun by package tourists during the summer. With cricket on Sundays and bars called the 'Pig and Whistle' this is not the place to discover the 'real Greece', but since it's often the destination for very good value charter flights, it's well worth considering. And parts of it are beautiful, especially in spring. Most of its roads are surfaced, and the views from the saddle are excellent. The most 'developed' (and least attractive) part is the 20 kilometres or so north of Corfu town.

The next island south is Levkas, far less popular but with some magnificent biking on its rough mountain roads. It's one of Greece's most accessible islands, joined to the mainland by causeways and a chain-ferry. It is possible to make a circular tour of the island using quiet narrow roads which wind along steep slopes (which rise to 1,158 metres in the centre) and there are several opportunities for swimming. The sign-posting is awful so it's best not to be too intent on any particular direction.

Moving on south, Kefallinia is the largest of the Ionian islands and can be reached by ferry from Patras and Levkas. Though it's rather less dramatic than its northern neighbour, it has a range of 1,000-metre mountains running along its spine, crossed in two or three places by small roads. Its very convoluted coastline gives continually changing views.

The Aegean Islands

In various confetti-like clusters these islands are scattered across the blue Aegean where they bask beneath a blazing sun, turning the rocky profiles of some of the more exposed ones a parched and buff brown for the summer months. Others are almost verdant. Many of the islands can be great fun to tour by bike (indeed the Greeks hire out bicycles on several) but it does not take long to run out of road. Some are so small you can ride every metre of road in a morning; others will provide a few days' leisurely cycling. The Aegean islands are not the place to plan long periods of continuous biking and are well-suited to sporadic velocipedean wanders interspersed with beach lounging, collapsing in cafés, visiting antiquities and mountain hiking.

Of them all, Rhodes probably offers the most scope for cycling, with a 200-kilometre ride around the perimeter of the island (mostly on tarmac) and the option of several more strenuous rides on unsurfaced roads through the central hills. It's one of the more colourful spots in the Aegean, with hibiscus and bougainvillaea contrasting with the silver-green of the olive groves. The main sights are the town of Rhodes itself, with its fourteenth-century Crusader castle and walls, and the acropolis above pretty Lindos. Fewer tourists travel to the south of the island.

Further up the Turkish coast, Kos, Samos, Chios and Lesbos all have enough roads and tracks for varied riding and the latter three are fairly wooded and less popular among tourists.

Among the Cyclades group, the mountainous islands of Andros, Tinos, Paros and Naxos have sufficient route networks to put together circular rides, or at least decent-length there-and-back excursions, though the scope is limited. On Andros for instance, the ride from one end of the island to the other is only just over 50 kilometres. Volcanic Santorini is one of the Aegean's most unusual spectacles, with the main town perched dizzily on top of a rim of precipitous cliffs; it's very crowded in summer.

Most parts of the Aegean are served by ferries from Piraeus, with small inter-island boats providing the means for island-hopping; if you plan to visit several islands, make sure in advance which ones are linked together. Some are not inter-connected, and you have to return to Piraeus in order to plug into a different ferry route. Unless you fly direct to the Aegean it's almost inevitable that you will have to pass through the doomed city of Athens. It's a nightmare of a place for a cyclist, with an eddying maelstrom of barging, hooting vehicles, sudden pot-holes and a sticky claustrophobic heat partly caused by the pall of curry-coloured smog which asphyxiates the city day and night. The once hallowed and beautiful 'Sacred Way' which ran from the capital to Eleusis, is now the most disgusting road in Greece and Eleusis itself is ravaged by industrial pollution. On all of my visits, Athens has come close to destroying the completely opposite images that the rest of the country seems so able to conjure up at every turn of the road.

Crete

The largest of the Greek islands, with some excellent, fairly hard cycling, and enough scope for at least a month's pedalling. Access is by plane direct to Heraklion, or by ferries from Piraeus to Chanea and Heraklion. Most of the roads are unsurfaced (though you can make a good tour which seldom leaves tarmac), so progress tends to be slow if you plan to see the best parts of the island. Crete's biggest towns are along the flatter north coast; the main road running its entire length has brought all the usual unsavoury tourist developments. But on the south coast the mountains more often than not fall straight to the sea, with occasional roads making their way down valleys to reach the shore. Some of the most scenic parts of the coast can only be reached by making there-and-back rides.

The western end of Crete is scenically the most appealing, with the

White Mountains, whose pale limestone glows a warm pink in the evening sun, dominating the landscape. The road between Platanos and Kepsalion which contours round the hillsides above Crete's west-facing coast provides one of many superb high-level (and bumpy!) rides, with the mountains above one elbow and the sea far below the other. The spaghetti-like roads which wriggle between the villages west of the White Mountains may be hard work, but they are thrilling too. Wind-bent stands of pine separate rocky crags and stony slopes and in sheltered corners terraced platforms of olive trees shelter from the wind. The local men still wear their traditional long black boots and baggy trousers and have those characteristic thick droopy moustaches.

High in the mountains is the unusual Plain of Omalos (one of the few bits of level riding south of Chanea), sunk between an all-encircling rim of mountains with no valley outlet. From its southern edges a road climbs to the head of the Gorge of Samaria, one of several formidable chasms which slash through the White Mountains, though this is the most accessible, and in fact the deepest gorge in Europe. The walk down the gorge from the 'Tourist Pavilion' (where bikes can be left) to the sea can occupy most of the day. At the bottom, most people take a small boat round the coast to Chora Sfakion (since there is no road); hardy types walk out to Chora Sfakion along donkey tracks or retrace their steps to the top of the gorge (to save making the return journey, some British club cyclists have apparently carried their bikes, including a tandem, the entire length of the gorge, 'riding' out along the coastal tracks!). Which ever way, it's not a trip to miss. (In winter and spring the gorge is a raging torrent and totally impassable).

The rest of Crete is an enchanting mixture of high mountains and broad plateaux; roughly midway along the island is the highest peak, Mt Idi (2,456 metres), snowy in winter and with a small rough road scaling its slopes. Just to the east of here are the island's main archaeological sites: the excavated Minoan city of Phaestos near the south coast, the old Roman capital of Gortys further east and beyond there the monastery of Arkades. Then a few minutes riding outside Heraklion (Venetian ramparts and chaotic traffic) is Crete's most famous discovery: the Minoan palace of Knossos, which might not be visually awesome or in a particularly pleasant location, but if you can actually grasp the fact that the throne rooms, frescoes, sewage systems and so on date from 1,400 BC, then it takes on an impressive significance.

Between Tzermiadon and the Dikti Mountains (superb mountain roads) is the Lassithi plain where 10,000 Cretan windmills pump water for the potatoes, and just east of here, near Kritsa, is the old Doric town of Lato. The south coast town of Ierapetra claims to be one of the sunniest in Europe, and sits at the neck of land which opens eastwards to provide more quiet and little used mountain roads.

The Highest Road in Greece

Making an airy crossing of the Pindus mountains between Ioannina in the west and Trikkala to the east, the road reaches a height of 1,705 metres at the Metsovon Pass.

Tour of the Peloponnese

A tour which will stretch imagination and emotion to the limit; a passage through ancient history, and through a landscape some would call perfect. It's based on the Peloponnese and explores the coast of Argolis, the extraordinary Mani peninsula and Arcadia's tranquil mountain valleys, calling on the way at classic sites like Epidauros, Bassae and Olympia, with optional detours to Mycenae, Mistras, Ancient Sparta and Delphi. Few of the roads are level, there are several major passes (at least three over 1,000 metres) to climb and sometimes there is no tarmac so it's not a tour for the faint-hearted. There is plenty of scope for making the route more adventurous, by adding loops or detours, or for reducing its length by using ferries or railways. The tour can be started or finished in either Patras or Athens; if you're landing at Athens' Ellinikon Airport, the city can be avoided by cycling direct to Piraeus. (If you want to visit Athens consider leaving your bike at Piraeus and taking the 20-minute electric train to Omonia Square). The many permutations of Greek ferry services offer ways of adapting this route; it's important you check ferry schedules before committing yourself to a particular route, as the times and services can change.

PELOPONNESE TOUR

Terrain: hilly/mountainous
Distance: 850 km (excluding detours)
Start/Finish: Athens/Athens
Scenery: **
Interest: **
Maps: Freytag & Berndt, Peloponnese 1:300,000 (Clyde Survey Leisure Map, Athens and the Peloponnese, 1:400,000, for Delphi detour and Athens district)

km	
	ATHENS
15	Piraeus

(alternative route by bike to Nauplia, via Eleusis, Megara, Corinth on old coast road [little traffic but spoilt scenery], Epidauros or Mycenae)

	ferry across Saronic Gulf
	Methana
44	Trachia
18	Epidauros
5	Lygurion
25	Nauplia

(detour north via Tiryns, Aj. Trias, Anyphion, Mycenae, Argos, Myli: 45 km)

33	Par Astros
53	Leonidion
26	Kosmas
16	X-rds 2km W Jerakion

(alternative route to Kalamata via Sparta [Mistras] and Taygetos Mtns cutting 100 km off route, OR detour SE to Monemvasia and rejoin route at Skala: 120 km)

25	Skala
18	Gythion
25	Areopolis

22	Exo Nymphion	27	Chalandritsa
14	Vathia	23	PATRAS

(detour to Cape Tainaron/
Matapan)

8	Gerolimin
21	Pirgos Dirou
11	Areopolis
85	Kalamata

(detour SW via Messini to Koroni,
Methoni, Pylos, Messini: 135 km)

56	Megalopolis
45	Andritsaena

(detour 10 km S to Bassae)

43	Krestena
14	Olympia
52	Langadia
25	Vytina
16	Panagitsa
22	Kato Klitoria
(30	Kalavryta)
28	Kato Vlasia

(ferry or train back to Piraeus
via Corinth Canal, or cycle back
along old road beside Gulf of Corinth
then beside Saronic Gulf: 200 km)

OPTIONAL DETOUR TO DELPHI
PATRAS

10	Rion
	ferry across Gulf of Corinth
	Antirion
9	Nafpaktos
47	Eratini
43	Amfissa
20	Delphi
46	Livadia

(train back to Athens avoids
partly unpleasant ride)

47	Thiva
49	Eleusis
24	ATHENS

Basic Information

Getting There

Air: international airports in Greece are Athens, Corfu, Heraklion, Rhodes and Salonika. Flight time from London to Athens is $3\frac{1}{2}$ hours.

Rail: limited connections with the rest of Europe, with two different routes from the UK to consider depending on which part of Greece you plan to tour. The London-Salonika-Athens option is suitable for the north, west and Aegean islands and takes roughly 70 hours (gruelling and the bike may arrive late), while the other option is to go to Brindisi in southern Italy (40-hour train journey) then take the 11-hour ferry to Corfu then Igoumenitsa on the Greek mainland. Brindisi ferries sometimes continue to Patras; the Italy option is thus suitable for touring the west, Ionian islands and Peloponnese.

Road: by main road Igoumenitsa is about 2,100 kilometres from Boulogne (via Brindisi in Italy).

Ferry: Greece has good ferry links with Yugoslavia, Italy, southern France, Turkey, North Africa and Israel.

Information Sources

National Tourist Organisation of Greece (NTOG), 195-197 Regent

Street, London W1R 8DL (tel: 01-734.5997). Invaluable general information booklet with notes of ferry services, useful maps and regional tourist brochures.

Local Tourist Bureaux: there are about 20 NTOG offices in the largest cities, at frontiers and on the most popular islands; the Tourist Police have a further 70 or so information offices in smaller towns and islands (addresses of these and NTOG offices in the free NTOG information booklet).

Greek Automobile & Touring Club (ELPA), 10 Messogion Street, Athens (Tel: 7791.615). Able to supply information on general touring matters, including roads and ferries, to AIT members.

Greek Cycling Federation, 28 Bouboulinas Street, Athens 147 (tel: 8831.414), administrative body for national cycle-racing.

Accommodation

Camping: camp-sites are not that frequently found in the best cycling areas, being geared to the needs of motorists and therefore close to the nastiest main roads, the biggest cities and most popular tourist sights. Generally they are too far apart to be linked by bike on a daily basis. Inland they are rare, with more on the Aegean coast than on the Ionian. Most are privately run, but the NTOG have a number of well-equipped and fairly expensive sites (they can cost more than a night in an inn, though they do offer 10% discount for holders of AIT cards or camping carnets), while the Hellenic Touring Club have some less expensive more basic sites. Rates may be lower out of season. A few addresses are in NTOG's information booklet; local Tourist Police and NTOG offices can supply information on sites in their neighbourhood.

Officially, wild camping is 'not allowed in any part of the country', yet at bicycle speeds it's impossible in many parts to link 'official' accommodation in one day's riding. Discretion is of paramount importance; the Tourist Police will move on – brusquely – camping outfits they find objectionable.

Youth Hostels: nearly 30 IYHA Hostels throughout the country, 7 on Crete alone; some are in interesting towns where hotels are expensive, or near historic sites where camping is difficult, so are good for the occasional night. They range in size from quite small buildings used mainly by climbers and hikers, to the big urban-dormitory type for anyone looking for a low-cost bed. A third have self-cooking facilities, while the rest offer meals which are usually good value, tasty and filling. Some of the mountain and coastal hostels have to be booked in advance. There are YMCA and YWCA hostels in Athens, Salonika and Rethymnon (YWCA only).

Inns/Pensions/Tavernas: normally less expensive and more basic than E class hotels, but good for character and local atmosphere.

Sometimes you may share a room with other travellers, which saves even more money. Also in this price bracket are rooms in private houses which are sometimes let (unofficially) at low prices. Local Tourist Police and NTOG offices can supply addresses.

Hotels: in six categories, from Luxury, then 'A' to 'E'; category E is about half the price of the Luxury hotels. Any establishment with 5 or more rooms has to have its prices cleared by the Tourist Police; rates are substantially less out of the tourist season. Again, the NTOG and Tourist Police are very helpful in providing addresses of low-cost hotels; just tell them the most you want to pay and they will provide addresses within that price bracket. Rock-bottom in Athens are the back-street hotels near Syntagma Square where you can sleep on the concrete roof for a fraction of the price of the Hilton, but with the same view of the Acropolis.

Advance hotel reservations can be made directly to the hotels in question, or to the Greek Chamber of Hotels, 6 Aristidou Street, Athens (Tel: 3233.501).

Weather

Very hot, dry and predictable in summer, with most places having temperatures well into the 30s during the two most scorching months, July and August. Only the very south of Italy, and parts of Spain can rival Greek heat; it's Europe's sunniest country. Temperatures are comfortable enough for taking a bike tour as early as April and as late as the beginning of November – though at the extremes of the cycling season nights are cold and the weather generally less settled. On the coast and islands the summer temperatures are moderated by sea breezes; inland it can be 5 or 6°C hotter. This, the dust and glare of pale rocks can make midday mid-season touring hard work. Winters are mild on the coast and islands but severe inland, especially in the north.

There's hardly any rain in a Greek summer, with dry (almost drought) seasons during July and August in the north, from May to August in the Peloponnese and from April to September in Crete. Nearly all the rain arrives in winter, with the west considerably wetter than the east. The mountains, especially in the north, catch a lot of snow which lies through to late April.

Prevailing winds between mid-May and mid-October are northerly and tend to get stronger through the day and die down at night; so if you have to bike northwards, do it early in the morning!

Other Considerations: Spring happens quickly, between late March/early April, and May, a lovely time when the landscape bursts briefly into fresh greenness, with a colourful quilt of Mediterranean flowers and blossoming almond trees. This is also the time of year to see the night-time lights of the fireflies, and is great for bike touring. The sea is warmest in July and August, and above 20°C from June to October.

Ferries to the northern Cyclades islands are very crowded around Assumption Day (15 August) as pilgrims head for Tinos.

Average Daily Maximum Temperatures (Centigrade)

	alt. in metres	J	F	M	A	M	J	J	A	S	O	N	D
Corfu	25	14	15	16	19	23	28	31	31	28	23	19	16
Trikkala	149	9	12	16	21	25	31	35	34	30	25	16	11

Cycling Information

Cycle Shops

The big cities of Athens and Salonika have several well-stocked shops which can supply good quality lightweight spares for derailleur bikes. Elsewhere the spares available tend to be for roadster bikes: brake cables, cotter-pins, tubes and tyres (27 x $1\frac{1}{4}$ are sometimes available, though in variable qualities; I've seen anything from an antique rubber Dunlop Sprint to a dubious-looking nylon '7 Stars' from Taiwan hanging on the wall), nuts and bolts, and not surprisingly puncture repair patches and rubber solution. These smaller shops are often disguised as motorbike/pushbike/general junk emporiums; on the islands, the bike-hire centres carry spare parts. Towns near flatter coastal areas and plains are more likely to have bike shops than those in mountain regions; Missolonghi, Trikkala, Nauplia, Tripolis, Gythion, Corfu, Heraklion and Chanea all have shops of some description. Prices for the same product can vary substantially from shop to shop, so if there's more than one in a town, look around.

Being a country where a 'precision tool' is often a hammer, it's best not to invite local 'mechanics' to actually repair your bike – though you'll find no shortage of advice if for a moment you look as if you have a problem. In the far south of the Peloponnese on the steep hill of a small coastal port, the freewheel on my bike tore itself to pieces. Within minutes I had a teenage interpreter and a gang of 'helpers' who took me on a tour of the back-streets where, through a dark doorway in a room heaped with coiled ropes, rusty sewing machines, car tyres, oars and a cascade of other dusty junk, I was introduced triumphantly to a small box *full* of spare freewheel parts for a bicycle! And the owner wouldn't accept a single drachma.

Cycle Hire

Normally inexpensive and confined to the islands – Kos, Corfu, Rhodes and Crete all have substantial fleets – bike hire concerns can supply machines on a daily basis, usually with some kind of deposit required. The bikes are mostly single-speed, with 'ladies" frames and 26″ wheels, sometimes with back-pedal brakes. Their design and levels of maintenance make them more suitable for rolling down to the beach than for prolonged excursions.

Transporting Your Bicycle

Bikes can be taken on Greek trains, which are not especially fast, comfortable or known for punctuality, with lines limited to the east of the country and the Peloponnese. You register your bike about an hour before departure and normally there is no charge. The Hellenic Railways Organisation (OSE) has information offices at Athens (1 - 3 Karolou St, Tel: 5222.491 and 6 Sina St, tel: 3624.402/6) and Salonika (20 Aristotelous St, tel: 276.382).

The various bus services reach some astonishingly remote parts of the country, and the local blue and white ones will carry bikes (though you're wholly dependent on the goodwill of the driver). All the island ferries will take bikes, usually for a modest charge.

Roads

The main through-routes generally have good tarmac, but they also carry most of the nation's traffic, especially those in the eastern portion of the country. In the north-west of Greece and in the Peloponnese these main roads are not generally offensively busy and can be a quick, if less interesting, means of crossing the country. Overall, traffic densities on Greek roads are well below the European standard, about on a par with Norway. Few foreigners venture onto un-metalled roads.

The best bike routes follow the secondary roads; often these have good tarmac, but they can include anything from fairly smooth oiled gravel, over which it's possible to ride quite fast, to roads of little more than river-bed quality. After heavy rain, great runnels cut up the surfaces and landslips add further interest. Dust can be a nuisance and in places the bouncing of lorries has created corrugations which are almost as impossible as Belgian *pavé* to ride a bike over. Since it's very difficult to predict what a forthcoming road will be like (though certain maps are helpful) it's best to plan short daily distances and not get frustrated if you have to walk the bike now and again. Changes of surface can occur suddenly, in the middle of nowhere and with no apparent reason; one moment you can be lurching between small boulders and the next gliding along on silky tarmac. After dark (a lovely time for biking in Greece) you need excellent night vision and good bike lights, because there are things to run into; one evening two of us shot over the handlebars having ridden straight into a massive pile of grit left in the road. Laughing after the soft landing, and looking at the two bikes standing upright with their front wheels neatly wedged into the yielding granules, we couldn't work out whether the roadman, the darkness or the *ouzo* should take the blame.

Gradients are usually reasonable, though some of the climbs and descents go on for many kilometres. Signposting is often non-existent (and sometimes in Greek script only); small roads can be hard to locate, the solution being to ask a local the way to the next village on your itinerary. Greek drivers like to drive fast and horn hooting is fashionable – mainly with the intention of clearing the road ahead of goats, dogs, donkeys and stray humans.

Maps

Note: village names, their locations and the position and courses of small roads and tracks differ from map to map; the free maps from NTOG are a helpful start, and show most of the ridable routes. The smaller sectional maps found in tourist leaflets handed out at Tourist Police and local NTOG offices are similarly useful.

General Planning

Geographia Pocket Map Series, Greece, scale 1:1,250,000. Compact and not too expensive, with good height shading, scenic roads and tourist sights.

Michelin No 980 Greece, scale 1:700,000. Good detail, scenic roads in green, spot heights and shading but inaccurate in places.

For Cycling

Kümmerly + Frey, Greece, scale 1:500,000. Normally too small a scale for detailed cycling, but this is the only thorough map which covers north-west Greece (it also covers the rest of the country so would do for general planning). Good height shading and useful information on probable road surface.

Freytag & Berndt, Peloponnese (scale 1:300,000), *Halkidiki-Salonica* (1:200,000), *Athens-Delphi-Euboea* (1:250,000), *Pilion-Skiathos-Skopelos* (1:100,000). The first of these four is vital for a tour of the Peloponnese; they all show roads and hills in good detail, and some tracks too. The shading helps identify hilly routes and flatter ones. They also have town and archaeological plans plus detailed tourist information.

Clyde Survey Leisure Maps, Crete (scale 1:275,000), *Rhodes* (1:120,000), *Corfu* (1:100,000). The best maps for cycling these islands with usually-correct information on road surfaces, location of tracks, clear hill shading and abundant tourist information. The *Athens and Peloponnese* edition (1:400,000) includes the north coasts of the Saronic Gulf and Gulf of Corinth.

Greek National Survey, scale 1:200,000. Expensive, very difficult to decipher (all annotations in Greek) but perhaps worth considering for local touring in areas (like the north-west) not covered by the tourist editions already listed. They are very detailed, with contours and hill-tracks shown.

Other large-scale maps: the local Tourist Police and NTOG offices sometimes have special editions available which cover the more popular Aegean islands; M. Toubis publish one of Santorini (at 1:36,000) and Mykonos (at 1:40,000).

SPAIN

Looked at over a pair of handlebars, Spain is a big country, not just because it is the second largest in Europe, but because the landscape has a scale and emptiness that create an aura of vastness; crossing the Netherlands by bicycle is a three-day jaunt, but to pedal across Spain can be a three-*week* journey. Unlike its neighbour on the other side of the Pyrenees, much of Spain's landscape does not have that cosy intimacy which guarantees new views every few kilometres; instead it has a grander, slower-moving succession of vistas. It is the interruptions in this vastness, and around its edges, that is where the best, most varied cycling is to be enjoyed. There are winding roads following tortuously rocky coasts and others which claw precipitously over high mountain cols; country byways roll through seas of orange and olive groves and there are river valleys too wide to see across. And there are the beaches — hundreds of kilometres, some of them swept and cleaned daily, others looking (and smelling) like a corporation rubbish tip. There are even a few less accessible, delightfully untrodden beaches.

The core of Spain is the *meseta*, a great austere plateau between

600 and 900 metres high which occupies most of the inner part of the country and above which rise a number of mountain and hill ranges known as *sierras*. The most significant ranges stretch obliquely across the centre of the *meseta*, separating Old from New Castile. The *meseta* can be a daunting place to ride a bicycle – it is a land of endless horizons at its most stark on the La Mancha tableland, the wandering-ground of Don Quixote and Sancho Panza. The edge of the *meseta* is marked by a rim of mountains, sometimes spectacularly sheer, such as parts of the Sierra Nevada in the south and Cantabrian Cordillera in the north. Between these mountains and the sea is a narrow strip of lower coastal land, often thinning to a fine shelf, generally fertile, with many more villages and roads than the interior. It is in the transitional zone, between the edge of the *meseta* and the sea, that the most interesting cycling is to be found; most of the roads in these parts are, however, hilly, so there is little point in choosing Spain for a bike tour if you have an 'exertion aversion'.

One of the greatest attractions of Spain is the rich historical and cultural legacy. Phoenicians, Carthaginians, Romans and Vandals all made their mark, but none so memorably as the Moors, the Moslem Arabs who stayed for 800 years. They introduced irrigation, oranges and almonds, the date palm, sugar cane and the cotton bush, and constructed castles, mosques, palaces and gardens which still survive. Indeed Spain is truly the 'land of the castles' – a reflection of the centuries of conflict between the Moors and Christians. Gothic cathedrals and great walled towns date from medieval times, their past recalled in museums and in a fabric little changed over the years.

Spanish weather varies with the different regions and you can choose between riding under clear blue skies of African intensity in the south or in cooler more tempestuous conditions in the north; Andalusia shares the same lines of latitude and weather as Algeria, and at the other extreme, Galicia has much in common with the climate of western France. Severe droughts periodically hit the centre of the country, ruining harvests and wringing dry the reservoirs; water can become very scarce.

One of the consequences of Spain's mixed history is that there is no such thing as a 'typical Spaniard'; the people vary in temperament and looks with their regions. The dark-eyed Andalusians tend to be friendly and outward-going, the Castilians paler and more reserved. *Mañana* however, is everywhere the Spanish catchword, taken as meaning 'tomorrow, or the day after, or the day after that ...'; it is used to devastating effect by Spanish officials intent on procrastination rather than co-operation. Mass tourism along the coasts encourages the locals to capitalise on spendthrift visitors (bikes should be locked when left), and here, too, foreign women are the target of unwelcome and persistent attention from the Spanish male. Inland, among the less-frequented villages and towns, a foreigner travelling by bicycle is the subject of curiosity, and often of heart-warming generosity.

Spain is a Catholic country, and arms and legs should be covered when entering a church. Politically, the country has, since 1975, gone through a radical transformation from dictatorship (the last in western Europe) to democracy; the least settled part of the country is the Basque region, where the separatist movement is involved in a bitter struggle with the national government – tourists are never intentionally involved, though Spanish police are notoriously jumpy as a result of the 'troubles'. English is not widely spoken inland, but is fairly common in coastal areas; French is often spoken in the north. Spanish is the accepted native tongue, but Catalan is spoken in the north-east and Balearics, Basque in the western Pyrenees and Galician in the far north-west. The currency is the *peseta*, divided into 100 *céntimos*.

Spanish food has little of the subtlety of neighbouring France, but it is varied and interesting. Different regions have their own specialities, though fresh fish, and a penchant for cooking everything in olive oil and garlic are common throughout the country. Shops can be hard to spot, and sometimes the only clues to their whereabouts will be a pile of crates or gas cylinders stacked outside a shady doorway; away from the coast and towns, supplies of food are rarer and less varied. Restaurants are classified by 'fork' gradings from one to five; a 'two-fork' establishment is normally reasonable value and quality. The *menú turístico* (also known as the *MT*, *menú del día* or *prix fixé*) is usually the best value meal. Spanish people eat late, lunch usually being around 2 or 3 pm and supper after 9 pm. Bars are found along the roadsides, and are an admirable place for a pause from pedalling; they open from early morning till past midnight, serving alcohol, coffee and soft drinks. *Tabernas* and *bodegas* are more basic establishments, serving wine straight from the cask. Good for a casual nibble are *tapas*, light snacks provided with your drinks or before the main meal as an appetiser.

Ride Guide

Cantabria and Galicia

An under-rated area which is a good choice for a tour if you want to cycle by coast and mountains without suffering the scorching summer heat across the rest of Spain; the north coast has damper, cooler weather which brings a lush greenness to the landscape. It is an area where impressive scenery makes up for the relative lack of cultural and historical sights; a verdant luxuriant landscape quite unlike the blasted dusty browns of central and southern Spain. From the UK, the

Plymouth-Santander ferry provides easy access, landing you right on the edge of excellent cycling country; alternatively you can take the train via Paris, to Hendaye/Irun, and thence along the north coast to any of a number of stations. Roads in Cantabria and Galicia are hilly, so low gears and good brakes (and strong legs!) are necessary. In some ways, pedalling through north-west Spain is harder going than cycling the Pyrenees because the hills follow each other relentlessly, with little time for drawing breath before the next climb; some gradients are steep. A tour here does, however, have the great bonus that you need never be far from the sea, so energetic biking can be tempered with lounging on the beach and swimming.

Cantabria, the eastern of these two regions, can be seen as a long strip of coast backed by the hills and mountains of the Cantabrian Cordillera, behind which stretch the vast, empty plains of Old Castile. The scenic (and literal) highspot of Cantabria is the section of the Cordillera known as the Picos de Europa, a range of wild and precipitous limestone peaks which rear spectacularly to 2,648 metres at Torre Cerredo. They are fairly compact, but several roads penetrate the Picos, providing enough scope for several days of unforgettable touring. You can ride through shady gorges and sheer-sided defiles such as those of Hermida and Los Beyos, and tackle some dizzy passes. The San Glorio pass reaches 1,609 metres (with a track from it to a fine viewpoint on Peña de Llesba). Close to the west there are good views from the Pandetrave Pass (1,562 metres), and near the top of the narrow Panderruedas Pass (1,450 metres) there are superb views from the Mirador de Piedrashitas. Stony jeep tracks *(pista para jeep)* through the Picos offer scope for adventurous rough-stuffers, and the hiking is excellent; one of my most enjoyable mountain walks has been from Fuente Dé, up an ancient track carved in the mountain-side, to a high, deserted green valley surrounded by gaunt snow-patched ridges of pale rock. On a subsequent trip two of us enjoyed a challenging day trip on unloaded bikes, starting at Potes, cycling down the gorge to La Hermida, then riding the jeep tracks through the heart of the Picos, via Beges, Sotres and then via a rain-lashed col and a plunging descent to Espinama and back to Potes. Westwards the Cordillera continues in a less spectacular fashion, but fierce enough to force the roads up to 1,500 metres in several places. Eastwards from the Picos, the Cordillera runs into the Basque mountains, themselves an outlier of the Pyrenees.

Between the Cantabrian Cordillera and the sea is a narrow strip of hills (since many are over 1,000 metres they could almost be mountains). Here the valley bottoms are quilted with small fields of maize and spotted with tiny red-roofed villages; woods and forests climb the valley sides. Many of the Cantabrian roads follow the rivers which rush down from the Cordillera, and these valleys offer the least strenuous cycling

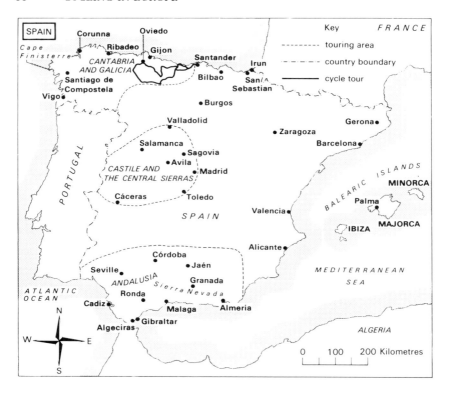

routes. And some of the downhill runs from the mountains to the sea are terrific: though a characteristic of the area is that winds get funnelled from the sea into the narrow valleys, sometimes making 'downhill pedalling' necessary.

The Cantabrian coast is one of low cliffs (steeper and more rugged to the west) with sandy beaches and the occasional inlet harbouring a small port. The largest sandy beaches are in the Santander area; these, and centres like San Sebastian and Santander, get very crowded in August. The most attractive section of coast is west from Santander (the Costa Verde), the town of Santillana del Mar with its old monastic buildings and well-preserved character being one of the main tourist attractions. Cantabria also has a number of caves, some like Altamira being famous for their prehistoric paintings. The areas around Bilbao, and south of Gijon, are quite industrial.

To the west of Cantabria, embracing the right-angle of coast above Portugal's northern border, is Galicia – a far-flung corner of Europe whose inaccessibility has preserved intact much of its scenic and cultural charm. It is a region which fits well with a tour of northern Portugal. Galicia's main attraction is its coast, washed on two sides by the muscular swell of the Atlantic and worn into a ragged fringe of peninsulas and long sinuous inlets known locally as *rias*. The western part of this coastline looks vaguely similar to those other spiny Atlantic extremities: Brittany, Devon and Cornwall, south-west Ireland and Scotland. Appropriately, the bagpipes are one of Galicia's native musical instruments.

This generally low and rocky coast is scoured by strong sea winds, with roads that are often exposed: as you round a headland, a comforting tailwind can turn to an irritating headwind. From Ribadeo to La Guardia on the Portuguese border you can ride on winding roads, seldom far from the sea and often following picturesque *corniches* which provide ever-changing views. Some of the more interesting rides are out along the peninsulas on 'there-and-back' roads – Cape Finisterre being one of the classic outings. The most popular part of the coast is the Rías Bajas from Muros south to Vigo, while the two main centres are the port of Corunna and inland, the holy town of Santiago de Compostela; Vigo has an impressive setting. Elsewhere the towns are small though industrious and the fishing ports of Galicia are the most important in Spain. Inland the granite upland is broken into several *sierras*, with hilly cycling through a wooded, green, though depopulated land.

Castile and the Central Sierras

Not an area that can congratulate itself on having the same variety of scenery that some of Spain's coastal regions can boast, but one that is worth noting for its many historical towns and villages. It is a land of castles and cathedrals, of Spanish tradition and of architecture dating back to Roman times. In summer the weather is scorchingly hot and in winter freezing and snowy, so the most practical time for bike touring is spring and autumn. Away from the main roads surfaces can be rough, with big distances between villages. Being on a main rail line, and with an international airport, Madrid is an obvious starting point for a tour; Cáceres and Salamanca also have good rail links.

The three main ranges of *sierras* which run from north of Madrid westwards to the Portuguese border separate the great arid rolling plains of the *meseta* into two halves; an important geographical dividing line. It is in these hills and mountains – the Sierras de Guadarrama, Gredos and Gata – and in their lower outliers, that the more interesting (and hilly!) roads lie. Here you can ride up to fine viewpoints, with pine woods adding variety and shade. There are several 1,000-metre passes.

But the main justification for touring here is to visit the historical sites of Castile, the 'land of the castles', and of neighbouring Cáceres province. Madrid is a natural focus, with national museums and art galleries, though the city itself, located by Philip II in the 16th century because it seemed central, is not especially notable; his grand palace of Escorial lies to the north-west in more pleasant surroundings. The major towns of interest are found in a 300-kilometre arc west from Madrid. Going anti-clockwise these are: Segovia (Roman aqueduct and Alcázar), Valladolid (fine buildings, San Gregorio College), Avila (old city with medieval ramparts), Salamanca (beautiful university town), Cáceres (medieval atmosphere) and Toledo (former capital of Castile and famous for its arms, cathedral and Alcázar). Many smaller towns and villages also have strong links with Spain's past: Peñafiel and Coca (east and south of Valladolid respectively) have fine castles while north of Segovia is the medieval fortified town of Pedraza de la Sierra. South of the Tagus, Alcántara has a Roman bridge, Trujillo was the hometown of many of the *conquistadores* and Guadalupe has an old battlemented monastery.

Andalusia

Often claimed to be the essence of the 'real Spain', the area which lies between the Sierra Morena and the Mediterranean and Atlantic coasts is a memorable land through which to travel by bicycle. Snow-capped mountains, magnificent cities and expansive plains bask beneath a sun which cannot be matched for predictability and intensity by anywhere else in Spain – or Europe for that matter. In fact, unless you can take the sun in unlimited amounts, think twice before touring Andalusia in July or August because temperatures can top 35°C; in my naïvety I first toured here in high summer and to escape the devastating heat had at times to ride in frenzied dashes between one patch of roadside shade and the next – early morning and evening turned out to be the only practical times of day for comfortable pedalling. The winter months can be a pleasant time of year to tour the low-lying parts of Andalusia. Secondary roads, in the hills and mountains especially, can have bad surfaces and water can be hard to find in more remote areas. Almeria, Seville and Malaga have international airports, the latter being a popular destination of low-cost off-season charter flights and well sited as a start/finish point for an Andalusian tour.

Andalusia was occupied by the Moors for longer than other parts of Spain, and the exotic Arab influence has lingered; there is much outstanding architecture. The three most celebrated Andalusian centres are Seville, the Andalusian capital and in many ways a synthesis of the entire region with its splendid cathedral and Giralda (once a minaret), Alcázar, parks, museums and colourful Holy Week which starts each Palm Sunday; Granada which has a lovely setting, Moorish buildings and magnificent 14th-century Alhambra (castle); and Córdoba with its 8th-century mosque, old Jewish quarter and Alcázar.

Córdoba and Seville sit in the broad valley of the Guadalquivir, the most fertile (and hot) part of Andalusia, which despite being semi-arid produces a rich variety of crops; groves of olive, orange orchards and fields of wheat, maize, sugar cane, tobacco and rice line the roads. The heat in this valley has to be felt to be believed: the daily temperatures top 30°C from June to September.

But it is in the hills of Andalusia that the most dramatic scenery is to be found – and the hardest cycling. High above Granada is the Sierra Nevada, a scaled-down version of the California range it gave its name to, rising steeply from the valley haze to clean coniferous-clad slopes, barren ridges and rocky peaks. This is the most impressive of the several *sierras* which line the Mediterranean coast, and includes among its summits Spain's highest mountain, Mulhacén (maps do not agree, but it is about 3,480 metres). Here too is Europe's highest road, one of the ultimate challenges for cyclo-mountaineers (see page 71). In one of the ranges to the west of the Sierra Nevada is impressively-sited Ronda, with a walled 'old town' and Moorish buildings – the town is also the focus of a number of exciting roads for cycling: to the east are the Chorro gorges where the river Guadalhorce cuts a sheer-sided channel through the limestone mountains while to the west are the Pileta Caves with ancient wall drawings. Other hilly parts of Andalusia with scenic cycling include the Sierra Cazorla east of Jaén, where you can pedal by woods and streams at the headwaters of the Guadalquivir, and parts of the Sierra Morena north of Seville; the attractive town of Aracena has caves and a castle.

In complete contrast, the area north-east of Almeria is as close to desert as you can find anywhere in Europe, a wilderness of scrub, sand and dun-coloured hills which starred in Lawrence of Arabia and several spaghetti-westerns. Few people cycle here, but anyone who does cannot fail to be impressed by its awesome lack of welcome: wind-blown sand drifts across the road and great washed-out wadis yawn cavernously across the plain. There is no shade, and on a bicycle under the noon-day sun you feel as lonesome and vulnerable as a parched cowpoke with a flock of vultures breathing down his neck.

Yet, a handful of kilometres away is the infamous Costa del Sol – the most visited and least Spanish part of Andalusia. Parts of this coastline are a hideous mess of cast concrete and tatty tourism, but there are still lovely sandy beaches (and rocky shores) which are unspoilt – usually those without car-parking facilities. The main resorts are west of Malaga; the words 'Torremolinos' and 'Marbella' ought to be sufficient warning. A main road follows the coast closely from west of Almeria to Algeciras, quite hilly in parts, busy in others, but well-surfaced. The

Rock of Gibraltar is a magnificent spectacle rising in triangular defiance from the sea mists, with a classic view to be had from across the Bay of Algeciras. 23 kilometres south-west of here is Punta de Tarifa, the most southerly point of mainland Europe, one of those places – like the North Cape of Norway – which is so satisfying to reach on a bicycle, simply because it is such a definable goal.

The Balearic Islands

Worth considering for a spring or autumn tour, and, of these two seasons, spring being the drier is a better bet; temperatures are pleasant by mid-March, by which time the 'rainy season' should be coming to an end. In summer the islands are crowded, and accommodation impossible to find unless booked months in advance. Access is easiest by direct flight to Palma, the Balearic capital – and often the destination of low-cost off-season charter-flights. Ferries ply between the Balearics and the mainland ports of Valencia, Barcelona and Alicante.

Majorca holds the greatest potential for cycling, and is an old favourite among racing cyclists, who set up 'training camps' on the island during early spring, using the varied terrain to practise hill-climbing and time-trialling, and to generally ride off the winter flab. The Puerto Pollenca area is a common centre for these camps. The sunny, mild winters bestow on the Balearics a lush almost sub-tropical vegetation, and, away from the towns and hotels, the hillsides are stepped with ranks of man-made terraces used for growing oranges and almonds, vines and olives. Majorca is about 75 kilometres by 100 kilometres, with enough roads for a week or two of varied cycling. Between the small, picturesque villages you can find yourself riding on anything from dead-flat, to rolling terrain, to Alpine style hairpins. The much-indented coast varies from spectacular, sheer limestone cliffs plunging to a clear sea, to the soporific lapping of peaceful waters against a gently sloping sandy beach. The most exciting cycling is in the two ranges of hills which lie either side of the island's central plain. Of these, the north-western hills are the most promising, with twisty scenic roads curling through pines high above the sea, that in places are quite exerting – the Col de Sóller reaches 900 metres. Two of the classic rides are the excursion out along the hilly road to the cliffs of Cape Formentor (the most northerly point on Majorca), and the spiralling plunge from the northern mountains down to dramatically-sited La Calobra. There are several celebrated caves to visit among the hills that line Majorca's south-eastern coast.

The other Balearic islands have relatively few roads, and limited possibilities for cycling. Minorca is the second largest in the archipelago, fairly low and windy, with stark white-painted buildings and an attractive coast, the north deeply indented by rocky inlets and the south blessed with many fine sandy beaches. Ibiza by contrast is relatively mountainous with a rugged, cliff-lined shore difficult to reach by road.

Spain's (and Europe's) Highest Road

Currently the highest point reached by a road in Europe, the 3,392-metre Pic Veleta in the heart of the Sierra Nevada range is also Spain's second highest mountain – not many metres below the top of neighbouring Mulhacén. The normal approach is from Granada, up a road to the south-east which involves 55 kilometres of virtually continuous climbing, through increasingly wild and rugged mountain scenery. The summit panorama is outstanding and on a clear day embraces such distant parts as Castile to the north and Morocco's Rif mountains far to the south. On a bicycle it is a testing challenge, but if you do reach the simple monument at the top, where the 'Lady of the Snows' stands over a simple stone arch, you can congratulate yourself on having pedalled the equivalent of over a third of the way up Mount Everest! Snows normally limit the 'open' season of this road to the months of July to early November.

Tour of Cantabria

An exciting tour based on the steep limestone mountains of northern Spain, with a bit of coastal cycling thrown in for variety. Roads are seldom level and there are some 2,500-metre passes to cross. Santander, the start/finish point, has a good ferry link with the UK and rail connections to Paris; Bilbao could also be used at the start/finish, though it would add to the total distance. The route could be shortened by returning from Oviedo to Santander by train. From Santander you ride for a short while near the Atlantic, with a chance for bathing at beaches such as the one at Comillas. But you soon turn inland, climbing steadily up a gorge into the heart of the magnificent Picos de Europa. There are opportunities here for leaving the bike and enjoying some mountain hiking, before tackling the 1,609-metre pass which leads you over to the southern side of the Cantabrian Cordillera. The route then heads west, before turning once again to cross the crest of the Cordillera, picking up the valley of the Nalón at Oviedo for another adventure in the high valleys of the Picos de Europa – this time over passes and through the gorges of their northern flank, before heading for Santander. Time permitting, the tour could be extended westwards to include the Galician coast and Santiago de Compostela.

CANTABRIA TOUR

Terrain: mountainous
Distance: 710 km
Start/Finish: Santander/Santander
Scenery: ••
Interest: •
Maps: Firestone Hispania, Mapas de Carreteras series 1:500,000 No 1. Firestone Hispania, Mapa Turistico series 1:200,000 No T21 (Picos de Europa/Costa Verde)

---

km	SANTANDER
33	Santillana del Mar

17	Comillas		*(to avoid extra mountain passes*
10	San Vicente de la Barquera		*go N via Infiesto and Arriondas*
12	Unquera		*to Cangas de Onis)*
11	Panes		
12	La Hermida		Puerto de Tarna
15	Potes	45	Puente de los Torteros

(detour to Fuente Dé: 49 km)

Puerto del Pontón

	Puerto San Glorio	22	Oseja
37	Portilla de la Reina	34	Cangas de Onis
19	Riaño	5	Corao
14	Crémenes	26	Arenas de Cabrales
12	Vegamediana	23	Panes
19	Boñar		
8	La Vecilla		*(use route of outward journey*
21	La Robla		*back to Santander, if you wish*
17	La Magdalena		*to avoid hills)*
19	San Petro de Luna		
16	San Emiliano	12	La Hermida
		18	Quintanilla
	Puerto de Ventana	13	Puentenansa
34	San Pedro de Taverga	16	Cabuérniga
11	Caranga		
20	Trubia		*(alternative route to Santander*
14	Oviedo		*via Cabezon de la Sal and Comillas*
10	Tudela		*and thence via outward route of*
9	La Felguera		*tour)*
3	Ciano		
		15	Villanueva de la Peña
(detour S to Carbayo)		16	Torrelavega
36	Campo de Caso	27	SANTANDER

Basic Information

Getting There

Air: international flights operate to and from Alicante, Almeria, the Balearics, Barcelona, Bilbao, Gerona, Madrid, Malaga, Santiago, Seville and Valencia. Flight time from London to Madrid is 3 hours.

Rail: connections with the rest of Europe are quite good, though there are only two main lines of entry, at either end of the Pyrenees, and on some services you have to change trains at the border. Journey time from London to Madrid (via Paris) is between 23 and 31 hours, depending on service.

Road: Dieppe to Andorra by main road is 990 kilometres.

Ferry: the Plymouth (UK) to Santander ferry takes 24 hours and is especially useful for riders wanting a relaxed journey to the touring areas of northern Spain. Other ferries link Spain with Portugal, the Canaries, Morocco, southern France and the Balearics.

Information Sources

Spanish National Tourist Office (SNTO), 57-58 St James's Street, London SW1A 1 LD (tel: 01-499.0901/6). General information leaflet, regional accommodation lists, annually-revised camp-site guide.

Local tourist bureaux: major towns, ports and airports have branch offices of the SNTO *(Oficinas de Información y Turismo);* elsewhere, there are smaller offices, usually identified by a *Turismo* sign.

Federación Española Ciclismo, Ferraz 16-5°, Madrid 8 (tel: 2420421). The national cycle-racing organisation.

Real Automobil Club de España (RACE), General Sanjurjo 10, Madrid 3 (tel: 4473200). A general touring club affiliated to the AIT.

Accommodation

Camping: there are many sites along the Mediterranean coast between the Pyrenees and Alicante; they are also frequent along the rest of that coast, along the north coast, around Madrid and along the Pyrenean foothills. Elsewhere sites are rare. Generally camp-sites have good facilities (they are government controlled), with modern installations, and most have a source of food – they can also be crammed with campers during the summer months. Camping carnets are no longer obligatory. A free map and list of over 600 sites is available from the SNTO, and more detailed information can be obtained from the *Agrupación Nacional de Campings de España* (ANCE, Duque de Medinaceli 2, Madrid 14 (tel: 2222830).

Spain has the kind of empty landscape that lends itself to wild camping – and in places there is no alternative. Officially, you are expected to ask the landowner's permission, and are not allowed to camp wild on river-beds liable to flood, in industrial, military or tourist areas, within 150 metres of a source of drinking water, unreasonably close to the roadside or within one kilometre of an official camp site. It is worth noting these restrictions because the Guardia Civil are notoriously diligent in their enforcement; I've had a couple of unnerving night-time encounters with this armed (and intimidating) branch of the police. Spain's excellent summer weather means that sleeping out (without a test) is both feasible and enjoyable.

Youth Hostels: there are about 110 hostels unevenly distributed through Spain. They are most frequent in the high *sierras* of central Spain (around Madrid), among the hills and mountains of the north coast and in the Pyrenees, and in these areas they are close enough to form a (limited) basis for a tour. Elsewhere, the distances between hostels are great. Sizes vary from 20 to 200 beds and standards are good; self-cooking facilities are rare though meals are usually provided (breakfasts are compulsory). Hostellers under 25 get priority in the event of a shortage of space. Additional information to that provided by the IYHF Handbook can be obtained from *Red Española de Albergues Juveniles,* José Ortega y Gasset 71, Madrid 6 (tel: 4019460, 4019518, 401300).

Pensiones and Hostales: these come in three grades, the two and three-star establishments being comfortable and inexpensive. One-star *pensiones* and *hostales* are basic. An *hostale-residencia* is an *hostale* without a dining room. In a similar price bracket are the *fonda* (inn) and *casa de huéspedes* (guest house). All these types of accommodation have a maximum limit for tariffs, and prices must be displayed in each room. Breakfasts often have to be paid for, whether you eat them or not. Officially-registered establishments are identified on their outside walls by blue plaques bearing a 'P' for *pensión,* 'Hs' for *hostale,* 'HsR' for *hostale-residencia,* 'F' for *fonda* and 'CH' for *casa de huéspedes;* stars following these initials indicate the grading. Unregistered rooms in private houses are known as *casas particulares.* SNTO can provide lists of some *hostale* addresses; otherwise obtain information from local tourist bureaux. Accommodation is very much harder to find during July and August, and in many small towns and villages there is none for visitors at all.

Hotels: standards vary from the cheap and basic one-star to luxury five star, classifications being determined by the Ministry of Tourism. Charges are per room, not per person and sometimes breakfast is compulsorily included in the tariff. Tariffs are displayed in each room, and the government sets a maximum; during July and August, hoteliers are permitted to raise their prices by 15%. In addition to privately-owned hotels there are a growing number of government-owned tourist hotels, *albergues nacionales* are found on main highways in more remote areas, and are of high grade and intended for motorists looking for an overnight stop, and *paradores nacionales* (2 - 4 star) which are luxuriously appointed establishments often located in restored historical buildings. *Refugios* are also government-owned, being basic hostel-type accommodation in mountain regions, intended for climbers and hikers. Regional hotel lists are available from the SNTO, and from local tourist bureaux.

Weather

Temperatures vary with region throughout Spain. The north coast is the coolest part in the summer, with pleasantly warm and sunny weather from June to September. On the high central *meseta* the warm season starts a month earlier and temperatures soar up into the 30's during July and August. The hottest weather is found in the south, where searing daytime temperatures can grill you on the tarmac and 'summer' lasts from March to November. Everywhere, August is the hottest month, with July a close second; unless you can cope with withering heat it is best to avoid touring the *meseta* and southern Mediterranean coastlands during these two months. Winters on the *meseta* and *sierras* are short and severe, but along the southern coast, and in Andalusia it is warm enough for cycling all the year round (January temperatures in Seville are about the same as April in southern England).

Most of the rain in Spain falls not on the plain but on the northern coastlands and Pyrenees. Galicia has a similar annual total of rain as does France's Brittany and England's Cornwall, much of it coming as drizzle or mist, though it concentrates on the autumn rather than summer months (in Corunna, May, June, July, August and September are all drier than London in August). The rest of Spain; the *meseta* and Mediterranean coast, receives hardly any rain in the summer, and not much in the winter – though snow falls on the high *sierras*. Throughout the country, July and August are the driest months.

During the summer, prevailing winds are north-westerly in the north of the country and southerly in the south.

Other Considerations: the tourist season runs from April to October, peaking in July and August, when roads will be their busiest – especially on the coast. Central and southern Spain are most comfortably, and enjoyably, visited in spring, when more moderate temperatures make city exploration more pleasant and when the blossoms are out. The 'orange-blossom coast' – Costa del Azahar – usually looks its best for a fortnight early in May. Like Portugal, Spain has many colourful religious festivals and processions which can be tied in with a bike tour.

Average Daily Maximum Temperatures (Centigrade)

	alt. in metres	J	F	M	A	M	J	J	A	S	O	N	D
Madrid	660	9	11	15	18	21	27	31	30	25	19	13	9
Santander	66	12	12	14	15	17	20	22	22	21	18	15	13
Seville	9	15	17	20	24	27	32	36	36	32	26	20	16

Cycling Information

Cycle Shops

Bike shops can be found in most large towns, and they usually stock a range of lightweight spares – though these will be mainly for racing, not touring bikes; Spain has a long tradition of cycle racing. Cycle-shops in villages are a rare discovery. Spares are metric dimensions, so items like 27 x $1\frac{1}{4}$ inch tyres and tubes are impossible to find.

Cycle Hire

Unlikely to be possible on the mainland, but there are several companies operating on the Balearic Islands.

Transporting Your Bicycle

As the *Guardian* newspaper once so rightly proclaimed 'The strain in Spain is mainly on the train'; for various reasons it is not worth considering a rail journey unless your timetable is as flexible as that of RENFE – *Red Nacional de los Ferrocarriles Españoles*. Journeys are slow and trains often run late; some of the rolling-stock is, to put it kindly, spartan, and feels as if it is being dragged over the sleepers rather than the rails. The national rail network is however quite thorough, with lines radiating out from Madrid. All the best cycling areas can be reached by train, and Spain has good rail links with France, via the two main routes at each end of the Pyrenees. The fastest and most comfortable type of train is the *Talgo;* after that, in declining order of speed and comfort, are the *expresso, rápido* and the *correo*.

Bikes can be taken free, as accompanied luggage, on the mail *(correo)* trains which travel at night, and although these are the slowest and most agonising at least they have the advantage that the bike travels on the same train as yourself. Bikes can also be taken on some of the faster daytime trains, but it is best to inquire 'on the spot' as information from other sources is invariably contradictory – whatever the official regulations say about taking bikes on trains, you are in any case at the mercy of the RENFE staff at your station of departure. My all-time worst journey was an attempt to get two of us the 150 kilometres (as the crow flies) from Algeciras to Seville, a modest ambition which led to a day of frustration with unco-operative station staff at Algeciras followed by a wildly jolting (but very scenic) train ride to somewhere called Bobadilla Junction, where, in the middle of the night, we were told our connecting train had broken down and that we would finish the journey by bus. Miraculously the bikes arrived two days later. The moral is to leave plenty of time: well before the train is due to depart, take your bike to the baggage office (if there is one) and have it registered as accompanied luggage. You are issued with a receipt which is used to reclaim the machine at the other end.

Long distance buses are operated by RENFE and private companies – some carry bicycles.

Roads

The secondary ('C') roads are the most enjoyable for cycling, with a minimum of traffic and surfaces which are usually acceptable. Spain's network of secondary roads is fairly thin compared to other European countries; only about a third the density of the UK road network so choices of route tend to be relatively limited. Surfaces on these smaller roads vary from smoothish tarmac to a patchwork of casually-filled craters. Potholes can be a menace; it never pays to swoop in relaxed abandon down a steep hill because there is always a chance that just around the next bend there is a cavernous and jagged-rimmed hole waiting to swallow that swiftly spinning fragile front wheel-rim (it happened to me in the Picos de Europa, a long way from home!). Cobbles still exist in some towns. On the rougher roads, horses, donkeys and mules are as common as cars.

The main ('N') roads have good surfaces, and often hard shoulders too, but they also carry most of Spain's traffic. Some of the smaller N roads inland can be empty enough for pleasant cycling, but as a general rule it is best to avoid them. Those along the most accessible parts of the coast can be particularly horrendous, as they carry volumes of foreign holiday traffic, as well as the locals. Sections of the Mediterranean coast road are a corridor of filth, the air heavy with diesel fumes and the sickly smell of run-over dogs, the hard shoulders strewn with grit and glass. Particularly bad are the sections from the French border through Barcelona to Tarragona, and in the north from Biarritz to Santander.

Some Spanish drivers have an annoying habit of creeping up behind you, giving an intimidating blast on their horns and then making a big show of overtaking; ride on the hard shoulder where it is feasible. Traffic increases at weekends, and especially on Saints' days and major football fixtures. Signposting is adequate in towns but sporadic in the country.

Maps

For General Planning

Kümmerly + Frey, Spain-Portugal, scale 1:1,000,000. Covers the whole Iberian peninsula in one bulky sheet; good height shading, major scenic roads and an attempt at marking good and bad road surfaces.

Michelin No 990, Espagne/Portugal, scale 1:1,000,000. Less expensive than the K + F, but also showing less road detail. Scenic roads and faint height-shading marked, plus a larger scale insert of the Madrid area.

For Cycling

Firestone Hispania, Mapas de Carreteras series, scale 1:500,000. Tend to be inaccurate, with roads and places wrongly marked, but for much of Spain these are the only readily-available maps of reasonable scale. 10

maps in the series (including Portugal); scenic roads and viewpoints marked but no height shading.

Firestone Hispania, Mapa Turistico series, scale 1:200,000. 11 maps (Nos T20 - T30) cover nearly all the Spanish coast, the Pyrenees, Balearics and Madrid area, showing most minor roads, selective height shading, tourist information, scenic roads and viewpoints. The backs of these maps have detailed town plans. Good for coastal cycling. A couple of special editions, Firestone Hispania R1 (1:300,000) and R2 (1:200,000) cover the Pyrenees and area to the south, showing most minor roads and with clear height shading.

Mair, Die General Karte, Costa Brava, Costa Blanca, Costa del Sol, scale 1:200,000. Covering three separate sections of the Mediterranean coast and a sizeable slice of the hinterland, these maps are more detailed than the Firestones, with all minor roads marked and some rough tracks too, plus height shading, tourist information, scenic roads and viewpoints.

Large-scale maps of the Balearics: apart from the 1:200,000 Firestone already mentioned, there is the Mair Majorca (and all the Balearics) at 1:150,000, the Clyde Leisure map of Majorca at 1:175,000, Firestone E-53 of Ibiza-Formentera at 1:75,000 and Firestone E-54 of Minorca at 1:75,000.

For Rough-stuff and Hiking

Mapa Militar de España series, scale 1,50,000. Expensive and covering a small area per sheet (30 x 18.5 kilometres), but useful for off-road riding and hiking. Contours, all roads and most tracks shown; series mostly revised since 1968 but some sheets more than 30 years out of date.

PORTUGAL

With one of the most pleasant climates in Europe, and some of the least crowded roads, Portugal has much to offer the cycle tourist. Much of its landscape seems to be scaled for cycling, with every day's riding offering new interest; there are broad river valleys with vine-clad slopes, airy plateaux and bare ridges, ancient walled towns, monasteries, cathedrals and palaces. For the rider looking for a challenge there are several 1,000-metre passes, whilst 900 kilometres of coast offer the chance of swapping the bike for a beach if the going gets too hard.

Portugal is not, on the whole, breathtakingly stunning in its scenery; it has a mellow blend of sights, colours and fragrances: heady airs laden with aromatic herbs and eucalyptus, hillsides of flowering broom and gorse, stands of cypress, cork and oak, and rolling forested slopes. The coast is mostly sandy beaches backed by dunes, farmland, pine woods, hills or lagoons, though there are some dramatic sections of cliffs just north of Lisbon and along the western part of the Algarve. The River Tagus acts as a dividing line, separating the more hilly north, with its steeper roads, more abundant vegetation and slightly cooler weather (on the coast), from the flatter south (not much land above 350 metres) with its fewer but more level roads, less attractive more agricultural landscapes and greater heat. The north has far more villages and towns, including most of those which are of historical interest; it also fits in well with a tour of Spanish Galicia.

With very much a rural economy, Portugal is a poor country by European standards, but also one whose charm is, as yet, untainted by twentieth-century 'progress'. Riding a rough track along the crest of a low range of hills – one of the many *serras* – I came across a squat, white-painted and mournfully-creaking windmill, its small triangular sails slicing through the balmy Atlantic air. Being nosey I pushed open the little door and went in. I was still standing there, hypnotised by the revolving, rumbling, meshing and graunching cogs, spindles and grind-stones when a man trod down the stone steps from above. Instinctively I expected to have to provide some sort of explanation as to why I was there, but the opposite happened and I was greeted like an old friend and shown with great patience how a trickle of grain poured onto the turning stone, and emerged on the floor below as a fluffy pyramid of flour so fine it dissolved in your mouth.

Friendliness, a welcome for strangers and an easy-going pace of life help create a restful mood; Portugal is no place for tight schedules or urgency – it is simply too hot to hurry. Language can be a problem unless you speak Portuguese or Spanish (which is quite similar in its written form). French is more commonly spoken than English, which at best is restricted to the Algarve and two major cities. About 90 per cent of the population is Catholic, and you should always cover your arms and legs before entering a church. Somewhat out of the ebb and flow of European money and politics, Portugal has managed to preserve its folk history; the costumes, dance and song, sports and community ebullience bubble and burst into colour and life during the many civic festivals held up and down the country. The riches and relics from the age of discovery when Portugal was a great maritime empire are still to be seen in the architecture and art of the cities and museums – the exuberant Manueline style being the most characteristic.

Away from the towns and coasts, the food available can be fairly basic; in the mountainous regions it can take several hours of biking to reach a shop, and water is sometimes scarce too. Generally however, roadside bars and cafés are common, staying open all day and much of the night. Some of them will sell snacks and simple meals. Fish in many different forms is popular on the coast and watching the catch come in is one of the prime pleasures in the many small ports. Restaurant meals are usually excellent value and of generous proportions – seafood and soups are a national speciality. The unit of currency is the *escudo* (1 *escudo* = 1$00), divided into 100 *centavos*.

Ride Guide

The North

By far the most varied and interesting part of the country for a bike tour, the north has terrain ranging from rolling agricultural lands to demanding mountains. Easier riding can be found by keeping close to the coast and along the many river valleys which cut through the area; pass-climbers can indulge themselves further east where roads reach 1,000 metres. Northern Portugal can also be linked with Galicia, just across the border, to make an excellent extended tour. Access is normally via Porto, which has an international airport and a good rail link with Lisbon; the city is Portugal's second largest, sitting impressively astride the Douro with several popular tourist sights.

Between the River Douro and the northern Portuguese border is the country's historical heartland; originally peopled by Celtic tribes 3,000 years ago, followed by the Romans, Christian Visigoths and then the Moors, after whose expulsion the County of 'Portucale' was given to Henri of Burgundy. His son proclaimed himself King of the Portuguese, ultimately bringing the country its independence. The landscape manages a striking change of character in the 150 kilometres between the coast and the eastern borders. Along the coast from Porto to the pleasant town of Viana do Castelo, with its port and old houses, is a string of small fishing towns, resorts, long sandy beaches, dunes and pine woods. Behind these, stretching for about 50 kilometres inland is an area of rolling wooded country, well served with roads and liberally sprinkled with villages and historic towns. Barcelos is well known for its pottery and fine old palaces; old walled Braga was the ancient capital of Lusitania and has palaces and a twelfth-century cathedral the oldest in Portugal; medieval Guimarães, the 'cradle of Portugal' has a very old castle; Amarante is attractively located overlooking the Tâmega, and Valença up on the northern borders has imposing defensive walls and the nearby viewpoint on Mt Faro.

Moving east from this rich, green hinterland you ride into the draughty, bare plateaux region of the Tras-os-Montes, the province 'beyond the mountains'. A scrubby, relatively un-developed area with few villages or roads, it is a stark contrast to maritime Portugal. What roads there are pick sinuous, often steep, routes between the various *serras* which run down from the uplands of Spain. The historic focus of this province is the walled frontier town of Bragança, its narrow medieval streets and houses largely intact. In the north-west are the dammed lakes of the Cávado valley, whose wooded shores can be followed on a well-surfaced road, and the barren heights of the Peneda-Gerês national park.

The Douro itself is one of this area's highlights with the valley

slopes of its upper reaches terraced and planted with the vineyards that produce port wine. Vila Real is the home of Mateus wine, and Lamégo just across the river to the south, has a castle, cathedral and palace. South of the Douro are the three Beira provinces, with bland, fairly flat coastal scenery, but which rise inland through the Serra da Lousã to the highest range in Portugal, the long thin Serra da Estrêla; often on a bike itinerary because it offers the most authentic mountain scenery in the country. Various roads struggle up on the steep flanks of the Estrêla, and the views (haze permitting) are especially dramatic because the surrounding countryside is so low by comparison. Above the pines, the slopes become broken and jagged, with granite cliffs and gorges, waterfalls and dammed lakes. Away from these high *serras* the landscape is rolling with vineyards, cereal crops, cattle and woods.

The main towns of interest in the Beira are Aveiro, the so-called 'Venice of Portugal', with its painted boats, lagoon, beaches and salt flats; the old university town of Coimbra (the 'Oxford of Portugal'!) with steep, twisting streets, old cathedral and famous museum; and Bussaco the scene of Napoleon's defeat by Wellington in 1810 and the site of an exotic national forest.

Estremadura

Sandwiched between the Tagus and the Atlantic with Lisbon at its southern tip, this virtual peninsula does not have the same interest or undisturbed charm as northern Portugal, but it can be a pleasant part of the country in which to spend a few days. The cycling is easier than further north, the hills not so high and the roads better surfaced. The countryside is gently rolling, with many villages gathered between fields of vines, vegetables and fruit. Here and there ranges of hills such as the Serras de Candieiros and Aire (both national parks) rise above 500 metres to add some variety; the roads and tracks which cross these isolated *serras* provide good views of the surrounding lower land. The coast changes from one of rocky headlands and small sandy bays in the south near Lisbon, to one of long uninterrupted strands of sand further north.

Seen from the saddle, Lisbon is a lethal noisy nightmare of traffic and roads, with tramlines and pot-holes looking for a chance to swallow a front wheel; on foot the city is more manageable and has a plethora of well-documented sights to see, not least of which is the general aspect of Lisbon itself, on a series of hills overlooking the Tagus. Approaching or leaving Lisbon southwards, some of the busier roads can be avoided by using ferries across the Tagus (bikes are not allowed on the fabulous suspension bridge anyway), and across the Sado between Setúbal and Tróia (ride the impressive upper corniche road along the south-facing slope of the Serra da Arrábida). The most visited tourist attraction of Estremadura is probably Sintra, over by the Atlantic 30 kilometres from Lisbon. By bike the least squalid exit from the city is along the sea-front, through Estoril (where at last the traffic eases); Sintra can be approached from the south, or more impressively from Cabo da Roca, the most westerly point of mainland Europe and, in the fashion of Britain's Land's End, a most appropriate and scenic place to reach on a bicycle (you can buy an illustrated 'Cabo da Roca' certificate proving you got there!). Several roads wind through the wooded and therapeutic heights of the Sintra hills, whose verges burgeon with mimosa, jasmine, camellias and arbetus; it is excellent though limited cycling, which can be made more interesting by excursions along tracks to the granite tors which stand on the summits giving wide views. The magnificent Pena Palace must be visited (leave your bike at the lower entrance to the Park and walk up through the secluded gardens) and though bursting with tourists, the town of Sintra itself is very picturesque.

Moving north up the coast, Ericeira, Peniche and San Martinho do Porto are all pleasant stop-overs, though the brightest gem on this section of coast must be Nazaré; huddled beneath a long sheer headland and facing a superb beach from which the gaily-painted fishing fleet flings itself into the surf, the town retains its Portuguese identity despite its obvious touristic charms. Nazaré makes a fine centre for exploring the towns and coasts within its bikable radius, with many bumpy and challenging tracks for the rough-stuff addict. Inland, some of the main places in Estremadura worth visiting are Mafra (huge monastery and palace), Tôrres Vedras (the 'Lines' built by Wellington as defence against the French are still visible and more recently, one of Portugal's most notable racing cyclists, Joaquim Agosthino, was born here), Obidos (dramatically fortified town), Alcobaça (twelfth-century monastery and abbey church), Batalha (a slightly younger monastery but one which displays some of Portugal's best Gothic work), Leiria (crafts and fine castle), and Tomar (ancient convent with some remarkable Manueline ornamentation).

The Algarve

The beaches are much better than the biking along this famous coastline, which only deserves mention here because it's warm enough for touring while much of the rest of Europe is still freezing, and because early in the year its fragrant blossoms can just redeem it. Once unknown, it's now heavily developed, with hotels, tourist complexes, villas, golf courses and so on, though these do thin out a little as you move west. The coast itself has long clear beaches in the east, which get separated and made more secluded in the west by rocky headlands. The riding is largely uninspiring compared to the rest of the country, and the main N125 road runs 2 - 5 kilometres inland for nearly its entire length, offering rare views of the sea; the beaches have to be reached by cycling down there-and-back side-roads.

The only really meritorious ride is out to Sagres (where Prince Henry founded his School of Navigation in the fifteenth century) and thence to Cape St Vincent, a wildly desolate headland bounded by cliffs and concluded by a lighthouse; the most south-westerly point of Europe. Inland, the hills, waterfalls and trees of the Serra de Monchique provide the greatest interest, with several small scenic roads, and one which climbs to a viewpoint at 902 metres. To the east of here, the somewhat lower shale hills of the Serra do Malhão are crossed by some pleasant (though very hot in summer) roads, and the ride following the western side of the Guadiana valley is attractive.

Portugal's Highest Road

Crossing the Serra da Estrêla between Seia and Covilhã, the highest road in the country (surfaced all the way) climbs to 1,991 metres on the summit of Torre, which is also Portugal's highest mountain. The summit is unfortunately memorable for its mess of ugly buildings, commercial stalls and wind-blown rubbish.

Tour of Northern Portugal

This route captures the essence of Portugal by including a bit of everything: the coast, ancient towns and a long ride through austere mountain scenery as the roads lead to the 'back of beyond' in the high plateaux country of Trás-os-Montes close to the Spanish border. From Bragança the route turns back and heads towards the Douro valley, a more congenial land of vineyards and villages, and riverside rests, and the home of the grapes which make port wine and delicious *vinho verde*. It's a tour with two distinct parts, starting off quite strenuous and hilly and finishing with 150 kilometres of much easier pedalling down the Douro to Porto. The optional detour takes a bite out of central Portugal and provides the chance for some exciting cycling through the country's highest mountains and visiting the old city of Coimbra and lagoon of Aveiro (trains provide several opportunities for shortening this detour).

NORTHERN PORTUGAL TOUR

Terrain: hilly
Distance: 620 km (excluding detour)
Start/Finish: Porto/Porto
Scenery: *
Interest: *
Maps: Michelin No 37, Portugal, 1:500,000
Instituto Geográfico e Cadastral, 1:200,000,
nos 1 & 2 (3 & 4 just; both necessary for
Serra da Estrêla detour).

---

km	PORTO
27	Vila do Conde
3	Póvoa de Varzim
25	Barcelos
18	Braga

*(detour SE to Mte Sameiro and
Bom Jesus; and via N101 to
Guimarães also)*

28	Cerdeirinhas
(detour N to Gerês)	
30	Venda Nova
50	Sapiãos
21	Chaves
42	Rebordelo
56	Bragança
37	N15/N102 junction

(*'short cut' on N102 via Moncorvo to Celorico on Serra da Estrêla detour saves 100 km but misses Douro valley*)

30	Mirandela
33	Murça
26	Riba Pinhão
10	Sabrosa
15	Pinhão
(24	Regua)
15	Lamégo

(*optional detour to Serra da Estrêla; see below*)

31	Resende
23	Cinfães
26	Castelo de Paiva
43	PORTO

(*Optional detour to Serra da Estrêla, Coimbra and coast: 490 km*)

	Lamégo
34	Moimenta da Beira
41	Trancoso
19	Celorico
28	Guarda
6	Vale da Estrêla
40	Manteigas

(*detour SW to Torre*)

38	Gouveia
24	Mangualde
13	Nelas

(*trains to Coimbra*)

30	Sta Comba Dao
29	Buçaco (Bussaco)
22	Penacova
22	Coimbra

(*trains to Porto*)

23	Cantanhede
15	Mira
27	Aveiro
8	Forte Barra

ferry across Ria de Aveiro

	San Jacinto
48	Espinho
16	PORTO

Basic Information
Getting There

Air: Portugal's international airports are at Lisbon, Porto and Faro, flight time from London to Lisbon being $2\frac{1}{4}$ hours.

Rail: limited connections with the rest of Europe, journey time from London to Lisbon about 38 hours.

Road: Coimbra is 1,660 kilometres from Dieppe by main road.

Information Sources

Portuguese National Tourist Office (PNTO), New Bond Street House, 1/5 New Bond Street, London W1Y 0BD (tel: 01-493-3873). General information booklet which includes a wine guide; limited accommodation lists.

Local Tourist Bureaux: these are found in major towns and coastal resorts and are usually called *Turismo*. By phoning the Lisbon Municipal Tourism Board on 369450 you can obtain information in English.

Automóvel Club de Portugal (ACP), Rua Rosa Araújo 24, 1200 Lisbon 2 (tel: 563931). A touring club primarily concerned with motoring, affiliated to the AIT, which publishes a very useful 'Road Condition Map of Portugal'. A tourist map of the Algarve is also available. ACP has branch offices in Porto, Coimbra, Aveiro, Faro and Braga, and has its own camping department.

Federação Portuguesa de Ciclismo, Rua Barros Queiros 39-1°-Esq., 11000 Lisbon (tel: 326215/322787). The national federation of cycle-racing clubs.

Accommodation

Camping: Camp sites are not frequent, and there are only about 60 official sites in the whole country. most of these are close to the coast, though unlike Spain and Italy, few are actually right next to the beach. The Algarve has the greatest number. Sites are usually of a good standard and camping carnets are sometimes required. Site locations can be obtained from *Turismo* offices and a list is published by the *Direcção-Geral do Turismo* (Av. António Augusto de Aguiar 86, 1099 Lisbon. Tel: 575015, 575066, 575164); also available from PNTO, though it is not often updated, and at the time of writing prices are about twice those stated in the list. It's usually easy to find places for wild camping; over 40% of the country is forested or unproductive.

Youth hostels: there are only 11 in the country, and most of these are found in the central part of Portugal between Porto and Lisbon. They are usually too far apart to link daily by bike so would have to be supplemented by other accommodation (much of which is not dissimilar to hostels anyhow). Except for the three Lisbon-area hostels, they are not large; most have self-cooking facilities.

Boarding Houses/Private Rooms: occasionally it is possible to find accommodation in private houses (addresses from *Turismo*), though much more common are establishments such as an *Estalagem, Albergues* and *Pensão*. These are graded from four stars down to one (the best are about the same quality as a 3-star hotel) and are more friendly than hotels; their facilities may be limited but they are inexpensive generally and in many respects ideal for bike tourists. *Pousadas* are slightly more classy, designed to provide local atmosphere and cuisine and found in converted historical sites and specially-constructed buildings. There are about 25 in the country, mostly off the normal tourist track. Addresses can be found in the regional accommodation lists (PNTO).

Hotels: graded on a five down to one-star basis, with prices controlled and displayed in each room. Standards are normally good and you don't have to pay the earth for a room with a shower; continental breakfast is included in the price. It's always worth looking around town for the best choice because outlook and ambience can vary considerably. I've paid the same for a superb room with a spectacular Atlantic view as I have for an airless cell whose walls reverberated all night to the sound of drunken sailors. Prices are higher in Lisbon and the Algarve, and are reduced out of season (November through to February). Local *Turismo* offices are helpful in providing addresses within your price range, and addresses are also found in the regional accommodation lists.

Weather

Sunny and hot in summer, with daily temperatures into the 20s from April till October along the coast, and from May till September inland. Porto and the northern coast are about 3°C cooler than Lisbon, the southern coast and inland valleys during the summer.

Nearly all of Portugal's rain arrives during the winter, mainly between October and May (wettest month November) and falls in fairly specific places: along the northern coast and around the Serra da Estrêla. Unseasonable weather is not uncommon on this high and exposed range; my own (September) ride over these lofty slopes was made all the more homely by the wind-driven mist which gusted horizontally across the road in true Irish fashion. The Algarve is the driest part of the country and even in winter has very little rain; the winters are so mild here that the Algarve is warm enough (by UK standards!) for a tour at any time of year. Faro's coolest month has temperatures not usually any lower than London in April. Throughout Portugal, July and August can be virtually guaranteed dry, with June a close runner-up.

Prevailing winds tend to be westerly or northerly, though (except for exposed coastal areas) most roads are sufficiently sheltered by surrounding hills for it to be difficult to predict general wind directions inland. The on-shore breezes can create impressive breakers.

Other Considerations: the sea is warmest in July, August and September, when it reaches 26°C on the west coast, one degree warmer on the Algarve. Spring starts early in Portugal, with the almond blossom of the Algarve looking its best around mid-January, though flowers and blossoms further north appear somewhat later. Many towns have colourful (and noisy) festivals lasting several days, between June and September, with folk-dancing, costumes, music, fireworks, bull-fighting (and the infamous 'bull-running' when the animals charge through the streets) and religious ceremonies. PNTO publish a calendar of dates and places. The grape harvest in and around the Douro valley takes place between mid-September and mid-October (may fluctuate with weather), and the trees of the north look especially fine in their autumn tints.

Average Daily Maximum Temperatures (Centigrade)

	alt. in metres	J	F	M	A	M	J	J	A	S	O	N	D
Coimbra	141	14	16	18	21	23	26	29	29	27	23	18	14
Porto	95	13	14	16	18	20	23	25	25	24	21	17	14

Cycling Information

Cycle Shops

A rarity not to be expected outside Lisbon and Porto, though being a keen cycle-racing nation, lightweight spares are available. Some motorbike/moped shops also stock spares for roadster bikes, and it may be possible to buy 27-inch tyres and tubes.

Cycle Hire

The tourist centres of the Algarve have shops which hire bikes; elsewhere it is unusual.

Transporting Your Bicycle

As well as the main north-south line and a couple to Madrid (all of which have regular services) there are a number of branch lines which can be useful in putting together a bike tour. The *Caminhos de Ferro Portugueses* (CP) run the railways and there are a variety of different services from *Rapido* (supplement payable) to the slower *Directo*. Bikes can be taken as accompanied luggage on trains; occasionally, when the luggage wagon is full, bikes will be put on a subsequent train.

Arrive at least half an hour before the train departs and take your bike to the *Bagagem* office where you will embark upon some entertaining bureaucracy which will take 5 or 30 minutes depending on how sleepy or busy the station officials are. Once I even had my bike compulsorily weighed, an entertaining piece of theatrics aboard a pair of scales normally used for measuring small boxes of fruit. (The final total of kilograms, only accepted after much intense squinting, seemed to have absolutely no bearing on the cost of transporting the bicycle. But it helped pass the time anyway). Where there is no *Bagagem* you should present your bike to the ticket office. After filling in the forms and label, and paying a small fare (meant to be a flat rate regardless of distance) you'll be given a receipt for the bike. Porters load it onto the train for you. When you reach your destination present the bike receipt to the train's guard, and he'll unload your machine. You can also register and send your bike as unaccompanied luggage, paying according to distance.

Some of the bus companies (which are independent, not national) will transport bicycles on the roofs of their vehicles; the services are not very fast or direct.

Roads

Surfaces range from appalling to quite good; with lots of spare granite lying around, the Portuguese originally built their road system using cobbles, and many excruciating stretches still remain. The north has worse surfaces than the south. Lisbon, Porto and Coimbra, the three largest cities, all have such bumpy roads and jostling streets it's often easier to walk. But surfaces are being improved and a road can change from being a nightmare of bone-jarring setts to quite smooth tarmac — although even this seems to get pot-holes. What is probably the country's only cycle-path runs by the main road north from Porto for a few kilometres.

Traffic volumes are among the lightest in Europe and are concentrated onto a few very obvious long-distance routes. On the smaller roads, out in the country, the cycling is very peaceful indeed, and you can ride for hours with no noisier companion than the rustling leaves.

Drivers like to hoot their horns and tend to drive fast. Sign-posting is sometimes non-existent or misleading and you may have to rely on locals for finding a road.

Maps

For General Planning

Kümmerly + Frey, Portugal/Spain, scale 1:1,000,000. Covers the whole Iberian peninsula in one bulky sheet; good height shading, major scenic roads and attempt at marking good and bad surfaces.

For Cycling

Michelin No 37, Portugal, scale 1:500,000. The most commonly used and most economical biking map, with the entire country on one sheet. A lot of very good roads for cycling are not shown but it does mark spot heights, steep gradients and scenic roads. Not much idea given of hilly areas.

Firestone Hispania Nos 1, 4, 7 and 9, scale 1:500,000. Not as detailed or as helpful as the Michelin, with Portugal on four sheets which also cover most of Spain. Scenic roads, spot heights and gradients shown.

Instituto Geográfico e Cadastral series, scale 1:200,000. Covering the country in 8 sheets, these are the best maps for detailed biking of Portugal, at a sensible scale which shows all roads and all the rough tracks which are likely to be ridable. Good height shading, contours and clear colouring provide a very precise picture of the terrain.

NORWAY

The scenery of Scandinavia gains in grandeur as you move west from Russia: flat and lake-filled in Finland, rising through the forests of Sweden, to culminate majestically in a 1,500-kilometre rampart of mountains which towers over the Atlantic swell like a battered but defiant sea-wall. For physical spectacle, Norway far outshines the other countries of Scandinavia and can lay claim to what is arguably the best coastal cycling in Europe.

This is a land of water and rock: water as thundering falls and cascading rivers, as glaciers and ice-fields, lake and fjord, rain and mist; rock as sheer granite cliffs and distant peaks, spiny promontories and lonely islets, as bumpy gravel road surfaces or as boulders strewn across valley floors by long-gone glaciers. You ride through a landscape of powerful dimensions; a place for the elemental cyclist, unafraid of hills and weather, roused by an untamed natural architecture that can bring feelings of its desperate inhospitability as well as sky-high ecstasy. The sky plays a part, bringing moods to the valleys with the passing of clouds, while north of the Arctic Circle the sun stays above the horizon all through the mid-summer night.

One inevitably gets drawn towards the coast, picking off fjords as one would English country churches or Swiss cols – or French bars! Even picture postcards cannot over-dramatise the awe of fjord-side pedalling: you speed along smooth tarmac beside steely placid waters hemmed in by towering rock walls which narrow the further up the fjord you get, till you are finally squeezed upwards and forced to climb some lofty pass. Or the road ends altogether and you hop on to a ferry; an indispensable accessory to Norwegian bike touring and in some parts the only way of actually seeing the most spectacular fjords. The coast is an incredible 20,000 kilometres long, all islands and inlets; Sogne Fjord, the longest of them all, snakes inland for 170 kilometres.

Inland you ride through a landscape of barren moor, mountain and forest. Only about 4% of the land is cultivated and the occasional patches of pasture and meadow that lie about the valley villages are all the more welcoming for their rarity. The solid wooden houses have an unpretentious rustic benevolence, and in June many bright petals sparkle beneath the lichen-covered stone walls which line the roads. Timber 'stave' churches blend into the forests they were cut from.

When planning a Norway tour it is a sensible precaution to plan lower-than-usual daily distances. The need to fit in with ferry schedules, the arduous hills and road surfaces, and the unpredictability of the weather do not benefit tight itineraries. And apart from that, spare hours can enjoyably be absorbed off the bike along the country's many superb hiking trails. Lightweight walking boots or shoes are well worth the pannier space.

Norway has only about one twentieth of the UK's population density, so people and places are thin on the ground; distances between shops and accommodation can be great. Norwegians themselves could not be more different from the comic-strip plundering and pillaging Vikings; they are reserved and polite, hospitable and humorous, and healthy lovers of the open air. It is not however the place to come to if you are looking for night-life and Mediterranean-style social electricity; entertaining is usually done in the home (remember to take off your shoes when entering a Norwegian's house). There are two languages, Nynorsk and Bokmål, and although plans are afoot to unite them in to one national dialect, both are still used. English is widely spoken in towns and tourist centres, less so in the country. Most Norwegians are Protestant, and the country has a stable constitutional monarchy and a high standard of living.

Food is expensive, hearty and basic, with fish (the best buy), cheese and meat, and many types of bread being most commonly on the shelves. Picnics can be extravagant affairs, especially if you are brave enough to experiment with the many sorts of sea-food. Try making your own *smörbröd*, a multi-ingredient sandwich. Eating out is a pricey business though some of the café-type establishments are affordable; in popular areas like the western fjords, cafés *(kafé)* are found at frequent intervals by the road. The unit of currency is the *krone*, divided into 100 *öre*.

Ride Guide

Sörlandet and Telemark

If you are looking for milder riding through more gentle scenery than that offered by the western fjords or the north, then the gentle slopes fringing the Skagerrak are appropriate. This is Norway's largest area of lowland as well as being its most productive agricultural region. Here too are over half of the population and most of the nation's industry. Roads and villages are frequent and there is a good choice of alternative routes; one of the more interesting options is to start at Oslo and head generally south-west then west, mixing coastal cycling with forays inland, finishing at Kristiansand or Stavanger, both of which have good ferry links with the UK.

The most obvious attraction is the Skagerrak coast itself – known as Sörlandet – with thousands of tiny islands and inlets set against gently rising tree-clad hills. It is an area much favoured by Norwegians as a holiday area, and quite unlike the vaster fjord scenery further west. Using secondary roads and ferries, nearly all of this coast can be cycled without having to stray onto the busy E18 highway. Small farms and fishing villages sit by the water, houses white-washed and neat. West of Lindesnes the coast becomes more rugged and fjords increasingly sinuous as mountains reach closer to the sea. The main town of this southern coast is of course Oslo, with its impressive Akerhus Fortress, museums and maritime traditions; the Polar ship *Fram*, the *Kon Tiki* and *Ra II* rafts, and three preserved Viking ships can all be seen. Some of the Sörlandet towns, for instance Kragerö and Lillesand, have especially attractive settings.

Inland, between the patches of rock and forest, small farms and hedges quilt the landscape and there are numerous lakes. Vestfold, the county on the western bank of the Oslo inlet, is known for its historical and cultural monuments, with rock carvings, old manor houses and stone churches. Looking down on these mild coastal lands are the ridges and plateaus of Telemark, where you still find the *stabbur*, or storehouse, lavishly decorated with carvings and 'rose paintings', and the 'stave' church, which is typically clad in overlapping wooden tiles.

The Western Fjords

Allowed just one visit in a lifetime to Norway, it would be very hard to resist the lure of what must be the most impressive coastal scenery in

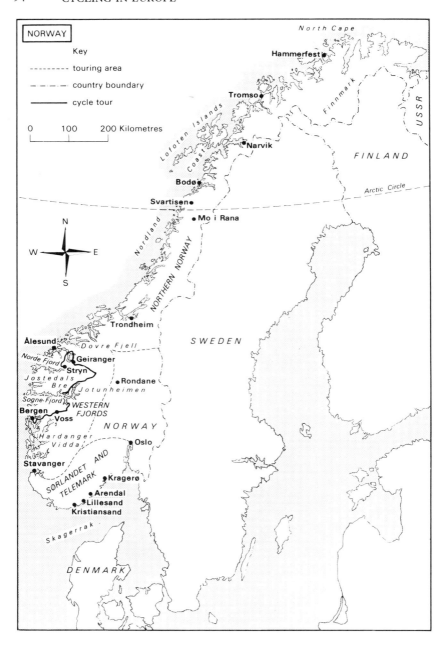

Europe. Especially as they are, from the UK at least, particularly
accessible with North Sea ferries running to Bergen (and Stavanger),
right on the doorstep of superb cycling country. Bergen itself is one of
the most attractive towns in Norway, with pastel-painted wooden houses
climbing up sharply from the quaysides. Roads can be exerting, with
some of the most protracted climbs in the country, and there is plenty of
opportunity for rough-stuff riding. Ferries (and occasionally trains too)
play a vital part in assembling a good route and cunning use of
timetables helps you avoid the traffic and find the most exciting roads.

The most spectacular sights lie roughly between Bergen and
Alesund. This is postcard Norway, with steamers gliding like tiny toys
beneath great walls of rock, of waterfalls hanging like wispy veils from
high valleys, of snowy horizons and of roaring cataracts that can
thunder down dark chasms flipping boulders and sending up a fine misty
spray. Wherever the slopes relent, the trees have been cleared and
replaced by clean green fields. You cycle in the continual presence of
mountains – some of them permanently snow-capped. One of the most
remarkable features of this area is the Jostedals Bre ice-cap, the biggest
in Europe, with several spectacular ice-falls spilling into the valleys
below from its lofty plateau-like surface. One of the great adventures is
to ascend to the level of this great ice-cap and gaze across its seemingly
endless bright-white surface; a dramatic foot-path (map and hut details
from Fjærland tourist office) climbs up to Jostedals Bre from
Supphelledalen, one of the valleys feeding the northern end of Fjærlands
Fjord, itself a branch of Sogne Fjord. The most remarkable of the
western fjords are Nærøy, Aurlands and Fjærland Fjords (all off Sogne
Fjord), Norde Fjord further north, Geiranger Fjord (perhaps the best of
all) south of Stranda, and Romsdals Fjord.

There are a number of rides in 'fjord-land' that must be mentioned
specifically, because (weather-permitting) they are so memorable. From
south to north these include the ride from Voss up peaceful Raundalen
and thence by train under the mountain to Myrdal from where there is
a rough but beautiful descent to Flåm and Aurlands Fjord. In the
adjacent valley there is an exciting (and better surfaced) ride from
Stalheim to Gudvangen. A couple of dramatic climbs in this region are
the road up from the end of Ulvik Fjord, and north of Voss the ascent
of Vikafjell, on the way to Viksöyri. If the weather is kind and it is one
of those rare days when the mighty peaks of the Jotunheimen are clear
of cloud, then the airy ride over the Sognefjell Pass (see page 98) from
Skjolden to Lom is a thrill, albeit an enervating one. Easier but no less
beautiful is the ride up to Briksdal (south of Olden, on Innvik Fjord)
where the most famous of the ice-falls tumbles down from Jostedals Bre
into a valley of tranquil lakes, meadows and flowers. Three other high,
dramatic roads are the one past Dalsnibba mountain (detour to summit

for views) to Geiranger, the 'Eagle' road between Geiranger and Eidsdal, and just to the north, the 'Troll' road from Valldal to Andalsnes.

Inland of the western fjords there are several areas which would complement a tour in these parts. South of the inner reaches of Sogne Fjord is a huge plateau, uninhabited and speckled with lakes and tarns, known as the Hardangervidda, crossed at one point by the impressive Geilo – Eidfjord road (and also by a railway line, beside which runs a rough track occasionally traversed by more adventurous rough-stuff enthusiasts, starting at Haugastöl on the Geilo – Eidfjord road, and finishing at Myrdal). Further north, the national parks of Rondane and Dovrefjell can be reached by road and are well worth a pause. The OC's *'Guide to Norway and Sweden'* (see appendices for address) carries much useful information on western Norway's high roads.

Apart from those already mentioned, the main passes of the western fjords and mountains are as follows (from south to north):

Halseheia (730 m) from Algård to Tonstad on road 45 east of Stavanger.

Lågefjell (917 m) on road 12 between Evje and the junction of the E76 and road 12.

Dyrskar (1,148 m) on a loop of the E76 between Röldal and the junction of the E76 and road 12.

Rölldalsfjellet (876 m) on the E76 between Röldal and Odda (use the old road to avoid tunnels).

Hardangervidda (1,358 m) on road 7 between Eidfjord and Geilo.

Three passes over 1,000 metres on road 8 between Rödberg and Geilo.

Osen (1,137 m) on road 52 between Gol and the junction with the E68.

Fille-fjelle (1,004) on road E68 between Lærdalsöyri and Fagernes.

Tyisosen (1,117 m) on road 53 between Hugostua (on road E68) and Ovre Ardal.

Valdresflya (1,390 m) on road 51 between Fagernes and Vagamo.

Videdalen/Mårådalen (1,139 m) on rough-surfaced road 258 between Lom and Stryn.

Djupvass (1,038 m) between the junctions of roads 15 and 258, and Geiranger.

Dovrefjell (1,026 m) on the E6 between Dombås and Oppdal.

Northern Norway

Norway continues for over a thousand kilometres north-east from Trondheim; a wild extravagance of rock and water, 80 kilometres wide in the south but narrowing to as little as 6 kilometres near Narvik. This long, thin, strip of immensely rugged land is the corridor which ultimately leads to the North Cape – the most northerly point of mainland Europe and the goal for countless motor tourists, and a few cyclists, each year. The long ride north is not one to be undertaken lightly; Trondheim to the North Cape is a road distance of 1,640 kilometres (by the quickest route), in places over rough gravel surfaces and passing through some barren parts where distances between habitation are great. It is the closest you can get to 'expedition riding' in Europe, moving as a self-sufficient lonely unit through a landscape that can change from being staggeringly beautiful to desperately inhospitable. Settlements cling close to the rocky, treeless coast, eking a living from the sea and sparse patches of fertile land. The interior is an empty wilderness, with some forest in the south, but becoming more bare as you move northwards, till scrubby birch gives way to tundra. The coast is rich in birdlife.

The main highway – and the only continuous one – up this coast is the E6. The discerning rider, with sufficient time, can assemble a much quieter, more interesting, route to the seaward side of the E6, using coastal ferries to link isolated sections of island and peninsula road. During July and August the E6 is busy with foreign tourists hammering up to the North Cape. An exciting alternative to the 'long ride' would be to take the train (or ferry) to Bodö or Norvik and tour the Lofoten Islands and northern Nordland coast.

Northern Norway has several highlights. Two days riding from the old Viking centre of Trondheim you enter the county of Nordland, with an impressively broken coast of bare islands and steep mountains which stretches all the way to the Lofoten Islands. Small harbours occupy sheltered spots. Many of this coast's more attractive places lie some way off the E6, and so remain unsullied during the tourist season. North of Mo I Rana you cross the Arctic Circle and at Holandsfjord the Svartisen Glacier almost reaches the water.

The archipelago of the Lofoten Islands is one of the more extraordinary sights of northern Norway; great granite peaks rise almost sheer from the water's edge, dwarfing the tiny fishing communities which, during the summer, are a hive of intense activity as hundreds of boats cram the sheltered harbours. Kebelvåg is one of the most attractive Lofoten villages. North of the Lofotens, the coast perceptibly turns away from the Atlantic and towards the Arctic. Tromsö is the main centre, and has been the point of departure for past Polar expeditions. And beyond Tromsö the Lyngen Alps are worth a pause. From here northwards you are restricted to the E6 as you approach the flat tableland of the North Cape, Hammerfest being the most northerly town in the world. South of here is the Finnmark plateau, a wilderness of lakes and rivers, sparse vegetation, reindeer, gnats and Lapps. It is crossed by few roads.

Norway's Highest Road

From Skjolden to Lom the main road crosses the 1,430-metre Sognefjell

Pass, sandwiched between the mighty Jostedals Bre ice-cap to the west and Jotunheimen massif to the east. From sea-level at Skjolden there are over 30 kilometres of climbing to the summit, the last section of which is over a rough gravel surface more often than not shrouded in cloud.

Tour of the Western Fjords

A ride by the best of Norway's famous fjords, starting and finishing at Bergen, which has regular ferry links with Newcastle-upon-Tyne in England. It is a tour which relies on suitable local ferry connections, and in two instances upon trains – so if you are riding to a tight schedule make sure you obtain in advance the appropriate timetables. Although parts of the route are level and on excellent tarmac surfaces, there are some major climbs and short sections of rough surfaces, so overall it is a fairly strenuous itinerary. Because of this a loop northwards to Geiranger can be left out if short of time or energy. Highlights of the tour include the escalatingly scenic ride (and train journey) from Voss to Flåm, the detour up lovely Fjærlands Fjord with the option of a couple of days hiking by the Jostedals Bre ice-cap, the mighty climb beneath snowy peaks over the Sognefjell Pass and a visit to Lom's 'stave' church. If you take the Geiranger loop there are superb views from the top of Dalsnibba mountain, then the chance of a ferry up majestic Geiranger Fjord and a ride over the famous 'Eagle' road. Finish by making the there-and-back ride up to Briksdal to goggle at the frozen avalanche of ice that hangs above a milky pool below the lip of Jostedals Bre. Arrange to make the first part of the ferry trip back to Bergen, along Norde Fjord, in daylight; it is a wonderful way to end the tour!

WESTERN FJORDS TOUR

Terrain: mountainous
Distance: 640 km (480 km without Geiranger or Briksdal loop)
Start/Finish: Bergen/Bergen
Scenery: **
Interest: *
Maps: Cappelen Bil-Og Turistkart 1:325,000 No 3-4

Km	BERGEN
25	Indre Arna
15	Trengereid
	train to Vaksdal

(avoids long and dangerous road-tunnel prohibited to cyclists

15	Dale
55	Voss
33	Mjölfjell

(to avoid rough-stuff take train from here to Myrdal)

10	Upsete
	train to Myrdal
19	Flåm
8	Aurlandsvangen
	ferry to Leikanger

(detour W to Hella, then ferry up Fjærlands Fjord to Fjaerland; rides up Boyadalen and Supphelledalen from where hike to Flatbrehytta by Jostedals Bre)

23	Sogndal
32	Gaupne
28	Skjolden
	Sognefjell Pass
83	Lom
19	Bismo
42	Grotli

(return to Bergen by taking rough-

surfaced road along Mårådalen and
Videdalen, then via Hjelle to Stryn –
see end of tour for Briksdal detour –
ferry back to Bergen; Grotli to Stryn :
66 km)

	8 Kjellstadli
	14 Hornindal
	26 Stryn
	18 Olden
	24 Briksdal
	24 Olden

9   Briedablik
12   Djupvasshytta
16   Geiranger
25   Eidsdal
     ferry to Stranda
29   Hellesylt
4   Tryggestad

(if ferries connect, cycle W to Innvik
or Utvik, and then ferry to Bergen; or
return to Stryn and take ferry)

18   Stryn
     ferry to Bergen
     BERGEN

Basic Information

Getting there

Air: there are regular international services to Bergen, Kristiansand, Oslo and Stavanger. Flight time from London to Oslo is 2 hours.

Train: a roundabout method of reaching Norway from the UK, via the Netherlands and Copenhagen, taking 34 hours to travel from London to Oslo.

Ferry: North Sea permitting, this is a thoroughly relaxing and simple, but time-consuming, way of travelling from the UK to the best biking areas. Ferries ply from Harwich and Newcastle, to Bergen, Kristiansand, Oslo and Stavanger. Newcastle to Stavanger takes 19 hours; to Bergen 25 hours.

Information Sources

Norwegian National Tourist Office (NNTO), 20 Pall Mall, London SW1Y 5NE (tel:01-839-6255). Hotel list and useful general information booklet which includes 'Midnight Sun' chart.

Local tourist bureaux: each Norwegian county has its own 'TTK' office which can supply by mail free information on their district; once in Norway there are over 150 local tourist information offices which can help with accommodation, local transport and sights etc. Addresses and phone numbers of both types of bureaux are listed in NNTO's general information booklet.

Den Norske Turistforening (DNT), Stortingsgata 28, Oslo 1 (Tel: 02-33.42.90). The national mountain touring association publishes special hiking maps with recommended tours and sells topographical maps and its detailed guide.

Mountain Holidays in Norway which includes information on huts and trails. Write to DNT for free map and information, stating mountain area of interest.

Norges Automobil-Forbund (NAF), Storgaten 2, Oslo 1 (tel: 02-33.70.80). A national motor-touring organisatipn, affiliated to the AIT. NAF also administers many of Norway's camp-sites.

Norges Cykleforbund, Hauger Skolevei 1, 1351-Rud, Norway (Tel: 02-13.42.90). The national cycle-racing organisation, with a bi-monthly magazine *På Hjul*.

Syklistenes Landsforening, (SLF) Majorstuveien 20, Oslo 3, Norway (Tel 02-44.27.31). Working to encourage cycling and improve cyclists' conditions under the slogan *'Pedalkraft giv Livskraft'* ('Pedal-power gives Life-power') the SLF has done much to help the urban rider and has several useful publications: their quarterly magazine *På Sykkel* has calendars, news and features, there is a fact-sheet in English *(Cycling Holidays in Norway)* for visiting foreign cyclists, and to date they have produced four route pamphlets (with English translations). These cover Oslo to Arendal, Oslo to Hemsedal, Röros to Fagernes and an interesting loop round the fjord country: *Möre og Romsdal, Sogn og Fjordane*. SLF can also supply books, guides and a cycle-map for the Oslo region: *Sykkel Kart Oslo og Akershus*.

Accommodation

Camping: there are over 1,300 camp sites in the country, mainly found along the coast and in the south. Official sites are graded from one to three-stars and are listed in a leaflet 'Camping Sites in Norway' obtainable free from the NNTO. Camping carnets are necessary for entry to, and obtain reductions at some sites. The distances between sites, and the hilly terrain mean that it is often necessary to camp wild; you are allowed to put up a tent for up to two days on uncultivated land no closer than 150 metres to a house or chalet. For longer periods you must ask the permission of the landowner except in areas of mountain etc far from human habitation, where you may stay for longer without permission. The lighting of fires is prohibited between 15 April and 15 September. Norway offers the wild camper some truly spectacular pitches, often in locations with far better views than the best hotels. Note that nights can be cold, even in the south during June and September.

Mountain huts (hytter) and chalets: useful for rough-stuff riders and anyone who fancies a bit of hiking, these huts are found on the main footpaths (usually marked or cairned), offering the bare necessities: a roof, blankets, wood or paraffin or gas for cooking. You pay on the spot, either leaving money in the tin or with the warden if it is an attended hut, and normally sleep in dormitory-style bunks. Having stayed in one of these excellent huts I can strongly recommend grabbing the bed furthest from the door – away from the draught and clear of that odd species of climber and walker who likes to set off before dawn accompanied by amplified grunting, rustling, and rattling of equipment.

Then just as you get back to sleep they come back for some rope or carabiner that is of course beneath *your* bunk. I remember one group whose equipment included three husky dogs – and at four in the morning they *do* make a noise! These huts have an international camaraderie not found in the more accessible types of accommodation. The DNT (see page 99 for address) publishes a guide book, *Mountain Touring Holidays in Norway* which includes information on huts, chalets and other mountain accommodation. Intended mainly for motorists, the more luxuriously appointed tourist huts and chalets can be found close to roads, sometimes incorporated into a camp-site. You use your own sleeping bag, but bunks, electricity and other facilities are provided; ask at the local tourist office or village for their whereabouts.

Youth Hostels: about a hundred hostels throughout the country, those in the western fjords and upper Telemark being close enough to reach by bike on a daily basis. North of Trondheim they are much farther apart and would have to be supplemented by camping or *hytter.* Standards vary: some are purpose-built with superb amenities and others are very basic. Sizes vary from 10 to 270 beds. Most hostels have self-cooking kitchens, but you are expected to provide your own pots and utensils; the meals provided – especially breakfasts – are substantial. Noisy school parties are a summer feature.

Private houses and farms: signs advertising rooms *(husrom* or *rom)* to let may be spotted by the roadside; costs are normally about the same as the cheapest hotels. Local tourist offices also carry lists for their area.

Hotels: expensive and found only in the accepted tourist areas. Breakfasts are not usually included; standards are high. Anywhere described as a *hospit, pensjonat* or *gjestehus* will be cheaper. The NNTO publish an annually-revised list of these types of accommodation, with prices and amenities.

Weather

The best time to visit is June (with May a possibility if you can put up with the chill and possibility of blocked roads) which though not being as warm as July and August is a lot drier, Oslo has twice as much rain in August as it does in May. September is acceptably warm but the chance of rain is greater than during the spring. Norwegian weather is warmed and dampened by the North Atlantic Drift current which brushes the entire coast, keeping the northern ports free of ice all the year round, and by the prevailing south-westerly winds. Where the rain falls depends largely on the shape of the land, so that the deep valleys and leeward side of islands, which sit in the 'rain shadow', are a lot drier than the other side. The Sogne Fjord area has five times as much rain as do the valleys 160 kilometres inland. Western Norway is wetter than the east, Bergen (ironically the first part of Norway many tourists see) is renowned for its rain and its residents are said to be recognisable anywhere by their mackintoshes and umbrellas. Snow lies on the ground from about November to February.

Other Considerations: the case for touring in June (and May) is made stronger by the fact that road traffic is less during these two months than in July and August, accommodation is less crowded, and these two spring months are the time of year that the fjord blossoms look at their best, while the mountains are still impressively snow-covered. Also, by early July the loathsome gnat hits peak form and if anything is worth avoiding it is these repellent creatures. They are especially prevalent in Finnmark and the north.

One of Norway's more remarkable spectacles is the Midnight Sun, which for a part of the summer in the north of the country, never sets; so you can ride your bike all night! The dates and places from which the midnight sun is visible for 24 hours a day are as follows:

Bodö	1 June – 13 July
Harstad (Lofoten Islands)	23 May – 22 July
Tromsö	19 May – 26 July
Hammerfest	14 May – 30 July
North Cape	12 May – 1 August

The most captivating moments are in the first or last weeks of these periods, when the sun sets then rises again within the hour. The incredible Northern Lights – or aurora borealis – are unfortunately best viewed from autumn through to spring north of the Arctic Circle; which is not the most congenial time or place for riding bikes in the higher latitudes of the northern Hemisphere.

Average Daily Maximum Temperatures (Centigrade)

	alt. in metres	J	F	M	A	M	J	J	A	S	O	N	D
Bergen	43	3	3	6	9	14	16	19	19	15	11	7	5
Oslo	94	-2	-1	4	10	16	20	22	21	16	9	3	0
Tromsö	102	-2	-2	0	3	7	12	16	14	10	5	2	-1

Cycling Information

Cycle Shops

Most towns have a cycle shop of some description, usually dealing with utility bikes; specialised parts for lightweight touring bikes and 27-inch tyres, are hard to find. Since the distances between towns are so great it is pointless relying on bike shops for solving mechanical problems; you have to travel self-sufficiently, with your own tools and stock of appropriate spares. Wheels especially take a hammering, so set off with a strongly-built pair, and take some extra spokes.

Cycle Hire

A number of tourist offices and hotels have bikes for hire, and most of these are listed in the NNTO'S *Where to Stay* brochure, together with telephone numbers. The machines available are intended for valley-floor wandering, not bold touring.

Transporting Your Bicycle

The Norwegian rail network is efficiently run by *Norges Statsbaner* (NSB) and is a scenic though expensive method of crossing the country quickly. Three main lines radiate out from Oslo – to Stavanger, Bergen and Bodö – all of which can be useful if assembling a bike tour. Oslo also has good connections to Denmark and Stockholm.

Bikes can be taken on most trains as accompanied luggage; the exclusions are the *Ekspresstog* (Express) trains running during the day between Oslo and Bergen, and between Oslo and Stavanger. On the Oslo to Bodö journey the bike may arrive on the following train. Bikes should be registered 20 minutes before departure (30 minutes at Oslo) and you load and unload the machine yourself. (On the slow, local two- and three-carriage *Persontog* trains I have loaded the bike with no advance registration, paying the guard once on the train and the bike travelling at the end of the aisle.) Note that some trains have push-button electric doors. A flat rate is payable for the bike, so if you have used the train for just a short journey – say to avoid a prohibited tunnel or nasty hill – the cost can be a fright. The same flat rate is payable for bikes sent as unaccompanied luggage.

The key to Norwegian cycling is the clever use of ferries – to avoid busy sections of road, to reach otherwise inaccessible little-visited corners, and to see the fjords from their best angle. They are also a very pleasant way of carrying you to or from a touring area. Bikes are often carried free, though there are modest charges on the longer routes. And unlike the poor motorists who have to queue up to board the car ferries, you can just ride straight to the front and embark with no fuss. My own favourites are the small, slow 'mail' boats which do not carry cars but thud amiably along the shores calling at all the isolated villages to off-load and load a wonderful assortment of goods. The boats are run with a pride and efficiency born of centuries of maritime tradition; half way across Sogne Fjord I remember asking the ferry's engineer if he had any spare oil for a bike chain that had been brutally eroded by gritty roads. The blond mechanic handed me a spotless oil-can in a clean white cloth before wiping the soles of his feet with another cloth and stepping back down into an engine-room which, had I seen it, would I am sure have positively gleamed with pristine endeavour.

The ferry timetables – *ruter* – are invaluable and can be obtained from local tourist and travel offices. The NNTO also supply an abbreviated Norwegian timetable, for car ferries only.

Most buses convey bicycles for half the passenger fare, and they operate over much of the road network. During the summer the luggage space on the buses can get filled up, so this form of transport should not be relied upon.

Roads

Surfaces on the main roads are normally of good smooth tarmac, though on passes of 1,000 metres and over you can expect oiled gravel. This is also found on secondary roads, and on northern section of the E6 to the North Cape. After dry spells the gravel can get very dusty, but it is usually smooth and well enough worn to be cycled without too much discomfort. The exceptions are newly laid gravel surfaces which are loose, bumpy and especially cruel to tyres. On any Norwegian tour, it is almost inevitable that you end up riding at least some gravel surfaces. As a general rule the south and east have more tarmac than the north and west. Ice and rain sometimes cause nightmare pot-holes in the gravel, so do not take the down hills too fast! Gradients are not on the whole too vicious, but the climbs can be very long; passes do not often top 1,000 metres, but frequently start at sea level. Hills are toughest in the mountains of the western fjords; up north around the Lofotens gradients are gradual or non-existent. A characteristic of Norway's mountains is that they are steeper on the west than the east, and so are the roads!

But more than surfaces, the greatest preoccupation – in the western fjords at least – is tunnels. They come in varying lengths but can be up to two kilometres, and are invariably dripping with water and totally black. Riding into them from the bright glare of daylight leaves you nearly blind, even with a powerful cycle lamp to 'see' by. The more predatory tunnels even have curves in them so that you can blunder on into the rocky rough-hewn walls, and some have deep channels at the edge of the tarmac, waiting to swallow a bike wheel. I hope this has put you off tunnels; they should be avoided wherever possible. Many of them have parallel sections of old road (occasionally perilously decayed) which can be used as bypasses; sometimes the way on to them is far from obvious. At tunnel entrances there should be a sign indicating length, and whether it is prohibited to cyclists. If there is no 'bypass' and a prohibited tunnel, the options are to hitch a lift with a passing vehicle or to use a bus or train. Another bikers' hazard to watch out for is the cattle grid (*ferist*) which can suddenly appear at the bottom of steep hills, the chance of crossing a *ferist* – which is much chunkier than those of the UK – at 50 kph and emerging with a full complement of nuts and bolts, dental fillings and panniers, is slight.

Traffic is not generally a problem, and Norway has only a third of the UK's density. It is seasonal, peaking in July and August, with the E6 (Oslo – North Cape) and E18 (Oslo – Stavanger) being the most busy. Both these roads should be avoided where possible. Much of the E6 can be bypassed by using ferries and sections of isolated road along the coast and islands to the west. Near ferry termini the traffic tends to move in waves, corresponding to the landing of the most recent ferry. And in some of the wider valleys there may be an alternative quieter road running on the opposite side to the main highway. Norwegian drivers are about on a par with those of Britain.

Roads are closed by snow in the western fjords from mid-October to late May; dates of specific roads are as follows:

Andalsnes – Valldal	Oct – June
Dragsvik – Eldalsosen	Dec – May
Eidfjord – Geilo	Oct – May
Geiranger – Grotli	Oct – June
Lom – Sogndal	Oct – June
Ringebu – Enden	Oct – May
Vinje – Vangsnes	Dec – May

Rough-stuff cyclists will be pleased to read Norway has a 'right to free access', which means you can move at will across uncultivated country.

Maps

For General Planning

Kümmerley + Frey, Scandinavia, scale 1:1,000,000. Covers Norway, Sweden and Denmark in one bulky sheet; good height shading, major scenic roads and an attempt at identifying good and bad road surfaces.

For Cycling

Cappelen Norge series, scale 1:325,000 and 1:400,000. The standard map for cycling in Norway, with a surprising amount of detail for its relatively small scale. Five sheets cover the country, the southern three at a slightly larger scale. Good height shading and tourist features marked (including viewpoints). Position of rough tracks shown but not in enough detail to follow safely on the ground.

Joint Operations Graphic (Ground) series, scale 1:250,000. Military maps showing in great detail contours, all roads plus tracks and footpaths but no tourist features!

For Rough-stuff and Hiking

Norges Geografiske Oppmåling 1:100,000 and 1:50,000 series, available from tourist offices and bookshops, these maps are very detailed, with contours and shading, and recommended hiking routes. Only cover selected parts of the country.

SWEDEN

Scenically Sweden plays second fiddle to Norway: the land of fjords and fjells hogs the steepest, highest, more spectacular western face of the great mountain chain which stretches from the Arctic Circle to the Skagerrak, leaving Sweden to make do with the much gentler more uniform eastern slopes. Climbs in Sweden are seldom long, and in the south, in Oland and Gotland, they are virtually non-existent; the roads are suited to the beginner looking for some mild pedalling. Skies are warmer and more settled than those of Norway, three-quarters of the country is forest and marsh, and it lends itself well to a camping (and youth-hostelling) tour.

As the crow flies it is about 1,500 kilometres from Malmö to northern Lapland; 2,400 as the elk trots (or bike rolls). The south is on the same latitude as Edinburgh, the north level with the Greenland ice-cap; a large span of the northern hemisphere which not surprisingly embraces some vastly differing terrain – the wheat fields and castles of Skåne could hardly be more different to the bleak tundra home of the reindeer herds. Sweden saves its secrets for the slow traveller: at 15 kilometres per hour along the smaller roads which twist along waterways and valleys you will come across the villages and farms, and can appreciate fully the myriad nuances of trees, water and rock.

Try exploring farm tracks, swimming, canoeing or sailing on the lakes (many lakes have the full range of water-sport activities fully catered for), hiking the trails through thick forests of spruce, pine and birch, searching for flowers in the meadows or picking berries. The short summer brings a profusion in the high mountain bogs (rare elsewhere) of cloudberries, bilberries, cranberries, crowberries, raspberries and strawberries. If you paint, sketch or take photos, then the traditional cupric-red timber buildings, the shifting greens of wind-blown forests, the solid grey granite, and the reflected blues of sky and water, make subtle and elusive images. To bring the greatest contrast into say two or three weeks of cycling, choose your area well. Possibilities include linking the Bohuslän coast with the central lakes of Värmland, riding by Lake Mälar then up to Dalarna, mixing Skåne with Småland (or northern Denmark), Lapland with Norway's Lofoten Islands ... and so on.

Taxes for Swedes are very high. The decades of neutrality have spared the country devastation by war (indeed peace is an art in Sweden) allowing the economy to steadily progress to today's high standard of living. It is the most prosperous (and largest) of the northern European countries. Education has high priority and many Swedes speak English. Most are Lutheran and the country has a stable parliamentary monarchy. Eating out is expensive – as is everything for most of us from the poorer countries. Supermarkets have a good variety of food and in preparing picnics you are spoilt for choice. Many supermarkets and department stores have their own self-service restaurants, which are more moderately priced, and most villages have a *kafé* where you can buy coffee and snacks. Anywhere called a 'bar' is nearly always a snack bar, not one which sells alcoholic drinks.

Ride Guide

The Bohuslän Coast

One of the more accessible parts of Sweden, forming an attractive cycling route between the west of the country and Norway, and linked (through Gothenburg) by ferry to the UK and northern Denmark. It is an area popular among Swedish holiday-makers, who come here to camp and stay in the hundreds of holiday homes and cabins which line the Skagerrak; July is the busiest month, when roads are crowded. The main E6 runs up this coast, from Gothenburg to Oslo, and the best cycling terrain is to be found on the westward side of this very busy highway, where you can pick a route which wriggles round the inlets, using ferries and bridges to reach the islands. These small roads provide 250-300 kilometres of riding between Gothenburg and the Norwegian frontier.

Bohuslän has a granite coastline broken into skerries, tiny islands and inlets, with secluded fishing villages nestling in sheltered rock coves. It is popular among bathers, yachtsmen and sea fishermen, and is well served by camp sites. Overall it has a more bare, wind-swept aspect than the east coast.

Gothenburg makes a natural starting point; Sweden's first port and second largest city. Just to the north is Kungälv, once a mighty border stronghold between Sweden and Norway, with the impressive ruins of the Bohus fortress rising above the trees and several well-preserved eighteenth-century wooden buildings.

Further up the coast from Marstrand – an attractive island resort and yacht harbour with a picturesque cobbled quay and white-painted wooden buildings – are the islands of Tjörn and Orust, linked to each other and the mainland by the three famous Tjörn bridges – themselves something of a tourist attraction. These heathery islands are an interesting diversion, with idyllic fishing villages like Rönnäng and Skärhamn (on Tjörn), red timber houses set behind racks of drying fish, and Mollösund on Orust. Across the Gullmaren inlet is the resort of Lysekil, and an hour's biking away the rock carvings of Brastad. Kungshamn and Smögen, set at the end of a peninsula jutting into the Skagerrak are perhaps the most interesting fishing ports on the coast, while some way to the north, Tanum and Tanumshede (east of Grebbestad) have some of Sweden's best rock carvings that are 3,000 years old.

The South

Not outstandingly scenic, but notable for its mild climate and easy terrain, which is more like Denmark or England's East Anglia than it is like the rest of Scandinavia; it has some of the warmest and driest weather in the country. It is particularly accessible, being on the route for cyclists travelling to and from Denmark; ferries cross from Hälsingborg and Malmö to Helsingör and Copenhagen. There is a good network of minor roads, and escaping the worst of the motor traffic is not usually a problem; the main roads are the busiest in Sweden.

The most southern of Sweden's provinces is Skåne, a region of gently undulating, very fertile plains, rich in history and occupied by ten per cent of the entire population. Its productive farms have earned it the nick-name of the 'granary of Sweden' and you ride through a gentle patchwork of colourful fields and beechwoods. This is also the 'chateaux country', with over 200 castles, fortified manor houses and stately homes, together with their attendant parks and gardens, many of them open to the public. Some of Skåne's more interesting features are the

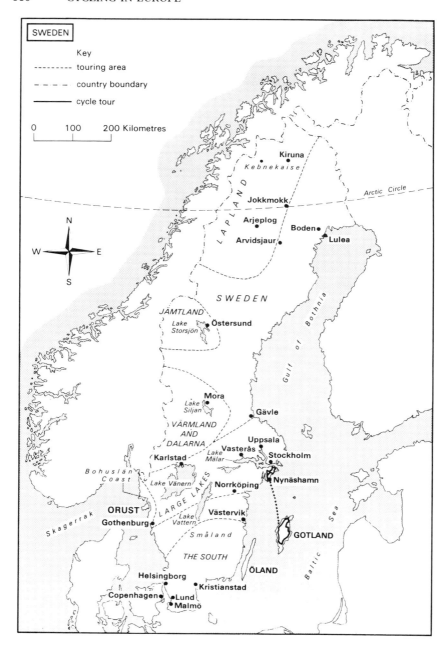

SWEDEN

Key

- - - - - - -   touring area

- - - - -   country boundary

————————   cycle tour

0   100   200 Kilometres

N
W — E
S

Kiruna

Kebnekaise

Jokkmokk

Arjeplog

Arvidsjaur   Boden

Lulea

Arctic Circle

L A P L A N D

S W E D E N

JÄMTLAND

Lake
Storsjön   Östersund

Gulf of Bothnia

Mora
Lake
Siljan   Gävle

*VÄRMLAND
AND
DALARNA*

Uppsala
Vasterås
Karlstad   Lake
Mälar   Stockholm

*Bohuslän
Coast*   Lake Vänern   Norrköping   Nynäshamn

ORUST

Gothenburg   Lake
Vättern   Västervik

Skagerrak   *L A R G E   L A K E S*

GOTLAND

Småland

Baltic Sea

THE SOUTH   ÖLAND

Helsingborg

Copenhagen   Kristianstad

Lund
Malmö

cliffs of the Bjäre peninsula (north of Hälsingborg); the Kärnan tower in Hälsingborg; the old university town of Lund; the geometric castle of Landskrona; the largest Scandinavian memorial to a Viking chieftain at Kåseberga (east of Ystad); while close to the coast south of Kristianstad is just one of the many fine castles of Skåne, that of Vittskövle.

A high range of wooded hills bounds Skåne to the north, bringing a touch of wildness to the landscape. This is the edge of the Småland plateau, which rises to form a low but noticeably upland region, of small, rocky farms, rivers, forests and lakes with moors and heath. Småland has few large towns, but many minor roads. It is mainly famous for its glass; 36 of Sweden's 44 glassworks can be found in an 80-kilometre radius of Växjö. Kalmar has a magnificent castle.

Off Småland's eastern coast are the two Baltic islands of Oland and Gotland. Oland, a birdwatcher's paradise and major migrant stop for arctic birds, is linked to the mainland by the longest bridge in Europe and has enough interest for a few days of relaxed riding. It is long and low (140 km by 16 km), blessed with reasonable weather and with a limestone core that attracts many types of rare flower. In summer a ferry links Oland and Gotland. Gotland is much larger and offers a lot more scope, its capital Visby in many ways being the 'pearl of the Baltic', important in Hanseatic times. Ancient walls encircle the city, with 44 defensive towers, merchant palaces and churches, and many medieval buildings. The island has over 90 lovely old churches and many prehistoric remains too; it also has a dense network of small roads which are ideal for cycling. A special sign-posted cycle-route encircles the island, picking out the most interesting parts and avoiding traffic. The north and west coast is lined with sandy beaches and in places some low rugged limestone cliffs and curious rock sculptures called *raukar*, can be found.

The Large Lakes

This is one of the more obvious parts of Sweden to head for with a bike, being gently undulating so not overly strenuous, and with several richly historic towns which complement an attractive though unremarkable landscape. Gothenburg lies at the western end of this lowland belt, Stockholm is at the east, so access is quite simple, with the opportunity to start in one city and finish in the other after a 'one-way' ride; the distance coast-to-coast is over 300 kilometres. Both the Bohuslän coast (see page 108) and the Baltic coast between Norrköping and Västervik (wildly indented with several good roads for cycling) make pleasant additions to a tour of the central lakes.

In the country you ride through a land of idly rolling fields and woods, and in places there seems to be a lake at every turn, their twinkling waters a welcome break from the sombre conifers, and a magnet for boaters and bathers. The two biggest lakes, Vänern and Vättern, are so huge they are almost inland seas, though busy roads along their shores take away much of their charm. Lake Vättern is the annual venue of what is now virtually a national institution among the cycling fraternity: the *Vättern Runt* (Around the Vättern) – a 305-kilometre ride involving over 10,000 cyclists, staged every June. Riders leave in groups of fifty at two-minute intervals, thus avoiding potentially dangerous 'bunching', and although it is strictly a non-competitive event, many try and cover the distance in as short a time as possible (if you are interested in joining a *Vättern Runt*, contact Vätternrundans kansli, Box 48, Motala, S-591 21, Sweden, or try the SCS – address on page 117).

But the most interesting large lake around which to base a cycle tour is Lake Mälaren, the great ragged fringe and island-dotted expanse of water which stretches for some 100 kilometres west of Stockholm, and around which the SCS has designed a special cycle route (see page 114). You can make your way round the perimeter of the lake, with excursions to the more accessible islands and to a number of historic towns which developed close to its shores centuries ago. These include the university town of Uppsala, with a cathedral, castle and old quarter, Sigtuna (old and picturesque, with massive Skokloster castle nearby). Vasterås (13th-century cathedral and nearby Tidö castle), and on the southern shore the little town of Mariefred and Gripsholms Castle which contains the largest collection of historical portraits in the world and a narrow-gauge railway run by enthusiasts. Stockholm itself is a civilised capital, with roads safe enough for exploration by bike (it has many well-signed cycle paths) and plenty to do and see (the old town, Royal Palace, view from the City Hall tower, preserved 17th-century man-of-war – the Vasa, the sculptures of Millesgarden and more besides).

Värmland and Dalarna

If you are looking for something Swedish which is a little more challenging than the gentle roads of the south, then these two provinces are the most accessible; Karlstad is on the main rail lines to Oslo, Stockholm and Gothenburg, and Värmland would fit in well with a tour of the Bohuslän coast. The main valleys trend north west to south east, so to avoid extra effort you can ride 'with the grain' of the country; many of the lakes have a quiet and a noisy side, with a main road following one of the shores, and a peaceful minor road on the other.

Both provinces are popular holiday regions, and both are known for their old traditions of folk-lore, dancing and costume. Värmland, to the south, has lush fields and attractive country villas, and is the home of some of Sweden's greatest writers; Rottneros manor, just south of Sunne is one of the best-known beauty spots. Western Värmland is an area of forests and narrow lakes with fast streams rushing down from the highlands towards Lake Vänern.

North of Värmland is Dalarna, the province which marks the boundary between the softer scenery of the south and mountains and forests of the north. The terrain is hilly, heavily forested and sprinkled with lakes, with tiny white churches and weathered timber farms adding colour. Dalarna's focus is Lake Siljan, a tourist honeypot, with the lakeside towns of Rättvik, Laksand and Mora the stickiest parts. Hand-carved ornaments, national dress, traditional song and dance entertainments concentrate here, and there is a folk-lore museum. The midsummer's eve celebrations are especially boisterous around Siljan; the copper mines of Falun can be visited. Northern Dalarna by comparison is fairly untamed, with some 1,000-metre peaks and many hiking trails.

Jämtland

Some 340 kilometres of cycling north from Dalarna's Lake Siljan, you reach another large lake which forms the focus of a tourist region – that of Storsjön, whose waterside town of Ostersund is the centre of Jämtland. The attraction here is the mountains which range along the Norwegian border, their rounded summits climbing clear of 1,000 metres (the highest is 1,766 metres). Few roads cross the area so its cycling possibilities are few indeed, but it is one of the scenic highspots on the long road north (or south) for those riders trying a Scandinavian 'end-to-end'. Jämtland's mountains are the most southerly peaks in Sweden of any size. Jämtland has also been described as an 'oasis of fertility' because a gap in the Norwegian mountains allows warmth and moisture to cross the divide, creating a more productive climate than the surrounding areas – and more precipitation!

Lapland

Like the north of Norway, a trip to Lapland on a bicycle is one into the realms of 'expeditioneering', with great distances between shops and villages, long deadly monotonous stretches of road with rough surfaces and a wild, largely unconquered landscape. It is also hard to reach. There is a main rail route up the Baltic lowlands to Boden and then Narvik, and the Norwegian rail route up the Atlantic coast to Bodö can also be used; in only six places north of Ostersund do roads cross the mountain chain between Norway and Sweden. And with the valleys heading in a parallel and south-easterly direction towards the Baltic, a ride up or down the country can be very exerting. Many of the roads follow river valleys, a few pressing on through to Norway. Mosquitoes are a problem, being particularly ferocious in July, so May, August and early September are the best times to visit.

The terrain ranges from mountainous along the Norwegian border, to slopes of forested hills split by rushing torrents, to a fairly level area by the Gulf of Bothnia where most of the towns are sited. Lapland has several attractions: the midnight sun, a vast emptiness unique in Europe, some fine mountains (for example in the national parks of Sareks, Padjelanta and Stora Sjöfallet), and of course the Lapps themselves – who live at the Lapp capital Jokkmokk (which has a museum), at Arvidsjaur (which has 70 Lapp cottages) and at Luleå Arjeplog and Karesuando. There is the chance of seeing herds of reindeer and of walking on the centrally-heated pavements of Luleå. Overall, Swedish Lapland is more of a hiker's then a biker's province; you have to be keen to visit with a cycle.

Sweden's Highest Road

In the Jämtland district south-west of Lake Storsjön is an unclassified gravel road which runs between the village of Ljungdalen, over the 975-metre summit of Falkvålen for Funäsdalen village, which is situated on Route 312 between Hede and Röros in Norway.

Tour from Stockholm to Gotland

An unusual tour, with two distinct parts separated by a 5-hour ferry journey (check the schedules before leaving home). It is an intricate route, relying on the expert guidance of the Svenska Cykelsällskapet's route booklets to pick a pleasant course out and back in to the Stockholm conurbation. Once clear of the city you ride generally southward through forested country to the peninsula port of Nynäshamn from where ferries run to the Baltic island of Gotland. From the medieval walls of Visby you cycle anti-clockwise the perimeter of the island, following the special cycle-route signs of the designated Gotlandsleden tour. Interesting diversions include the boat trip from Klintehamn to the 'bird island' of Stora Karlsö, visits to the huge ancient fortress of Torsburgen, and to numerous ancient churches, farms and fishing villages. Once back on the mainland you can either use your outward route to get you back to Stockholm, or follow the longer alternative suggested. In both cases the special route booklets and excellent Gotland cycling map (Esselte Kartor) are essential aids to locating quiet unspoiled roads.

STOCKHOLM TO GOTLAND TOUR

Terrain: undulating/hilly
Distance: 573 kilometres
Start/Finish: Stockholm/Stockholm
Scenery: **
Interest: *
Maps: Esselte Kartor 1:100,000 Stockholm Stora Fritidskartan, Esselte Kartor 1:100,000 Cykel & Turistkatra Gotland, Svenska Cykelsällskapet 'Nynäsleden' route booklet, and the No 2 'Mälardalsleden' route booklet.

Km	STOCKHOLM
14	Stortorp
5	Länna
8	Lissma

2	Ekedal
3	Ostorp
1	Adran
4	Prästängen
3	Väländan
3	Högelund
9	Kristinelund
7	Sorunda
9	Marsta
8	Norsbol
7	Nynäshamn

Ferry to Gotland

	Visby
6	Axelsro
3	Högklini
3	Hallbros
2	Västerhejde
2	Sion
3	Stenkumla
2	Gardrungs
12	Ajmunds
4	Sanda
6	Klintehamn
7	Fröjel
3	Sandhamn
10	Hammarudd
4	Burge
1	Bjärges
2	Hägur
2	Sandholme
3	Lindarve
2	Hägsarve
2	Snausarve
4	Hallvide
4	Hablingbo
1	Hagsarve Medebys
5	Hallvards
6	Nisse
3	Marbodar
5	Näs
1	Båtels
5	Skäls
2	Fidenas
3	Roes
3	Frisgarve
5	Skradarve

5	Eke
4	Smissarve
5	Malms
5	Kärne
7	När
3	Kauparve
6	Utalskog
6	Ljugarn
2	Vitvär
4	Ardre ödekyrka
8	Grogarns
6	Sande
3	Ostergarn
7	Trosingsgärdet
3	Osterby
6	Bendes
4	Hammars
3	Aurungs
5	Buters
3	Hörsne
4	Nedbjärs
3	Vallstena
5	Bäl
5	Hejnum
3	Rings
9	Othemars
3	Spillings
1	Osterby
11	Hellvi
5	Valleviken
6	Rute
6	Fleringe
2	Lundarhage
6	Krokungs
7	Kappelshamn
5	Västös
4	Hallshuk
3	Nors
8	St Häftings
4	Hangvar
12	Stenkyrka
5	Pajse
3	Tjauls
5	Lummelunds
4	Brissund
3	Själsö
5	Gustafsvik
3	Visby

	Ferry to mainland	7	Berga
	Nynäshamn	2	Arsta Havsbad
7	Norsbol	8	Växjö
8	Märsta	2	Högsta
9	Sorunda	11	Spirudden
7	Fituna	3	Vissvass
8	Brink	7	Raksta
4	St Uringe	5	Alby
4	Sandsborg	4	Bollmora
7	Prästänen	4	Alta
4	Tungelsta	8	Nysätra
5	junction with route 73	6	STOCKHOLM

Basic Information

Getting There

Air: Sweden has major airports at Gothenburg and Stockholm; London to Stockholm is a $2\frac{1}{2}$ hour flight.

Rail: not a very convenient method of travelling to Sweden as the journey involves both trains and ferries from London to Harwich and the Hook of Holland (or London to Dover and Ostend) and thence via Copenhagen. London to Gothenburg and Stockholm takes 22 – 25 hours.

Ferry: Felixstowe and Newcastle have fairly frequent sailings to Gothenburg, travel time 23 – 25 hours, a reasonably painless (providing the North Sea is being kind) way of starting a tour.

Information Sources

Swedish National Tourist Office (SNTO), 3 Cork Street, London W1X 1HA (tel: 01-437-5816). Free literature includes a useful general information brochure (which has the addresses of regional tourist offices), tourist map, camp site and hotel lists and regional leaflets.

Local tourist bureaux: there are about 200 tourist information offices – *Turistbyrå* – throughout the country identified by the international 'i' sign. They are very co-operative, and can help with finding accommodation and the supply of local maps and guides; some also have details of cycle routes. Their addresses are availablr fron SNTO.

Cykelfrämjandet, Stora Nygatan 41-43, (Box 2085) 103 12 Stockholm (tel: 08-11.83.67). Affiliated to the AIT and concerned mainly with cycle-touring in Sweden; *Cykelfrämjandet* has co-operated with the regional tourist offices to produce selected cycle routes for nearly every region of the country. The routes, which are described in Swedish, come in plastic folders and can be from one day to a week long; they can be obtained from *Turistbyra* and direct from *Cykelfrämjandet*.

Svenska Cykelförbundet, Åsögatan 122 (Box 4163), 102 62 Stockholm (tel: 08-743.06.85). The national federation of amateur and professional cycle-racing.

Svenska Cykelsällskapet (SCS), Box 6006, S-163 06 Spånga (tel: 08-751.62.04). Proclaiming itself the 'organisation for all cyclists' SCS has an impressive cycle-touring programme. For visiting foreign riders their most useful service is the series of prepared routes. These include the *Mälardalsleden* map booklets (a set of 7 routes booklets, written in Swedish, covering 2,100 kilometres of cycling in the area around Lake Mälaren west of Stockholm, with notes on bike shops, food stores, bathing sites, restaurants and so on), the 350-kilometre *Gotlandsleden* way-marked cycle-route around the island of Gotland, with blue and white road signs indicating the direction to be taken and a supporting route guide, and the 80-kilometre *Nynäsleden* routes. The compilers of these notes are bike experts and have chosen the smallest and quietest of roads (and sometimes tracks too), using local knowledge to suggest ways which a foreigner would normally never discover in a short holiday. The recommended routes out of the Stockholm built-up area are especially helpful. These booklets can be bought directly by mail from the SCS or from Esselte Kartcentrum (see page 121) and obtained in the local tourist offices. Key maps are available showing the areas covered by each booklet. SCS also arrange conducted three-hour bike tours of Stockholm with English-speaking guides and each year (in July) conduct 'rolling cycle camps' *(Cykelrallyt)* in various parts of Sweden, which attract over 100 riders and to which foreign participants are welcome. The SCS quarterly magazine *Cykel* carries news of touring events, new publications, product reviews and so on – in Swedish of course!

Svenska Turistföreningen (STF) Vasagatan 48, Box 25, S-10120 Stockholm (tel: 08-227200). This organisation administers Swedish youth hostels and can provide about 25 cycle tours, from 80 to 250 kilometres in length, which include accommodation, maps and meals; information from the STF or local tourist offices. STF also carries information on mountain stations, huts and trails. Affiliated to the AIT.

Accommodation

Camping: there are nearly 600 approved and classified (by the Swedish Tourist Board) sites in Sweden, identifiable at their entrances by a sign bearing the words *Kontrollerad av Sveriges Turistråd*. South of a latitude roughly level with Gävle, sites are quite plentiful, particularly by the coast and lakes; north of here they are much thinner on the ground. On most sites a camping carnet is required. Standards are high, with sites graded from one to three star; very often the one-star sites are the most pleasant, with amenities which have to include showers, laundry facilities and hot water. The 2 and 3 star sites are frequented by caravanners, and the latter grade has a restaurant sauna and car wash! Over 80 of the sites have bikes for hire. 250 sites have 'camping cabins' which can accommodate 2 - 6 people and are equipped with a hot plate, utensils and so on. Most sites are open from mid-May to September, though a few do not open till early June. Basic details of all these sites are given in the SNTO's free brochure *Camping in Sweden,* but for more information buy the *Campingboken* (from book-shops in Sweden or ask SNTO for the address of the UK distributor).

Wild camping is a natural pleasure in Sweden, and it is easy to find delightful spots for a tent. Sweden has a 'right of common access' which allows you to camp without permission for one night on any uncultivated, un-fenced land provided it is not near habitation. Otherwise the land-owner should be asked. The 'rights' do not extend to breaking down trees for fires, though they can be lit provided there is no risk of the fire spreading. There may be prohibitions during periods of drought. Mosquitoes are an occupational hazard whilst camping in Sweden. They seldom get the chance to sink their fangs into a moving cyclist, but if you choose to camp in the wrong place they will get you. They are a menace in Lapland below the treeline, in July, what they like most is to be shut into a tent at night with a camper who thinks she or he is alone. Once on the Baltic coast I woke up having slept with these venomous acupuncturists and it took a good couple of hours to prise my eyes open, my face was so swollen. A good insect repellent is a worthwhile investment, and try to camp in the open, away from damp and leafy spots.

Youth Hostels: there are over 220 hostels run by the STF, with a concentration of them in the south; roughly south of Gävle they are mostly close enough together to reach on a daily basis by bike, but in the north they are a great deal further apart. Standards are high, and most hostels have family rooms and self-cooking facilities; some offer meals. From mid-June to mid-August they can get crowded (often with school groups) so you should book against the chance of being turned away. In addition the STF have 8 mountain centres (listed in the IYHA handbook) and a number of mountain huts along hiking trails.

Rum: a *Rum* sign by the roadside indicates an establishment with a room to let for the night; rather like a bed-and-breakfast but sometimes without the breakfast. The cost is usually about three times that of youth-hostel charges, but you can save if you can share a room. Local tourist offices have the addresses.

Working Farms and Cottages for Rent: renovated accommodation is available in a number of working farms, normally for about twice the youth-hostel rate per night. Some farms have self-catering facilities, and a list is available from: Land, 105.33 Stockholm. Very popular among the Swedes themselves are the fully-furnished cottages/chalets/log cabins which can be rented by the week and used as a fixed centre for a holiday. There are 20,000 of them, (frequently in attractive lake-side, mountain or forest settings) and they make a good base for a family cycling holiday. Details from the SNTO.

Hotels: not cheap, but of high standard. Most tourist offices have a *Rumsförmedling* or *Hotellcentral* service which will help in finding overnight accommodation. In the cities there are student hostels which are excellent for low-budget nights and the out-of-town motels can sometimes be good value. A free hotel list (with prices and facilities) can be obtained from the SNTO.

Weather

Sweden has a very pleasant climate for cycling and although the summers are not very long, they compare favourably with the UK; and are noticeably warmer than Norway; June, July and August see the highest temperatures with July the warmest of all. May and September are cool, but not prohibitively so. In summer the daylight can extend to 19 hours, with no 'night' at all during June and July in the north.

Because it sits in the 'rain shadow' of the Norwegian mountains, Sweden is much drier than its western neighbour and Stockholm receives less rain than London; eastern Sweden is much drier than the west. What rain does fall tends to do so in sudden heavy downpours, and autumn is drier than the spring. The dampest months are July and August. August water temperatures in the Baltic are around $16 - 18°C$ and in the Lakes $20 - 22°C$.

Other Considerations: May and June are tempting months, being dry and warm, with the mountain rivers in full spate, the wild flowers and shrubs flowering, and the trees fresh and green. In July Sweden goes on holiday, with many businesses, restaurants etc closing down.

Average Daily Maximum Temperatures (Centigrade)

	alt. in metres	J	F	M	A	M	J	J	A	S	O	N	D
Jokkmokk	257	-10	-8	-2	4	10	16	20	17	11	3	-3	7
Västerås	18	-1	-1	3	10	16	21	23	21	16	9	4	1

Cycling Information

Cycle shops

Most towns have a cycle shop of some description, and usually one which can also handle repairs; cities like Stockholm have several shops, including lightweight specialists who carry high quality touring and racing spares. 27-inch tyres can also be found, but make sure you start a Swedish tour with good tyres because some of the secondary roads have rough gravel surfaces.

Cycle hire

Bikes can be hired in many places: 82 of the sites listed in the 'camping in Sweden' brochure (free from SNTO) rent bikes and many of the tourist offices do as well.

Transporting Your Bicycle

Sweden has an extremely efficient rail system, with a fairly thorough rail network in the southern part of the country. Bikes can be taken on trains; you buy a ticket for the bicycle then take it to the baggage office and register it to your destination. Station staff load and unload the bike, which may take 24 hours to reach its destination (48 hours during July and August). A flat rate is payable regardless of distance which can work out expensively if your journey is a short one; if your bike weighs more than 25 kilograms you pay more.

Bikes can be carried to the larger islands on most of the inland ferries, and also on the country buses, which usually have a special bicycle-carrying rack fitted to their fronts.

Roads

Surfaces range from smooth well-maintained tarmac on the main trunk roads and more important secondary routes, to gravel on most lesser roads, the better ones being oil-bound. Very often these are no problem, but they can get broken up, pot-holed, and in dry weather, dusty. The smallest roads can have a sandy surface which on a thin-tyred bike is hard work. The rougher surfaces are more common in the north than south. Sweden's city engineers are relatively enlightened, so cycle-paths in the bigger towns are common; you ride on your own segregated lane, or more commonly on one shared with pedestrians. Traffic lights and special road markings help you across busy intersections; in Västerås there are 85 kilometres of segregated paths, with 75 cyclists' tunnels and bridges and 1,000 parking racks. Stockholm has good facilities too. Sign-posting is generally good.

You may come across signs warning of elk or deer on the road but such obstructions are disappointingly rare – keep your eyes open at dusk however. Traffic is heavier in the south than the north, and it is sensible not to ride on the more important trunk roads (although many do in fact have hard-shoulders which can be used); overall however, Sweden has only half the volume of cars on the road compared to the UK.

The ancient Swedish philosophy of *Allemansrätt*, or 'every man's right' allows you to cycle on rough tracks at will, provided you do not damage the property across which you are travelling, and provided you close gates and keep out of military zones closed to foreigners (these are signed).

Maps

For General Planning

Kümmerley + Frey, Scandinavia, scale 1:1,000,000. Covers Sweden, Norway and Denmark in one bulky sheet; good height shading, major scenic roads and an attempt at identifying good and bad road surfaces.

For Cycling

Esselte Kartor Länskarta series, scale: 1:300,000. Detailed enough for general cycling but with insufficient road information for exploring the nooks and crannies; covers Sweden in 8 sheets. Most roads are marked, with some tracks too (though not in enough detail to follow them), height shading, many tourist features, scenic roads in green, viewpoints and intermediate distances (main roads only).

Esselte Kartor Tourist/Cycling maps, scale 1:100,000. Excellent for cycling, these special editions now cover the Stockholm area, Gotland, Gothenburg and Malmö, with one in the pipeline for the Mälar area. Each sheet covers a large area, with all minor roads shown, major tracks (though you would need a larger-scale topo map to follow them), tourist features (including camp-sites, historic sights, viewpoints and bathing places), restricted military areas and ferry routes. The Gotland edition has the designated "Gotlandsleden' cycle-route (followed by the suggested tour on page 114) marked as well.

For Rough-stuff and Hiking

Topografisk Karta över Sverige series, scale 1:50,000 (1:100,000 in the north). Very detailed indeed, though compared to the British Ordnance Survey series, each sheet covers a fairly small area. Contours, all tracks, and geographical features shown, but no tourist information. These maps are essential if you are venturing off the beaten track, or need detailed route information for escaping say Stockholm.

Note: The Esselte Kartor maps, the 1:50,000 'Topo' series, and SCS route booklets mentioned on page 117 can all be ordered or bought direct from Esselte Kartcentrum, Vasagatan 16, S-111 20 Stockhokm. Tel: (08) 11.16.97 or 11.16.99.

DENMARK

Mild, charming and safe, Denmark lends itself well to bring the venue for a first tour abroad. The roads are on the whole gentle, can be adequately tackled with a three-speed roadster, and the weather is similar to that of the UK. And while there is nothing spectacular about Denmark, it *is* crammed with interest on the sort of human scale that makes it difficult to ride for long without climbing off the bike to peek at some roadside curiosity. It is also a 'civilised' country where people are ready to help and where a maze of minor roads and cycle-paths keeps you clear of traffic. Access from the UK is straightforward: just a 20-hour boat trip from Harwich (or Newcastle) to Esbjerg, or a 2-hour flight from London.

Denmark is only about half the size of Scotland, so in just a two- or three-week tour it is possible to get a real feel for the country; it is the smallest of the Scandinavian countries and is so compact that no point is more than 65 kilometres from the sea. You can ride through a gently undulating landscape with just enough hills to keep you wondering what might be around the next corner. The farming is intensive, with co-operative businesses producing butter, bacon, eggs and poultry for export; in places the fields are broken by grasslands and the lovely beech woods that feature so much in Danish art. Small lakes fill the hollows, and the coast is in parts attractively indented with fjords or lined with excellent sandy beaches.

The people of this mellow homely land are friendly and full of humour, ready for a laugh, and exponents of the work-hard-play-hard ethic. The Danes know how to enjoy life and 70% of the population own bicycles. Like Sweden they have a high standard of living, though it has been built on farming rather than industry; Danish people are country-folk at heart. They have excellent social services. English is spoken by most and it has been the first foreign language at schools for a long time. Most Danes are Lutheran and the country is run as a parliamentary democracy, with a monarchy for added colour.

While to an outsider Denmark might seem something of a pedallers' paradise, the $2\frac{1}{2}$ million cyclists who live and work here do not see things quite so rosily. In fact, to many Danes the humble biker gets a very raw deal and in recent years a lot of this indignant energy has been channelled into a rapidly-growing organisation called the Dansk Cyklist Forbund – a national body devoted to improving facilities and safety for cyclists. Aside from the lobbying of transport authorities, fighting for reduced air pollution and protecting the rights of child cyclists, the DCF has a reputation for such newsworthy demonstrations as painting crosses on the roads at accident sites to 'commemorate the fallen in the traffic war', getting arrested for marking their own cycle-lanes onto highways and drawing a staggering 25,000 people to annual bike days. So when you ride peacefully along a new section of cycle-path, spare a moment's thought for the cyclo-campaigning Dane – and for the DCF!

Food is one of the joys of biking in Denmark, with shops bulging with fresh produce; picnics can become long drawn-out affairs. If you are having meals supplied for you, the breakfasts will not be disappointing, and will provide a good calorific investment for the day's pedalling. Lunches are traditionally *smörrebröd*, an open sandwich which might contain any of 200 possible fillings usually selected from meat, fish, cheese, vegetables and eggs. If you are not planning on leaping straight back on the bike, *smörrebröd* should be enjoyed with beer. *Aquavit*, the other national drink, is a potent spirit distilled from potatoes or grain. The famous Danish pastries make good mid-morning – or afternoon – snacks and can be bought in a *konditori* or *bageri*. Restaurants are plentiful and of a high standard, but they are also fairly expensive; the unit of currency is the *krone* (kr), divided into 100 *öre*. Nearly all shops and restaurants close at lunch-time on Saturday for the entire weekend, so make sure you have adequate supplies.

Ride Guide

Jutland

With the port of Esbjerg on its western coast, Jutland is often the first taste of Denmark for visiting cyclists. This long peninsula, some 300 kilometres from the German border to its northern tip, is the only part of Denmark attached to mainland Europe, and is often passed over by tourists on the way to the more obvious charms of the island archipelago. It is also narrow, and to ride across the peninsula from Esbjerg on the west to Kolding on the east takes no more than a morning. Cycling in Jutland is not hard, and nature's only real attempt to hamper cyclists is the winds which can blow in strong gusts from the North Sea – sometimes bringing fog as well. These can be especially trying in the west.

The peninsula is divided into two by a long low ridge of hills running down its centre. The scenery to the west is not especially inspiring, being a flat expanse of farmland, marshes and heather, though the coast, with its backing of sand-dunes, has some of the finest beaches in the country; these stretch north from Esbjerg all the way to Skagen. The small islands of Römö and Fanö are well known for their beaches and the latter has two well-preserved old villages: Sönderhö and Nordby. Just across the water from Fanö is the mainland town of Ribe with what is probably the most authentic medieval atmosphere of any Danish town; it has a 12th-century church and the oldest inn in the country – dating from the 15th century.

Eastern Jutland is by contrast quite hilly and attractive, with a coast of inlets and estuaries known as *förde* – although they are quite unlike the fjords of Norway. The land here is more fertile than over on the west, with brick and timber farms settled over well-ordered fields and a thick maze of tiny roads excellent for biking. The highlight of eastern Jutland is the area around Aarhus, Denmark's second city, with a port, university and 12th-century cathedral. Two peninsulas eastwards of Aarhus is the small port of Ebeltoft, with its medieval streets, while on the other peninsula the Mols hills are an interesting diversion. Inland from Aarhus is a chain of lakes which eventually reach Silkeborg; this is Denmark's 'Lake District' with good cycling in the adjacent woods and a popular holiday area. Here too is Yding Skovhöj, Denmark's highest point – all of 173 metres!

Moving north you get to one of Jutland's most unusual features: Lim Fjord – a vast inland waterway covering some 1,500 square kilometres and stretching from the Kattegat to the Skagerrak, most of it less than 4 metres deep. The northern shore of the island of Mors is interesting with good views from the cliffs of Hanklit and Salgerhöj. Aalborg, the main town of northern Jutland is worth a pause, with Jens

Bang's superb Renaissance house, a cathedral, monastery and 16th-century castle. Jutland tapers off into the Spit of Skaw, an area of dunes and windy moor at the end of which sits Skagen, a town of character and a long-time artists' haunt.

Fünen

The second largest of the Danish islands is a fairytale land of castles and half-timbered buildings, with soft countryside which has earned it the tag of 'Denmark's Garden'. There are no hills to speak of, so biking is not exerting, and there is an intricate net of minor roads to enable you to get well off the beaten track. In many ways Fünen is at the focus of the best cycling in Denmark, linked by ferries to the other islands of the archipelago, and to eastern Jutland; it makes a good place to base a tour.

This is an idly rolling landscape, with ancient inns, attractive harbours and good beaches. Odense, the main town, is the birthplace of Hans Christian Andersen, and today his house and a museum relating to his life are open to the public. The 13th-century cathedral in the city is one of the most notable Gothic buildings in the country. If you ride east fom Odense for about 20 kilometres you reach Ladby, the site of a Viking burial ship, with some good coastal cycling in the neighbourhood. The south of Fünen is known for its old châteaux, often built in a Renaissance style and set in mellow parkland; Egeskov, between Ringe and Stenstrup, is one of the most celebrated, built on an island in the 16th century. The two main resorts of southern Fünen are Fåborg and Svenborg, delightful old towns with many wooden buildings, woods and gentle hills to the north.

Of the various islands of the southern archipelago which can be reached from Fünen, ÆErö is one which should not be missed. Try and visit out of the tourist season so that you can enjoy the lovely 18th-century port of ÆErösköbing with its cobbled streets and half-timbered houses. It is also the home of 'Bottle' Peter Jacobsen who is claimed to have invented the craft of building model ships in bottles. Connected to Fünen by bridge is the little island of Tåsninge with superb views from the top of the church tower at Bregninge, and on the long thin island of Langeland historic Rudköbing is pleasant.

Zealand

This is the first target of tourists visiting Denmark – who nevertheless stick to a well-worn trail of the principal sights, leaving much of the countryside undisturbed. It is a gently undulating island, with many beech woods, lakes and historic towns, and fields of sugar beet and wheat. Copenhagen is a major attraction – it is gay and vibrant, a mixture of old preserved town and sophisticated city, and compared to most European capitals a pleasant place for riding a bicycle.

The peninsula north of Copenhagen contains the most visited sights. At Helsingör you can visit Hamlet's castle, and take ferries to Sweden 4 kilometres away, and north of here the sandy coast has good bathing. At Fredensborg there is the Royal Palace set in a grand estate, and at Hillerød, 9 kilometres away, you can visit Frederiksborg, one of the most outstanding Renaissance châteaux in Denmark. Roskilde was the ancient capital of the Danish royalty, and has a 12th-century cathedral and a Viking ship museum.

Of the three main islands which hang off the bottom of Zealand, Lolland and Falster are flat and intensively farmed (they have the best soils in the country), but Mön by contrast is the second highest (after Bornholm), with the dramatic (by Danish standards) limestone cliffs of Moensklint lining its eastern coast.

Bornholm

This rocky island, four times further from Denmark than it is from Sweden, simply does not fit into the geographical character of its host country. Seven hours by ferry from Copenhagen, Bornholm lives a life of its own, some 30 kilometres by 20 kilometres in size, with enough small roads to give about a week's cycling. Ferries also link Bornholm to Ystad, in Sweden.

The weather-beaten granite of which the island is made lends an air of scarred ruggedness, and the interior is quite hilly, especially in the north, where the coast is marked abruptly by towering granite cliffs; those of the Hammeren headland are especially impressive. And just south of here are the ruins of medieval Hammershus fortress. Much of Bornholm's coast is rocky, with tiny picturesque fishing villages occupying sheltered corners; Allinge on the north coast is one of the best known. The south coast is milder, with long sand strands at Dueodde. Historically Bornholm's greatest prize is its four round churches, which were built in the 12th century as a defence against pirates as well as a place of worship.

Denmark's Highest Road

On the main road between Skanderburg and Horsens, in eastern Jutland, is the village of Tebstrup. The highest road in Denmark runs from Tebstrup, north-west to the village of Yding, reaching its highest point (171 m) where it detours to the tower and restaurant on Ejer Baunehöj, the second highest hill in Denmark.

Tour of the Islands

A route for pedalling gently, picking a delightful course through the maze of tiny back roads which so characterise the Danish countryside; you need good maps and lots of time to make the most of this tour. Hills are not usually severe, and a three-speed sit-up-and-beg bike is adequate transport for the types of terrain covered. The tour starts and finishes at Copenhagen in order to concentrate on the archipelago of eastern Denmark; it could however be adapted to suit riders arriving by ferry at Esbjerg – riding east from the port via Holsted, Stationsby, Vejen and Lunderskov you could join the route at Middelfart, follow it through the islands of Fünen, Ærö, Langeland, Tasinge and Zealand, to leave it at Silkeborg in Jutland, heading back to Esbjerg in a south-westerly direction. This is a particularly versatile tour and can be adapted to various lengths. If it is too long for you, cut off the visits to Ærö, Langeland and Tasinge, or use a train for the section between Aarhus and Middelfart. Follow the tour in whichever direction pleases you.

ISLAND TOUR

Terrain: undulating
Distance: 700 kilometres
Start/Finish: Copenhagen/Copenhagen
Scenery: *
Interest: **
Maps: Geodaetisk Institut/Mair Die
Generalkarte 1:200,000 series nos 2, 3 & 4
or Geodaetisk Institut 1:100,000 series nos
1513, 1514, 1414, 1315, 1314, 1214, 1213,
1212, 1312, Aerö sheet, 1412, 1413.

COPENHAGEN
6	Hellerup
20	Rungsted
19	Helsingör
6	Gurre
5	Tiköb
6	Fredensborg
9	Hilleröd
6	Tulstrup
4	Nejede
10	Ramlöse
11	Melby
10	Hundested

Ferry to Jutland

	Grenå
11	Alsrode
5	Glatved
8	Hyllested
3	Gravlev

(special cycle-path)

11	Ebeltoft
7	Lyngsbæk Strand
	(Mols Bjerge)
9	Vistoft
5	Tved
5	Sködshoved

Ferry to Aarhus

	Aarhus (south of
	Braband Sö)
10	Arslev
3	Lyngby
3	Borum
8	Skörring

7	Sorring
15	Silkeborg

(alternative route to
Horsens on special
cycle-path)

4	Virkland
12	Himmelbjerget
4	Gammel Rye
10	Vissinggård
2	Tönning
5	Vestbirk
3	Torp
6	Lundum
4	Lund
6	Horsens
5	Boller
2	Uth
7	Stenderup
6	Store Dalby
5	Daugård
7	Bredballe
5	Vejle
10	Skærup
5	Follerup
2	Herslev
10	Erritsö
7	Middelfart
7	Gamborg
6	Föns
11	Sönder Aby
7	Sandager
9	Assens
6	Ebberup
5	Snave
7	Strandby
8	Fladsled
6	Osterby
4	Fåborg
6	Katteröd
4	Pejrup
	(east side of
	Brændegård Lake)
15	Lydinge Möller
3	Espe
3	Herringe
4	Volstrup
3	Egeskov

6	Stenstrup	2	Galdbjerg
3	Kirkeby	4	Langå
5	Hvidkilde	4	Svindinge
4	Svendborg	4	Frörup
		5	Kogsbölle
	Ferry to Ærö	4	Holckenhavn
	ÆErösköbing	2	Nyborg

(detour to visit west
ÆErö via Breginge, Skovby,
Söby, Leby and Breginge to
rejoin route at Dunkær: 30 km)

			Ferry to Zealand
			Korsör
7	Vodrup	6	Halseby
7	Dunkær	5	Vemmelev
9	Marstal	8	Slagelse
		6	Vedbysönder
	Ferry to Langeland	7	Boröd
		4	Sorö
	Rudköbing	8	Store Ebberup
8	Bjerreby	13	Haraldsted
3	Lundby	6	Valsölillegård
5	Valdemarsslot	8	Ny Tolstrup
4	Vindeby	3	Sælöse
2	Svendborg	7	Gammel Lejre
4	Björnemose	3	Gevninge
4	Skårup	4	Herslev
4	Langdysse	2	Kattinge
3	Gudme	7	Roskilde
		8	Hedehusene
		25	COPENHAGEN

Basic Information

Getting there

Air: Copenhagen's international airport is about 10 kilometres cycling from the city and $1\frac{3}{4}$ hours flying time from London. Some international flights also serve Aarhus airport.

   Trains: there are three main rail/ferry routes between London and Copenhagen: via Dover and Ostend, and via Harwich and the Hook of Holland, both of which take around 24 hours, and thirdly via Harwich and Esbjerg which takes 27 hours. There is also a route from Newcastle-on-Tyne to Copenhagen (via Esbjerg) which takes 25 hours.

   Ferries: daily car ferries run between Harwich and Esbjerg (19 hours), and on a less frequent basis between Newcastle-on-Tyne and Esbjerg (19 hours).

Information Sources

Danish Tourist Board (DTB), Sceptre House, 169/173 Regent Street,

London W1R 8PY (tel: 01-734.2637/2638). A good selection of information includes described tourist itineraries, a special guide to package cycling holidays and a free map.

Local Tourist Bureaux: all towns and tourist centres have local information offices *(Turistbureauet)* − about 175 of them country-wide. Those identified with the international 'i' sign have fixed hours, a multi-lingual staff and can reply to written enquiries, while the others offer more limited services. A full list of all *Turistbureauet* addresses and phone numbers is available from the DTB.

Danmarks Cykle Union, Idraettens Hus, 2600 Glostrup (tel: 2-455555). The national federation of cycle-racing clubs.

Dansk Cyklist Forbund (DCF), Kjeld Langes Gade 14, 1367 Copenhagen K (tel: 01-14.42.12). One of the most effective bicycle organisations in the world, with aims which include defending cyclists' rights, increasing road safety and encouraging cycle-touring. Services to members include a bi-monthly magazine *Cyklister*, touring information and specialised publications, among them the excellent guide book (in Danish) *Cykelferie i Danmark* and a unique national cycling map (see page 135. Both publications are available by mail from the DCF.

Accommodation

Camping: with about 500 (approved) sites scattered across the country, there should be no problem finding a pitch for a tent, and standards of amenities are high, with some of the more luxurious sites equipped with saunas, swimming pools, restaurants and so on. The approved sites are graded from one star (basic and low cost) to three star (laundry, shop on site etc). Most sites have an open season which runs from 1 May to 1 September, though about 70 remain open through the winter; half the sites have huts (some fully furnished) for rent, though these normally have to be booked well in advance.

All approved sites require campers to be in possession of a camping pass; either obtain an International Camping Carnet before you leave home (which does as a camping pass, as well as allowing you to stay on the 26 sites of the FDM − *Forenede Danske Motorejere:* the Danish motoring organisation − and occasionally getting you discount rates on approved sites) or buy a visitors' camping pass from the first Danish site you visit. The most detailed guide to sites is that of the Danish Camping Committee, which has explanatory text in English and is widely available in book-shops and at camping sites; alternatively it can be ordered by post (apply to *Det Danske Lejrpladsudvalg,* Skjoldsgade 10, DK-2100, Copenhagen 0).

Wild camping is not easy in Denmark, because it is heavily cultivated, and by Scandinavian standards densely populated; you need to obtain permission from the landowner before putting up a tent away from an official site.

Youth Hostels: like the camp-sites, these are plentiful, of a high standard, and are an excellent type of accommodation on which to base a tour. There are about 90 hostels distributed in all the corners of the country, so you can cycle virtually anywhere and never be more than a day's riding from a hostel; sometimes they are only two or three hour's apart. Most are fairly large, specially adapted, or built, establishments with good facilities; nearly all have members' kitchens and all but a very few provide meals (though a handful offer breakfasts only). Most hostels also have family rooms. Between late June and early August it is wise to book in advance.

Private rooms: the English type of 'bed and breakfast' is not usually found, but one can sometimes find private houses with a room to let; ask at the local tourist office for their accommodation list.

Farmhouses/Holiday Homes: both can be good for fixed-centre touring, making a comfortable homely base for exploring the local countryside. The farmhouse accommodation is let by the week, and is much favoured by families; you eat with the hosts and are free to wander round the farm. The holiday homes are normally wooden chalet-style builldings (or old converted dwellings) in rural settings, by woods, lakes or the sea. They are privately owned and usually fully-furnished, with three categories covering a span of amenities and prices.

Inns: the renowned Danish *kro* (inn) makes a memorable overnight sanctuary after a day's pedalling, often in an old building in the heart of a village or town, reasonably priced with sumptuous breakfasts. Some are quite expensive, other out-of-the-way establishments less so.

Hotels: the most expensive accommodation, though occasionally it is possible to find cheaper hotels away from the main roads and tourist centres. There is no grading system, and the best guide is to compare price and facilities in the DTB's *Hotel Guide;* it lists over 1,000 addresses, including hotels, inns, motels and pensions, and is revised annually. Away from Copenhagen the local tourist offices are able to find and book rooms for foreign visitors. And if you tour out of season (before June and after August) it is often possible to obtain big discounts on hotel prices. Two useful sources of low-budget accommodation are the Mission Hotels which are good value, clean, no-frills establishments, and the various addresses obtainable from the Use-it office in Copenhagen which among other services can help you find a place to suit your purse within the city. They are found at Magstræde 14, Copenhagen V (tel: 31.36.12); The student residence halls *(kollegier)*, empty during the summer, are popular among thrifty travellers.

Weather

Denmark has the mildest weather in Scandinavia, with short winters and summers not dissimilar to those of eastern England, though spring comes a little later, usually mid-April to early-May. The touring season extends from May through to September, with July and August the warmest months; sometimes even hot. Rainfall is fairly low, partly because there is no high land to catch those soggy Atlantic clouds, though cloudy weather is quite common. West Jutland is more likely to produce rain than elsewhere, and in the summer this often makes an appearance as shortish thunderstorms. By far the wettest month is August, with June, July and September noticeably drier. Being low-lying, Denmark is exposed to the wind, and there is seldom a day without a breeze; the prevailing winds are westerlies, with many of the farms protected by belts of trees planted as wind-breaks.

Other Considerations: spring has a lot in its favour, with the beech trees bursting into fresh greenness and the various types of accommodation uncrowded. Danish schools have summer holidays from about 20 June to 10 August so that most family holidays take place during July. Sea temperature reaches 18-20°C.

Average Daily Maximum Temperatures (Centigrade)

	alt. in metres	J	F	M	A	M	J	J	A	S	O	N	D
Copenhagen	9	2	2	5	10	16	19	22	21	17	12	7	4
Vestervig	19	2	2	5	9	15	18	20	20	17	12	7	4

Cycling Information

Cycle Shops

You are never too far from a bike shop in Denmark, and most towns have a choice of several, including specialists who can handle repairs and supply quality lightweight spares. Of the 800 or so in the country, about 50 can offer a comprehensive lightweight service, including building to order, while at the other end of the scale some shops are mainly moped stockists and the bicycles are a sideline.

Cycle Hire

Quite a common amenity, the best source of information being the local tourist offices; the DTB also publish an annual activity holiday brochure, which includes a map of cycle-hire locations and brief information. It is sometimes possible to hire a tandem. You need proof of identity, and may be asked to leave a deposit. The DSB (Danish State Railways) have hire bikes available at a limited number of stations between 1 April and 31 October each year; in Copenhagen and North Zealand these are Klampenborg, Lyngby, Hilleröd and Helsingör, and

on Falster, bikes can be hired at Nyköbing station. In all cases it is wise
to book ahead.

Transporting Your Bicycle

The Danish State Railways (DSB) run a clean, efficient, rail network,
with lines reaching all corners of the country, including the larger
islands; sadly they do not have a progressive attitude towards the
carriage of bicycles. Most rail carriages do not have luggage compartments so bicycles cannot be accompanied and have to be sent in advance
as registered luggage. Take your machine to the station of departure at
least one day before you plan to travel, present your own passenger ticket
and buy a ticket for the bicycle. You leave the bike in the hands of DSB
staff who consign it to a special luggage train; there may be delays which
mean a wait at the destination for the bike to arrive. Bicycles arrive at
their destination a maximum of 2 - 3 days after being consigned. The
charges for the bike vary according to distance. To make things even less
convenient, it is only possible to register bicycles between the major
stations (these stations are listed on the reverse of the DCF's
Cykelferiekort). Bikes can also be sent as unaccompanied luggage (i.e. if
you are not travelling by train yourself) for a slightly higher scale of
charges, a service which extends to all rail stations, not just the larger
ones.

On Denmark's few private railways there is a more enlightened
attitude, and on 14 of these branch lines bikes can be carried on the same
train as yourself, for a charge which varies according to distance. These
lines, and useful details like costs and the number of bikes each train can
carry, are listed on the reverse of *Cykelferiekort*.

Ferries are a natural (and fun!) part of a Danish bike tour; on some
the bike travels free, but on most there is a modest charge. Again, the
useful *Cykelferiekort* carries helpful information, showing all the
regional, local and island ferries, the charges for bikes, frequency,
duration of sailings and so on.

Many buses carry bicycles, though the number each can take varies
from 2 to 10 so you may not find space first time. A smallish charge is
payable for the bike, the same whatever the distance. *Cykelferiekort* has
a brief guide to the services and charges.

Roads

Surfaces on Danish roads are on the whole excellent, even on minor
thoroughfares, though cobbles still exist in some towns. At the time of
writing, a new system of road numbering is being introduced. The prefix
'A' has now been discarded, though many of the roads still have the same
numbers; there are now three categories: E-roads (which include

motorways), prefixed 'E' with green and white signs; primary roads with one- or two-digit numbers in black, on yellow boards; secondary roads which have three-digit numbers on white boards. Sign-posting is good on all roads.

Traffic densities per kilometre of road are only half the level of densities in the UK, and busy roads are something that can be avoided without too much trouble. Main roads close to towns have heavy traffic, especially during rush-hour (and during July and August), but once out in the country, on the smaller back-roads, you can bike in peace and tranquillity. Many of the main roads are in any case monotonous straight drags (where you notice the wind most) with little of the charm that can be found on their tributaries.

But while overall traffic is half that of the UK, bike ownership per 1,000 of population is double; the Danish bike rider has an enviably loud voice when it comes to road planning. Many of the towns have cycle-paths running parallel to their main roads (their use is compulsory), and these can be invaluable for picking a safe route out of the suburbs towards the countryside. Rather like Amsterdam, Copenhagen is a bicycle-city with (by UK standards) good facilities for cyclists and intersections thronged with spinning spokes during commuting hours. (A DCF census once counted 13,500 cyclists daily crossing a Copenhagen bridge). Make sure you have a copy of the DCF's *Cykelferiekort*, which shows all the roads which have adjacent cycle-paths. This map also marks the specially constructed cycle-ways, which run independently of the roads. At crossings preceded by a blue sign with the words *For gående* you should give way to pedestrians. The rules for turning left in Denmark do not follow the UK convention: you must stay on the right-hand side of the road until you are opposite the road down which you want to turn. If traffic is passing you, halt the bike and wait for a gap; you must not pull out into the centre of the road. Bike felons have rich pickings in Denmark, (especially around railway stations) with 100,000 bicycles a year being reported as missing – so lock it when you leave it!

Cycling is permitted on most paths and tracks, unless a sign expressly forbids it.

Organised Tours

Popular with newcomers to overseas bike touring, Denmark is well served by companies offering packaged pedalling holidays. The DTB have detailed brochures describing the tours and listing the addresses for making bookings. Most tours last between 4 and 14 days, with the maximum daily distance 45 - 60 kilometres. You are not shepherded around in groups, but choose your own day for starting and ride with whom you wish. Inclusive in the price is an itinerary, accommodation in youth-hostels or hotels (full or half-board), all meals, extras like ferry tickets and the loan of an equipped bicycle; there are discounts if you bring your own machine.

Maps

For General Planning

Bartholomew/Mair Denmark, scale 1:1,000,000. A compact little map clearly showing the areas of higher and lower land, with a few tourist features like camp-sites, viewpoints and scenic roads. Many smaller roads not marked.

For Cycling

Dansk Cyklist Forbund, Cykelferiekort, scale 1:510,000. An invaluable map, specially designed to help you choose cycle-routes in Denmark. It shows recommended cycling routes, the locations of custom-built cycle-ways and identifies roads which have adjacent cycle-paths. The reverse has useful information such as a youth-hostel list, the addresses of tourist offices, a key to Geodætisk Institut maps, lists of the trains, ferries and buses which carry bicycles – and it is all in English!

Kümmerly + Frey, Danemark, scale 1:300,000. Could be used for cycling, though it does not show all the minor roads. No height shading, though some tourist features like camp-sites and youth-hostels are shown.

Geodætisk Institut/Mair Die Generalkarte series, scale 1:200,000. The GI is the Danish 'Ordnance Survey', and this map series is available in a Mair cover or in its original GI form. Virtually all roads are shown, in enough detail to use for touring. Although some tourist features are marked (camp-sites, hostels, museums etc) there is no indication of scenic roads or height shading. Four sheets cover the country.

Geodætisk Institut, scale 1:100,000. The best maps for cycling use, showing all roads and much incidental detail too; ideal for detailed local exploring. 32 sheets cover the country.

FINLAND

Suomi, the 'land of fens and lakes' offers a limited though unusual type of cycling. What hills there are do not make exerting pedalling, and for a country of its extreme northerly latitudes – Finland is level with Alaska – the summer weather can be remarkably kind. You have to be sure of your interests before choosing Finland for a bike tour; this is a large and empty land where distances between villages and towns can in some parts be measured in hours of cycling. The scenic surprises and human curiosities that so frequently occasion a pause in other parts of Europe, are further apart in Finland. But there are compensations, particularly for those with an affinity with water since there are plenty of opportunities for bathing, boating and wind-surfing.

Nearly one and a half times as big as the UK, the scale of Finland is fairly awesome for the self-propelled traveller, the feeling of inter-minableness being encouraged by the relative 'sameness' of much of the landscape. Most often you ride through an undulating land of forest, bared rock, marsh and waterways, with views which normally only open out over the lakes – of which there are some 60,000. In the centre and east, lake and channel lock inextricably with isthmus and promontory in an intricate maze of land and water.

About 70% of the land is forested and a further 10% is covered by water. The long coast is fragmented into several archipelagos of islands, backed by a narrow coastal plain whose prized soil is deep and rich enough for cultivation. Behind this is the great central lake plateau, whose forests ultimately give way in the far north to a bleaker tundra landscape. The only high land appears along the boundary of Finland, Sweden and Norway, in northern Lapland; a third of the country lies north of the Arctic Circle and the Midnight Sun shines through the summer months. The Finns have carved little pockets of habitation from this harsh environment, with isolated wooden farms in the clearings and towns which can boast a progressive and clean architecture.

By most countries' standards the Finnish summer cannot be regarded as much more than a hiccup in an extremely long and severe winter, a season so bitter that the daily ferries which ply between Stockholm and Turku are sometimes prevented passage by an iced-over Baltic. Not surprisingly, the people who live in Europe's most northern and easterly country have developed a reputation for endurance and fortitude; they are healthy, fair-skinned, fair-haired, reserved but helpful, and hardworking. How many of these attributes are encouraged by the taking of saunas is impossible to say, but any who daily boil in a steam-bath, whisk themselves with birch twigs and then plunge into a cold lake (or snowdrift) have at the very least to have developed a companionship with extremes – a theme which recurs through the country and culture.

Originally coming from Asia, the Finns now have a language which is hard to master and which has little in common with the other Scandinavian languages; quite a number do speak Swedish, and English is widely spoken in the towns. Nearly all the population belong to the Evangelical Lutheran Church, and the country is a republic with an ardently preserved neutrality.

The main meal of the day is normally taken between 5 and 7pm, and lovers of porridge will be pleased to know that this glutinous Gaelic fuel is a minor national dish; so are salty Baltic herrings and a hard rye bread called *ruisleipa*. Service station cafés can be a useful stop-gap when you are riding between towns. The unit of currency is the *markka*, (FIM) divided into 100 *pennis* (P).

Ride Guide

The Eastern Lake District

A unique area where land and water mesh in a haphazard jigsaw; as far

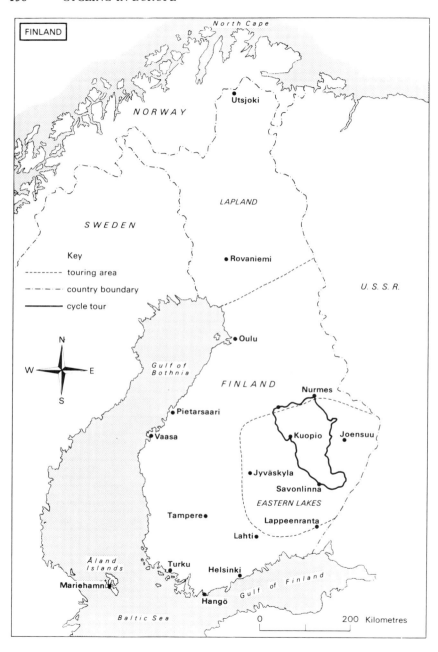

east as Leningrad and on the same latitude as Greenland. It takes a train journey from Helsinki to reach, or 200 kilometres of cycling, and as with most of Finland it is not the place to visit with a bicycle unless you have a 'wilderness affinity'. Villages and towns can be three or four hours cycling apart. It is not however especially exerting, as hills are short and seldom steep.

When the great ice sheets retreated north they left a land pocked by thousands of irregular shallow depressions which subsequently filled with water, some to form vast lakes, others mere pools. The low belts and hummocks, along shores so convoluted it is hard to tell where one lake ends and the next begins, are occupied by stands of pine, spruce and birch; and in places the glaciers left long sinuous ridges of moraine, which today snake across lakes like lengths of casually tossed rope. Roads have to pick tentative routes along ridges and between lakes, rivers and waterways, while towns often perch delicately on tiny islands. In forest clearings wooden farm buildings stand grey with age and weather. You ride in the constant company of trees and water.

Savonlinna is the main centre of attraction, an old town which grew up around the magnificent medieval castle of Olavinlinna. Nearby at Kerimäki is the world's largest wooden church, with seating for 3,300 and just east of Savonlinna is a 7-kilometre long gravel ridge, a relic from the Ice Age, along which the old road runs. At the southern end of the great Saimaa Lake System – itself a powerful attraction for water-borne tourists – is the town of Lappeenranta, with its restored 17th-century fortifications, and to the north-east the celebrated falls of Imatra (now harnessed for hydro-electric power, and only unleashed on summer Sundays). North of Joensuu, the capital of the province of North Karelia, is the lake of Pielinen, notable for Koli, the 347-metre high peak which dominates its western shore providing a rare panoramic view over eastern Finland.

Lapland

You have to be committed to cycle here, especially as Finnish Lapland cannot match the fine coast and mountains that so dramatise the horizons of Norwegian and Swedish Lapland. Most cyclists who have toured here have done so because it was *en route* to or from the North Cape; it takes a dedicated Arctic cyclist to make the long journey for Finnish Lapland alone. You need to travel self-sufficiently, with the possibility of several days cycling between supplies of food and roofed shelter. The main routes are tarmac or concrete; others are rough.

North of the head of the Gulf of Bothnia the land rises to a 300-metre plateau, and as you move further up into the Arctic so the stunted forest gives way to bare rock and swamp, and a tundra of heather and bog, lichens, mosses, and in the valleys stands of dwarf alder, birch and willow. There are fewer lakes than in the south, but many rounded bare-topped hills; it is a barren wilderness. But you can meet the Lapps and see herds of roaming reindeer, and in the most northerly town of Utsjoki there are seventy days of uninterrupted daylight from mid-May onwards. Mosquitoes are rife.

Finland's Highest Road

In the far north of the country, the main E78 highway heads north-west via Karesuando reaching the highest point (566 m) on a Finnish road at a signed spot 16 km south-east of Kilpisjärvi; 25 km south-east of the border with Norway. By Kilpisjärvi is Saana, at 1029 m, one of Finland's highest mountains (good views).

The Eastern Lakes Tour

This route concentrates on the lakes and archipelagos of eastern Finland, with a short foray into the hills to the north. There are no long climbs (apart from the ascent of Koli), though in parts the roads are continually undulating. Kuopio is 5 or 6 hours from Helsinki by train; Savonlinna would make an alternative start/finish point for the tour but is further by rail from Helsinki. The tour can be shortened by omitting the Lapinlahti loop. From Kuopio you head south-east through the maze-like archipelago of the Saimaa Lake System, to Savonlinna with its magnificent fortress. From here you can take a short loop to visit the well-known gravel ridge of Punkaharju and great wooden church of Kerimäki. Heading north to Lake Pielinen, you can cycle up Mount Koli for a rare panoramic view, moving on by the lakeside to Nurmes. From Lapinlahti you return to Kuopio via the western snores of Lakes Onkivesi and Kallavesi.

TOUR OF THE EASTERN LAKES

Terrain: level/undulating
Distance: 680 kilometres
Start/Finish: Kuopio/Kuopio
Scenery: *
Interest: *
Maps: Suomen Tiekartta 1:200,000 nos 9, 6 and 8

KUOPIO	
12	Puutossalmi
6	Juonionlahti
25	Mäntymäki
13	Leppävirta
21	Varkaus
24	Pohjoiskyla
21	Rantasalmi
28	Punkaharju
20	Kerimäki
9	Anttola
15	Makkola
53	Junction of Routes 476 and 471
7	Vihtari
15	Sarvikumpu
28	Kontkala
30	Polvijärvi
36	Ahmovaara
10	Koli
4	Mt Koli
4	Koli
8	Savikylä

20	Nunnanlahti	26	Korpinen
12	Juuka	19	Varpaisjärvi
16	Vuokko	21	Lapinlahti
26	Nurmes	5	Akkalansalmi Ferry
		10	Junction with Route 564
(for quick route back to Kuopio take		21	Tuovilanlahti
roads SW via Siilinjärvi: 124 km)		16	Pulkonkoski
		24	Lamperila
49	Rautavaara	27	KUOPIO

Basic Information

Getting There

Air: Helsinki is Finland's main international airport; 2 hours 50 minutes flying time from London. The only really practical way of travelling from the UK to Finland.

Rail: you would have to have a good reason to use trains to reach Finland from the UK; London to Stockholm is 25 hours, and the ferry on to Turku is a further 11 hours.

Ferry: Services operate across the Gulk of Bothnia between Sweden and Finland: Skellefteå to Pietarsaari takes $5\frac{1}{2}$ hours; Umeå to Vaasa $4\frac{1}{2}$ hours; Sundsvall to Vaasa $8\frac{1}{2}$ hours and Kapellskär – Mariehamn – Naantali 10 hours. Daily ferries ply between Stockholm and Turku (11 hours) and Stockholm and Helsinki (15 hours). There are also ferries between Finland and northern Germany (Travemünde).

Information

Finnish Tourist Board (FTB), 66 Haymarket, London SW1Y 4RE (tel: 01-839.4048). A wealth of useful free brochures include general travel information, accommodation, regional itineraries, calendars and so on. FTB's *Sports in Finland* leaflet includes some details on participation in the popular mass bike tours (such as the annual ride round Lake Päijänne north of Lahti) and of packaged individual bike tours.

Local Tourist Bureaux: all major towns have a city tourist office *(Matkailutoimisto)* which can help with accommodation, supply brochures on local attractions etc (their addresses are listed in the FTB's general information booklet). Some of these local tourist offices (such as Porvoon Maalaiskunnan, Matkailuneuvonta; Rihkamakatu 3, SF-06100 Porvoo 10, tel: 915-146-133 X 238) can supply described multilingual cycle-routes for their regions as well as inclusive cycle-holiday packages. Travel agencies are called *Matkatoimisto.*

Suomen Pyöräilyliitto, Topeliuksenkatu 41a, 00250 Helsinki 25 (Tel: 90-418493). The national federation of Finnish cycle-racing clubs.

Touring Club of Finland, Kansakoulukatu 10, 00100 Helsinki 10 (tel: [9]0-694 0022). A general touring club catering mainly for motorists and affiliated to the AIT.

Accommodation

Camping: Finland has about 350 camp sites with an even sprinkling across the south of the country but fewer and more isolated clusters in Lapland. Most are situated by water. Standards are good, with sites being classified like Swedish ones into three gradings, which must be displayed at the camp entrance. A one-star site has all the basic washing and WC facilities while the three-star ones have 24-hour security, recreation facilities, hot water etc. The main camping season runs from late-May/early-June to the end of July, and at weekends during this period popular sites may become crowded. The FTB publish an annually revised (and free) site list. Many sites have camping cottages also.

Wild camping is not officially allowed without permission from the landowner, and neither is lighting open fires.

Youth Hostels: there are about 130 hostels in the country, close enough together in the Eastern Lakes to use as a basis for a bike tour, but elsewhere they are usually more than a day's riding apart; there are around 20 north of the Arctic Circle. Most hostels are fairly small, with family rooms (which are in heavy demand), while some of the larger ones are accommodated in empty schools. Hostel saunas are common, most hostels have members' kitchens and about half of them provide meals of some description. Opening months are restricted in most hostels to roughly 10 June to 15 August, a small proportion staying open through the winter.

Farmhouses, Holiday Cottages, Holiday Villages: very popular among vacationing Finns, and worth considering if you are looking for a fixed-centre holiday. There are about 160 farmhouses where you can take full-board, eating with the hosts and spending time helping in the fields if you like; most are in the centre and the east, and on the Aland islands. Holiday cottages can work out less expensive – there are 5,800 of these ranging from primitive fishing huts to luxuriously appointed villas. All are fully furnished. Holiday villages are less rustic, being groups of bungalows which can sleep anything from 2 to 5 people. The FTB can supply free brochures with details concerning advance booking.

Hotels: fairly expensive, often in new buildings with amenities which of course include the sauna. There is no official grading; many include breakfast in their price. An annually revised list is obtainable from the FTB. Less expensive are the 'summer hotels' which occupy empty university accommodation between 1 June and 31 August. These are found in the major cities.

Weather

Summers are short and briefly warm; winters are long and the most severe of any European country. July is the warmest month (it can even be quite hot) with Helsinki's temperatures about the same as London, though June and August are noticeably cooler (by 2 or 3°C). In July the north is about 3°C cooler than the south, and this is really the only sensible month for cycling in Lapland. So, for the southern part of Finland, the touring season is roughly mid-June to mid-August. Summer rain is generally light, and for short periods. Prevailing winds are westerly, but northerly in Lapland.

Other considerations: the days are long in June, July and August, with the north bathed in the curious pale yellow light of the Midnight Sun for several weeks in the summer; you can see it at the northern tip of Finland between mid-May and the end of July. Even in Helsinki there are nearly 20 hours of daylight during the summer. Mosquitoes are at their worst between Midsummer's Day and the middle of August, and during this period you need to take full precautions; the severity of their attacks varies from year to year. The deciduous trees of Lapland usually look their best during the second and third weeks of September, when the first frosts turn the leaves.

Average Daily Maximum Temperatures (Centigrade)

	alt. in metres	J	F	M	A	M	J	J	A	S	O	N	D
Pallasjärvi	278	-9	-9	-4	2	8	15	19	16	10	2	-3	-6
Tampere	84	-5	-4	0	7	14	19	22	20	14	7	2	-2

Cycling Information

Cycle Shops

Not found often enough to rely upon, so aim to travel with adequate spares and tools. Biking has been seeing a modest boom in Finland since the early eighties, so the spares situation is steadily improving; shops in the bigger towns may stock lightweight components. 26- and 28-inch tyres are more readily found than 27-inch, and Finland is one of the only places in the world where you can buy special bicycle snow tyres with tungsten steel studs.

Cycle Hire

Quite a widespread amenity, especially found at tourist centres like the Åland islands, Hangö, Jyväskylä, Kuopio, Lappeenranta, Nurmes and

Tampere. Youth hostels frequently have hire fleets, and to a lesser extent so do holiday villages, camp sites, hotels and tourist information offices; the FTB has a list of the latter source of rental.

Transporting Your Bicycle

Trains can be of invaluable assistance in getting to and from a touring area in Finland; lines radiate out from Helsinki, with main routes to Oulo in the north, Turku, Kuopio and Imatra, and there are a number of branch lines too. Most trains will carry bicycles, the loading and unloading being done by railway staff. You pay for the bike according to distance, there being a minimum and maximum fare. If you want to sent it unaccompanied, you register it at the baggage office and pay the same rate. If you have any specific queries, contact Finnish State Railways, Vilhonkatu 13, Pb 488 00101 Helsinki 10 (tel: Helsinki 7071).

In Lapland, where rail routes are fewer, buses provide an alternative. For a reasonable fare you can have your machine transported on the bus roof. In places you can find that the lake ferries (some of which take bikes) add interest to a day's ride.

Roads

Around half of Finland's road network is surfaced with asphalt or oiled-sand, the remainder mainly being gravel, sand or a mixture, which can deteriorate in wet weather to bumps and runnels, and in dry weather to dust. The better surfaces are in the south, on the main roads, while in the north even the major routes may be oiled sand or gravel. Tyres need to be in good shape before a tour. Around the cities and towns of the south, cycle-paths are quite common, and help you avoid the traffic; Helsinki, Turku, Tampere, Lahti, Espoo and Jyväskylä all have cycle paths.

Overall, Finland's roads are the least crowded in Europe, most of the traffic concentrating on the southern main roads; the route from Helsinki westwards to Turku, then northwards up the coast is among the busiest. Drivers are generally considerate, and used to the Finnish style of bike conspicuousness, with bright orange arms sticking out from rear carriers and plenty of reflectors.

Maps

For General Planning

Kümmerly + Frey, Finland, scale 1:1,000,000. Shows the whole of Finland, plus northern Norway and northern Sweden on one sheet. Good height shading, scenic roads, plus viewpoints and some camp-sites.

For Cycling

Suomen Tiekartta series, scale 1:200,000. The only maps for detailed cycling, covering the country in 19 sheets and showing a rare wealth of information: tourist information offices, camp sites, cafés, hiking routes, hostels and swimming places, with contours, but no scenic roads, gradients or height shading.

FRANCE

Who can help loving the land which has more minor roads than any other in Europe? Yes, France is as close to a bikers' paradise as one can get; it has an unparalleled diversity of scenery, a choice of climates, an indefinable ambience that makes cyclists feel at home – and it's only an hour across the water from Britain. Such are France's star qualities that you can pick it for a first continental tour because you feel it's an easy place for a novice, yet years later you will still be choosing it because there always seems to be one more challenging part worth another bike tour. It *is* a big country, in fact the biggest in Europe and roughly equivalent to the combined areas of the UK, Germany, Belgium, Luxembourg and the Netherlands. It's also unique in that it stretches from the Channel to the Mediterranean; France's northern latitude is the same as Southampton, and Perpignan is comfortably south of Florence.

The 'little' roads of France are a delight (appropriately enough they're called 'D' roads) and are the master-key to discovering the country on a bicycle. With the large-scale map you can ride for hundreds of kilometres without suffering traffic, many of the byways being so peaceful that you can picnic on the verge without a thought. Where you *look*, you *find:* south of the Dordogne is a little-visited valley called the Célé which meanders quietly between steep limestone bluffs as it wends its way down towards Cahors. Along the wooded valley floor is a road which bends and curls with the river, the D41, angled at a relaxing downhill tilt and along which four of us pedalled one still September morning. Across the river lay Espagnac-Ste-Eulalie, a defensive huddle of medieval houses with huge oak beams and steeply-pitched red-tiled roofs. Pushing open heavy studded doors we could explore their creaking interiors, climbing to the balcony of a lofty watch-tower for a view up the valley, carpeted in tree-tops. In one musty upstairs room rested piles of maize glowing golden in shafts of dust-speckled light which lanced down from tiny windows; with the deftness of a conjurer France's D roads can throw you back hundreds of years.

Scenically France has a bit of everything: majestic glaciers and great idle rivers, wild rugged coast and clear bubbling streams, forests and fields, flat-as-a-pancake roads and others that climb over 2,000-metre passes, fearsome gorges and mild valleys, broad monotonous plains and soaring jagged peaks. Its archaeological sites range from megalithic to Roman to Renaissance and its weather from blustery damp to searing heat.

But most of these are obvious lures, and France is more subtle than that. There is an intangible charm which magnetises bikers – the street cafés like pit-stops along the roadside, the comradely calls from French cyclists, the food, the wine, acceptance of the bicycle as something more than a toy, the empty countryside (France has half the population density of the UK) and the old French buildings which, like its bikes, still look elegant even when they're dilapidated.

There are few cyclists who can deny an obsession with food once on tour, and French shops are a spectacular source of replacement calories for ravenous riders. The enormous *'hypermarchés'* (such as the *'Mammouth'* chain) normally offer the best value-for-money. Picnic lunches are a challenge to the imagination, and choosing which cheese, what vegetables, and how much fruit, can prove as time-consuming as the final feast. And if picnicking in France is an art, then trying to fit a *baguette* on a bike is an inexact science! At first glance these long thin loaves look an ideal shape for carrying on a bike; after all they're not dissimilar to a fat frame tube. But you can strap them to the bike frame, slot them into a pannier and tie them across a luggage carrier to no avail because they *always* seem to bend, snap, then bounce off down the road, no matter what you do. The only safe solution is to ask before leaving the *boulangerie* for the loaf to be cut into two more manageable pieces.

Most cafés open from 7 am through to midnight, and are an ideal refuge. If it's rainy, too hot, too windy, or cold, you're thirsty, a bit peckish or you want somebody to talk to then pull on the brakes in the next village and indulge! Cafés advertising *casse-croûtes* or *sandwiches* offer snacks as well as the normal range of hot and cold, alcoholic and still drinks. You can save money by imbibing at the bar – if you sit at a table expect to pay up to 50% more. Many cafés have television – useful for watching the *Tour de France* during July. Establishments called *Brasseries* are good for impromptu meals and snacks at most times of day too. French resturants have an enviable reputation and in each town (and many villages) you'll find one that provides a freshly cooked meal at most hours of the day. The dishes labelled *menu à prix fixé*, *menu touristique* or *plat du jour* are usually the best value. Another favoured cyclists' haunt (generally found by main roads, away from major towns) is the *relais routier*, a chain of transport cafés (of higher standards than UK ones) used mainly by lorry drivers. Food is plentiful and modestly priced, and many offer accommodation too; they are identified by a distinctive blue and red sign, and listed in an annual guide available from most book shops.

Apart from sharing an appreciation of bicycles, eating a lot and watching bike races, the French wave their arms when they talk, and some wear berets. 95% of the population are Catholic and expect visitors to cover their arms and legs when entering churches. Most have been taught English as a second language, but will never admit it; you will be expected to try speaking French. To make things more complicated, Basque is spoken in the south-west, Breton in Brittany, German in Alsace and Catalan in Roussilon.

The French always seem vaguely surprised that other nationalities can ride bicycles too, for they see themselves (with some justification) as world experts. This is the home of great racing cyclists like Louison Bobet and Bernard Hinault, and of nationally-revered cycle-tourists like Paul de Vivie. From the humblest two-wheeler being bumped over the cobbles of Artois to the glittering lightweights of the *cyclo-sportifs*, the bike has earned a respected place on the road. France is a republic, and its currency, the French *franc*, is divided into 100 *centimes*.

Ride Guide

Lower Normandy

A good choice for a first foreign tour; easy to reach via the Channel port of Cherbourg, or via Le Havre and Dieppe to the east. The terrain can best be described as gently rolling, fairly undemanding for biking, with lots of small uncrowded roads. It's a small-scale landscape with enough variety and interest to suit anything from a few days' holiday to a more extended tour which includes parts of Brittany too.

Very roughly, Lower Normandy lies west of Lisieux, a mainly rural region with a coastline of cliffs and beaches. The most scenic parts are the Cotentin peninsula, which has many attractive roads, small fishing villages and some rocky coast (and miles of beaches too), and a couple of slightly more hilly areas inland. The first of these, the Normandy *bocage*. is south of St-Lô, where small green fields, thick hedges, clumps of woodland and sunken lanes create a quiet and intimate landscape. On a grander scale are the hills and steep valleys of *La Suisse Normande* through which the River Orne winds.

Off the bike there is plenty to do; it is an area for idling. Local cheeses include Camembert, Pont-l'Evêque and Livarot; there is cider, cream and *calvados* (apple brandy) and a rich history. Celts, Gauls, Britons and Normans have lived and fought here, leaving sites such as Bayeux with its cathedral and tapestry, Mont St Michel, historic Caen and a galaxy of manors, castles, cathedrals and abbeys. Relics of the Second World War invasion can be found from the Orne to the Cotentin.

North and east of Lisieux, and across the Seine is Upper Normandy, which has some pleasant though unremarkable cycling; there is an attractive ride west from Dieppe through St Valéry-en-Caux and Fécamp to the cliffs of Etretat.

Brittany

If Normandy can be taken as the novice's touring primer, then Brittany is the next stage on; inland it is similar but grander than Normandy and its coast is in places wildly exhilarating. The cycling can be challenging, with steep (though not usually long) gradients inland, and nagging headwinds. The rewards are great; Britanny's insularity to some extent restricts the motor-hordes and it's fairly easy, especially inland, to find quiet roads. Main roads near the popular resorts are very crowded in summer. There are lonely hill areas for the adventurous and lots of scope for swimming. Brittany's scale and shape make it ideal for a two or three week tour and even one week is long enough to see a bit of everything; Roscoff (ferries from the UK) makes an excellent start/finish point and the port of St Malo is handy for cycling eastern Brittany.

Like a piece of torn lace floating on the Atlantic, Brittany has an extraordinarily intricate outline – similar to the English county of Cornwall, though much larger. The coast – some 1,200 convoluted kilometres of it – is mostly rocky, broken here and there by sheltered bays (often sandy) and long winding inlets with harbours. Handfuls of islands and islets lie offshore. Some of the most dramatic cycling is out along the many windswept headlands and in places the cliffs rise to 90 metres. Often the shore can only be reached by narrow 'there-and-back'

roads, the 'back' nearly always being uphill! The most exciting sections of coast are found roughly west of Roscoff and Quimper where the savagery of the reefs and cliffs is given a sombre power by melodramatic place-names such as 'Bay of the Dead'. The coastal scenery between Roscoff and St Malo also has a rugged beauty (and includes the well-known high-spots of the 'Armorique Corniche', 'Bretonne Corniche' and 'Emerald Coast') but it is more accessible than the western peninsulas and draws more tourists. One of the most unusual sights of the southern coast is the great inland gulf of Morbihan, with several small roads following its ragged fringe.

Inland Brittany is chequered with small fields, hedges and woods similar to the *bocage* of Normandy but with some bare and windy ridges adding welcome variety. Tiny hamlets and villages speckle the landscape, linked by small lanes, often sunk between high banks and used by little more than local farm vehicles. On a bike you can thoroughly lose yourself and get well away from the twentieth century. The bare windy slopes of the Montagnes d'Arrée rise to 300 metres, with small roads over their crests giving fine views. These, and the parallel ridge of the Montagnes Noires to the south provide an interesting complement to coastal riding.

Brittany not only looks similar to Cornwall, but its people are Celtic too; proud stock who hauled up the famous *menhirs* of Carnac on the south coast. Despite the arrival of the tourist industry and atomic power stations, many of the old ways of life and tradition remain, including occasional religious processions: *pardons*. It's also been the home of some of France's greatest bike-racing idols, among others Jacques Anquetil and more recently Bernard Hinault. Brittany's *crêperies*, where you can buy wafer-thin pancakes with assorted fillings, are excellent for replacing lost calories!

The Loire Valley

I've a cousin who claims you are not properly abroad till you've crossed the Loire, and in several ways the lazy arc of the Loire really is the threshold of truly 'foreign' parts. As you ride down from the chilly north through the plains of wheat fields and forests, the placid brown waters of France's longest river mark the point on the journey south where weather becomes noticeably warmer and drier (hopefully!) and where the architecture is indisputably foreign. For cyclists the Loire valley and its environs are specially significant because it is one of the very few parts of Europe which is both flat *and* interesting.

The lure of the Loire châteaux has made the region one of France's premier tourist attractions, but there is far more to enjoy than turrets and courtyards, Renaissance riches and mirror-surfaced moats. The various tributary valleys that join the Loire – such as the Vienne, Indre, Cher, Loir and Mayenne – provide better cycling than much of the great river itself. The valley of the Loire is in parts uninspiring, being broad and featureless, and it's best to ride selected sections such as the southern bank between Angers and Tours, and base the rest of the tour on other valleys and the very pleasant landscapes between. The entire area is well served by small, quiet 'D' roads and it's easy to escape from cars. It is an area of big skies and gentle farmland, generally low, and in places quite wooded, with river bluffs and gentle undulations occasionally lifting the roads to give modest views. Poplars and willow line the meadows with vineyards and orchards across the warmer south-facing slopes. The dullest area is the cereal plain north of Orléans; south of this city is the Sologne, an expanse of heather and marsh with thousands of tiny ponds and lakes. By contrast the Collines du Sancerrois, just to the east, are quite sharp with attractive though exerting cycling roads.

'Châteaux fever' can be quite debilitating after a while, and often the old 'family chateau' with plaster peeling and windows awry, which can appear out of the blue at the end of an unassuming country lane, can be more enchanting than the preserved art-form with its car-parks and crowds. Try mixing visits to Azay-le-Rideau, Blois, Chambord, Chenonceaux, Loches *et al* with lesser-known sights. Similarly, the many small and charming riverside villages are as alluring as the historic honeypots of Angers, Chinon, Tours, Châteaudun, Vendôme and so on.

Massif Central

This is the complete opposite of the flat, open, straight-road landscape of northern France. There is hardly a level kilometre of tarmac, with roads twisting and turning, rising and falling between each village and town. The riding is often strenuous, with plenty of hill-climbing, sometimes steep and in parts long-drawn out too. Some of the cols, which can reach 1,000 metres, can take a morning to conquer. Clermont-Ferrand is a popular starting point for a Massif Central bike tour: it's on the main rail line from Paris and a mere quarter of an hour's cycling from the railway station takes you to the first slopes of the Auvergne. Ignoring the effort required, this is cycle-touring country *par excellence* with a maze of tiny minor roads uncluttered by cars and a countryside blessed with peace and scenic variety.

The Massif Central is big! I once spent six weeks bike-exploring here, on a tour which did not cross even half the horizons. There are several distinct sub-regions. To the south-west of Clermont Ferrand is the Auvergne, a long strip of high land (mostly national park) through which poke the *puys* – a range of extinct volcanoes. It's a desolate, much forested area which sometimes looks a bit like Scotland, and it is slowly coming back to life after decades of sapping depopulation and poverty. There is exciting potential for rough-stuff cycling and hiking. The most famous Auvergne peak is the Puy de Dôme, a near perfect volcanic cone with a spiral road (sadly closed to bikes) climbing to its summit – a superb viewpoint and the scene of some historic stage finishes in the Tour de France. Further south, the Puy Mary has several fine roads scaling its heights, culminating in the 1,582-metre Pas de Peyrol (from near the top of this mountain you can ride for 400 kilometres, nearly all of it downhill or level, to Bordeaux and the Atlantic – via Aurillac and the valleys of the Rance, Célé, Lot and Garonne).

West of the Auvergne is the region of the Perigord, and the river Dordogne – a hilly green limestone land split by gorges and undermined by caverns. Brive-la-Gaillarde and Cahors make good start/finish points for a tour, and are on the main Paris rail line. There's more than enough here to occupy two weeks of cycle-touring: museums, old churches, châteaux, cliffs and caves and quiet orchard-filled valleys are roadside company. Domme, Les Eyzies, Rocamadour and Padirac are all favourite tourist haunts but there are hundreds of other less visited gems. Some of the rivers which curl and twist down from the heights of the Massif Central towards the Bay of Biscay have some really delightful small roads by their banks. The beauty of the Dordogne is well known, but the lovely little valley of the Célé is relatively undisturbed and parts of the Lot are dramatic. In summer the area around the Dordogne is probably the busiest part of the Massif Central. To the north of Perigord is Limousin, a region of rolling, verdant, more tame countryside.

The south-eastern edge of the Massif Central is marked by the broad diagonal swathe of high land known as the Cévennes. They stretch for over 150 kilometres from St Etienne to hesitate north of Montpellier before continuing as the Lacaune range. In several places the peaks of the Cévennes top 1,500 metres. It's a lonely region once tramped by Robert Louis Stevenson and his reluctant donkey, with few main roads but a profusion of exciting minor roads ideal for cycling. Biking is quite hard work, and in summer it can get very hot. Two of the region's most outstanding features are the Gorges de l'Ardèche (canoes can be hired to explore them properly) and the Gorges du Tarn, both of which are followed by impressive roads. There are a multitude of lesser gorges, ravines and exposed ridges to ride beside, and some challenging 1,000-metre passes. Much of the Cévennes is cloaked with cool pine forests; there are chestnuts, clear mountain rivers, rock-walled valleys, and even in summer the lower slopes remain green. Exceptions are the barren limestone plateaux of the Causses de Sauveterre, Causse Méjean, Causse Noir and Causse du Larzac in the southern Cévennes. These bare treeless heights are separated by narrow winding valleys; one of the least populated parts of France. The Cévennes tie in well with a tour of the historic lower Rhône valley and Provence.

The Vosges

This hump-backed range of hills is not really extensive enough for more than a week or so of riding, but it would conveniently fit in with an itinerary including the Black Forest of Germany just across the Rhine to the east, or the ridges of the Swiss Jura to the south. Both Belfort (at the southern end of the Vosges) and Strasbourg (to the north-east) are on main rail lines from Paris. The Vosges are about 15 kilometres long, separated into two portions by the major valley at Saverne; the southern half ('High Vosges') rises to about 900 metres, steeply on the Rhine side and more gently in a series of terraces on the west; rounded and bare summits – locally called *ballons* – sit above forested slopes. The northern 'Low Vosges' are less dramatic, being more of a heavily forested plateau split by steep-sided valleys.

There is plenty of scenic cycling in the Vosges, harder work in the south, but more rewarding; roads like the specially designated Route des Crêtes, which snakes along the high ridges, offer good views. And there are some really stiff climbs. The hairpinned approach to the Ballon d'Alsace is a well-used Tour de France terror for example. Local specialities include cheese, a lovely light wine from the slopes above Colmar and kirsch produced from cherry orchards around Epinal.

The French Alps and Provence

From the Lake of Geneva southwards, a 350-kilometre chain of mountains provides France's toughest and most spectacular cycling. It is a huge area, narrow and highest in the north, broadening and declining as it runs down towards the Mediterranean, with enough scope and variety to provide weeks of touring. In just a fortnight you would have to concentrate on one particular part, rather than try and see a bit of it all. It's quite an accessible area, with international airports at Geneva and Marseilles and main-line trains running into the mountains at places like Grenoble and Chambéry. Excursions can also be made into the Italian Alps and Switzerland from this area. Roads are well surfaced, but in some parts care has to be taken choosing routes; in the high Alps there are so few roads that traffic is funnelled into just a few valleys – notably those that link the main French and Italian cities. Elsewhere the French Alps (compared to say those of Switzerland) are notable for their very great choice of excellent cycling roads. Briançon and Grenoble are good towns for basing a fixed-centre tour.

Between Lake Geneva and the River Durance (near Gap) are the highest summits: the Savoy Alps, one of Europe's mountain highlights. Here glacier-sculpted granite forms such giants as Mont Blanc, (at 4,807 metres, the highest mountain in Europe) and snow and ice cover these peaks all the year round. Valleys here are deep, often with forested sides, small villages and hamlets clinging to the sunny south-facing slopes above the chill of the valley floor. West of Mont Blanc, along the western shore of Lake Annecy, a superb cycle route has been built along the course of an old railway line; for 15 kilometres or so a strip of smooth tarmac curls without gradient beside the waters and below the peaks. Further south, where rainfall is less, the landscape is more parched. This is an area of mighty mountain massifs through which roads thread along narrow valley-bottoms or spiral heavenwards to scale famous cols like the Galibier and Izoard. A day's cycling here is three-quarters measured toil and one quarter ultimate thrill. The 'pass guides' of the O.C.D. are an excellent aid to discovering the lesser-known passes in this part of France – many of them reaching dizzy heights.

To the west of the Savoy Alps is a broad curve of lower Alps, rugged but on a lesser scale than their neighbours, with more roads to choose from and generally less severe cycling. Highlights of this Alpine hinterland include the forested Vercors Massif (many grinding hairpinned climbs) which is laced by narrow, fairly quiet roads; interesting rides including a visit to the Gorges du Bourne.

South of the Durance the Alps become more broken up, giving a chance for several high cols to be opened up to spectacularly engineered roads; here there is some magnificent cycling, often on roads unspoilt by traffic and in spendid weather. The mighty passes of the Allos, Cayolle and Restefond are all well over 2,000 metres. From here to the Mediterranean the mountains get gentler; in fact if you freewheel down the Col de Cayolle and follow the River Var to the sea, you get 124 kilometres of virtually uninterrupted downhill! Further west there are several 'mini ranges' and plateaux crossed by little-used roads. One of them is Mont Ventoux; it was on the verge of the N574 from Carpentras, near the summit of this notoriously gruelling climb that Britain's racing cyclist Tom Simpson died from exhaustion in the 1967 Tour de France – a memorial now stands on the spot, carved from Tarn granite and subscribed to by readers of *Cycling* magazine.

South of the Alps is Provence, which lends itself to being combined with a tour of the Cévennes (just across the Rhône), with the French or Italian Alps, or with the Riviera. Avignon and Marseilles have rapid train links with Paris, and the latter is an international airport too. Provence roads are hilly, though with the mountains trending east-to-west effort can be saved by cycling with the lie of the land, following the river valleys. The roads often cross the 300-metre contour.

The attractions of Provence – apart from its settled weather – are its rich and diverse landscape, and its many historical sites. While milder parts are characterised by terraced slopes of vineyards and orchards, by little red-roofed villages perched on hilltops or nestling in green valleys, there are more rugged areas with deep gorges and pale dessicated ridges; the Gorges du Verdon (Grand Canyon du Verdon) are notably impressive, and further west the Luberon range (a national park) has several good, though steep, roads for cycling. The towns of the lower Rhône have a wealth of interest, including Roman remains; Aix-en-Provence, Arles, Avignon and Orange are all worth a visit. It is difficult to visit the coast without getting tangled up in traffic, and most of the famed Côte d'Azur is followed by busy N roads. Out of season it's more tolerable, and the minor roads inland are always quieter. The Camargue, where the Rhône meets the Mediterranean, is well worth adding to any tour of the area (being flat it makes a welcome change!).

The Pyrénées

This is thrilling and relentless cycle-touring (or should it be cycle-mountaineering?) country, with some of the steepest and longest climbs in Europe. The attraction of the Pyrénées is one of physical challenge; a personal duel with gravity played out on roads which zig-zag skywards in endless switchbacks, climbing dizzily over the warm and friendly valleys to cross chilly cols above the snow-line. Both ends of the Pyrénées have good rail connections with Paris. Consult the O.C.D's *Pyrénées Guide* for details of individual passes and rough-stuff routes.

The Pyrénées stretch for about 400 kilometres, though to cover them from end-to-end by bike the distance is very much longer; the infamous *Raid Pyrénéen,* a standard ride which takes in 18 of the major passes between Hendaye on the Atlantic, and Cerbère on the Mediterranean, is 710 kilometres long. More significantly it involves 15,000 metres of climbing! (Details of *Raid Pyrénéen* from Cyclo Club Bearnais, 64000 Pau, France; enclose an International Reply Coupon.) The Pyrénéen range is long and thin, with the highest passes in the central section, roughly between Andorra and Pic d'Orhy (south-west of Oloron-Ste-Marie); here some of the mountains top 3,000 metres and are snow-covered all the year round, and the passes can reach 2,000 metres. The highest pass in the Pyrénées is the 2,407 Port d'Envalira in Andorra, one of those sneaky ascents which makes you think you've reached the summit then, bang! – just around the corner a pile of impossible-looking hairpins tell you it is far from over yet.

The western Pyrénées are lower and less spectacular than the centre, with milder passes and lusher vegetation; the centre and west receive a lot more rain than the east which has Mediterrean-type weather. Road surfaces vary considerably, with those on the Spanish side of the border being worse.

Corsica

One of Europe's best biking islands, offering adventurous, strenuous cycling for the rider who likes to mix mountains and coast. Views from the saddle are superb as most of the roads are high level, climbing and descending tortuously between the island's many precipitous valleys. The physical scale, steepness and drama of the island make it an especially exciting place to visit with a vehicle as diminutive as a bicycle. The scenery makes up for the lack of archaeological and cultural attractions. Gradients are long though comfortable; the roads follow the routes of centuries-old pack trails. Surfaces are rougher than mainland France, and in places pot-holed; on a bumpy road over a col on the west coast I remember passing some graffiti painted on a rock which proclaimed 'Once a Route Nationale – now a mule track!' and a little further on the same artist had added to the road sign warning of 'Unstable hard-shoulders' the cryptic comment 'since 1950!' The main points of entry to Corsica – Bastia, Ajaccio, Calvi, L'Ile Rousse and Propriano – all make good start/finish points for a two-week circular tour of the island.

Corsica also has two railway lines which link Bastia, L'Ile Rousse and
Corte, on which bikes can be carried; the views from this quaint line are
impressive.

About the size of Wales, Corsica squats a stone's throw from
Italian-governed Sardinia, and about 150 kilometres from the French
mainland. Its mountainous nature gives rise to a wide range of
vegetation and scenery; as you cycle up from sea-level, you pass through
a thick tangle of waist-high *maquis* – impenetrable thorny scrub – then
at around 750 metres move into cool dark forests of beech, chestnut and
pine. Flowering shrubs and herbs fill the air with a heady fragrance
during the spring. Above 1,500 metres the trees thin and grassy Alpine
pastures lead up to shattered ridges; this you have to see on foot
however, since the highest road (the Col de Vergio, east of Porto) 'only'
reaches 1,464 metres. To bike the north-south route up the centre of the
island is a dramatic experience; one of those roller-coaster rides where
you are either in bottom gear at 10 kph or freewheeling at 60! Steep
unfenced drops are often by your wheels, with little villages huddled at
the few junctions. My favourite Corsican pass is the Col de Bavella, in
the south, which is reached after a long climb through pine woods.
Dominating the pass is the fang-like ridge of the Aiguilles de Bavella,
whose granite towers glow pinkish in the sun, beckoning you on towards
that elusive summit. The helter-skelter freewheel down the east side of
the pass drops 1,218 metres in 30 kilometres straight into the Mediterranean – you need good brakes! The west coast has superb cycling (best
enjoyed outside July and August) with jagged cliffs, headlands, harbours
and occasional sandy bays. The east coast is relatively dull, with an
endless sandy beach and a narrow, cultivated coastal plain.

Only 2% of Corsica is used for farmland, and over a third of the
population live in Ajaccio and Bastia, so it is a wild and empty land with
considerable distances between shops and accommodation. (Happily,
banditry has receded into folklore and there is little chance of pedalling
into the midst of a fiery local feud.) Since the Bronze Age people have
eked a living from this 'mountain in the sea' and artefacts are strewn
over the island; there is a striking community of megalithic figures at
Filitosa in the south, while Cargèse retains its Greek character. There
are numerous fortified 'torri' and some really splendid Genoese bridges.
Romans, Vandals, Ostrogoths, Lombards and Pisans have all sampled
life on Corsica, and Napoleon was born here. Some of the towns are
especially striking: Bonifacio has an extraordinary cliff-top site, Calvi
has an immense citadel, the one-time capital of Corte has a shambling
elegance and L'Ile Rousse a picturesque slumbering harbour.

Rough-Stuff in France

From canal towpaths to old drove roads and high mountain cols, there is plenty of scope for riding off-the-tarmac in France. Much of the fun is in finding your own tracks, using a suitable large-scale map such as the IGN 'Green' or 'Orange' series (see page 177). Common sense and discretion will tell you which tracks can and cannot be used – typical signs prohibiting access are *Propriété Privee and Défense d'Entrer* (the other common woodland sign is *Chasse Privée* which indicates that extermination of the local wildlife is a pleasure reserved exclusively for the landowner). Many of the older canals have wide, smooth towpaths which are superb for cycling, and you can find odd stretches of tranquil level pedalling from the Canal Latéral à la Loire, to the Canal du Midi.

Much more arduous (and definitely not for the inexperienced) are the rough tracks crossing Alpine cols. There are a rich crop of these in the French Alps (and France's other mountain ranges too) with conditions which vary from smooth, compacted gravel to steep, loose boulders where the bike has to be carried. Among those in the Alps frequented by cyclists are the Col de Coux (1,924 metres) from Champéry to Samoëns, the neighbouring Col de la Golèse (1,671) from Morzine to Samoëns, the steep and tunnelled Col de la Charmette (1,277) north of Grenoble (from St Egrève to St Laurent), the Col de Granon (2,413) just north of Briançon, and the Col de Parpaillon (2,788), so much of a cycling favourite it is the subject of the regular Rallye du Parpaillon, organised by the Gap cycling club. The pass is between Embrun (south of Briançon) and La Condamine Châtelard. Very much harder than the Parpaillon is the Col de Boucharo in the Pyrénées, which can be used to cross an otherwise long and impassable section of the mountain chain, from the top of the new road above Gavarnie, into Spain via Bujaruelo, to rejoin the tarmac at Puente de los Navarros.

French Alps Pass Guide

Pass (height in metres)	Location	Comments
Agnel (2,744)	Château-Queyras – Casteldelfino (Italy) (SE of Izoard)	narrow, steep, quiet, poor surface.
Allimas (1,352)	Gresse – St Michel (SW of Grenoble)	narrow, wooded, quiet.
Allos (2,240)	Barcelonnette – Allos	picturesque, narrow and quiet with superb views; hairpins on south side.
Aravis (1,498)	La Clusaz – Flumet	narrow, superb scenery, hairpins.
Bataille (1,313)	Léoncel – Col de la Portette (Vercors Massif)	pleasant, narrow and wooded

Bayard (1,248)	Chauffayer – Gap	fairly easy and busy, steeper on S side.
Bleine (1,439)	St Auban – Grasse	picturesque, narrow and quiet, hairpins on N side, good views from top.
Cabre (1,180)	Die – Aspres-sur-Büech	pleasant, views.
Cayolle (2,327)	Barcelonnette – St Martin-d'Entraunes	narrow, picturesque, quiet.
Champs (2,095)	Colmars – Chastelonnette	very narrow, picturesque, hairpins.
Chauvet (1,126)	La Charce – Col de la Saulce (E of Nyons)	narrow, picturesque, quiet.
Colombière (1,618)	Cluses – Le Grand-Bornand	wooded, pleasant.
Cou (1,116)	Thonon-les-Bains – Habère-Poche	narrow, picturesque, quiet, superb views.
Crêt de Chatillon (1,699)	Annecy – Leschaux	wooded, good views from top.
Croix de Fer (2,068)	Col du Glandon – St Jean-de-Maurienne	narrow, picturesque, quiet, great views. Scenic detour on east side along minor road via Col de Mollard (1,638 m).
Croix-Fry (1,477)	La Clusaz – Manigod	narrow, picturesque, quiet, very good views.
Cyclotouristes (1,330)	Albertville – Molliessoulaz	an appropriate name for a quiet col.
Echelle (1,766)	Briançon – Bardonecchia (Italy)	quiet, rough surface on Italian side, superb views.
Festre (1,441)	Agnières – La Cluse (NW of Gap)	narrow, quiet, picturesque, views.
Font-Belle (1,304)	Sisteron – Thoard	narrow, picturesque, quiet.
Galibier (2,645)	St-Michel-de-Maurienne – Col du Lautaret	one of the classic Alpine cycling cols, with a monument to the creator of the Tour de France, Henri Desgranges, at the summit; superb views, tight hairpins.

Gets (1,163)	Taninges – Morzine	quiet, ski resort at top, views
Glandon (1,924)	La Chambre – Allemont (SW of St Jean-de-Maurienne)	narrow, picturesque quiet, good views.
Graille (1,597)	Valbelle – St Etienne (SW of Sisteron)	narrow, picturesque, quiet, good views.
Granier (1,134)	Chambéry – St Pierre-d'Ent	pleasant, wooded, quiet.
L'Homme Mort (1,211)	Séderon – St Trinit (east of Mt Ventoux)	narrow, picturesque, quiet, views.
Iseran (2,762)	Val d'Isère – Lanslebourg	the highest pass in the Alps, picturesque, good views, several unlit tunnels on N side.
Izoard (2,360)	Briançon – Château-Queyras	historic associations with Tour de France, with monument to Fausto Coppi; many hairpins, barren scenery, superb views.
Joux-Plane (1,713)	Morzine – Samoëns	narrow, picturesque, quiet.
Larche (1,991)	Jausiers – Demonte (Italy)	quite busy, fairly easy, picturesque.
Lautaret (2,057)	La Grave – Briançon	busy, pleasant, good views on W side.
Luital (1,263)	Grenoble – Sechilienne	steep on S side, narrow, picturesque.
Madeleine (1,933)	S of Feissons – La Chambre	narrow, picturesque, quiet, steep on N side.
Menée (1,457)	Les Oches – Menée (E of Die)	picturesque, narrow, quiet, views from top.
Mont Cenis (2,083)	Lanslebourg – Susa (Italy)	very busy.
Montets (1,461)	Vallorcine – Chamonix	quiet, picturesque, fine views to S.
Montgenèvre (1,954)	Briançon – Cesana-Torinese (Italy)	very busy, views.
Morgins (1,370)	Abondance – Monthey (Switzerland)	picturesque, narrow, quiet.
Moutière (2,454)	Bayasse – St-Dalmasse-le-Selvage (SE of Barcelonnette)	new road, picturesque, linked by track to Restafond/Bonnette.

Noyer (1,664)	Poligny – Col de Rioupes (NW of Gap)	narrow, pretty, quiet, steep on W side.
Pommerol (1,072)	La Charce – Rosans (E of Nyons)	picturesque, quiet.
Pontis (1,301)	Pontis – Le Lauzet-Ubaye (SE of Gap)	narrow, quiet, picturesque, good views over Lac de Serre Ponçon.
Petit St Bernard (2,188)	La Rosière – La Thuile (Italy)	fairly busy, good scenery.
Porte (1,325)	St Pierre de Chart – Grenoble	pleasant, wooded, narrow, view on S.
Portette (1,175)	St Martin-le-Colonel – Vassieux-en-Vercors (Vercors Massif)	pleasant, wooded, quiet, views.
Restefond/Bonnette (2,802)	Jausiers – St Etienne-de-Tinée (W of Barcelonnette)	the highest tarmac road in France and in the Alps (the pass itself is at 2,715 m), narrow, hairpins, superb views.
Rioupes (1,438)	Col du Festre – St Bonnet (NW of Gap)	narrow, picturesque, quiet.
Cormet de Roseland (1,922)	Beaufort – Bourg St Maurice	narrow, picturesque, quiet.
Rousset (1,367)	Vassieux-en-Vercors – Die (Vercors Massif)	picturesque, narrow, quiet, hairpins, views.
Saisies (1,635)	Flumet – Hauteluce (SW of Megève	narrow, picturesque, quiet.
St Martin (1,500)	Valdeblore – St Martin Vésubie	narrow, picturesque, quiet.
Télégraphe (1,570)	St Michel-de-Maurienne – Col du Galibier	pleasant, wooded, hairpins.
Turini (1,607)	St Martin Vésubie – Sospel	wooded, narrow, quiet, hairpins.
Valberg (1,669)	Guillaumes – Beuil	narrow, quiet, picturesque.
Vars (2,111)	Guillestre – Jausiers	narrow, picturesque, views on S side, hairpins.
Mont Ventoux (1,909)	Malaucène – Sault-de-Vaucluse	picturesque, barren, superb views to Alps and Pyrénées, Tom Simpson memorial.

Pyrénées Pass Guide

Pass height (in metres)	Location	Comments
Alto Laza (1,125)	Ochagavia (Sp) – Isaba (Sp)	narrow, picturesque, quiet, good views.
Ares (1,513)	Prats-de-Mollo – Camprodon	busy.
Aspin (1,489)	Espiadet – Arreau	picturesque, narrow quiet, superb views.
Aubisque (1,709)	Laruns – Col de Soulor	picturesque, quiet, good views, an old favourite among cyclists.
Boixois (1,380)	Organa (Sp) – Tremp (Sp)	good views and scenery.
Bonaigua (2,072)	Salardu (Sp) – Esterri-de-Aneu (Sp)	fine scenery, hairpins, narrow quiet, good views.
Fabas (1,470)	Castejón (Sp) – Laspaules (Sp) (SE of Benasque)	narrow, picturesque, quite, views.
Ibañeta (Roncesvalles) (1,057)	St-Jean-Pied-de-Port – Burguete (Sp)	quite busy.
Jau (1,513)	Prades – Roquefort-de-Sault	narrow, picturesque, quiet, good views.
Jou (1,560)	St Llorenc (Sp) – Solsona (Sp)	narrow, quiet.
Larrau (1,573)	Larrau – Ochagavía (Sp)	narrow, picturesque, quiet.
La Trape (1,111)	Pont-de-la-Taule – Aulus-les-Bains	narrow, quiet.
Mente (1,331)	St Béat – Henne-Morte	very narrow, quiet, picturesque.
Paillères (2,001)	Ascou – Mijanès (E of Ax-les-Thermes)	very narrow, quiet, picturesque.
Péguère (1,375)	Massat – Burret (W of Foix)	picturesque, one of the harder Pyrénéen passes.
Perves (1,350)	Pont de Suert (Sp) – Sentereda (Sp)	narrow.
Peyresourde (1,569)	Arreau – Bagnères-de-Luchon	narrow, picturesque, quiet, good views.

Pierre St Martin (1,578)	Arette-la-Pierre-St-Martin — Isaba (Sp)	narrow, quiet, very pleasant.
Port (1,249)	Massat — Tarascon-sur-Ariège	narrow, picturesque, quiet.
Portet (2,215)	above St Lary (S of Col d'Aspin)	new road, one way only.
Portet-d'Aspet (1,069)	Fronsac — Audressein	steep, hairpins narrow, quiet, picturesque, good views.
Port d'Envalira (2,407)	l'Hospitalet — Soldeu (Andorra)	highest pass in the Pyrénées, good scenery, many hairpins, superb views, busy.
Portillon (1,293)	Bagnères-de-Luchon — Bossost	a lovely cycling pass, narrow, quiet, good scenery.
Pourtalet (1,792)	Gabas — Escarilla (Sp)	fine scenery, narrow, superb views.
Puerto de Cotefablo (1,423)	Broto (Sp) — Biescas (Sp)	picturesque, 1-km summit tunnel.
Puymorens (1,915	l'Hospitalet — Ur	fairly busy, picturesque.
Quillane (1,714)	Formiguères — Mont-Louis	fairly easy, pleasant.
Somport (1,632)	Urdos — Los Arañones (Sp)	busy, picturesque, good views.
Soulor (1,445)	Col d'Aubisque — Arrons	picturesque, superb views.
Tourmalet (2,115)	La Mongie — Barèges	one of the best for cycling in the Pyrénées and regularly included in the Tour de France, superb views, side road from top up Pic du Midi de Bigorre.

Note The high passes are only open between mid-June and early October — and can occasionally be closed by bad weather during the 'cycling season'.

Tour of Central France

A route of great variety which visits three very contrasting areas of France; the ride begins in the cradle of Renaissance architecture, passes through a high and empty mountain region and finishes in warm secluded valleys riddled with the cave-dwellings of early Man. From the flat lands of the Loire valley, and visits to some of the most spectacular châteaux, easy pedalling takes you south-east to meet the foothills of the Massif Central. From there it's increasingly strenuous as you climb up among the forests and old volcanic peaks of the Auvergne, though over the last third of the tour the pedalling becomes easier as you follow the gorges and flat-bottomed valleys westwards out of the Massif Central. To avoid unnecessary gradients the route follows valleys where possible, and consequently it is the kind of ride that makes you friendly with certain rivers: after leaving the Loire you follow in turn the Indre and Creuse, then the infant Truyère, the Lot and the Célé, finally picking up the Lot again for the last few kilometres. The tour could easily be altered (and shortened) to follow the more touristy Dordogne instead of the Célé and Lot, in which case an obvious finish point is Brive-la Gaillarde. Alternatively the tour can be shortened by starting at Clermont Ferrand (picking up the described route at Fontanas, just west of the city). Both Tours and Cahors (and Brive-la-Gaillarde and Clermont Ferrand) are on the main rail line from Paris. There are many opportunities on this tour for rough-stuff riding and hiking (notably in the Auvergne where there are several long-distance footpaths).

CENTRAL FRANCE TOUR
Terrain: flat/very hilly
Distance: 760 kilometres (excluding detours)
Start/Finish: Tours/Cahors
Scenery: **
Interest: *
Maps: IGN Red Series 1:250,000 Nos 106, 111, and 110 (just) or Michelin 1:200,000 Nos 64, 68, 72, 73, 76, 80 (just) and 79

km	TOURS
	(detour W to Villandry, Azay-le-Rideau and back to Montbazon via the Indre: 57 km)
2	St Avertin
10	Veigne
22	Azay-sur-Indre
12	Loches
1	Beaulieu-les-Loches
8	St Germain
15	Servolette
1	Châtillon-sur-Indre
21	Mézières-en-Brenne
27	St Gaultier
1	Thenay
10	Argenton-sur-Creuse
14	Gargilesse-Dampierre
5	Cuzion
11	St Jallet
3	Crozant
12	Dun-le-Palestel
16	St Vaury
13	Guéret
20	Ahun
2	Le Moutier-d'Ahun
9	St-Martial-le-Mont
6	La Rochette
8	Aubusson
18	Pontcharraud
21	Giat
12	Herment
18	Gelles
15	Ceyssat
	Col de Ceyssat
10	Fontanas
4	Manson
4	Laschamp
11	Randanne

(detour SW to Le Mont Dore	11 Chaudes-Aigues
and Puy de Sancy, then SE via	16 Pont de Tréboul
Courbanges to rejoin route	11 Paulhenc
at Besse-en-Chandesse: 44 km)	9 Laussac
	6 Barrage de Sarrans
20 Murol	11 Brommat
12 Besse-en-Chandesse	8 Lacroix-Barrez
(marked on IGN map as	23 Entraygues-sur-Truyère
Besse-St-Anastaise)	15 Vieillevie
28 Condat	20 Port-d'Agres
23 Allanche	23 Capdenac-Gare
13 Neussargues-Moissar	7 Figeac
22 St Flour	33 Marcilhac-sur-Célé
12 Viaduc de Garabit	20 Conduché
20 Maurines	29 CAHORS

Basic Information

Getting there

Air: the main international airports in France are at Bordeaux, Geneva, Lille, Lyons, Marseilles, Mulhouse/Basle, Nice and Paris.

Rail/Ferry: the easiest continental country to reach from the UK, and only $1\frac{1}{2}$ hours ferry journey across the Channel at its closest (Dover – Calais). All the French Channel-ports (Dunkerque, Calais, Boulogne, Dieppe, Le Havre, Cherbourg, St Malo and Roscoff) are on rail lines giving ready access to the rest of the country; most lines converge on Paris and the capital can only be avoided by taking cross-country trains and probably changing *en route.*

Information Sources

French Government Tourist Office (FGTO), 178 Piccadilly, London W1V 0AL (Tel: 01-4917622). Useful literature includes a calendar of events, regional hotel and camping lists and a guide to the *Logis de France.*

Local Tourist Bureaux: called *Offices du Tourisme* or *Syndicats d'Initiative* and sprinkled liberally across the country; there is one in nearly every town and resort. They often have useful literature not available from FGTO and can advise on accommodation, camp sites, restaurants and so on. For advance information on specific regions of France you can write to any of the 24 Regional Tourist Committee offices (addresses from FGTO). A new centralised accommodation-booking service – the *Service Réservation Loisir Accueil* – has been set up on a *département* basis to reserve and provide information on local *gîtes ruraux, chambres d'hôte* and camp sites (and on organised cycling holidays too). The service is free and in each *Loisir Accueil* ('Leisure

Welcome' office) there is usually an English speaker; their addresses and phone numbers are available from the FGTO and in the *French Farm and Village Holiday Guide* (see 'Gîtes de France').

At the time of writing, at least one of these Comités Régional de Tourisme was publishing leaflets with recommended routes and accommodation for the cyclist; the *Bretagne* office offers *Randonnée a Bicyclette* guides based on selected centres such as Brest, Lorient, Nantes, Rennes, Saint Brieuc, Quimper and Vannes, staying in *gîtes d'étape.*

Fédération Française de Cyclisme, 43 Rue de Dunkerque (B.P. 11-10), 75462 Paris Cédex 10 (tel: 285.41.20). The national federation of cycle-racing clubs, publishing a regular journal *La France Cycliste.*

Fédération Française de Cyclo-tourisme, 8 Rue Jean-Marie Jego, 75013 Paris (tel: 580.30.21). The French equivalent of Britain's CTC, with over 2,000 cycle-touring clubs under its umbrella and publishing each spring a 100-page calendar of touring events, a biannual handbook (with recommended accommodation addresses) and a regular (10 issues a year) magazine *Cyclotourisme* which includes lists of coming events. Affiliated to the AIT.

Touring Club de France. 6-8 Rue Firmin Gillot, 75737 Paris Cédex 15 (tel: 5322215). A national organisation covering all forms of touring (mainly motoring), affiliated to the AIT.

La Voix du Nord, a daily newspaper distributed in northern France, which has among other things the routes and details of local major and minor bike races – handy if you're trying to fit a tour in with some race-spectating.

Le Cycle, 59 Avenue de la Grande-Armée, 75782 Paris Cédex 16 (tel: 500.25.72). A sizeable magazine with technical and racing-oriented features on most pages plus a *Cyclotourisme* section devoted to more arduous aspects of touring (including *randonneur* riding) and a *Col Dur* feature which focuses on specific mountain passes.

L'Equipe, available from French newsagents this daily sports newspaper gives good coverage to cycling and is a useful aid if you're fitting some race-watching in with your tour.

Miroir du Cyclisme, 126 Rue Lafayette, 75461 Paris Cédex 10 (tel: 246.92.25). One of the best bike-racing magazines in the world, known for its good colour photography and race analysis.

Accommodation

Camping: generally it's easy to find camp-sites in France, though they obviously concentrate along the coast and in prime tourist areas such as the Dordogne; there are 7,000 official sites, graded from one-star to four-star. A typical three-star site will have hot showers and decent toilets, whereas some one-stars have no more than a cold-water tap and the dreaded French hole-in-the-floor 'toilet'. The most pleasant sites are without doubt the small ones. During the summer (especially August) the main coastal sites get overcrowded, if not full up, though a cyclist can often persuade a site manager there's room for 'just one more small tent'.

A new boon for itinerant cyclists is the increasing number of *'camping à la ferme'* and *'Aire Naturelle'* sites, usually out in the country and run by locals or a farmer, offering just the basic facilities and very often uncrowded and peaceful even in the height of summer. The *Fédération Nationale des Gîtes Ruraux de France* recognises a number of *Gîte-Camping-Caravanning à la Ferme* sites which are small and secluded (a maximum of 20 people per site is permitted), located on working farms away from main roads and railways. They have all the basic facilities and as a general rule rent by the week during the high season (15 June – 15 September) but daily at other times; these *gîte* sites are ideal for low-cost fixed centre touring and especially suitable for people (eg families) who may want to experiment with a fairly 'safe' form of cycle-camping before venturing out on more ambitious bike tours. Quite a number of *Gîte-Camping-Caravanning à la Ferme* sites are listed, with photos and amenity details, in the *French Farm and Village Holiday Guide* (see *Gîtes de France* for address). Many towns also have a municipal camp site. The best source of information for finding the quietest sites is the local Syndicat d'Initiative, which will often have site locations not listed in the big commercial guides; the local *Mairie* is also a good bet. Probably the most detailed listing is that of the *Fédération Française de Camping & Caravanning* (in French) which has 8,400 addresses including some *Aire Naturelle* sites (available from FFCG, 6 The Meadows, Worlington, Bury St Edmunds, Suffolk, UK and 78 rue de Rivoli, 75004 Paris). Both Michelin and Letts also publish campsite guides. Note that on some official sites, and in National Forests, a camping carnet is required; on some sites it may entitle you to a 20% discount.

Being such a rural country, wild camping in France is not only feasible but most enjoyable; most farmers are very amenable to a polite request. Wild camping is illegal in National Forests.

Youth Hostels: there are about 170 IYHA hostels in France, distributed unevenly; in Brittany, the central Loire valley, Dordogne, Vosges and French Alps they are generally close enough to each other to be comfortably linked by bike, but elsewhere the distances are greater and they are mainly useful as a supplement to other types of low-cost accommodation. Standards can vary from grim to good. Nearly three-quarters of the hostels are categorised 'large' (favoured by groups and schools), leaving only a quarter as 'standard' and sadly a mere handful of 'simple' establishments; a fair number have space adjacent to the hostel available to campers at reduced rates. Nearly all have self-cooking facilities. Children between 7 and 14 have to be accompanied by a parent and are only admitted with prior approval of the warden. The French hostel federation encourage you to book during July and August; in practice it is often possible to find a bed 'on the night'.

Gîtes d'Etape: favoured by backpackers but also a good option for bikers passing through an area. A *gîte d'étape* falls partway between a youth-hostel and a *gîte de France*, being a converted country building (anything from a stable to village house), sometimes with a warden, other times unattended, with stays normally restricted to three days. Sleeping is in dormitories, in your own sleeping bag, and there are basic cooking and washing facilities. While booking in advance is safer, it's sometimes possible to find space merely by turning up (or phoning earlier the same day).

Gîtes de France: in many ways the unique French *gîtes* are perfectly suited to the bikers' needs: they are inexpensive, self-contained, self-catering, simply but adequately equipped and found in rural locations, either out in the country or in small villages. They come in an amazing variety of shapes and sizes: some are rustic restored cottages, others parts of farmhouses or a village house – they may have space for just a couple or room for a group of 12. The accent is on providing a temporary home for visitors who like to feel they can be part of the French landscape, and offer a private and personalised sanctuary into which a tired cyclist can withdraw after a day pedalling the local lanes. *Gîtes de France* are privately owned but have to meet certain basic requirements laid down by the *Fédération Nationale des Gîtes Ruraux de France.* They are usually rented out by the week and it's essential to book well in advance for the months of July and August (High Season) and during these two months you normally have to book a minimum fortnight's stay. Rates are reduced for Low Season which runs from September to June except for mountain areas where a Winter Season runs from December to April. The annually revised and invaluable English-language *French Farm and Village Holiday Guide* (published and available from McCarta Ltd, 122 King's Cross Road, London WC1X 9DS, (tel: 01-278-8278) lists the *Gîtes de France* by region with prices, facilities, a photo of each etc, and clear details on how to make a booking. The FGTO and *Féderation Nationale des Gîtes Ruraux de France* (34 rue Godot-de-Mauroy, 75009 Paris) can also supply information and a handbook of addresses (the *'Guide Officiel des Gîtes Ruraux de France').* The FFCT has even bought its own *gîte* in the Auvergne, and this can be made available to *bona fide* cycle-tourists from overseas (contact FFCT for details).

Chambres d'Hôte: similar to the good old British 'bed and breatfast' the chambre d'hôte is a furnished guest room whose owner (living on the premises) offers breakfast, and sometimes a midday or evening meal also.

On the back of the expanding *gîtes* movement, the *Fédération Nationale des Gîtes Ruraux de France* is officially recognising a growing number of *Gîtes Chambres d'Hôte;* 'bed-and-breakfasts' in farmhouses and villages off the main routes. Minimum stay is normally one week – though this may be shorter out of high season – and rooms should be booked in advance. A fair number of *Gîtes Chambres d'Hôte* are listed and fully described in the *French Farm and Holiday Guide* (see *Gîtes de France* above), which also gives booking details. FGTO and the *Fédération Nationale des Gîtes Ruraux de France* also provide information.

Logis/Auberges: there are more than 3,500 budget-priced, sparse but comfortable *logis* (inns) throughout France; they are sponsored by the government so have a minimum standard, and come in 1 and 2 star grades. There is hot and cold water in each room, cooking is regional and *logis* tend to be situated off the beaten track. Over 600 smaller and ungraded *auberges* (less expensive and more rudimentary than *logis)* are included in the scheme. Very often you will be expected to eat at the *logis* or *auberge.* A booklet detailing the scheme is available from the FGTO and from the *Fédération Nationale des Logis et Auberges de France* (25 rue Jean Mermoz, 75008 Paris). A free list, the *Guide de Logis de France* is published each March and is available from the FGTO (state region of interest).

Hotels: there are five grades, the 1 and 2 star establishments normally being adequate and good value for the passing cyclist. Hotels abound throughout France and often provide good food too. You pay by the room, not by the person, and the tariffs have to be posted in each room; breakfasts (not usually substantial enough for a day's biking) are sometimes included in the tariff. Some *patrons* will expect you to take the hotel's evening meal. The 1-star hotels are especially popular in tourist areas and will fill up early in the day; if you want to play safe, book in advance. Off-season reductions may be as much as 20-40%. Hotel staff in France are normally understanding in their provision of safe overnight bike parking.

Other good-value accommodation can be found in 'no-star' hotels, at some of the *Relais Routiers* chain and at cafés which will often have a couple of rooms to let for a night. Any establishment displaying a sign *'Chambres'* is indicating the availability of a room to let.

Weather

Tropical winds from the south, depressions and the Gulf Stream from the west, plus a very varied geography combine to make France's climate extremely diverse, with different regions experiencing very different types of weather.

Brittany and Normandy have similar weather to that of south-west

England. It rains on about half the days in each year, this being concentrated in the west – though Brest for example has rather less rain in July and August than Plymouth. Prevailing winds are westerlies, which can sometimes blow up strong and make cycling hard work.

The remainder of lowland France – between the Bay of Biscay and Massif Central and between the Channel and Massif Central – have summer temperatures slightly higher than Normandy and Brittany, with colder winters. Heat-waves rarely last long and rainfall is more seasonal, coming more in winter than summer (Paris and London have similar rain characteristics). The west coast is exposed to the Atlantic winds, though fortunately for cyclists the roads of Les Landes are to some extent sheltered by the huge forests. The weather of the Massif Central is a more severe version of eastern France conditions; it can be very wet indeed, and windy on exposed slopes and valleys. Clermont Ferrand (Massif Central) and Grenoble (French Alps) have virtually identical temperatures all the year round.

The most predictable weather is found in the south and on Corsica where summer conditions are reliably sunny, hot and dry, with mild, moist winters (conditions in the higher mountains are obviously less predictable). Be ready however during spring and autumn tours, for sudden downpours, which usually clear quickly. In the French Alps and Pyrénées, weather is influenced by altitude, with temperatures dropping as you climb higher. The Pyrénées are generally hotter and drier than the Alps (though damper at their western end).

France's most infamous wind is the *mistral*, which blasts southwards down the lower Rhône valley (especially south of Montélimar) coming mainly in the winter and spring. It can last for several days at a time and affects Marseille for an average of 100 days each year.

Other Considerations: What time of year you tour in France depends a lot on where you are going; the warmest season in Provence lasts three months longer than does Brittany's for example. Mid-July to the end of August sees the greatest crowds at seaside resorts, on the coast roads and at main inland tourist areas; if you are planning a tour of the Loire châteaux or the Dordogne, you'll find the principal sites much quieter outside these two months. Also avoid during this period areas where roads are limited and traffic therefore concentrated, such as Corsica and the French Alps. School holidays in France are between late June and early September. Spring in France has all the usual colourful fragrant floral advantages, with apple blossom in Normandy and broom and heather in Brittany at their best during April and May. Provence looks it most colourful in spring and autumn (when it has a second blossom season), but is fairly uniform during the summer heat. France's many forests take on soothing hues of golden-brown during the autumn with the trees of the north turning a month earlier than those of the south. The grape-harvesting season is normally late-September to early October, depending on the weather.

Average Daily Maximum Temperatures (Centigrade)

	alt. in metres	J	F	M	A	M	J	J	A	S	O	N	D
Brest	98	9	9	12	13	15	18	19	20	18	15	11	9
Clermont - F	329	7	8	13	16	19	23	25	25	22	17	11	7
Montélimar	73	7	9	14	18	21	26	29	28	24	18	12	8

Cycling Information

Cycle Shops

Shops are plentiful, with major cities and towns having a choice of several ranging from lightweight specialists to clunker-menders. Off the beaten track a cycle-shop of some description (often combined with a moped store) will be found in most small towns and big villages. Motor garages sometimes stock a limited range of spare parts as do cycle-hire centres in tourist areas. Bicycle parts in France are metric dimensions, so some threads, wheels (tyres and rims) etc will not be compatible with 'Imperial' dimensions; a 27 x $1\frac{1}{4}$-inch tyre is nearly impossible to find.

Most shops will carry out repairs and in my experience French bike mechanics are both competent and very amenable. They understand bikes and will (usually) tackle a repair 'on the spot' if you mix diplomacy and desperation in the right proportions. On more than one occasion it's been the warm-hearted patience of a French bike mechanic that has got me out of a fix – either being happy to root out a single pedal spindle to replace a snapped one or another time being prepared to painstakingly rebuild a 30-year-old tandem freewheel using strands of spring-steel he cunningly fashioned from a discarded piece of brake-cable. And his price for making mobile our ancient two-wheeler was ... "Rien"!

Cycle Hire

Cycle hire *(location de bicyclettes)* businesses frequently operate from bike shops, hotels and holiday villages – especially near the coast, and the FGTO can supply a regional listing of addresses. The biggest operator is the French Railways (SNCF) with its *Train & Vélo* ('Rent-a-Bike') scheme (leaflet, which includes list of stations, from London office of SNCF: 179 Piccadilly, London W1V 0BA, tel: 01-409-1224; or from FGTO) which has fleets of hire-bikes at over 170 stations. The machines are mostly 'unisex' design, with lights, luggage racks and locks though some stations have more sophisticated ten-speeds. Identification and a deposit are required and you can book a bike by writing in advance to the station of your choice; the rate-per-hour drops the longer the period of hire. Bikes normally have to be returned to the station of origin, but arrangements can sometimes be made to leave them at a different station.

Transporting Your Bicycle

France's mainly electrified rail network (the largest on the continent) is run efficiently by the SNCF (*Société Nationale des Chemins de Fer*) with lines reaching all parts of the country; trains can be a handy complement to a French bike tour.

Bikes can be taken free of charge as accompanied luggage (*bagages à main*) on most rail routes – but only at restricted times and on certain types of train, primarily those operating over relatively short distances. To find out which trains these are, either phone or visit the London Passenger Enquiries office of the SNCF (179 Piccadilly, London W1V 0BA, tel: 01-409-1224) or ask at a main travel agent, main British Rail information bureau or, of course, at the appropriate railway station in France; all these sources will refer to the five SNCF regional timetables (*Indicateurs Officiels* – also on sale at French railway stations) where trains which take bikes as accompanied luggage are identified above each column of train-times by a small symbol of a bicycle. When taking a bike on a train as free accompanied luggage, you are responsible for its loading and unloading; sometimes there is a special luggage-waggon for bicycles.

On trains which will not carry bikes as free accompanied luggage you will have to register the bike, sending it as unaccompanied luggage (though sometimes the bike will actually travel on the same train as yourself). Arrive at the station at least half-an-hour before the train departs and take your bike to the *Bagages* or *Bagages (Consigne)* office. Present your passenger ticket, fill in the form provided and pay a flat charge (regardless of distance); guard your bike registration document with your life. Railway staff then assume responsibility for your bike, loading it and unloading it and you will next see it at the *Bagages* or *Bagages (Arrivée)* office of your destination, where you present the registration document and reclaim the machine. You can expect a delay of up to 24 hours before the bike becomes available at its destination (48 hours in peak periods) and up to 5 days on international services where more than one train is involved (hence claims by impatient cyclists that 'SNCF' really stands for 'Sometimes/Never Cycle Freight'!) When you register your machine, insist that the baggage staff state which train it will travel on, so you know when it will arrive. Registering a bike as unaccompanied luggage is a truly risky business if you are touring to a tight schedule. If you are registering your bicycle in advance, add the words 'à l'avance' to the luggage label, to avoid paying warehouse charges on arrival.

At the time of going to press the SNCF are running an experimental scheme at 20 stations, whereby cyclists are obliged to wrap their bikes in a cardboard box for transporting on trains. This 'service' is free if you wrap the bike yourself; or you can pay for it to be wrapped by station staff. Initial reports are that bikes get more damaged being thrown about in these boxes than under the established system of wheeling them. A new brochure *Guide du train et du velo* (from French stations) details this and other developments in the bike-on-train saga.

If you are making a journey via Paris (which has no through rail routes; only termini) do not register your bike through the capital as unaccompanied luggage because the delays at the far end can be substantial. Instead, register it to your terminal of arrival in Paris, reclaim it, cycle across the city to your terminal of departure and re-register the bike to your final destination. This will cost more than registering straight through but avoids the delays caused by the SNCF moving the bikes across the city by truck. (If you are going for the ride-and re-register option, leave plenty of time to cross Paris and deal with the registering bureaucracy.)

A final caution: before boarding the train remember to date-stamp your passenger ticket at one of the automatic machines (or ticket collector) found at the platform entrances – or you will subsequently be asked to pay a 20% surcharge.

By telephoning the SNCF London office you can find out in advance about any special fare concessions – some, like the *Carte Couple*, can be useful money-savers.

Local bus services are commonplace, and those buses equipped with roof luggage-racks may take bicycles; in the Alps a charge may be made.

Roads

With the densest road network in Europe and half the average traffic density of the UK it is easy to see why France is so well suited to cycle-touring. It has a maze of 'D' *(Départemental)* roads, a very broad classification which includes everything from long, straight, quite busy drags between towns and large villages to single-track byways which wriggle through undisturbed countryside linking the occasional hamlet or farm. In fact a D road is roughly equivalent to all the UK's 'unclassified' roads, its 'B' roads and the smaller of its 'A' roads. The best D roads conjure up images of narrow curls of tarmac between burgeoning banks of foliage and hedgerows thick with blackberries waiting to be picked by the dallying traveller, the quiet occasionally ruffled by one of those Citroëns which look like corrugated-iron chicken-coops, careering past on some urgent rustic mission.

It's these D roads which are of course the key to finding France by bike; all are tarmac surfaced though conditions can vary. In places (such as the lesser-populated parts of Brittany and Corsica) the road-edges get frayed and you have to expect the odd hole; bad patches are usually preceded by a *chaussée deformée* sign. Cobbles can still be found here and there, particularly in the north-east of the country.

Aside from *autoroutes* (motorways, on which cyclists are banned) France's busiest route-ways are the 'N' *(Route Nationale)* roads which are the major trunk routes between towns and cities and the equivalent to Britain's A roads. While some N roads are not actually that busy (and some even have hard shoulders which can be useful for biking) there is not much joy or point in using a noisier, smellier and more hazardous highway when the network of D roads is so ideal. At the time of writing about 5,000 kilometres of N roads are in the process of being re-designated as D roads, so for a while there may be irregularities on maps and signposts concerning road numbering; it also means that there will be some new D roads which carry substantial traffic. The *gendarmerie* may object to your riding two abreast on 'N' roads.

Smaller than D roads are the RF *(Route Forestière)* roads, found in national forests and initially built to provide forestry workers with access to otherwise remote woodlands; many are now surfaced with tarmac and provide excellent biking into fine scenery (in Corsica, some of the best cycling is on these roads). The unsurfaced RF routes can be atrociously muddy in wet weather.

French drivers are on the whole considerate and safe; traffic is worst during July and August, especially at weekends. The *Bison Futé* (Clever Buffalo) scheme is run by the Ministry of Transport to ease traffic congestion, and apart from manning the 80 information bureaux it annually publishes a map (available from FGTO or petrol stations in France) which marks the areas of major traffic jams and charts the days of the year which have the heaviest traffic; the map is quite useful for showing you where *not* to cycle. Signposting in France is good.

There are surprisingly few cycle paths in France and where they do occur you must use them if there is a sign *Piste Cycliste Obligatoire*. In popular tourist areas you can come across signposted cycle routes, chosen for their good scenery and peacefulness. Roads signed *Route Pittoresque* are often good for biking.

Bibulous bikers beware of exceeding a blood alcohol level of 80mg/100ml because if you haven't already fallen off your bike the police may take you off it and invite you to pay a fine or go to prison!

French Events

When it comes to turning bike touring into organised recreation, with certificates, cups and medallions to be claimed, the French are specialists. Each weekend, up and down the country, there are a myriad of organised rides ranging from short, easy family affairs to very long-distance hard-riding bashes against the clock. Foreign cyclists are made welcome to all these events.

Randonnées are organised by local cycling clubs (notably those affiliated to the FFCT), and attract anything from 50 to several hundred riders. Commonly the organisers have prepared a choice of different-length routes to suit riders of varying ability; typically there might be rides of 35, 60, 90 and 150 kilometres. Starts are usually early in the morning: you pay an entry fee and are issued with route instructions and a *brevet* card which has to be stamped at designated controls along the route. You ride with whom you like, so there's plenty of opportunity for making new friends, and you ride at your own speed – though normally there is a maximum time limit for completing the ride.

In the more serious *randonnées*, riders are given individual times for completing the route, and the distinction between racing and touring can become a little smudgy. The most famous of these is the Paris-Brest-Paris, held every fourth year over a 1,200 kilometre route. And at the other end of the country, and an equally big touring fixture, is the *Brevet du Randonneur des Alpes*, a spectacular bi-annual ride over some of the more dramatic passes that is held in July.

On the small, local *randonnées* you can join in by merely turning up on the day and signing on, but on the bigger events which draw cyclists from the whole country, and which are obliged to have limited fields, you have to submit an entry in advance.

Some *randonnées* exist as a permanently acknowledged route which can be ridden individually at any time of the year. The most famous are the FFCT's *'Diagonales de France'*, which are specified rides between the 'corners' of France, described as the 'pinnacle of *randonneur* achievement'; the 1,392-kilometre Brest to Menton has to be completed in 116 hours. And over a shorter but more severe route the infamous *Raid Pyrénéen*, in which you ride the entire length of the Pyrénées from Hendaye to Cerbère, involves 700 kilometres and 18 passes, to be cycled in under 100 hours. By contrast, the hybrid Flèche Velocio is a ride undertaken by teams who pedal a minimum of 350 kilometres to the location of the FFCT's Easter meets.

Audax events are rather different, and you ride in controlled bunches under the eye of a *Capitain de la Route*, and at a maximum speed of 22.5 kph.

In addition to all these one-day and hard-riding events there are the relaxed rallies of the FFCT such as the *Pâques-en-Provence* (Easter in Provence), staged on Easter Day and held in a different Provençal village each year, and the *Semaine Fédérale*, the FFCT's week-long gathering around late July/early August, which regularly draws 4,000 riders.

So as you can see, there is a rich assortment of organised 'touring' events to choose from. There are several ways of getting 'plugged in' to *randonnée* and *audax* news. Joining Audax UK (address on page 301) the British branch of a Paris club who paradoxically organise *randonnée* rather than *audax* events, will put you in touch with other cyclists who already ride French events, and the AUK newsletter carries advance notice of some *randonnées*. Membership of the FFCT brings you an annual calendar of the major French *randonnées* plus the magazine *Cyclotourisme*, which regularly lists coming events. If you are keen on mountain *randonnées*, then the newsletter of the UK section of the *Ordre des Cols Durs* will be helpful. The British magazines *Cycletouring* and *Cycling* sometimes carry news of forthcoming *randonnées*, and the French magazine *Le Cycle* has a regular calendar of the major events.

Maps

For General Planning

Michelin No. 989, France, scale 1:1,000,000. Shows the entire country (including Corsica) on one sheet. All major roads marked, with distances but no height shading.

Kümmerly + Frey, France, scale 1:1,000,000. Good height shading, with scenic roads, some tourist information, Corsica too.

For Cycling

Institut Géographique National (IGN) Red Series, scale 1:250,000. The best cycling maps of France, giving a clear picture of the terrain, this series (the country is covered in 16 sheets) is excellent for most types of touring except rough-stuff. Also some of the very smallest roads are omitted. Each sheet covers a large area, with excellent height-shading, viewpoints, tourist information, distances and scenic roads marked.

Recta Series, scale 1:250,000. Covers France in 15 sheets, with scenic roads, tourist information and distances, but no height shading. Some potential rough-stuff routes marked, but otherwise not as useful a series as the IGN.

Michelin 1:200,000 Series. Another old favourite for cyclists – low-cost and lightweight with detailed road information but nothing like the geographic picture the IGNs manage. Only those sheets (38 cover the country) marked *'Avec Relief'* have height shading; they all have gradient 'arrows', distances, some tracks, scenic roads, viewpoints and tourist features. Their long thin shape means you can cycle across a map a day so you can end up with a bag full of them at the end of the tour.

(Note however that Michelin have got round this problem partly by producing special 1:200,000 editions of certain regions (eg Brittany, Auvergne & Limousin, Nord and Ile de France) which cover much larger areas and work out cheaper and more convenient than the standard 1:200,000's).

Institut Géographique National (IGN) Green Series, scale 1:100,000. 74 maps in the series, covering the whole of France, with contour lines, height shading, and rough tracks and an overprint of long-distance walking routes. An ideal series for detailed local cycling, rough-stuff, and fixed-centre touring. In collaboration with the FFCT, IGN produce a special edition – *Circuits Cyclotouristiques dans la Région d'Ile de France* – with 51 recommended cycling circuits outlined in red on a 1:100,000 base map.

For Rough-stuff and Hiking

Institut Geographique National (IGN) Orange Series, scale 1:50,000. The French equivalent to the British Ordnance Survey 1:50,000 series, but covering much smaller areas per sheet and working out quite expensive. All footpaths and tracks shown, contours, height shading but no tourist features. Based on these maps the *Didier Richard* series (covering the French Alps south of Besançon) and the *Randonnées Pyrénées* (covering the French Pyrénées) are more economical with an overprint of long-distance footpaths and tourist information.

THE NETHERLANDS

The Netherlands is an obvious choice for an undemanding and rewarding introduction to continental biking: the country is quick and inexpensive to reach from the UK and its network of cycle-paths makes cycling safe and relaxed. To make the most of the Dutch landscape, you have to be sympathetic to vast skies, lots of water, insistent winds and flatness. The loveliness of the Netherlands is not grandly obvious in the manner of the Swiss Alps or Brittany coast, but is to be found in the subtle *mélange* of light, history and culture. Dutch art, architecture and civil engineering all beg appreciation.

Neat and tidy, this country is so compact that even pedalling gently, it can be crossed in three days. Perhaps it is the shortage of space that makes the Dutch so careful of their environment; if the entire population of Australia was crammed into an area the size of Scotland, that would give you an idea of the population density.

The west of the country is more urbanised than the east, and it is less flat in the south and south-east. Except for the industrial parts of

Limburg, it is fair to say that most of the Netherlands is good for cycling. A network of over 10,000 kilometres of cycle-paths cross the nation, though their meandering courses and varied surfaces make leisurely dawdling more appropriate than high-speed cycling. An added bonus is that the cities can be safely explored by bike – unlike many of Europe's big centres.

Like the English, the Dutch can be reserved, though once through with the hand-shaking they are extremely friendly, ready to help and advise. They are, after all, experts at the bike game; about two-thirds of the population own bicycles, and they are used for commuting, shopping, business and for getting to school. It's not unusual to see two on one bike. While one part of the nation has its senses tuned to the fortunes of its racing stars and to such burning issues as aerodynamic time-trial frames, the vast majority of Dutch people treat the bike as a humble vehicle to be bumped along cycle-paths on the way to town or country. Climbing onto the saddle is as natural for the Dutch as pulling on a pair of shoes is for the British; some 40 per cent ride a bike daily.

In common with the other Benelux countries, several Dutch towns appear under more than one name. 'The Hague' is really ''s-Gravenhage' or 'Den Haag', 'Flushing' is 'Vlissingen' and ''s-Hertogenbosch' is sometimes called 'Den Bosch' – useful to know when you try to find them on a map. And 'Holland' is actually the name given to just a couple of provinces, not to the whole country. Many Dutch people speak English, and French and German are widely understood. Thirty-seven per cent of the population are Roman Catholics, slightly more are Protestant; paradoxically Dutch society is both strictly religious and very permissive. It is a constitutional monarchy, with Queen Beatrix as nominal Head of State.

Dutch food is great cyclists' fuel! They are keen on carbohydrate and eat heartily: their cheese, milk, yoghurt and bread are delicious, and as fresh vegetables can be bought everywhere, picnics are a delight. Outdoor markets are cheaper than shops or supermarkets. If you need a quick snack, try a sandwich shop *(Broodjeswinkel)* where you can buy rolls with a tremendous variety of fillings, or try a street vendor selling chips *(Frites)* with mayonnaise. *Automaaten,* where you can buy hot food day and night, can be found in most towns and railway stations. Meals at a standardised price can be eaten at restaurants offering tourist menus – indicated by a sign bearing a fork wearing a hat and a camera. Quantities are normally generous, and quality excellent; Indonesian restaurants are good value. In Amsterdam there is a new breed of establishment, called an *Eetcafé;* a cross between a restaurant and a café, generally boisterous and good value. Bars stay open all day and half the night; the Dutch unit of currency is the *Guilder* (also known as the *Guilden* or *Florin),* divided into 100 *cents.*

Ride Guide

North and South Holland

For many visitors, these two provinces epitomise all that is expected of the Netherlands and so it is a good area if you are planning a short tour. It's also easy to travel to: by plane direct from the UK or by boat to Vlissingen or Ostend, then by bike via Zeeland. And it is the most densely populated part of the Netherlands, so biking here tends to be more oriented around cultural and historical centres than in undisturbed countryside. Here more than anywhere you will be confined to cycle-paths. It is absolutely flat, trim and neat, and is the largest area of polder (reclaimed land). Dykes, ditches, canals and windmills abound.

While Amsterdam is undeniably the star attraction, don't let it overshadow the many other places of interest. Haarlem (old town), Broek (lovely harbour), Monnikendam (boats), Volendam (painted houses), the island of Marken (local costume) and Edam (cheese) are all worth fitting into a tour of North Holland. In the north-east of the province, Hoorn and Enkhuizen (orchard country) have harbours and an old-world atmosphere. North-west of Amsterdam is windmill country around Zaandam, tulip fields around Limmen, the cheese market at Alkmaar and cattle market at Schagen. And when you are drunk with culture, turn your wheel towards the island of Texel (ferry from Den Helder).

The largest and most southern in the group of Wadden Islands, Texel has plenty of roads and many kilometres of scenic cycle-paths. There is a delightful ride, mostly on cycle-paths, which circles the entire island, sometimes by the sea, along dykes, through woods and by the dunes; Texel VVV can supply a useful cycling map. The same VVV have also devised for cyclists a 55-kilometre 'bird-route' (with an itinerary in English) which links the island's nature reserves. Texel is quite crowded during the summer.

The Netherlands' best sandy beaches are to be found along the coast of North Holland; Bergen, Egmond, Castricum and Wijk being popular centres. There is some pleasant riding in the dune reservation of Kennemerduinen, just west of Haarlem.

Amsterdam is *the* cycling city of Europe. Everywhere you turn there are bicycles. They clutter the canal railings, rattle along cobbled streets and surge in colourful gaggles from the special cyclists' traffic lights. Window-cleaners carry ladders on them, kids carry friends on them, dogs sit in handlebar baskets and vegetables protrude from panniers. It's a celebration of sanity; thousands of spoked wheels quietly revolving round the city with messages of fun, health and practicality. Two-thirds of the Amsterdam population own bicycles. You only have to imagine what would happen to Amsterdam if all those cyclists changed to cars, to realise what went wrong with Europe's other cities.

Six hundred bridges, 90 islands, canals whose still waters reflect trees and step-gabled houses break the city into so many intimate corners. Indoors there are galleries brimming with Rembrandts and Van Goghs, over fifty museums, 7,000 buildings under the care of the National Trust, a Royal Palace, concerts, churches ... the list is endless.

The province of South Holland is dominated by the *Randstad* ('ring city'), a kind of controlled megalopolis the Dutch have nurtured from the Hague, Leiden, Amsterdam, Utrecht, Dordrecht and Rotterdam to form an urban ring around preserved countryside. It's an area of some diversity: all the towns have different characteristics and there is still plenty of intact 'Dutch' landscape: low, canal-crossed pastures dotted with windmills and small lakes. Several broad, winding rivers with adjacent roads and cycle-paths complete the scene. If you are touring in the period mid-April to early May, try and take in the flower fields around Sassenheim, Lisse and Hillegom, south-west of Amsterdam, and also the flower auctions at Aalsmeer.

Rotterdam has been rebuilt since its devastation in the last war and is interesting for its broad avenues and purpose-built bike systems (though it has little else in its favour). By contrast, an hour's cycling away to the north-west is Delft, one of the best preserved Dutch towns with canals, courtyards and convents, old mansions and museums, and it is the origin of the famous blue Delft china.

The seat of the national government, The Hague, sits on the coast surrounded by gardens and parks, with many grand buildings. There is a lovely ride north-east through the woods and sand-dunes about Wassenaar, to Leiden, birthplace of Rembrandt, and home of one of the world's greatest universities. Southern Holland's main coastal resorts are Katwijk and Noordwijk. Inland, Gouda (cheese), Kinderdijk (reputed to have the greatest concentration of windmills in the world), Sliedrecht and Alblasserdam are all worth slotting into an itinerary.

Veluwe

Not a large area – about 40 kilometres north to south – but an attractive district to explore by bike when you have tired of the big open spaces. Woods, sand, heather, and even a few hills, congregate here to bring a touch of wildness to an otherwise thoroughly tamed country. Veluwe (in English: 'bad land') is sparsely populated and is criss-crossed by cycle-paths and walking trails; many of the roads are closed to motor traffic. There are some pleasant villages and the town of Apeldoorn (Het Loo Palace) is a big tourist centre. Between Apeldoorn and Arnhem to the south are the national parks of De Hoge Veluwe and of Veluwezoom, and the Kröller-Müller Museum containing 300 Van Gogh paintings.

On the southern edge of the Veluwe, Arnhem has memorials, and a museum (at Oosterbeek), to the airborne invasion of 1944. To the east of Zwolle, within easy cycling distance of the Veluwe, are the Lemmeler 'Mountains', some wooded hills. And on the opposite side of the Veluwe are East Flevoland and South Flevoland, the two most recent polders to be reclaimed from the IJsselmeer, and now rich farmland.

Zeeland, North Brabant and Limburg

Zeeland lies on the route if you are biking the North Sea coast to or from the Channel port of Ostend in Belgium; a province of estuaries and islands, with old churches and harbours, orchards and farms. Worth visiting are Veere (architecture) on Walcheren, Goes (old town) on South Beveland and Zierikzee (boats and 16th-century town hall) on Schouwen-Duiveland).

Zeeland's motto is 'I struggle and emerge', a maxim born of the tragedy and reward that the sea has brought this province. Now the Zeelanders have the Delta Plan; an ambitious scheme to close the mouths of some of the wide inlets and create broad freshwater lakes which will provide much-needed drinking water, act as a sea defence, help navigation and link the isolated islands by a road system.

The part of North Brabant which sits south of the River Maas has a distinct Belgian flavour, with woods and moor, reedy ponds and sandy rises, but little of the flat polder land found further north. The larger towns of the province are industrial – though inconspicuously so – but some, like 's-Hertogenbosch with its cathedral, have fine features. Traditionally hospitable, North Brabant has many cycle-paths running through its countryside.

Interesting localities include the area around Tilburg: to the north is a large tract of wind-blown sand-hills, the Loonse and Drunense Duinen, and also the medieval town of Heusden; to the east is Oisterwijk with fens, small streams and bird sanctuaries. Between the rivers Maas and Waal is the unusual Biesbos (boat trips up the creeks), and east of Eindhoven are some preserved marshlands (Groote Peel).

In the southern tip of the province of Limburg – that ungainly appendage which juts into Belgium – is the only genuinely hilly bit of the Netherlands. With valleys and trees, sloping meadows and rivers, it can add pleasant variety to a Dutch tour, though there are fewer cycle paths here. Central Limburg is heavily industrialised; the old and fortified city of Maastricht is the centre for the province.

Friesland, Groningen and Drenthe

These three provinces lie in the quietest corner of the Netherlands, tucked away up north and well-served by cycle-paths. Compared to the rest of the country there are few main roads, and Friesland in particular has an intricate network of twisty minor roads. For centuries these provinces have squatted like an impertinent fist thrust out into the North Sea, cut off from the through-traffic of northern Europe and relatively untouched compared to the more accessible parts of the Netherlands.

In the right weather, the most striking way of cycling into this area is by way of the cycle-path along the astonishing Afsluitdijk the thirty-kilometre dyke which separates the salt-water Waddenzee from the freshwater IJsselmeer, linking North Holland with Friesland. The dyke is completely exposed to the elements, and the direction of the wind will decide whether you fly euphorically over the waves with not a care in the world or suffer an interminable slog. If it's blowing true to form, it's best to ride the dyke from west to east.

Friesland has its own 'lake district' of *meers*, canals and waterways, with woods and moors, old towns and pretty villages set on man-made mounts *(terpen)* to protect them from flooding. There is a strong independent spirit here, and the locals have their own language *(Friese)* and signposts are bi-lingual. It was here that the man who founded New York, Pieter Stuyvesant, was born. Hindeloopen, Sloten and Leeuwarden are all pleasant towns.

From Harlingen, Holwerd, and Achutsluis (on the Dutch/German border) ferries (which take bicycles) run out to the Wadden – or Friesland – Islands. These long, low pieces of land rose in the 14th century from the North Sea, as mere sandbars, and have been growing ever since. They all have enough roads and cycle-paths to make them feasible for bike exploration, have important nature reserves and fine sandy beaches. (The biggest of the islands, Texel, is approached from North Holland, and is described earlier).

To the north of Friesland is the historic province of Groningen: countryside dotted with villages perched on small hills, surrounded by flat meadowlands crossed by dykes. The barns here are some of the largest in Europe. Eastern Groningen introduces some hill and heath to the landscape; for cycling, the south-east of the province is probably the most attractive. The town of Groningen boasts a university, Gothic, baroque and Renaissance architecture, and has museums and castles on its outskirts. To the north, Uithuizen has a notable castle.

For the Dutch, Drenthe is *the* cycling province. It has over 350 kilometres of cycle-paths, is quiet, largely unspoilt and has plenty to interest. Peaceful rivers, meadows and woods mix with marsh and moor speckled with hundreds of tiny lakes. Many of the farms are ancient, and the province is known for its prehistoric *hunebeds*, assorted megalithic heaps which can be found concentrated between Emmen and Groningen.

Worth tacking onto a tour of Drenthe is a small area just to the south-west, bordering IJsselmeer. Giethoorn is a small village of bridges and water, and Urk, on the waterfront, was once an island out in the old Zuiderzee and is now on the newly-arrived mainland of the North-East Polder. Urk has narrow streets, fishermen's cottages and colourful traditional costumes. There is a pleasant ride northwards from here towards Lemmer, along cycle-paths beside reed-fringed dykes.

The Netherlands' Highest Road

In the far south-eastern tip of Limburg sits Vaals, and from the southern edge of this small town a minor road leads up the slopes of the Netherlands' highest peak: Drielandenpunt is all of 321 metres high and rests on the meeting point of the Dutch, German and French borders, offering wide views of all three countries.

Local Cycling Routes

Various Dutch organisations have compiled cycling routes based on their local knowledge. Most of them are circular and can be very helpful in planning fixed-centre tours and for taking day trips out of particular towns. The itineraries are usually in Dutch, but very often the route can be adequately followed using the sketch maps supplied with the package.

ANWB: has two types of scenic cycling routes – those which have been described in special leaflets and which are also sign-posted (in blue, with a hexagonal motif) on the ground, and those which are only described in a booklet. Of the former type there are 9 leaflets describing a total of 44 routes, Of the 'described only' routes (which are rather harder to follow unless you read Dutch) there are 6 booklets covering 89 routes. Distances for these routes range from 20 to 50 kilometres. The booklets and leaflets c·n be bought from the ANWB local offices (and head office) and from VVVs.

Stichting Fiets!: has researched over 200 routes in the Netherlands and these are described in a series of folders called *Ontdek Nederland op de Fiets* (Discovering the Netherlands by Bike). A total of 19 folders cover different areas, each containing 11 or so routes. A large scale map such as the ANWB 1:100,000 would have to be used with these routes unless you can read the Dutch directions. These folders can be bought from local ANWB offices and VVVs or direct from *Stichting Fiets!* (mention area of interest).

VVVs: many local VVVs have devised their own scenic cycling routes which can be used for exploring the neighbourhood. Set tours can often be supplied, which include a map and detailed description of the ride. Text is usually in Dutch but those available at VVV offices along the North Sea coast, at Amsterdam and Rotterdam, are also printed in English, French and German. Amsterdam for example has a recommended bike route for exploring the city itself plus two others for taking day rides out of the city; Rotterdam VVV offers five routes in and around that city, of between 20 and 45 kilometres, while up at Texel the VVV can supply a map and information for following the 'bird route'.

Nederlandse Spoorwegen: as already mentioned, the Dutch railways can supply about 60 different local routes of between 20 and 50 kilometres, radiating out from certain stations. These are described in the *NS Dagtoerisme* brochures.

A final route worth considering is the *Sentier de Grande Randonnée 5* (GRS) a long-distance path which starts at Bergen op Zoom youth hostel and follows a mixture of way-marked rough tracks, cycle paths and small roads to the Belgian hostels of Zoersel, Nijlen, Diest and Bokrijk/Genk.

A Tour of Historic Holland

A classic bike tour of the Netherlands, encircling the expansive IJsselmeer, whose waters are gradually being pushed back by ambitious projects to turn them into polders and rich farmland. This most unusual inland lake is fringed by many old towns dating from the days of the Hanseatic trading league, pretty fishing villages and many serene corners where your only company will be whispering reeds and wheeling birds. Nearly all of the route can be ridden on cycle-paths, away from the traffic, and there are plenty of off-bike diversions: the dunes and beaches of the North Sea coast, bulb district, bouncing Amsterdam, the great 'Encircling Dam', the canals, castles and cathedrals of old Holland, forests of Het Loo and De Hoge Veluwe national park and the windmills of Kinderdijk. To take advantage of prevailing winds, the route is best cycled clockwise. Although we start below at the Hook of Holland, Amsterdam is an equally good start/finish point.

HISTORIC HOLLAND TOUR

Terrain: flat
Distance: 700 km
Start/Finish: Hook of Holland/Hook of Holland
Scenery: *
Interest: **
Maps: ANWB Toeristenkaart Nos 1,2,5,6,7

Km HOOK OF HOLLAND
21 The Hague

(detour to Delft)

20	Katwijk
12	Leiden
10	Sassenheim
5	Lisse
18	Haarlem
23	Amsterdam
20	Marken
8	Monnikendam
7	Volendam
5	Edam
20	Hoorn
24	Enkhuizen

(optional ferries across IJsselmeer to Staveren and Urk, thus cutting out northern section of tour)

23	Medemblik
27	Den Oever

(detour west to Den Helder and island of Texel)

	Afsluitdijk
5	Makkum
10	Workum
17	Stavoren
31	Lemmer
14	Kuinre
11	Blokzijl
10	Giethoorn
12	Zwartsluis
16	Kampen
16	Elburg
15	Nunspeet
13	Elspeet
4	Uddel
20	Hoenderloo
15	Otterlo (via Kompagnieberg)
20	Barneveld
19	Nijkerk
8	Bunschoten
16	Naarden

12	Muiden	10	Schoonhoven
4	Weesp	1	Nieuwpoort
12	Vreeland	22	Kinderdijk
10	Breukelen	2	Krimpen a/d Lek
20	Utrecht	15	Rotterdam
5	De Haar	5	Schiedam
10	Woerden	6	Vlaardingen
10	Oudewater	6	Maasluis
7	Haastrecht	19	HOOK OF HOLLAND

Basic Information

Getting there

Air: Rotterdam and Amsterdam's Schiphol airport have regular services to and from the UK, flying time from London to Schiphol being one hour.

Rail/Ferry: the shortest ferry route from the UK to the Netherlands is from Harwich to the Hook of Holland (about 8 hours). Services also run from Hull to Rotterdam, Great Yarmouth to Scheveningen, and from Sheerness to Vlissingen (Flushing). Ferries also link Amsterdam with Gothenburg and Kristiansand. There are scheduled services up and down the Rhine linking Rotterdam and Amsterdam with Basle and Strasbourg. By train, Amsterdam is 11 hours from London, Rotterdam is 10 hours (both via Harwich and the Hook of Holland). The Netherlands has excellent rail links with other European cities.

Information Sources

Netherlands National Tourist Office ((NNTO), Savory and Moore House, 2nd Floor, 143 New Bond Street, London W1Y 0QS (tel: 01-9367/8/9/0). A calendar of principal events (including the big bike gatherings), thorough information booklets including 'Holidays on two Wheels' and 'General Information' which has the vital list of provincial VVV addresses

Local tourist bureaux: marked by blue triangular 'VVV' signs and providing anything from accommodation addresses to suggested cycle routes. The Dutch tourist authorities are more tuned in to the needs and interests of cycle-tourists than any other country; many of the local offices sell special cycling maps, can hire cycles and arrange complete bike holidays. Some have calendars of cycling events. VVVs are often found near railway stations and are open from at least 9 am to 5 pm Monday to Friday, and 10 am to 12 noon on Saturdays. Those offices that display the 'i' (Information) sign in addition to the VVV symbol can supply information on the whole country. You can write to local VVV offices by addressing the envelope to 'VVV' followed by the name of the town and province. VVV is pronounced 'Fay-Fay-Fay' and is seldom referred to by its full title; which for the inquisitive is *Vereniging Voor Vreemdelingsverkeer.*

Koninklijke Nederlandse Toeristenbond (ANWB), Wassenaarseweg 220, PO Box 93200, 2509 BA The Hague (tel: 070-264426). The ANWB is a general touring organisation (catering mainly for motorists) similar to the British Automobile Association. Literature is in Dutch, but their maps and cycle routes (see page 195) are invaluable aids to a bike holiday. They have about 50 local offices (their addresses can be obtained from ANWB head office). Affiliated to AIT.

Koninklijke Nederlandse Wielren Unie, Polanerbaan 15, 3447 Woerden. (tel: 03480-11544) The national cycle-racing body.

Nederlandse Rijwiel Toer Unie (NRTU), Postbus 326, 3900 AH Veenendaal (tel: 08385-21421). NRTU is the Dutch equivalent of the CTC; a national union of cycle-touring clubs. Its annual calendar, *Fietsevenementenprogramma* (printed in Dutch) costs about F15 and lists dates and organisers' addresses of nearly 5,000 club events (to which foreigners are invited). It also lists the addresses of its 230 clubs and lists the 350 recommended cycling routes in Netherlands and across Europe which have been researched by NRTU and are sold for a nominal price. NRTU's regular periodical *De Rijwieltoerist* carries news and information of cycle-touring in the Netherlands. NRTU cannot send itineraries to foreigners. Affiliated to the AIT.

Stichting Fiets! Europaplein 2, 1078 GZ Amsterdam (tel: 020-440944). Represents the Dutch cycle industry and provides maps, routes (in Dutch), a list of cycle hire firms and a helpful information sheet called *Cycling in the Netherlands* which among other things lists the national, provincial and regional addresses of the VVV offices.

Fiets magazine, Lijnbaansgracht 309, 1017 WZ Amsterdam. Glossy Dutch journal covering all aspects of cycling

Accommodation

Camping: There are plenty of camp-sites throughout the country; some 2,000 in all. Standards are good: most have showers, shops (which tend to be expensive) and launderettes. You are expected to provide proof of identity (a Camping Carnet will do). The NNTO can supply a free list of about 350 sites, and the ANWB publish their detailed *Kampeerplaatsen in Nederland.* VVVs can provide helpful information on local sites, and many of their offices publish their own thorough local lists. About 70 camp sites spread across the Netherlands have grouped themselves together under the banner of the *Sticting Gastvrije Fietscampings* (GFC). Distances between these sites are 15 to 50 kilometres and each is intended to offer the cycle-camper an 'optimum in service'. Information and booking forms from: *Stichting Gastvrije Fietscampings*, Rijksstraatweg 117, 7231 AD Warnsveld (tel: 05750-22483), or from local VVV and ANWB offices. Wild camping is not the simplest way of spending the night in the Netherlands, because every square metre of land seems spoken for — though in the west it's slightly more hilly and wooded. It's therefore necessary to ask the landowner's permission in all cases.

Youth Hostels: The distances between the Netherlands' 56 IYHF hostels are small enough to be easily cycled in a day, with a strong concentration along the North Sea coast and islands; here they are no more than 20 kilometres from each other. They tend to be large (there are only 10 'simple' hostels), and are rather spoilt by big groups of visitors. Anyone who has tried to sleep through a raucous school disco after a day pedalling into horizontal rain will know what I mean! Only 9 hostels have members' kitchens, and all 56 provide meals. A minimum age of 6 is stipulated.

Kamphuizen/Kampeerboerderijen: these 'camping houses' and 'camping farms' have more in common with long-stay youth hostels than with tents and 'roughing it', and are mostly used by youth groups. They might be worth considering for a fixed-base holiday with family or friends. The camping house is a permanent recreation centre while the camping farm is normally part of a working farm and is only open for a part of the year. Accommodation in both is a mixture of dormitories and smaller rooms (separate for women and men). The NNTO can supply a list of 200 *kamphuizen* and *kampeerboerderijen*, though there are several hundred more throughout the country.

Hotels: The Netherlands has large numbers of small guest houses and private rooms for passing travellers; the best way of finding these is to ask at local VVV offices. Hotels are clean and efficiently run, often by staff who speak English. The old grading system of five categories, with '1' being the most luxurious, is being replaced by the Benelux hotel classification with rates establishments on a scale from 1 star (the most modest) to 4 star (the most expensive). Prices have to be displayed at the reception desk and in the rooms; unlike in France, you pay per person, not per room. NNTO and ANWB can supply hotel lists.

Weather

Rainfall is spread fairly evenly through the year, with June through to September being the warmest months, and the south of the country being a couple of degrees warmer than the north and coast. Overall, the weather is similar to that of northern England; fairly changeable and inclined to be damp. Summers can be bright and sunny, winters gloomy and wet. Winds can blow strong and constantly, for there is no high ground to check their progress. They come mainly from the south-west, west and north-west, occasionally from the north or north-east.

Other Considerations: the bulb season, when you can catch the crocuses, daffodils, tulips and hyacinths in bloom, usually lasts from the end of March to mid-May. The main tourist season stretches from early May until the end of September, with a peak between about 3 July and 29 August.

Average Daily Maximum Temperatures (Centigrade)

	alt. in metres	J	F	M	A	M	J	J	A	S	O	N	D
Urk	2	3	3	7	12	16	19	21	20	18	13	8	5

Cycling Information

Cycle Shops

There is a bicycle shop is virtually every town and large village – more than 5,000 in all. Most carry out repairs and many hire out machines too. Spare parts are metric sizes. Shops specialising in lightweight racing and touring equipment are fairly common.

Cycle hire

This is the cycle-hire country of Europe: single-speeds, tandems, cycle-bags and childrens' seats can be rented just about anywhere. Like the Belgians and French, the Dutch operate a train-and-bike hire scheme. Some 80 stations hire out machines; during the holiday season it is advisable to phone the station in advance, and at some stations, prior reservation is mandatory. Reductions are offered for holders of valid rail tickets (buy at your station of arrival a reduced *fietskaartje);* a hefty returnable deposit may be requested. More than half the 'train-and-bike' stations also provide free cycle-touring maps of the vicinity, marked with suggested routes ranging from 18 to 50+ kilometres and 8 of the stations have tandems for handicapped people. The booklet *Fiets en Spoor* gives details (in Dutch) about the entire scheme.

There is also a multitude of private hire firms and many bicycle shops have machines for rent, including tandems. Specialist firms are often found close to the railway stations. *Stichting Fiets!* sell a list of 750 hire addresses, and local VVVs have their own detailed lists. The Dutch for 'bicycle hire' is *Fietsverhuur.* In the western provinces of Gelderland and Overijssel there is a handy scheme called 'Rent a Bike' involving some 3,000 hire machines: provided you hire the bike for at least three days, it can be returned to any of 50 firms in the scheme (details in 'Rent a Bike' brochure from VVVs).

Transporting Your Bicycle

Nederlandse Spoorwegen (NS) run a quick and clean rail system, reaching all corners of the country. The booklet *Fiets en Spoor* (available from railway stations, VVVs and from the NS at Moreelsepark 1, Utrecht) details all you need to know about taking bikes on Dutch railways – though it's written in Dutch. Nearly all Dutch rail routes (except a few in the province of South Holland) are open to bike transport, though various conditions apply according to the time of day bikes can be carried (not during rush hours: 7 - 9am, 4.30 - 6pm Monday to Friday) and which types of train they can be carried on. Some stations only handle bikes between July and September. Certain local stopping trains have no capacity and some Intercity trains have space for only 4 or 5 bikes; these can get full during peak season, and it may be quicker to travel by a slower local train than wait for the next Intercity which has space for your bike. *Fiets en Spoor* has a useful map marking the lines and stations which cater for bikes, whether accompanied or unaccompanied.

Charges for the bicycle are high, and are scaled according to the length of journey; insurance can be bought for a surcharge. Bicycle tickets are bought at the same time as the passenger ticket; some ticket offices close before 6pm. You travel on the same train as your bike, loading it and unloading it yourself; you are expected to advise the conductor that you are putting a bike in his luggage compartment. If you cannot spot the conductor go ahead anyway (push the button to open automatic doors) and tell him or her once you are aboard. If the luggage compartment is full, you have to wait for the next train.

During the Dutch summer holiday season (28 June – 30 August), unaccompanied bikes can be sent on special bicycle freight wagons which operate between certain stations (see *Fiets en Spoor*). This service runs only on Mondays, Wednesdays and Fridays and it takes two days for the bike to reach its destination – three days if a weekend intervenes. When you buy the bike ticket, station officials should be able to tell you when your machine will arrive. Fares are about £1 less than if the bike is accompanied. Insurance cover for the bike can be bought for an extra charge. It is not possible to take bikes on buses, but Dutch ferries do provide a service, sometimes free.

The Cycle-path Society

The Dutch have done for the bike what the Venetians did for the boat; they have given a simple, low-cost, ecological method of transport a number one slot in their life-style. To get from one place to another the Venetians use canals, the Dutch use their cycle-paths. And, just as you can gondola uninterrupted from one side of that Italian city to the other, so you can pedal the length and breadth of the Netherlands free of the hateful motor-car; Dutch cycle-paths form an intricate spider's web of routes, delicately laid over one of the busiest landscapes in the world. Some are former tramways.

They come in various shapes and sizes; at the start of a section of cycle-path should be a sign telling you whether the path's use is compulsory or optional. A compulsory cycle-path is marked by a sign with a white bicycle on a blue background. You have to use such a path and are prohibited from riding on the road which runs alongside. These paths sometimes follow the 'wrong' side of the road; where there is not enough space for a cycle-path on each side of the road, you have a two-way path on just one of the sides. A sign *Fietsers Oversteken* warns of the point where a cycle-path crosses from one side of the road to the other. A hedge or embankment normally separates the path from the road. Compulsory paths are shared by mopeds.

Also in this 'compulsory' category, and most often found in towns, is the cycle-lane: part of the road identified by a solid or broken white line painted onto the surface to separate bikes and mopeds from other traffic, and marked with white painted bicycles at regular intervals. It's a sin of the highest order to stray across the white demarcating line of your lane. At really busy intersections it can be difficult to spot the entrance to the cycle-lane or path you next want to use; many such junctions are made safer and easier to cope with by special cyclists' traffic lights which indicate when you should move forward. Where a cycle-lane or path crosses a road in a built-up area, in theory the cyclist has the right to cross the road while other vehicles give way (unless the junction is controlled by traffic lights). In places, special tunnels and bridges carry the cycle-path under or over a highway.

An optional cycle path is marked by a small rectangular black sign bearing in white letters the word *Rijwielpad* or *Fietspad*. These are generally the most enjoyable types of path as they often strike out across country, well away from roads. Sometimes they are constructed purely for recreational use, and tend to congregate in tourist areas. Thankfully mopeds are only allowed to use optional paths if they have their motors switched off.

Until you ride on a Dutch cycle-path you may wonder why one of the world's foremost cycle-racing nations pedals around on fat-tyred leviathans made of drain-pipes and panelled with a few square metres of chain-guard, rather than flyweight thoroughbreds. But the Dutch know their cycle-paths, and their heavy black roadster bicycles soak up the bumps that years of winter frosts and soggy soils have left behind. The most common surfaces are bricks laid end-to-end, or concrete slabs, which can get dislodged over the years. Some resemble minor earthquake zones. Elsewhere, cycle-path surfaces range from compacted gravel or earth on some of the scenic optional paths, to smooth tarmac on the well-used compulsory paths. Cycle-lanes normally have good surfaces, sometimes of small bricks laid in a herring-bone fashion and called *klinkers*. Bumpy cycle-paths are not something normally worth thinking about, but I mention them here because, for once, the proud owners of heavy-duty shopping bikes will find their machines better suited to the terrain than the riders of sensitive lightweight touring-bikes.

There are a couple of cycle-path hazards to be aware of: bicycles and mopeds. If knees were noisy there would be no problem – but (for most of us) they work quietly and it's therefore not possible to hear an approaching cyclist. So the Dutch use the cycle-bell with alacrity; it's especially useful on the narrow cycle-paths where you may approach another cyclist (or a pedestrian) from behind and need to warn them that you're about to overtake. Pedalling solitarily along in cloud cuckoo land talking to the butterflies and dreaming of cream cakes, there's nothing more startling than to suddenly become aware of another person who's crept up unnoticed behind your left shoulder.

Far more appalling are the mopeds – the dreaded *bromfiets*. They can brush past your elbow from behind, or scream out of the sun straight at you. Listen for the approaching engine drone; if it's low-pitched it will take half-an-hour to arrive and probably pass safely; a high-pitched note heralds a local in a hurry and it's best to be prepared for evasive action; a shindig of shrieking discordant drones marks the imminent arrival of a posse of teenagers travelling at Mach 2 and it's best to shelter behind the nearest hedge!

Note that pedestrians are permitted to walk on cycle-paths where there is no footpath, though cyclists are meant to have priority. Mopeds are the only type of motor-vehicle which do not have priority over bicycles.

Route-finding along cycle-paths is made simpler by the Dutch penchant for thorough sign-posting. At junctions look for a white sign with the town or village, and distance, in red lettering with a little red bicycle; these point out the route of the cycle-path. Sometimes paths are indicated by stumpy, knee-high concrete 'toadstools'. As a general rule, the sign-post should be used as an accessory to a good map (see page 195) rather than as an alternative.

Roads

After France, the Netherlands has the second-most dense road network in Europe – though fortunately cyclists have to make little use of it. But sometimes there is no cycle-path; traffic can be very heavy on main roads during morning and evening rush hours, and on Sundays. Out in the country there are very many minor roads which can be fun for cycling; most are well-surfaced but be prepared for occasional stretches of fierce cobbles in some villages – a sign *Slecht Wegdek* warns of uneven paving.

The Dutch drive their cars quickly, and per kilometre of roads, there are more cars in the Netherlands than in Britain – generally Dutch motorists are adept at overtaking cyclists safely. Cyclists are usually treated with respect by other road users.

Cycle Parking

If you are worried about leaving your bike unattended in large towns, or want to park it somewhere safe for a few days, ask at a VVV office for the nearest cycle-storage depot *(Rijwielstallingen)*. These are privately owned, and for a small charge your machine will be garaged and looked after by an attendant. Alternatively, try the town's main railway station; over 100 Dutch stations have bicycle storage sheds under or adjoining the main building.

In towns, cycles are not meant to be left unattended at the kerb; the practice is to push them into a rack or lean them on a wall.

Bicycle Museums

Batavus Museum, Heerenveen, Friesland. A unique collection of machines depicting the history of the bicycle.

De Waag Museum, Deventer, Overijssel. Includes displays from H. Burger's first bicycle factory.

National Automobile Museum, Raamsdonksveer, North Brabant. Old velocipedes among the history of transport displays.

Organised Tours

Numerous companies lay on organised cycling tours: some merely provide a map describing the route, and a hotel list, while the others supply a bicycle complete with all accessories, full-board accommodation, a van to carry your luggage and even a money-back guarantee if it rains too much!

Several provincial VVV offices organise cycling holdiays, among them Friesland, Overijssel, Texel and Gelderland (who have several holiday packages printed in English). A bicycle, maps, panniers, and full or half-board accommodation are usually supplied.

The Dutch railways (NS) arrange week-long trips which include bike hire, hotels and train travel to and from the touring area, and the Dutch youth hostel organisation (NJHC: *Nederlandse Jeugdherberg Centrale,* Prof Tulpplein 4, 1018 GX Amsterdam) arrange a hostelling/biking package which includes a bike you're allowed to keep.

If it is the company of group touring you are after, consult the NRTU annual calendar *(Fietsevenementenprogramma)* or ask at VVVs for details of club cycle-touring events to which foreigners are invited. Very popular are the four-day cycle-tours *(Vierdaagsen)* from fixed bases in attractive parts of the country, for example the Veluwe (from Ede), in North Brabant (from Hoeven), and in Drenthe (from Assen and Hoogeveen). Each year around July, the LAURA (Leiden, Amsterdam, Utrecht, Rotterdam, Alphen) rides attract UK riders; this 4 day cycle-touring event has been running for nearly 40 years, taking the form of two rides each day (of 100 kilometres or 150), with controls set up to stamp cards, medals awarded on completion and social events in the evenings. Advance warning is usually given in the UK magazine *Cycling,* and of course it is listed in NRTU's calendar. The Dutch 'National Cycling Day' takes place in May, with rides staged from many towns. Some local newspapers, for example *Utrechts Nieuwsblad, Het Parool, Nieuwe Utrechts Dagblad* and *Amersfoort Courant,* have regular cycling columns which can be used for gleaning information on local cycle-touring events and races.

Maps

For General Planning

ANWB, Fietsroutekaart Nederland, scale: 1:500,000. An invaluable map for general planning, showing the national grid of major 'through' cycle-paths, with intermediate distances and as a bonus the full address list of all local ANWB offices, from where their maps can be bought (at a lower price than the bookshops). Can be bought by mail from ANWB head office.

Michelin, No. 408 Netherlands, scale 1:400,000. Lightweight and modestly priced, with limited tourist information, including some scenic roads. Town maps of Rotterdam and Amsterdam at 1:100,000 plus an index of towns and villages.

Kümmerly + Frey, The Netherlands, scale: 1:300,000. A clear map which includes tourist features like windmills, bulb fields and recommended beaches, scenic roads and campsites. Railways clearly marked.

For Cycling

Michelin Nos 5, 6, 1, scale 1:200,000. Do not mark cycle-paths so adequate only for road-riding, giving a very limited idea of the cycling possibilities. They do however give an overview of the country at an affordable price and compact size. Information on the cycle/pedestrian ferries (marked as *bac*) may be out of date.

ANWB, Toeristenkaart Series, scale 1:100,000. The only map worth considering for serious exploration of the Netherlands by bike, drawn largely with cyclists in mind. It marks all types of cycle-path (*fietspad* on the key) outlines in green those that are specially scenic and even shows the locations of cycle-path signposts! Other detail is very thorough, they are accurate and pleasing to the eye. 13 sheets cover the country. Available from ANWB head office by mail, or from their local offices, VVVs and bookshops.

VVV Maps: Very often the local VVV offices publish their own large-scale maps covering their immediate neighbourhood. These are often very clear, showing the local cycle-paths in even greater detail than the ANWB maps, pointing out the scenic ones and highlighting local points of interest.

BELGIUM

Belgium is perhaps too often overlooked as a good area for an easy, low-cost tour; its image of wind-swept, grey, steppe-like plains regularly interrupted by neat little villages belies a certain charm and depth of interest which reveals itself especially to the slow traveller. It's a small country, and it's possible to cycle from border to border in just a couple of days. It is also convenient to the UK.

One of Belgium's quainter characteristics is the 'national' boundary which splits the country into two, along the industrial belt between Liège and Tournai. To the north of this belt live the Flemish people, and to the south, the Walloons. And they speak different languages. The same divide separates the flat lands and cultural riches of the north from the hills and scenic merits of the Ardennes, to the south, so that a bike tour which takes in parts of the north and south is sure to be varied. It's a good country for a beginner's tour, providing the winds are kind.

Much of Flanders is barely higher than the choppy surface of the North Sea it rests against, and the winds can sweep across this plain either blowing you along with all the carefree abandon in the world or pushing against you making pedalling a misery. Nothing's more dispiriting than riding against the wind; it's worse than rain, heat, or the steepest of hills; even the cold is preferable to a headwind. Maybe its the apprenticeship spent pushing gales which helped produce great racing cyclists like Schotte, Steenbergen, Ockers, Van Looy, Maertens and the greatest of them all, Eddy Merckx. Belgium has had more world champions over the last 50 years than any other country and exciting round-the-houses races *(critériums)* crop up in town-centres throughout the season; watch the wall posters.

This is also the second most densely populated country in Europe, with 9.8 million people jammed into an area only 1½ times the size of Wales. In the north there seems to be a village or hamlet every kilometre. The people of Flanders – the Flemings – speak Dutch while the Walloons of southern Belgium (Wallonia) speak French. German is spoken in the Eupen and Malmédy area in the east of the country. English is fairly widely understood in Flanders, and Brussels especially. Most Belgians are Catholics and, like Britain, the country is a constitutional monarchy.

Like France, this is good picnic country, with plenty of the necessary raw materials such as fruit and vegetables, easy to find. Cheap snacks to fill the energy-gap in the middle of the morning or afternoon, can be bought at *Fritures* and *Snackbars,* while *Pâtisseries* sell cakes, pastries and coffee. Bars are open all day; beer-drinking is something of a national hobby. The Belgians are big eaters, and restaurant fare is generous, rich and expensive. The main meal of the day is usually eaten at midday; steak and chips is popular and there are several specialities for the more adventurous palate, such as rabbit and prunes. In the towns there is normally a good selection of Italian, Greek, Yugoslav, Chinese and Indian restaurants. Belgian breakfasts are meagre and don't stretch much beyond coffee, roll, butter and jam; some hotels offer an 'English' more-miles-per-mouthful breakfast. The currency is the Belgian *Franc* (BF), divided into 100 *centimes;* prices are much higher in the cities (notably Brussels) than in the Ardennes.

Ride Guide

Flanders

This isn't somewhere that would normally deserve a place in the 'Ride Guide' but I'm including it because, despite its ordinary scenery, Flanders' closeness to the UK has made it a popular area for short bike tours, and a common pushing-off point for longer European rides. Zeebrugge and Ostend are obvious ports to start from, while Dunkerque, just across the French border, and Vlissingen (Flushing), a couple of hours biking into the Netherlands are also convenient.

Flanders is flat; very flat. Excepting those unfortunate days when the North Sea winds are sweeping unchecked over the dykes, cycling is easy and a single-speed or three-speed shopping bike is perfectly adequate; in fact a lumbering roadster with pudgy tyres is far more suited to Flanders' cobbles than a tight ten-speed. The 65 kilometres of coast has long sandy beaches and a string of resorts, backed by sand dunes then a strip of polder land reclaimed from the sea and laced with canals and drainage ditches. Most of inland Flanders is intensively farmed, with endless market gardens, and oceans of cabbages split by long straight roads and unsurprising villages.

There's more for the intellect than the eye in Flanders. Bruges is one of Europe's classic attractions; a kind of land-bound Venice with a network of canals criss-crossing the town, whose medieval atmosphere is mercifully little changed. There are step-gabled houses, palaces, a 13th-century belfry, museums and a cathedral. Seven kilometres north-west along the Canal de Bruges à L'Ecluse (bike along the tow-path) is Damme, with a preserved medieval quarter. Ghent, the capital of East Flanders, has many antiquarian attractions including a 13th-century cathedral, belfry, Cloth Hall, a fine castle and museums. Further west, Ypres is a sombre focus of the First World War battlefields.

Between the plains of Flanders and the Ardennes are a couple of varied areas. The Campine consists of the provinces of Limburg and Antwerp, and like Flanders it is flat though the landscape is broken up by heathery moors, small lakes and ponds, patches of pine and wandering streams. Plenty of small, quiet roads cross the area, and on its western edge is the huge port of Antwerp, home of Rubens and Van Dyck, with museums and a world-famous zoo.

Just south-east of Brussels is a triangle of gently hilly terrain, the Forêt de Soignes, its beeches lovely in autumn. West of Brussels is a low range of hills imaginatively called the 'Flemish Ardennes', though they are only about 150 metres high! Some of their slopes are climbed by notorious (among racing cyclists) cobbled lanes of lung-bursting steepness. Fierce climbs like the Mur de Grammont, Volkegemberg, Koppenberg, Taaienberg, Kwaremont and Kemmelberg are known all too well by the professional riders who struggle up them in the classic races of Het Volk, Tour of Flanders and Ghent-Wevelgem.

Ardennes

It's odd to find a country split into two such contrasting regions; you really know that you've left Flanders and entered the Ardennes when your obsession with wind direction is replaced by an earnest interest in the length of hills. Never having cycled over anything higher than an East Anglian railway bridge, the Ardennes, my first taste of continental

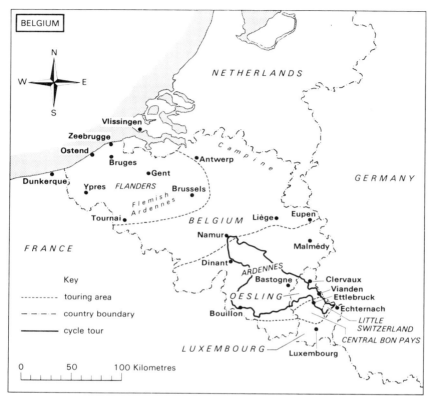

slopes, had a profound impact: I discovered the unrestrained joy, the pure delight, of freewheeling down long hills. I also made some discoveries about cycling *up* those hills-that-last-forever – but, like any emotional trauma, the details have faded with time!

As the bike goes, it's about 200 kilometres from the coast to the Ardennes (that's about the same distance as Birmingham to London), so these hills are convenient to the UK and make a good alternative to, say, Normandy or Brittany. Whereas the Flemish in the north like their roads straight and level, the Walloons in the south opt for corners and gradients. The result is a more interesting cycling terrain. Roads are well-surfaced, and there are plenty of small winding lanes to take you away from it all. Gradients can sometimes be steep and some of the climbs, where the roads rise to the top of the plateau, are fairly prolonged. The Ardennes is a popular holiday region, and it looks its best out of the tourist season, when the foliage is fresh and green in spring or golden brown in autumn.

Touring the Ardennes can take you through three different countries, Belgium, France and Luxembourg, and with the delightful Eifel region being a natural extension, Germany makes a fourth. The hills begin south of the Sambre and Meuse rivers, at first gentle and rolling with farmland and woods, but growing in stature until they rise to the main Ardennes plateau at around 400 metres. To the north-east, by the German border, they reach 670 metres at the Hautes Fagnes. It's a worn landscape, with bare, rounded hilltops, smooth ridges and steep valley-sides clothed in thick forests of pine, spruce, birch and larch. Half the Ardennes plateau is covered by trees, much of it plantation. Winding streams fill the valley bottoms and occasional outcrops of rock add variety.

Three of the 'gateway' towns to the Ardennes all merit a pause: Liège is known for its old alleys and citadel, churches, mansions and squares, Huy, too, has fine churches and Namur to the west has 18th-century houses and a citadel. In the Ardennes themselves, several towns have developed as resorts. Dinant and Anseremme sit attractively on the Meuse (lovely riding by the river provided the road is quiet). Nine kilometres south of Dinant, in the village of Falmignuel, is the "Premier Musée du Cycle", containing 300 old bicycles. Bastogne has the "Nuts" museum with relics of the Battle of the Bulge, Bouillon in the south has an imposing castle set among deep woods on the pretty river Semois and St Hubert has a fine basilica. But the best-known Ardennes attraction is the Grotte de Han, where the River Lesse has followed an underground course through the limestone, forming caverns which can be explored by boat. Rochefort nearby has a castle. To the north-east, where the Ardennes take on a German aspect, the town of Spa has been a source of mineral water since the third century; Stavelot has ancient tanneries by the river, and abbey ruins.

A couple of Ardennes highlights are in the neighbouring countries. Crossing the border in the south-west, the River Semois curls delightfully between rounded slopes and can be explored by bike on surrounding lanes or by foot on the many paths. The environs of the River Sûre in northern Luxembourg are similarly attractive. The two main off-bike diversions in the Ardennes are canoeing (ask at tourist offices about hiring) and walking – there are a number of well-marked 'GR' *(Grande Randonnée)* routes throughout the Ardennes.

Belgium's Highest Road

The highest road in the country crosses the Hautes Fagnes-Eifel national park, passing the 694-metre Signal de Botrange roughly halfway between Eupen and Malmédy. The views are extensive.

Tour of the Belgian Ardennes and Luxembourg

Under 12 hours by train from London, and about 60 km from Brussels, the historic town of Namur sits right on the edge of the Ardennes and makes a convenient start/finish point for a bike tour. The route sticks mainly to the smaller roads, picking a devious course through the valleys and over the hills as it makes it way south and east towards Luxembourg, visiting the Meuse, caves of Han and lovely Semois valley. In the Grand Duchy, the Sûre valley is explored (note that Luxembourg is on the same rail line as Namur, and makes a good point to shorten the tour) before heading back for the slopes and forests of the Ardennes, and a journey by the Ourthe valley. It's a pleasant, mentally undemanding tour, though some of the hills are quite long! In parts careful map-reading is needed because the Belgian lane network gets intricate. The tour could be expanded to include Germany's Eifel district and a corner of France.

BELGIAN TOUR

Terrain: hilly
Distance: 560 km
Start/Finish: Namur/Namur
Scenery: *
Interest: *
Map: Michelin 1:200,000, no. 4

---

km	NAMUR
7	Dave
13	Yvoir
8	Dinant
2	Rocher Bayard
3	Dréhance
3	Furhooz
4	Vêves
2	Celles
4	Conjoux
6	Chevetogne
16	Rochefort
6	Han-sur-Lesse
7	Resteigne
3	Chanly
9	Daverdisse
14	Bièvre
6	Houdremont
13	Membre
10	Rochehaut
9	Corbion
8	Bouillon
4	Noirfontaine
7	Dohan
9	Mortehan
4	Herbeumont
7	Ste Cécile
3	Chassepierre
4	Martué
6	Chiny
6	Suxy
12	Léglise
18	Martelange
5	Bigonville
5	Hochfels
2	Boulaide
3	Pont Misère
19	Esch-sur-la-Sûre
14	Göbelsmühle
10	Michelau
8	Erpeldange
3	Ettelbrück
2	Schieren
13	Larochette
3	Heffingen

(detour SW to Luxembourg city)

5	Reuland
7	Mullerthal
5	Consdorf
10	Echternach
6	Berdorf
8	Beaufort
5	Reisdorf
11	Vianden
6	Stolzenbourg
8	Schinkert
10	Wilwerwiltz

11	Clervaux	17	Hotton
4	Maulusmillen	7	Deulin
4	Asselborn	5	Pt. Han
10	Buret	8	Gros Chêne
8	Houffalize	11	Havelange
12	Nadrin	10	Ohey
2	Belvedères des 6 Ourthe	6	Gesves
2	Nadrin	12	Namêche
13	La Roche-en-Ardenne	9	NAMUR

Basic Information

Getting There

Air: Belgium's international airports are at Antwerp, Brussels, Charleroi, Liège and Ostend. Brussels is an hour's flying time from London.

Rail/Ferry: Brussels has good connections with other European centres and is about 9 hours train journey from London. Zeebrugge and Ostend have daily ferry services to Dover and Folkestone, crossing times between $3\frac{1}{2}$ and 4 hours. Felixstowe and Hull have less frequent services to Zeebrugge and Ostend.

Information Sources

Belgian National Tourist Office (BNTO), 38 Dover Street, London W1X 3RB (tel: 01-499-5379). Can supply a free map, accommodation lists and a general information magazine.

Local Tourist Bureaux: called *Dienst voor Toerisme* in Flanders and *Syndicats d'Initiative* in Wallonia.

Ligue Vélocipédique Belge, Avenue du Globe 49, 1190 Brussels (tel: 3430008). Responsible for Belgian national cycle-sport.

Touring Club Royal de Belgique, Rue de la Loi 44, 1040 Brussels. Covers all forms of touring, affiliated to the AIT.

Accommodation

Camping: there are over 500 sites in Belgium, mainly along the coast and in the Ardennes; they are fairly thin on the ground in the north of the country. BNTO publishes a free list of about 400 sites, identifying four categories. The one-star sites are perfectly adequate, with basic facilities, while the four-star establishments have other-worldly luxuries like restaurants and sports grounds. Fees (which tend to be expensive) are higher in the summer, and along the coast.

In the forests and corners of the Ardennes it's fairly easy to find inconspicuous plots on which to spend the night, but north of the

Sambre and Meuse rivers wild camping is difficult (81% of Belgium is used for agriculture and housing). Ask permission before camping on land which is obviously used. Belgium's variable weather makes sleeping-out without a tent a chancy business.

Youth Hostels: Belgium's 37 IYHF hostels are spread quite evenly across the country and are in easy cycling distance of each other; the country lends itself to a youth-hostel based tour. Most hotels are large (the average is 96 beds), about half have members' kitchens and nearly all provide meals of some sort. Breakfasts are normally unavoidable and insubstantial – you have to pay for them whether you want them or not. There are two organisations: *Vlaamse Jeugdherbergcentrale* administers Flanders' hostels and *Centrale Wallonne des Auberges de la Jeunesse* the southern ones. Flanders hostels tend to be institutionalised, catering for schools and large groups, while Wallonne hostels are more expensive, but easier-going and more intimate.

Other Hostels: in addition to the IYHF hostels, several other organisations run budget accommodation. *Les Amis de la Nature* (Rue de l'Enseignement 24, B-4800 Verviers, tel: 330545) have 10 hostels, *Centrum voor Jeugdtoerisme* (Diestsestraat 235, B-3000 Leuven, tel: 226530) have 39, *Centre Belge du Tourisme des Jeunes* (Rue Guimard 1, B-1040 Brussels, tel: 5125447) have 17 and *Het Natuurvriendenhuis* (Provinciestraat 53, B-2000 Antwerp, tel: 361862) has 5. BNTO publish a free booklet containing the addresses of these hostels and also a list of 'unofficial' hostels which are not administered by any association but which offer budget accommodation in an atmosphere free of IYHF regulations. Brussels had 8 such hostels.

Hotels: embrace a whole range of accommodation, from the conventional hotel, to the *Pension, Hostellerie, Auberge* and *Gasthof.* These are spread across the country, and can be found in small towns and villages. Establishments approved and listed (in their free guide) by BNTO display a distinctive BNTO sign on their outside walls; there is no official grading, though some hotels have the 'star grading' if they've adopted the new standard Benelux classification. Prices are displayed in the rooms and at reception, and you pay by the room rather than by the person; prices may be slightly reduced out of the tourist season (July and August). Brussels prices are astronomical.

Weather

Temperatures are similar to those of southern England, though a little warmer in summer and cooler in winter, with more bracing conditions in the Ardennes. July and August are the warmest months, April and May are drier than the summer and autumn months. Rainfall in the north and east is less than that in the west, and Flanders weather tends to be hazy and damp, with frequent rain showers and some thunderstorms in summer. Overall, the eastern parts of the country have better weather. Prevailing winds are westerly, and can be dispiritingly strong across the northern flat lands.

Other Considerations: the main tourist season is understood to run from the beginning of July to the end of August; beaches and beauty spots will be most crowded then, and the main Ardennes towns busy.

Average Daily Maximum Temperatures (Centigrade)

	alt. in metres	J	F	M	A	M	J	J	A	S	O	N	D
Brussels	100	4	7	10	14	18	22	23	22	20	15	9	6

Cycling Information

Cycle Shops

There are something like 6,000 cycle shops in Belgium – though very often they combine with being moped retailers too. There is a shop in every town and most big villages. Some open on Sunday mornings. Most will handle repairs and carry spares (usually metric sizes) for racing, touring and 'utility' bikes. If you have trouble finding a shop, look in the yellow pages of a telephone directory under *Bicyclettes* (in Wallonia) or *Rijwielen* (Flanders).

Cycle Hire

There are lots of companies in Belgium who hire out bicycles, many being listed in the brochures of the provincial tourist boards (details from BNTO). The biggest and most comprehensive scheme is that operated by the Belgian National Railways (SNCB): at 42 stations throughout the country it is possible to hire a bike which can be returned to any of 108 designated 'handing-in' stations – so the bike does not have to be returned to the station from which it was hired. There are reduced rates for holders of train tickets, and further reductions for hire longer than three days. Bikes can be booked in advance by phone or letter. Full details are in the *Train + Velo* leaflet, available from the SNCB (rue de France 85, 1070 Brussels). SNCB also organise *Minitrip- Velo* two- and three-day holidays in several locations, where bicycles, board and lodgings are provided. The UK office of SNCB (Belgian National Railways, 22/25A Sackville Street, London W1X 1DE) can supply information in English about most aspects of hire, *Minitrips* and general train travel.

Transporting Your Bicycle

The Société Nationale des Chemins de fer Belge (SNCB) runs one of the densest and most reliable rail networks in Europe; it takes under four hours to cross the country. Bikes can be carried as accompanied luggage on most trains, though not on international trains if the journey is to be within Belgium, and neither do the SNCB guarantee to accept bikes on the *Automotrices Electriques* and *Autorails,* which have limited space.

Tickets for the bike are purchased from the luggage office, though on local trains the guard may issue the bike ticket. On journeys within Belgium you load and unload the bike yourself, and this also applies for any changes of train *en route* (be sure to buy a bike ticket for the entire journey, or you may have to pay a supplementary charge when you change trains). Between any two Belgian stations the charge for bicycles is a standard rate regardless of distance.

For sending a bike as unaccompanied luggage (within Belgium, and between Belgium and other European countries), the charge is based on distance. The bike is registered at the station of departure on presentation of a valid passenger ticket, and will be loaded by station staff. Within Belgium, an unaccompanied bike may take up to two days to make its journey.

SNCB do not seem keen on encouraging cycle-tourists to take bikes on trains, and it's no coincidence that the charge for hiring a bike from their 'Train + Velo' scheme is actually less than the cost of taking a bike on a train. For a daily charge, bikes can be garaged in the 'left luggage' of railway stations.

Bikes cannot be carried on Belgian buses.

Roads

Belgium has more motor-vehicles per kilometre than any other country in Europe, and more than twice the traffic density of the UK, yet cycling is so endemic that visiting motorists are warned in one of the most respected guides to the country that 'cyclists can be a hazard'! Belgium has the highest accident rate in Europe.

Traffic is especially heavy on main roads between large towns; major routes along the coast and in the Ardennes are crowded during high summer and at weekends. Luckily, Belgium has a great many tiny minor roads and cycle-paths, so it's not difficult to keep out of the way of the car.

Surfaces on main and secondary roads are generally good so long as they are tarmac. But they can, especially in towns, villages and on the smallest roads, switch abruptly to the most horrendous species of cobbles you're likely to find anywhere in Europe. Such is their scale that in Dutch-speaking areas they are endearingly referred to as *kinderkopjes* (children's heads); riding over Belgian *pavé* is like sliding down the stairs on your bottom holding on to a pram full of bricks. Your teeth rattle like castanets, arms turn to jelly, your pump falls off and your buttocks feel as if they're being massaged by a pile-driver.

Level-crossings and tram-lines are other obstacles to steer clear of. Surfaces of cycle-paths vary from concrete slab to brick, and can be nice and smooth or cracked, pitted and strewn with gravel or glass. It is compulsory to use cycle paths where they occur. Normally they run adjacent to the highway, sometimes completely separate; other times they are only a form of hard shoulder separated from the traffic by a white line. The better paths are one-way but where space is tight, you end up riding on a two-way path, even sharing with pedestrians. A blue sign *Fietsers Oversteken* indicates that the cycle-path is about to cross the highway and continue on the other side. Most major roads have cycle-paths though they are less frequent in the Ardennes; and whatever their pitfalls, they are infinitely preferable to tussling with the traffic.

Places are well sign-posted, though several have two names, one for each language. A few examples are: Antwerpen (Anvers), Huy (Hoei), Ieper (Ypres), Liège (Luik), Mons (Bergen), Ronse (Renaix), Tournai (Doornik) and Vise (Wezet). It's worth remembering that in the north, the canal tow-paths can provide interesting and quiet routes; in the Ardennes there are numerous rough hill-tracks.

Maps

For General Planning

Michelin No. 409, Luxembourg/Belgium, Scale 1:350,000. Modestly priced and lightweight, showing scenic roads, some minor roads, occasional spot-heights but no indication of gradients. Good large-scale inset maps of Brussels, Antwerp and Liège plus a useful town and village index.

Mair Gedetailleerde Kaart Belgie, Scale 1:250,000. Shows scenic roads and some minor roads, frequent height indicators but no gradients.

For Cycling

Michelin Nos 2, 4 (1), Scale 1:200,000. The standard cycling maps for Belgium and Luxembourg, with all the smallest tarmac roads marked, gradients, tourist information and scenic roads. Cobbled roads and potential rough-stuff routes are marked as roads of 'unsurfaced or of doubtful quality'. Sheet 1 mostly covers the southern Netherlands, with a small sliver of Belgium north of Turnhout; sheet 4 includes Luxembourg and the French Ardennes.

Note: Sheet No. 101 of the excellent French IGN 1:250,000 series covers a sizeable chunk of Belgium south and west of Brussels, but including the Semois valley in the southern Ardennes. The rest of this sheet covers north-east France.

LUXEMBOURG

No bigger than Wiltshire, Luxembourg is literally a miniature country with all the scaled-down ingredients found in the larger European nations. It has its own capital – a centre for culture and administration, its own industrial heart-land and its own 'mountains'. And of course the best way of exploring a miniature landscape is slowly, by bicycle!

Although there is enough here for a week of biking, with hiking too, Luxembourg can profitably be fitted into broader cycle-tours which include the Ardennes of Belgium or the Eifel hills of Germany. It's no more than four days easy cycling from the Channel ports and is easily accessible by plane and train. I once visited Luxembourg having cycled down from the Hook of Holland via Maastricht and the Ardennes, a varied and pleasant route which starts easy and gets harder as you approach the hills! The northern half of Luxembourg is the most attractive.

Sharing borders with two of the world's greatest cycling nations it's inevitable that Luxembourgians should be keen followers of the sport. But they're enthusiastic *cyclo-touristes* too, and at weekends gaily-clad riders whisper along *chemins ruraux* headed for their favourite watering-holes. It's also a country of hikers, with many way-marked trails cob-webbing the woods.

To help preserve their identity, the Luxembourgians have devised a language which nobody can understand: *Letzebürgesch*, a kind of German. French is however the official tongue, and most speak English. German is also widely understood. Two-thirds of the population live in the capital and the industrial south, so the rest of the country is fairly un-crowded. Nearly all are Catholic. 'We wish to remain what we are' is a national motto understandably highly regarded in a country of low taxes and prices; it's run as a constitutional monarchy, the head at present being Grand Duke Jean.

Luxembourg has good food for calorie-starved cyclists and it can be bought at reasonable prices: lots of cheeses, cooked meats, vegetables and fruit for picnics, and pastries are a speciality. Many cafés not only serve drinks but inexpensive, wholesome meals at midday and in the evening. Restaurants abound, on their own and in hotels; local dishes include black pudding and Ardennes ham. Breakfasts at hostels and hotels can be less than enough sustenance for a day's cycling. The currency is the Luxembourg *Franc,* divided into 100 *centimes.* Belgian money can be used in Luxembourg, but not *vice versa.* (If you're just biking through Luxembourg rather than staying a while, and you are going to, or from, Belgium there is little point in acquiring Luxembourg *francs;* it's better to rely on Belgian money. And make sure you use up or change all your Luxembourg money before leaving the country.)

Ride Guide

The Oesling

The Oesling (Luxembourg Ardennes) is really an extension of the larger Belgian Ardennes, and if the Grand Duchy is a country-in-miniature, the Oesling is a bike-touring-area-in-miniature, for it can comfortably be crossed by bike in one day (40 kilometres as the crow flies) and is dotted with pockets of interest. Only two main highways, the N7 and N15, (both of which carry heavy traffic) cross Oesling, and to the side of these routeways are many twisty minor roads snaking along river valleys and climbing over the tops. Gradients can be steep but are seldom long.

The Luxembourg Ardennes are slightly lower than their Belgian neighbours, but have the same rounded, often bare, summits and flat skylines. Rivers like the Sûre cut winding and deep valleys into the plateau, their steep slopes clothed in dense woods of oak and spruce. Castles, gorges, sinuous rivers and small picturesque villages contribute to the colour. Towns like Clervaux and Vianden exude an obvious medieval charm and there are especially grand castles at Beaufort and Bourscheid. Numerous long-distance footpaths link villages and towns, usually way-marked, while the youth-hostel organisation maintains a network of inter-hostel paths way-marked with white triangles.

Central Bon Pays & Little Switzerland

Between Ettelbruck and Luxembourg City is a pleasant rolling landscape guarded by castles and crossed by many small rivers and minor roads. In the west, the pretty little valleys of the Attert, Eisch and Mamer all have delightful lanes (with relaxed gradients) following their courses. There are impressive castles at Hollenfels and Bourglinster.

In the east of this area is a tiny enclave of woods, small cliffs, ravines and falling streams affectionately dubbed 'Little Switzerland'. To catch the real flavour of this picturesque pocket you really have to leave the bike behind and take to the footpaths along valleys like the Hallerbach and the Gorge du Loup. This forms part of the Germano-Luxembourg national park designated to preserve the natural beauty of this border area. The nearby town of Echternach is choked in August and at weekends.

Luxembourg city, the capital, makes a pleasant break from pedalling if you're keen on sight-seeing. The city sits above sheer cliffs overlooking the valleys of the Alzette and Petrusse. Once a formidable fortress, many impressive remains survive. There are parks, the Promenade de la Corniche, Grand Ducal Palace, cathedral and National Museum to explore.

Luxembourg's Highest Road

The CR 308 climbs to 549 metres by the 'Tour Napoléon', 12 kilometres outside Martelange, on the route to Eschdorf (north-west of Ettelbruck).

Five Countries in a Day

In mountaineering circles there is an oft-sneered-at breed of climber referred to as the 'peak bagger'. Symptomatic of the peak bagger is an insatiable lust for 'knocking off' summits, keeping an obsessive tally of the conquests and using them for fuel in one-up-man-ship contests during evening sessions in the valley-floor pubs. And since goals-and-achievements (and obsessions!) are as much a part of cycling as they are of mountaineering, I have noted below a suitable challenge for the 'country bagger'.

There are only a couple of routes in Europe where you can cycle through five countries in one day. By far the easiest is that which links the Netherlands, Germany, Belgium, Luxembourg and France. The most

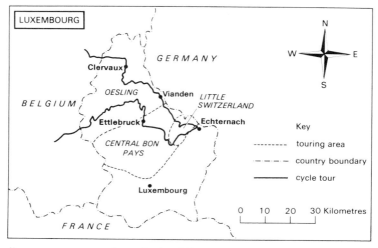

direct route passes through the following places: Vaals (Netherlands), Aachen (W. Germany), Eupen (Belgium), Malmédy, St. Vith, Wemperhaardt (Luxembourg), Ettlebruck, Luxembourg City, Hesperange, Evrange (France).

It is a ride of 172 kilometres, entirely on main roads, though passing through attractive countryside. And if you are not only a country-bagger but a peak-bagger too, then your passion for goals can be indulged to the full by deviations from the ride to scale the highest point in the Netherlands (Drielandenpunt) and the highest point in Belgium (Signal de Botrange) both of which lie within a kilometre of the above route.

Luxembourg Tour

This has been combined with a tour of Belgium and can be found in the Belgian Chapter.

Basic Information

Getting There

Air: Luxembourg airport is six kilometres outside the capital and about two hours flying time from London.

Rail: good connections with other European cities, and with the UK via Ostend and Brussels. Journey time from London to Luxembourg is about 12 hours.

Road: Calais to Luxembourg City by main road is about 400 kilometres.

Information Sources

Luxembourg National Tourist and Trade Office (LNTO), 36/37 Piccadilly, London W1V 9PA (Tel: 01-434-2800). Camp site and accommodation lists plus handy information booklet on the Grand Duchy.

Local Tourist Bureaux: offices of the *Syndicat d'Initiative* can be found in tourist centres and most towns, and are identified by a sign bearing a blue knight against a white background. Apart from the usual service of supplying information on local accommodation and places of interest, some also sell maps and have notes on local hiking trails.

Federation du Sport Cycliste Luxembourgeois (FSCL), PO Box 2253, Luxembourg *or* 26 rue de Cessange, Leudelange, Luxembourg (tel: 37383). The controlling body for national bike racing.

Union Luxembourgeoise de Cyclotouristes, 39 rue de l'Etoile, F-57190 Florange. Headquarters for Luxembourg's cycle-touring clubs, affiliated to the AIT.

Accommodation

Camping: Luxembourg is well-endowed with camp-sites, particularly in the north; there is seldom more than 20 kilometres of cycling between sites and in popular areas they are mere pedal-revolutions apart. LNTO lists over 120 official sites, and divides them into three categories according to amenities offered (charges for a Category 3 site may be as little as a quarter those of a Category 1). They tend to be less expensive than Belgian sites; charges are posted at camp entrances.

Officially, wild camping is frowned-upon unless it is done with the permission of the land-owner. It's easier to find isolated patches in the northern 'Oesling' part of the country than in the south.

Youth Hostels: there is a close-packed cluster of ten hostels, near enough to each other to form the basis for an easy cycle-tour; they can be linked by rides of 10-20 kilometres. At the time of writing there is still no hostel north of Vianden, neither are there any close at hand in neighbouring France and Belgium which can be used when exploring the northern top of the country. Hostels tend to be large, with about 100 beds (the mega-hostel in Luxembourg City has 300 beds, a laundry room and a disco!). Priority is given to hostellers under 35, and cyclists get prioroty over motorists – naturally.

Gîtes: a network of holiday homes (for unmarried people only) are spread over Luxembourg, and they can be useful if you're planning a fixed-centre tour. All have fully-equipped kitchens. Details from: *Gîtes d'Etape Luxembourgeois,* 10 rue des Tanneurs, Wiltz.

Hotels: ranges from traditional hotels to less expensive *auberges* (inns) and *pensions* (boarding houses). Prices in Luxembourg City are higher than elsewhere; it may be possible to obtain reductions out of the tourist season. Free annually-revised Hotel/Auberges/Restaurants/ Pensions list from LNTO.

Weather

Similar temperatures to the south of England, but with cooler winters, especially in the higher north of the country, where snow can lie for up to three or four weeks. Luxembourg is generally drier than neighbouring Belgium and The Netherlands, while the north of the country tends to catch more rain than the south, but by way of compensation gets clearer skies. May and June are the sunniest months; the prevailing winds are from the south-west and north-west.

Average Daily Maximum Temperatures (Centigrade)

	alt. in metres	J	F	M	A	M	J	J	A	S	O	N	D
Clervaux	454	3	4	9	12	17	20	22	20	18	13	7	4

Cycling Information

Cycle Shops

Most towns have cycle shops with spares, who can also handle repairs. Dealers seem used to touring bikes; one of the most 'successful' breakdowns I've been involved in was resolved in Luxembourg by an incredibly co-operative bike-shop man who not only had a replacement freewheel in stock which actually fitted the hub in question, but was also only too willing to transfer the bigger (and in the Ardennes, vital) sprockets from the shattered freewheel to the new one, so that the gear set-up still had its wide ratios. And he didn't charge much either.

Cycle Hire

Basic utility-style bikes can be hired by the hour, day or week in Luxembourg City and in tourist centres like Berdorf, Vianden, Echternach, Diekirch and Reisdorf. LNTO can supply specific addresses.

Transporting Your Bicycle

Rail lines of the *Chemin de Fer Luxembourgaise* (CFL) radiate out from Luxembourg City in five directions, amply serving the country and linking with the rest of continental Europe. Trains are frequent. Bicycles can be carried (as accompanied luggage) when space is available, and a (very low) flat rate is payable regardless of distance; you buy a 'bicycle card' from the ticket office and load and unload the bike yourself. For a higher charge (scaled according to distance) you can have the bike sent as unaccompanied luggage, handled throughout by CFL staff (take it to the luggage registration office); if the journey involves a change of trains the bike may take a day longer to arrive. For an extra charge insurance cover can be arranged for the bike. Cycles can be garaged in the 'left luggage' offices of stations for a daily charge.

Bikes cannot be carried on buses.

Roads

Compared to most European countries, Luxembourg has a very dense network of minor 'cycling' roads; in parts there's a junction every kilometre. So it's relatively easy to escape the traffic provided you like using maps. Luxembourg's roads have only a quarter the traffic density of Belgium's though in summer the main 'E' and 'N' roads are very busy indeed, and should be avoided. Surfaces and sign-posting are good.

In the area of 'Little Switzerland', a couple of cycle-tracks have been constructed, largely beside main roads, to link popular touring centres. These are: Echternach to Diekirch (28 kilometres), Vianden to Reisdorf (12 km) and a third is planned between Echternach and Bech. Especially over the summer weekends, this area is rather spoilt by motor-coaches and holiday traffic.

Maps

For General Planning

Note: being so small, Luxembourg tends to get tacked onto the edges of maps of Belgium, Germany and France; the three maps listed below can also be used for touring Belgium.

Michelin No. 409, Luxembourg/Belgium, Scale: 1:350,000. Modestly-priced and lightweight, showing scenic roads, some minor roads, occasional spot-heights but no indication of gradients.

Mair Gedetailleerde Kaart Belgie, Scale 1:250,000. Shows scenic roads and some minor roads, frequent height indicators but no gradients.

For Cycling

Michelin No. 4, Mons-Luxembourg, Scale 1:200,000. The standard cycling map for Luxembourg, with all the smallest tarmac roads marked, gradients, tourist information and scenic roads. Lightweight and reasonably priced.

Geokart No 64, Grand Duché de Luxembourg, Scale 1:100,000. A good map for local biking, with all minor roads, some footpaths and tracks and some tourist features, including scenic roads. All of Luxembourg on one sheet, plus detailed town and village index.

GERMANY

The land of the Brothers Grimm cannot boast wildly spectacular coastlines or mountains oozing glaciers, but it does have a unique romance: fairytale castles, huge and mysterious forests, picturesque towns and villages, secret gorges and dreamy rivers. It is a country which does not often have you rocking back in your saddle with the kind of astonished awe fired by the immensity of fjords or Alps; the rewards are more to be found in the subtler territory of moods and ambience, for this is an intimate rather than extravagant geography.

My most readily recalled image of biking in Germany is of a fleeting encounter on a steep and winding forest road which, the day being hot and me being in no hurry, I was walking gently up leaning on the bike and half looking for a spot to take lunch and a nap. It must have been the contrast of colour that caught my eye because that morning the world was limited to the grey of empty tarmac, blue sky and greens of the leaves. In a patch of sunlight, knee-deep in grass and haloed by the branch of a beech, stood a tiny fawn. Surprise froze us both and although it cannot have been more than a second before the deer bounded from view, the purity of that moment, has printed itself on my mind clearer than any photograph.

The easiest cycling is to be found in the flat northern part of the country, though with the exception of the eastern side of Schleswig Holstein, this is probably the least scenic portion of Germany. South from Dortmund the high land begins and cycling requires more effort as range after range of hills follow each other down to the biggest peaks in Bavaria. Most of the ranges top 500 metres, and some are as high as 1,000 metres; all are ideal for exploration by bike. Very conveniently, some of the best cycling areas are close to the western and southern borders, where they can be toured in conjunction with equally good areas of Belgium, Luxembourg, France, Switzerland and Austria.

The dwellers in this verdant land are traditionally known for the neatness, love of order, diligence and comradely cheer that Germans call *'Gemütlichkeit'*. I have always enjoyed their boisterous humour, honesty and supreme helpfulness. The Germans are also credited with a healthy reverence for nature – their affection for trees, running water and animals has been nurtured over the generations by folk-lore and legend. But paradoxically they are also the most motor-oriented nation in Europe, with 7,000 kilometres of *autobahn,* 28 million cars (Britain is second in the car league with a mere 18 million), and a manic lust for driving them far and fast. Fortunately there is a re-awakening of interest in environmental matters; in the newspapers, politicians look for electoral mileage by being photographed riding bicycles, and the 'Greens' are blossoming.

German food is rich and hearty: dumplings, potatoes, bread, ham, pork and of course *Wurst* – the infamous sausage that comes in all shapes, sizes and colours, hot or cold and which is superb raw-material for picnics. The white wines, especially those from the Mosel and Rhine, are some of the best in the world and can be sampled at a *Weinstube, Weinhaus* or in the dim vaults of a town hall *(Ratskeller).* Refreshing after a long hot ride is a *Stein* of beer, of which the Germans seem to drink enormous quantities. The chain of Reformhaus stores sell vegetarian and health foods and the Aldi supermarkets offer the best value for money.

English is widely spoken throughout, and for schoolchildren this is the first language they learn (note that the German letter "ß" may be substituted for "ss"). Roughly half the population is Catholic, the other half Protestant, and the country is a federal republic. Compared to other European countries Germany is expensive – the unit of currency being the *Deutsche Mark* (DM) which is divided into 100 *Pfennig* (Pf).

Ride Guide

Schleswig Holstein

No more than an 18-hour ferry journey from Harwich, England, this

GERMANY

DENMARK

North Sea

SCHLESWIG HOLSTEIN

• Flensburg

Kiel •
Plön •

Lübeck •
Hamburg

Bremerhaven •

Lüneburg •

EAST GERMANY

NETHERLANDS

Hamelin •

Paderborn •
Dortmund •

Harz Mountains

Sauerland/
Westerwald/
Taunus

Kassel •

Leine/Weser

CENTRAL UPLANDS

BELGIUM

Bonn •

Koblenz •

Vogelsburg
Rhon

EIFEL and HUNSRÜCK

• Frankfurt

LUX.

Mainz •

Wurzburg • Bayreuth •

Bamberg •

CZECHO-
SLOVAKIA

FRANCE

Heidelberg •

Odenwald   Spessart

Nuremburg •

EASTERN FORESTS

Baden
Baden •

Stuttgart •

Regensburg •
Donauwörth •

N

Black
Forest   SWABISCHE

ALB

W   E

Freiburg •

Rottweil •

Ulm •

Augsburg •

Passau •

S

• Munich

Key

• Salzburg

Fussen

BAVARIAN   ALPS

touring area

AUSTRIA

country boundary

cycle tour

0   50   100   150   200 Kilometres

northern province is both convenient and sufficiently flat to be a good
choice for a first foreign tour. It also offers pleasant riding for anyone
cycling from Denmark towards central Germany (or vice versa), and it
can be explored as part of a tour which uses as its end-points

Bremerhaven and the Danish port of Esbjerg (both having ferry links with Harwich).

This is an area dominated by water and the expansive skies so typical of East Anglia. Arable land and clumps of woodland are dissected by drainage dykes and a wealth of small roads, while many of the main roads have adjacent cycle-tracks or lanes. It is also heavily populated, (Hamburg is Germany's second largest city) and as you pedal the byways there seems to be a village or hamlet every couple of kilometres.

The eastern side of Schleswig Holstein is better than the west for cycling, being more sheltered from the wind and richer in scenery. While the west is a flat monotony of marsh, ditch and dune, the east is perceptibly undulating, sprinkled with lakes and woods and lined with beaches. The highlight is Holsteinische Schweiz (the 'Swiss District'), around the attractive towns of Plön and Preetz where lakes congregate in a rather more scenic version of the Norfolk Broads. The highest point hereabouts is 164-metre Bungsberg, at the base of the peninsula leading to Oldenburg. (The roads just north of Lübeck tend to get very crowded).

Schleswig Holstein has several historic Hanseatic ports worth a visit, among them Lübeck (the most interesting), Flensburg and Husum. South of Lübeck, the Lauenburgische national park has some pleasant roads for cycling, more lakes, and the fine towns of Ratzeburg and Mölln.

If you want to cycle south from Schleswig Holstein towards the Central Uplands, the most attractive route lies via the heather, gorse and woods of the Lüneburg Heath (both Lüneburg and Celle are worth a pause). Note that you can avoid Hamburg (unpleasant cycling if you cannot cope with traffic), by using the various ferries which cross the Elbe. To the east there is the small Zollenspieker ferry, just north of Winsen about 15 kilometres from Hamburg and convenient for Lüneburg Heath, and to the west there is a handy crossing between Wischhafen and Glückstadt.

The Central Uplands

This very large region (300 x 200 kilometres) is a real mixed bag, for the geography of central Germany is so jumbled that it's difficult to separate the various areas. Several major blocks of hills, extensive forests, many rivers and a predominantly rural aspect create a landscape which is pleasant without being jaw-droppingly spectacular. Much of it is seldom noticed by the tourist hordes, and the wealth of small roads make it easy to escape from traffic. Cycling here can be as hard as you want it to be, for there are plenty of opportunities to ride high, yet if you want to avoid exertion the numerous valleys and flatter plateaus have fairly level roads. The more interesting cycling areas are noted below, starting in the north.

The Harz Mountains. Inelegantly truncated by the East/West border, the rounded, forested outlines of the Harz provide limited though attractive cycling along minor roads – sometimes along valleys past reservoirs, other times climbing steeply to viewpoints. Cycling scope can be increased by using the many *Wanderwege* of the area, which can range from well-surfaced forest tracks to narrow bumpy paths. Signposting on these trails (primarily intended for walkers) is characteristically excellent, though one has to be wary not to interfere with logging teams. The main tourist town for the Harz is the old silver mining settlement of Clausthal-Zellerfeld (which has the largest wooden church in Europe), while beautiful Goslar is worth a visit. Both Braunlage and Osterode have half-timbered town halls and throughout the Harz there are several caverns open to the public. Weekends (especially Sundays) draw day-trippers to the Harz in droves, so try to plan rides for the weekdays. Würmberg (971 metres) is the highest peak.

Leine/Weser. Between the Harz mountains and the ridge of the Teutoburgerwald over by Paderborn, are the parallel rivers of the Leine and Weser. Although not exactly level, this is one of the easier cycling areas of the Central Uplands, with quiet roads meandering through fertile farmland and the opportunity to follow the banks of either of these two great rivers as they wend their way north towards Bremen. Between the rivers is some higher wooded land, now a national park; Hamelin (Hameln) to the north has associations with the famous Pied Piper legend, and the Rat Catcher's house still stands.

This gentler terrain continues southwards beyond Kassel, following the idle wanderings of the River Fulda to its source in the Vogelsberg.

Sauerland, Westerwald and Taunus. The western side of the Central Uplands is occupied by three blocks of high land separated by the rivers Sieg and Lahn and filling in the area between Dortmund in the north and Frankfurt am Main in the south; their western edge is defined by the Rhine.

Sauerland, the northern block, is lower and more broken than the other two, and is made busy at weekends by people fleeing the industrial Ruhr just to the north. By contrast, the hills (Rothaargebirge) tacked onto its eastern edge reach most of the way to Kassel, topping 800 metres around the skiing and hiking centre of Winterberg, and offering good cycling opportunities.

Westerwald, in the centre, has a better variety of scenery than Sauerland, with unusual volcanic forms, woodland and the romantic, much visited castles and towns of the Lahn valley.

Taunus, in the south is probably the most attractive of all three blocks. It is an area of fine forests and steep hills, well-supplied with scenic roads for cycling. South-facing slopes are painstakingly terraced and planted with vineyards, and the *Weinberge* (wine hills) of these hills are well known for their quality product.

Vogelsberg, Hohe Rhön, Spessart and Odenwald. To the north-east of Frankfurt, Vogelsberg is a great igneous lump (in fact the largest basalt mass on the continent), surrounded by forests of spruce. Small roads wind across the slopes and the highest point is 774-metre Taufstein. Unfortunately chopped by the East/West border Hohe Rhön rises to 1,016 metres on the Wasserkuppe (excellent views) just north of Gersfield and has a good network of roads which can be used to explore its woods and slopes.

Between Hohe Rhön and Odenwald are the gentler hills of Spessart with beech and oak lower down, and conifer at the higher levels. The southern part is especially scenic, with the option of a pleasant ride along part of the River Main's north bank.

To the south-west of Spessart, hilly Odenwald stretches for about 50 kilometres from Darmstadt to Heidelberg. It's like a miniature version of the Black Forest, nothing like so high (all under 600 metres), about a third of its area forested and the rest occupied by pastures, isolated farms and small villages. It has a fairly dense network of winding, picturesque, roads which are best cycled during weekdays; at weekends Odenwald is a refuge for people from neighbouring Rhine cities. The roads to the east of Odenwald tend to be quieter than those to the west. Interesting places include Michelstadt, Miltenberg, the cultural centre of Darmstadt, and the old university town of Heidelberg with its fine location and castle. The pretty Neckar valley on the southern edge of Odenwald is worth a ride if you can face the traffic – though cycle-lanes for part of the route alleviate the discomfort.

Eifel and Hunsrück

West of the Rhine and separated from each other by the River Mosel, are two blocks of hills: the Eifel and Hunsrück. The northern block, Eifel, is the more attractive of the two and provides more cycling opportunities. Together with northern Luxembourg and the Belgian Ardennes (of which Eifel is a continuation) this area is a fine choice for anybody looking for striking scenery, some challenging pedalling, plus the bonus of three different countries within a day's ride of each other – all 250 kilometres from the English Channel. Eifel is mostly around 450-600 metres high, with thick woods and sharp slopes dropping to incised river valleys. Its most unusual feature is its numerous crater lakes which have formed in the eroded stumps of old volcanoes. Called *Maaren*, the best known are Laacher See (west of Andernach) and Pulvermeer, which is one of several which are south of Daun. Eifel's highest point is the 747-metre Hohe Acht, near Adenau. Freewheeling off Eifel eastwards into the Rhine gorge you can visit Bonn (the German capital, birthplace of Beethoven), touristy Königswinter, Linz and Koblenz.

Hunsrück, south of the Mosel, is somewhat smaller than Eifel, and is dominated by a long ridge of 700-metre hills, heavily wooded and crossed by several small roads. Hunsrück does however rest against the most dramatic section of the Rhine gorge, that bit between Bingen and Koblenz, at its most narrow and romantic by the town of St Goar. In Hunsrück too is the highest road in Rhineland – some 22 kilometres westwards along the B422 from Idar-Oberstein a small side-road turns left up to 816-metre Erbeskopf. The Mosel itself is a deeply cut, pleasant river, and traffic permitting, the section downstream from Traben-Trarbach is an attractive ride.

Because of the heavy tourist traffic that the Rhine gorge attracts between Bonn and Mainz, cycling this river's banks is not the most tranquil of pastimes. If however you are keen to catch the castles, viewpoints, vineyards and impressive presence of this great river, try mixing it with rides (albeit comparatively strenuous) in the surrounding hills. At several points you can switch banks using the small car ferries.

If the Hunsrück hasn't sated your appetite for hill-climbing, then turn south to take in the forests and slopes of Pfälzer Wald (Palatinate Forest), a favourite tramping ground for hikers, and also possessing a picturesque selection of small roads. The national park reaches its steepest and highest in the east, and tails off southwards into the smaller, lower, rolling district of Wasgau.

The Eastern Forests

For some 250 kilometres south from the junction of the West German/East German/Czech border to the interesting town of Passau, the strip of country east of the river Danube and Naab is occupied by a band of forested hills known in parts as Frankenwald, Fichtel-gebirge, Oberpfälzer Wald, Bayrischer Wald and Böhmer Wald. It's a little visited area, and one which is now protected for most of its length by national parks. Small scenic roads can be used for biking the area and there are plenty of paths for hiking. The highest hills (Grosser Arber rises to 1,486 metres) are to be found right on the Bohemian (Czech) border around the town of Zwiesel.

At the confluence of the Danube, Inn and Ilz is Passau, with a fine cathedral which has the largest church organ in the world (17,000 pipes); Regensburg too has numerous attractions.

West of the Eastern Forests is an area generally known as Franconia, not scenically outstanding, but very pleasant, mild countryside, more or less empty but for woods and farmland, but including the interesting cities of Coburg, Bamberg, Bayreuth and Nuremburg, and three extensive national parks.

Schwäbische Alb

From the north-east, where it climbs from the Nördlingen 'basin' and the Romantic Road, to the south-west where it faces the Black Forest across the waters of the Neckar, Schwäbische Alb (also known as the Schwäbische Jura) stretches for some 160 kilometres. Its width – about 40 kilometres – is defined to the south by the River Danube and to the north by the Neckar. Often ignored as a touring area, these limestone hills are delightful and not overly strenuous for cycling: quiet, rich in castles, old towns and villages, sporting characteristic red-painted half-timbered houses, romantic ruins, caves, spiny crags and clumps of woodland which are best appreciated during an autumn tour.

This is a milder, more pastoral landscape than many I've suggested for Germany, and it is a good complement to a tour of the adjacent Black Forest and Fränkische Alb immediately to the north-east. It also fits conveniently into a ride up (or down) the Romantic Road or along the Danube. The town of Stuttgart has good rail and air links with the UK and is a handy starting point.

The steeper scarp slope of Schwäbische Alb is along its northern edge where cliffs and crags drop to the River Neckar. Roads are plentiful and it is not difficult to pick routes which follow peaceful rural byways – and the whole region is blessed with a multitude of unsurfaced tracks which provide fine scope for rough-stuff cycling. There are also many way-marked hiking trails.

Some of the roads get quite high: the Lochen Pass (highest in Schwäbische Alb) clambers up to 920 metres just south of Balingen, while south-west of here are the loftier summits of the region, among them Lemberg (1,015 metres), the highest, just east of Rottweil. The castle of the aristocratic Hohenzollern family stands grandly about 15 kilometres north-east of Balingen.

Lower, easier cycling can be enjoyed down in the many picturesque valleys, two of the most beautiful being the Bära which flows southwards into the Danube at Fridingen, and further east the Grosse Lauter which flows southwards towards the Danube from Münsingen. Busier, and on a much bigger scale, is the section of Danube from Sigmaringen to Tuttlingen, where it flows through a deep winding gorge whose walls vary from sheer rock to steeply scaling woods. Here and there the road is forced to tunnel. Castles perch on crags, among them the dramatic eleventh-century Schloss Wildenstein (part of which is a youth hostel) and those at Bronnen and Werenwag. No less impressive is the great Benedictine abbey of Beuron.

There are many other places in or near Schwäbische Alb worthy of a few hours out of the saddle – among them Ulm (beautiful cathedral), Tübingen (university town), Reutlingen and Nördlingen. South of

Reutlingen, around the village of Erpfingen, is the main area of caves, many of which can be visited.

Beyond the Romantic Road town of Donauwörth and a pleasant addition to a tour of Schwäbische Alb is the large Altmühltal national park. Covering an area about 80 by 40 kilometres, the park has plenty of small quiet roads, and includes an interesting ride along the banks of the River Altmühl as it wriggles from one side of the park to the other. It ties in well with a tour through the Eastern Forests.

So far, all the cycling around Schwäbische Alb that I've mentioned is on the hilly side, but there is one fine tour in these parts which – while not being effortless – is very suitable for those who would like to mix easy pedalling with a spot of swimming and soaking up the Bavarian atmosphere. This is the four or five day ride down the Danube, best started in the west at say Donaueschingen on the flank of the Black Forest. The ride then meanders downstream, cutting to and fro across the river to keep to the smaller roads, and passing through places like Tuttlingen, Sigmaringen, Ehingen, Ulm, Donauwörth, Ingolstadt and Regensburg, from where you can circle back through the Altmühltal national park and Schwäbische Alb, or press on to Passau.

The Black Forest

Just as the Welsh are being grandiose when they label those undulations north of Swansea the Black 'Mountains', so the Germans are being downright devious when they call a range of hills nearly twice as high as the Welsh Mynydd du, the Black 'Forest'. I cannot have been the only cyclist who has first set eyes on that lofty basalt rump which rears from the east bank of the Rhine, and wondered if I had come to the right place. Forests, after all, usually go more *along* than *up!*

So, Schwarzwald is hilly, with roads that are seldom level; climbing and winding their tortuous way through thick, dark woodland and breaking out here and there into grassy clearings. Gradients are often steep, and I found them as hard work as those of the Alps. The moody conifers, dank and gloomy when in cloud but sighing and mysterious under a breezy blue sky, can be depressing or intoxicating. They are livened by tumbling streams, and in places the trees disappear altogether to be replaced by heady views. Sheltered in valley corners, the smaller villages are often very attractive, with ancient farms and pretty little cottages.

Some 100 kilometres long and 50 wide, the Black Forest is a neighbour to some of central Europe's cycling high-spots: just across the Rhine are the Vosges; to the east is Schwäbische Alb; the Alps are south and the Jura south-west. The Forest is sparsely populated, its hill-tops blunted (many of them over 1,000 metres) and grassy, their slopes rounded, bleak in winter and higher in the south than the north. South of Freiburg the scenery becomes more varied, with less tree cover, small lakes and more frequent meadows. And here too is the bald summit of the Forest's highest point – Feldberg at 1,493 metres. Whereas the west tends to rise abruptly, the eastern edge of the Black Forest merges gently into rolling farmland.

One of the reasons that Black Forest cycling can be so strenuous is that the flatter valley routes are heavily motor-laden and to avoid such unpleasant company one has to literally 'take to the hills'. A willingness to tackle extra climbs and kilometres is handsomely repaid by an absence of cars and crowds. Minor roads snake scenically up valley sides, over cols and along ridges. Some of the busier valleys are also spoilt by ribbon developments of hotels and tourist shops.

Since the early 1900s when well-heeled industrialists and royalty flocked to the Forest's spas, it has been a popular tourist centre. Towns like Baden-Baden, Kurhaus, Freudenstadt, Triberg and Freiburg are now important centres. Tourism is thoroughly exploited. Woodcarving is the region's traditional export, seen at its worst in the billions of vulgar cuckoo clocks on offer, and at its best in the delightful carved signposts one finds along road and trail; a sign to a brewery might be decorated by a delicately worked brewer's dray led by a buxom barmaid clutching foaming tankards.

The Black Forest has one of the densest networks of hiking trails in Europe and is well-suited to off-road cycling. Many of the trails are sign-posted or way-marked; surfaces vary from smooth well-graded grit to muddy inclines too steep for easy progress. Many of the trails have small rudimentary *hütte* which can be used for sheltering and picnics; often they have an outside concrete plinth and pile of timber which can be used for making fires (care needed!).

Bavarian Alps

Sandwiched between the Austrian Alps and the rolling hills of southern Germany, and stretching from Lake Constance (Bodensee) in the west to Salzburg in the east, is the long, thin strip of the Bavarian Alps. The convolutions of the border and the limited number of roads in the area mean that the Bavarian Alps and Austrian Tyrol are effectively knitted together as touring areas. As the trend of the rivers is south to north, cycling along the length of the Bavarian Alps can involve a lot of climbing and descent.

Germany's Alps can be divided into three parts: in the west are the Allgäuer Alps, a region of beautiful mountain scenery with many peaks above 2,000 metres, situated between Lake Constance and the River Lech. Pastures are lush here, partly a result of the frequent drenchings of rain they receive. Less spectacular, but nevertheless pleasant, are the lower areas north of Wangen and Füssen. A 20-kilometre ride south-west from Oberstdorf takes you into the heart of an anomalous enclave of Austrian territory which can only be reached by road from Germany, so the inhabitants of Mittelberg use the *Deutschmark*.

The central part of the Bavarian Alps has the best scenery. Here, jagged limestone ridges are cut into pinnacles and arêtes. Sombre precipices cast shadows across high cirques. Zugspitz (2,961 metres), the highest mountain in Germany, sits astride the border south-west of Garmisch-Partenkirchen, whose twin villages are a mecca for skiers and skaters during the winter months. This part of Bavaria is very popular in summer so the best cycling is to be had on the narrower, steeper roads.

From just south of Oberammergau (painted houses, woodcarving, Passion Play), a road heads west past Linderhof (one of Mad Ludwig II's extraordinary castles), crosses the border into Austria and joins the main road south of Füssen – a delightfully situated town with a castle. Just east of Füssen is one of Europe's most romantic and photographed castles: Neuschwanstein sits on a bluff, an expression of unrestrained architectural romance with turrets and towers and balconies looking over forest, lake and mountain. At the eastern end of this central portion of the Bavarian Alps is the lake of Chiemsee on which can be found the third of Mad Ludwig's castles. It sits on a low island surrounded by trees, unspectacular in location but huge in scale. Bikes can be carried on the island's ferry.

The third and most eastern part of the Bavarian Alps is the Berchtesgaden area south of Salzburg. It is a popular resort, for here the Dolomitic limestone soars above 2,500 metres to form a rock amphitheatre around the enchanting lake of Königssee. Just east of Berchtesgaden, on Obersalzberg, was Hitler's mountain eyrie, demolished after the war. This is an area which naturally falls in with a visit to nearby Salzburg or a tour of pretty Salzkammergut.

The Deutsche Alpenstrasse runs from Lindau to Königssee, and while it is an indication of where the good scenery can be found, it also attracts the traffic and stays in Germany, whereas the better biking route crosses to Austria. The whole of the Bavarian Alps is excellent for hiking and there are several nature reserves.

North of the Alps proper, the 'Foreland' is an area of woods and rolling countryside, some of it attractive, and centred on the regional capital Munich. The city is within an easy day's riding of the Alps (50 kilometres), and has good air connections with the UK, and rail links to the rest of Germany.

Germany's Highest Road

The highest surfaced road in Germany is the 1,231-metre Feldberg Pass on the route from Titisee to Todtnau in the Black Forest. The summit of the Feldberg (the highest Black Forest peak) can be reached by footpath from the road.

Tour of Southern Germany

A route full of history and atmosphere, which starts in Würzburg and heads south through fairly easy terrain, linking the old towns of Germany's 'Romantic Way' – though on roads far quieter and smaller than those normally used by travellers of this renowned tourist trail. At Nördlingen the route splits, and you can either follow the Romantic Way to its conclusion at 'Mad' Ludwig's Bavarian castles in the Alpine foothills, or turn west and take a more varied course through the Schwäbische Alb, down to the Danube and then over the Black Forest to finish near the Rhine, at Freiburg. Many of the roads used on this tour are tiny; most appropriate for meandering travel and good map-reading! Würzburg, Freiburg and Reutte (south of Füssen) are all on rail lines.

SOUTHERN GERMANY TOUR

Terrain: hilly
Distance: 630 km (Würzburg - Freiburg);
400 km (Würzburg - Füssen)
Start/Finish: Würzburg/Füssen
Scenery: *
Interest: **
Maps: Mair Deutsche Generalkarte,
1:200,000 nos 16, 19, 22, plus nos 21 & 24
for Freiburg option, no 25 for Füssen option

km	WURZBURG
10	Winterhausen
7	Ochsenfurt
8	Hopferstadt
8	Aub
7	Frauental
6	Creglingen
3	Münster
10	Schwarzenbronn
8	Rothenburg
3	Gebsattel
5	Diebach
8	Schillingsfürst
4	Dombühl
5	Archshofen
6	Feuchtwangen
2	Kaltenbronn
4	Larrieden
8	Dinkelsbühl
11	Tannhausen
20	Wallerstein
6	Nördlingen

(see below for route to Füssen)

19	Neresheim
21	Heidenheim
15	Gerstetten
25	Nellingen
10	Laichingen
12	Donnstetten
7	Böhringen
14	Münsingen
7	Buttenhausen
14	Hayingen
7	Zwiefalten
10	Riedlingen
9	Binzwangen
13	Scheer
11	Sigmaringen
20	Hausen
16	Fridingen
8	Bärenthal
10	Egesheim
8	Böttingen
7	Dürbheim
5	Spaichingen
8	Schura
5	Tuningen
14	Donaueschingen
6	Wolterdingen
9	Bregenbach

15	Neustadt	8	Münster
6	Titisee	7	Thierhaupten
24	Todtnau	22	Augsburg
	Schauinsland	15	Gessertshausen
32	FREIBURG	8	Fischach
		12	Konradshaufen
ALTERNATIVE TOUR FROM		15	Ettringen
NORDLINGEN, THROUGH		14	Igling
'ROMANTIC WAY' TOWNS TO		8	Landsberg
FUSSEN		5	Stoffen
	NORDLINGEN	9	Reichling
10	Fessenhelm	8	Denklingen
12	Harburg	17	Burggen
4	Ebermergen	10	Lechbruck
3	Wörnitzstein	16	Buching
6	Donauwörth	8	Schwangau
14	Marzheim	4	Hohenschwangau
8	Rain	4	FUSSEN

Basic Information

Getting There

Air: Germany's international airports are: Berlin, Bremen, Cologne/Bonn, Düsseldorf, Frankfurt, Hamburg, Hanover, Munich, Nuremberg and Stuttgart. Flight time from London to Frankfurt is one hour.

Rail/Ferry: Apart from flying, the quickest way of travelling to northern Germany is by ferry from Harwich to Bremerhaven or Hamburg (17-18 hours). For central and southern Germany, the rail-ferry-rail combination is London - Dover/Folkestone - Ostend - Cologne (connects to all parts of Germany). All of Germany's best cycling areas can be reached by train. Journey time from London to Cologne by ferry and rail is about 15 hours. The north German ports have good ferry links with Norway, Denmark, Finland and Sweden.

Information Sources

German National Tourist Office (GNTO): 61 Conduit Street, London W1R 0EN (tel: 01-734 2600). Handy general planning maps, regional information, calendar of events etc.

Local tourist bureaux: found in or close to the railway station in most towns and resorts, and called *Verkehrsämter.* They open during normal business hours, but in some cities remain open in the evenings and at weekends. For a nominal fee they can make local hotel bookings.

Allgemeiner Deutscher Fahrrad-Club (ADFC), Postfach 107744, 2800 Bremen 1 (tel: 325656). The national organisation striving to improve the lot of the German cyclist by campaigning for better cycle paths and facilities, and publishing the bi-monthly magazine *Radfahren*.

Bund Deutscher Radfahrer, Otto-Fleck-Schneise 4, 6000 Frankfurt am Main 71 (tel: 6309222). The only national cycling organisation to have survived the earlier crises of this century, BDR co-ordinates German cycle-racing.

Tour magazine, Postfach 308, 7410 Reutlingen. Beautifully-presented German monthly magazine covering all aspects of cycling, with regular features on touring in Germany and abroad.

Accommodation

Camping: there are over 2,100 camp sites in Germany, which are normally open from May through till September, most of them concentrated in Bavaria, the Black Forest, Oberpfälzer Wald, Odenwald, the Rhineland and Harz/Weserbergland. Germans are inveterate campers and ramblers, so all outdoor recreation areas are well-supplied with highly organised (maybe a bit *too* organised), tidy, clean sites with comprehensive facilities. In such areas it isn't difficult to reach a camp site every night. In general, they are expensive by European standards; about 400 sites stay open during the winter in skiing regions. The German Camping Club classifies sites according to scenic merit, noise levels, facilities and so on, and lists about 1,600 of them in their official guide (available from German Camping Club, Mandlstrasse 28, D 8000 Munich 23; cost about 16DM). Holders of International Camping Carnets are entitled to a 10% reduction on DCC sites.

Wild camping is feasible in the southern part of the country which is better endowed with forest and hills than the north; permission is required from the landowner or police. Heavy dews and the possibility of overnight rain make sleeping out without a tent a chancy option.

Youth Hostels: Germany, the home of the youth hostel movement, which began here in 1909 as the *Jugendherbergen*, now has more hostels than any other European country. There are about 550 spread fairly evenly, and normally close enough to each other to be within daily biking distance. They are most abundant in the Black Forest and Sauerland, and thinnest on the ground between the River Danube and Bavarian Alps. Priority is given to hostellers under 27 years, and in Bavaria the maximum age limit is 27 (except for leaders of youth groups or families). The only snag with German hostels – which tend to be rigidly organised – is that the 'youths' who use them often take the form of huge and rumbustuous school parties. Unless you have alternative types of accommodation in reserve, it's best to book in advance.

Bed-and-Breakfast: a *Zimmer Frei* sign outside a house indicates the availability of a room for the night.

Inns: small local inns *(Gasthaus* or *Gasthof)* can often be a relaxed, homely and relatively inexpensive overnight option; most touring areas are well-supplied with inns, which have been used by holidaying Germans for decades. Prices are generally lower as you move away from big towns. *Fremdenzimmer* and *Pensionen* are also usually good value for money.

Hotels: expensive, scrupulously clean and neat no matter how big or small; Germany's hotels are categorised into over eighty classes! Quality is indicated from 'I' (luxury) to 'III' (economy), while a letter 'G' indicates only breakfast is served, 'P' indicates meals are served to guests only and 'R' shows that the hotel's restaurant is open to the public. Double rooms work out at less than twice the price of single rooms. GNTO can send a selective hotel guide which gives an idea of prices; the massive (and expensive) official German Hotel Guide is published annually. During festivals, fairs or international exhibitions (of which there are many) it can be impossible to find accommodation for miles around unless previously booked.

Weather

Germany's summer weather is generally agreeable with temperatures averaging a fairly uniform 17-18°C throughout the country, the south being prevented from being markedly warmer than the north because of its overall higher altitude. The warmest spots tend to be the low, sheltered valleys of the south-west.

Rain shows an annoying preference for being most noticeable in the summer, peaking in July, though most lowland towns are no damper than a southern English city. Hilly areas can get twice these amounts, a periodically sodden example being the Black Forest and Bavarian Alps (both getting twice as much rain as London in July), though unlike traditional British drizzle, German rain comes in quick thunderstorms, often with hail.

Winters are mild in the north-west, getting increasingly severe as you move across the Central Uplands towards the Alps, where snow can remain on the ground as late as March.

Prevailing winds tend to be westerly in the north of Germany, while further south the jumble of hills and valleys makes predictions difficult. The south-east, around Regensburg, is known for its calmness.

Other Considerations: the spring-time blossoms of the orchards around the Rhine, Pfalz and Neckar are at their best during April and May, while a tour around the Rhine, Mosel and other wine-producing areas from about the end of September to early October brings the possibility of joining in with local wine festivals, the best of which are the less-commercial ones in small villages (details from GNTO). The

Oktoberfest in Munich – several days of uninterrupted swilling in beer cellars – takes place in late September/early October. The Bavarian winter sports season runs from late December to late March.

Average Daily Maximum Temperatures (Centigrade)

	alt. in metres	J	F	M	A	M	J	J	A	S	O	N	D
Freiburg	259	4	4	11	15	20	22	24	24	21	14	8	5
Kiel	3	2	3	5	11	15	19	22	21	18	13	7	4

Hiking

Being a nation of hikers, Germany has a superb network of way-marked trails, and there are many supporting maps and guides available. Routes are marked by coloured patches and in selected villages there are notice-boards depicting the surrounding trails and the appropriate colour codes and distances. The most popular areas are the Bavarian Alps, Black Forest, Eifel, Odenwald, Spessart, Sauerland and Harz.

Cycling Information

Cycle Shops

The bike is enjoying a real comeback in Germany, and shops (for both spares and repairs) can be found in all towns, and most large villages – though availability of lightweight components is limited to towns which have racing clubs. Until recently, $27 \times 1\frac{1}{4}$ tyres were standard in Germany (and it is still possible to buy them sometimes), but now the German trade has 'gone metric' and the accepted tyres are 32-622 to match 24-622 rims.

Cycle Hire

Back in 1964 Deutsche Bundesbahn (the Federal Railway) made it possible to hire bicycles at eight stations chosen for their attractive surroundings; a Munster cycling club offered to provide machines and keep them in order. Today a modified version of the scheme operates from spring to autumn at 200 stations – all chosen for being close to suitable cycle-touring terrain. The daily charge is reduced by 50% on production of a valid rail ticket to that hire station. Reservations can be made in advance. GNTO can supply a list of the stations.

The German word for cycle-hire is *Fahrradverleih*, companies being listed in the commercial section of telephone directories.

Transporting Your Bicycle

Deutsche Bundesbahn's thorough rail network is one of the best in

Europe, electrified and reaching all the good cycling areas. Carriage of bicycles is limited to those trains which have luggage vans; this excludes InterCity trains and the slow two-carriage local services. (If you need to know which trains have luggage vans before you go abroad, ask at a good travel agent to see the bulky *DB Kursbuch*, which is published twice a year and lists these trains). Under a new scheme, some commuter lines now have special trains made available for cyclists at weekends – space permitting.

If the bike is to be taken on a train as accompanied luggage, you need to buy a *Fahrradkarte* (bicycle ticket) for a flat charge regardless of distance, and you are then responsible for loading and unloading the bike yourself, which includes any transhipment *en route* if you have to change trains. Sent as unaccompanied luggage the charge is higher (but is still a flat rate regardless of distance) and the bike may arrive up to a day later. The useful 'German Federal Railway Planner' (free from GNTO) gives a helpful idea of costs and times of train travel in Germany.

In many places on the large rivers it is possible to cross over by means of an *autofähre* (car ferry) – which will always convey bicycles.

Roads

Per square kilometre Germany has many more roads than does the UK; the home of the *Autobahn* actually has the fourth densest road network in Europe. This, and the fact that Germany has no truly impenetrable areas where nature has successfully thwarted the engineers, means that the country is particularly rich in small rural roads ideal for cycling.

Surfaces are good throughout the country, with northern Germany, the Black Forest, Rhine Valley and Bavaria having slightly better surfaces than elsewhere. Cobbles can still be found in some smaller towns and villages – occasionally left in place deliberately to preserve historic character.

Traffic won't be a nuisance on the small rural roads, because most of Germany's considerable volume of long-distance vehicles stick to the *Autobahn* and *Bundesstrassen* (state or 'B' roads; like British 'A' roads). Weekends during school holidays (July to mid-September) sees traffic peaking in the tourist areas, and some become completely spoilt by day-trippers. Very sensibly, the German government has banned all lorries from the roads at weekends during July and August, and over public holidays. As a whole, Germany has about the same amount of traffic as the UK; generally there is a lull between noon and 2pm while holiday-makers pause for lunch – so if you want to ride a particularly scenic stretch of road free of the stench of exhaust, try eating early or late.

Sign-posting is good, but tends to be haphazard in towns.

Germany's pressure group, ADFC, has a daunting task in trying to improve cycle paths. Towns often have cycle-paths extending through the suburbs, and paths will sometimes run adjacent to busy roads for many kilometres; but their surfaces can sometimes be in poor condition or strewn with debris. Use of them is compulsory. In places, instead of a segregated path, a white line is painted on the road to separate cyclists from other traffic – watch out for parked cars on these. Another thing to watch for is the paths which force you to cycle 'against' the flow of traffic; when the path ends you have to be careful as you re-cross the road to regain your rightful side.

Unless they are indicated as being private or are obviously for pedestrians only, you can generally cycle on rough tracks or paths.

Germans drive fast and aggressively, and pedalling peacefully down a seemingly quiet byway, a Mercedes hurtling past at six times your speed has about the same effect as Concorde flying through the rigging of your hang-glider. Riding two-abreast on main roads is frowned upon and could mean an on-the-spot fine.

Bringing order to otherwise unruly motor-hordes the Germans delight in designating tourist *Strassen* which link together many kilometres (sometimes hundreds) of scenic highways. Thus we have Swäbische Weinstrasse, Harz-Heide-Strasse, the Bergische Route, famous Romantische Strasse and many others. Unless you don't mind the heavy traffic, keep clear (or ride parallel routes) of all but the most enticing parts during the tourist season.

Some towns are known by an Anglicized name, such as Braunschweig (Brunswick), Köln (Cologne), München (Munich) and Nürnberg (Nuremberg). German maps (including those free ones from GNTO) use the German spellings.

Organised Cycling Holidays

A number of regional tourist offices in Germany organise cycling holidays – an address list of these offices can be obtained from GNTO.

Maps

For General Planning

Michelin No. 987, Benelux-Germany-Austria, Scale 1:1,000,000. Very small-scale encompassing six countries and a useful map for planning a long tour.

Philips International No. 3, Germany, Scale 1:1,000,000. Really a motoring map, but clearly marks all the national parks in Germany.

RV (Reise-und Verkehrsverlag), Germany, Scale 1:800,000. Embracing both West and East Germany with good detail and helpful height shading. It's a good indicator of where not to cycle since it marks recommended tourist roads. Also shown are useful things like view points, interesting towns, a few campsites etc.

For Cycling

Mair, Deutsche Generalkarte series, Scale 1:200,000. Covering West Germany in 25 sheets these are the standard cycling map, being an easily manageable size, printed on strong paper and excellently detailed, with height shading, gradient arrows, major footpaths and tracks, a myriad of tourist information and a key in English; tourist itineraries and town-maps on the reverse side. Like the Michelin 1:200,000 series, these become expensive if you're cycling long distances in straight lines (each covers an area about 80 x 160 kilometres) – at the time of going to press, Mair maps cost three times as much as the Michelin of the same scale.

Michelin Nos 202, 203, 204, 205, 206, Scale 1:200,000. Less detailed, less up-to-date and less expensive than the Mairs, covering a strip down the western border of Germany (including the Black Forest). Identical in format to the French series.

For Rough-stuff and Hiking

RV, Schwarzwald Nordblatt, Mittelblatt, Südblatt, Scale 1:75,000. Three beautiful maps, invaluable if you're planning to explore the Black Forest in detail, and covering the entire area between Pforzheim and Basel in the three sheets. Contours, shading, footpaths, tracks, 'wood-and field-ways suitable for cycling', waymarked trails (together with their colour symbols), hostels, camp sites and much else besides.

Landes-Topographische Karte series, Scale 1:50,000. The same scale as the British Ordnance Survey series, but the sheets are smaller and more manageable. Covers the whole of Germany, with contours, height shading, way-marked paths and much incidental detail.

Kompass Wanderkarten series, Scale 1:50,000. Detailed maps covering selected parts of Bavaria, the Black Forest and south-east Germany, aimed at tourists.

SWITZERLAND

Sitting in the centre of the continent, with an overall altitude head and shoulders above any other European country, landlocked Switzerland has more than its fair share of spectacular scenery. And while it has neither the highest mountain nor highest road in Europe, it does have an unparalleled concentration of peaks and high passes. For the col-climbing cyclist the Swiss Alps are one of the ultimate challenges, yet the remaining two-fifths of the country are far from dull: the Jura have a relatively untouched highland serenity which surprises most visitors while further south there are historic cities and Switzerland's own Lake District. It's a country for the fit rider, for there are few areas where roads are level; the higher you ride the grander the views so to make the most of this country you need to enjoy the hills – or at least not hate them!

By a curious coincidence, Europe's highest country is virtually the same size as its lowest: the Netherlands. But there the similarities end, for some 20% of Switzerland is covered by mountain, snow or ice, and lakes, and another 25% by forest. Unlike the Dutch, who are spread thickly across the whole of their country, most Swiss are jammed into the restricted central belt.

Aside from their image of making watches, yodelling from flower-decked hillsides, supping fondue and knocking back kirsch, the Swiss are unbelievably clean, and much of the countryside has an almost clinical quality, with swept roads fringed by tidy fences, close cropped grass and pristine hillsides. The still waters, frosted peaks and sparklingly clear air help create an atmosphere of health and vitality. A national characteristic is the ability to turn seemingly desolate territory into profitable enterprise. Massive HEP schemes, ambitious road and rail tunnels, improbable bridges, the serpentine passes, hotels on mountain ledges, and a unique knack for marketing tourist attractions, are all making or saving Swiss cash. It's the only country in the world where the most uncomfortable aspect of mountaineering is having to travel in a cable-car full of tourists.

Slightly more than half the nation is Protestant, most of the remainder being Roman Catholic, and no fewer than four languages are spoken: German in the centre and north-east, French in the west, Italian in the south and the old Swiss tongue, Romansch, in the far east. Most Swiss are bilingual and a great many speak English so sign language is redundant! The French and Italian speakers are rather less formal than those who speak German. A neutral country, Switzerland is a democratic republic, divided into 25 administrative *cantons.*

The Swiss *franc* (Sfr) is divided into one hundred *centimes* and has the enviable reputation of being a 'strong' currency, which is good news for the Swiss when *they* travel but not nice for the rest of us when we visit their country and have to pay their prices – Switzerland is expensive. Camping or youth hostelling, biking off the tourist track and shopping in Migros supermarkets (signed by a large orange 'M' and often having lower cost self-service meals) are ways of preserving cash. Restaurants are expensive, but generally of a very high standard indeed, with regional food specialities corresponding partly with the four linguistic areas. Hot food is normally served at limited hours only. Inns and bars are plentiful, and a popular evening rendezvous. It is illegal to drink standing up, so wait at a table rather than at the bar to be served.

The Swiss are ardently law-abiding and nowhere more so than on the road, so in the land where even the bicycles have number plates, be sure to use the bicycle lanes where they exist, and do not ride on prohibited roads or tussle with trams.

Ride Guide

The Jura

Wriggling untidily through this long thin range of upland is the

French/Swiss border, but for the sake of neatness we are going to treat the entire Jura as being Swiss (the French, after all, have more than enough hills of their own already).

The Jura mountains occupy a gentle diagonal crescent some 240 kilometres long and 80 wide, curving around the northern shores of Lakes Geneva and Neuchâtel. They are an unusual and rewarding bike touring area, less developed than the Alps, and less polluted by the attentions of motorists who – fortunately for the Jura – tend to gravitate towards the glamour and glaciers next door.

The hills are arranged into a series of parallel ridges which are at their highest looking out across the plateau of Mittelland, getting lower as the ripples move out towards France to eventually peter out in the plain of the Saône. The Crêt de la Neige (1,700 metres), just above Geneva, is the highest point in the Jura. The south-eastern slopes (facing Switzerland) are much steeper than those facing France, which sometimes form gently-sloping plateaux rather than distinct valleys. In places these long folds of limestone have been eroded to form a sharp ridge *(crête)* or been split at right angles to create a steep-sided valley *(cluse)* or gorge. Relatively few people dwell in the Jura, but there are plenty of cows and even more trees. Gruyère cheese is made at Dôle and Pontarlier and lumbering is important. Forests of spruce, larch and fir spread across the steep hillsides while much of the flatter plateau areas are covered with well-tended fields of grass.

Needless to say, riding 'with the grain' of the Jura is much easier than riding against it. The long valleys and broad plateaux provide fairly level cycling, and once up, the superb ridge-top roads often stay high and level for miles on end. A ride from one end of the Jura to the other, following the higher ridges and deeper gorges is hard to beat. Waterfalls and small lakes contribute to the interest, and the whole Jura is laced with tiny, quiet, roads. Off the bike, the forests are full of trails (it's a popular cross-country skiing area in winter) and there is plenty of scope for hiking.

To watch at dawn from the high crest of the Jura above Lake Geneva, as the sun edges over the horizon to throw light across the magnificent spread of the Alps ranged as far as the eye can see is a spectacle – and a treat – worth pedalling for.

Mittelland

Between the Jura and the Alps and stretching from Lake Geneva to Lake Constance is an area of lower undulating country: the Mittelland or Central Plateau. With many lakes and an abundance of small villages this can be a pleasant – though still fairly strenuous – alternative to the more spectacular adjacent uplands. It is crossed by a great many main

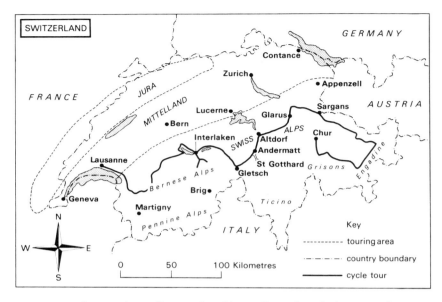

roads, too busy for comfortable cycling, though between these are numerous small back roads.

Mittelland has one of the world's highest population densities, and includes historic Berne (the federal capital), Zurich (Switzerland's largest city) and Lucerne with its medieval atmosphere. Thuner See and Brienzer See by Interlaken, and the clutch of lakes just east of Lucerne, are attractively set against mountain backdrops, though only a few of their popular shoreline roads are quiet enough for pleasant cycling.

The Swiss Alps

Despite their picture-postcard image of glittering ice, broad snowy sweeps and roaring rivers, the most famous range of mountains in the world are surprisingly green. Typically, an Alpine valley has an intensively farmed floor, then coniferous forests on the lower slopes, grassy pastures above that, then summits of rock, snow and ice. The Swiss Alps are also a highly developed playground; for skiers and skaters in the winter and for mountaineers, sightseers, hikers – and cyclists of course – in the summer. So peaceful cycling has to be sought with a mix of travellers' cunning and perceptive map-reading. The O.C.D. pass guides are helpful planning aids with sketch maps and details of most cols over 1000 metres.

On the school atlas the heavy brown band separating Switzerland from Italy always looks an impenetrable mountain barrier, but since the earliest times the Alps have been a vital routeway, though nowadays it is motor vehicles not pack animals which are funnelled down the deep valleys. The busiest roads are those of the great transverse route along the Rhône valley over the Furka and Oberalp passes and along the Rhine valley, and the four routes leading south from this: from Martigny over the Great St Bernard pass to Aosta, from Brig over the Simplon to Domodossola, from Andermatt over the St Gotthard to Bellinzona and from Chur over the San Bernardino to Bellinzona.

Try to avoid these routes altogether, or tackle them early in the morning or during the lunch period when traffic will be lighter.

Much of the natural splendour of these busy passes has been lost forever by new motorways which slice up the slopes – though at least these do take the pressure off adjacent routes. Riding over the legendary St Gotthard, once a tortuous snake of lumpy cobbles, is nowadays like pedalling over the English Pennines on the M62.

The art of Alpine biking is to pick the passes which are most inconvenient to cars; those that are narrow, violently hairpinned with indifferent surfaces and no guard rails are good bets. Much of the fun lies in taking *culs-de-sac* up deserted mountain valleys – often these smaller roads are uncluttered by traffic and will lead you to quieter parts not found on through-routes. As in most mountain regions, your mobility increases vastly if you enjoy a spot of hiking.

The Swiss Alps can be split into two parts at the point in the middle where they are pinched narrow by the St Gotthard pass. The western half has some of the most notorious, highest peaks in the Alps, among them the Jungfrau, Eiger, Matterhorn and Monte Rosa, at 4,634 metres Switzerland's loftiest mountain and the second highest in Europe. These spiny summits soar out of two enormous massifs: the Bernese Alps (or Oberland) to the north of the Rhône valley and the Pennine Alps (Valais) to the south, bordering the Italian frontier. While both are mountaineering areas *par excellence* they do pose real problems for the biker. There are simply very few roads hereabouts – in fact the Bernese Alps stretch for some 100 kilometres with no road crossing their high snowy cols.

So both to the north and south of the Rhone, the best cycling routes are up the dead-end valleys. A classic ride is to turn off the Brig-Sion road at Visp and pedal southwards up the Mattertal valley to Zermatt where you can leave the bike and walk up to the Gornergrat viewpoint (3131 metres) to gasp at the Matterhorn, Monte Rosa and assorted glaciers. And Interlaken, further north, is the kicking off point for another spectacular detour, up the sheer sided valley to Lauterbrunnen, then down and up to Grindelwald with its many views of the Eiger, Mönch and Jungfrau (try the expensive but astonishing train ride inside the mountain, up to Jungfraujoch). Zermatt and Grindelwald are both very popular motoring excursions, but there are plenty of lesser known detours to make.

Between the bulk of the Bernese Alps and the lower plateau of Mittelland is a 'foreland' of mountainous country, not as wildly impressive as the peaks to the south but nevertheless very attractive. Tiny roads thread along wooded slopes, often climbing steeply to passes like the Jaun (1509 metres). Closer to Bern the roads become denser.

East of the St Gotthard, the Swiss Alps broaden out and are cut through by far more roads than in the west and so the options for biking are much greater. Here it is possible to link pass after pass with no need to retrace, especially if you take the odd loop into Italy. Here too are some of the narrower quieter passes like the Albula and Klausen. The glaciated skylines of the Grisons and Glarus Alps are magnificent, and further south-east the lovely valleys of the Engadine are warmer and drier than most of Switzerland, and occupied by ski resort towns like St Moritz and Pontresina.

North of the Alps proper, and just south of Lake Constance, is the Appenzell district, well supplied with scenic, steeply graded roads, green pastures and pretty villages, and topped by the 2,502 metre Santis, by the Chräzeren Pass.

Pass Words

Swooping down the curling tarmac ribbon of an Alpine pass, a patchwork of grassy pastures below, glaciers at your elbow, the wind in your hair and not a pedal to turn for twenty kilometres, is one of the great 'highs' of continental cycling. Hairpin after hairpin is turned, as the road feels its way downward, and steeply cambered corners hang out over thin air with nothing but a row of stumpy granite pillars between you and eternity.

Like a skier spying a route down the *piste* you are always concentrating on the turn ahead; calculating how sharp it is and how much to slow down; keeping an eye on the car grinding up below you, judging it so you don't meet him on the corner; braking surely, picking a precise track into the bend, checking you're going slow enough to finish the bend (it's aways the last part of a hairpin that causes the scare); watching for that lethal patch of slippery gravel or water, then swinging upright into the straight as with an energy of its own the bike surges forward and you release the brakes.

A mountain pass, a bicycle and speed are an intoxicating cocktail, best sipped not gulped. Left to its own devices a bicycle can freewheel at 80 kph, yet the safe speed for negotiating a tight Alpine hairpin may be as slow as 10 kph. Always keep a check on your speed – as Hannibal said when one of his elephants overshot a hairpin: 'At least he won't do *that* again!' So don't go too fast because cyclists, like elephants, don't get a second chance to misjudge a hairpin bend.

Pass riding can be made infinitely more enjoyable if you are able to leave your luggage behind for the day. There is an exhilarating difference between dragging a pile of panniers up a pass, and pedalling unencumbered, light and free. The bike responds to effort, and there is an energising simplicity about biking un-burdened in the mountains – together you're an economical, highly mobile partnership. It's also true to say that the fitter you are the more enjoyable you will find pass riding.

But pedalling a bicycle up an Alpine pass is not half as hard as it sounds. Like the man who refused to cross the river at its widest point because it looked so big, not realising the widest point is also the most shallow, the Alps are wrongly regarded as being one of the toughest cycling areas in Europe. I've always found a day of pedalling up and down the short sharp hills of Devon far harder work than a day easing myself over an Alp. It is all a matter of rhythm and gearing (see pages 36-7).

Measure the distance from your starting point to the top of the pass, so that you know roughly the scale of your goal – on the big passes you can expect up to forty kilometres of continuous uphill, so it is worth spending the previous night close to the start of the climb. Have a hearty breakfast and keep topped up with food and drink during the ride. Be sure to take your time over the opening kilometres and ignore the temptation to set off with an expensive burst of early-morning exuberance which may later leave you rubber-legged with 28 hairpins to go to the top. The astonishment of passing motorists is always a morale booster, and encouraging yells from car windows help eat the metres – I've had bags of sweets handed me by benevolent motorists as they drive by.

When continental racing cyclists struggle over a snowy summit soaked in sweat they often stuff newspapers up the front of their jerseys to ward off the chill of the impending downhill plunge. After stopping to admire the view and so on, it's even more important to wrap up warm for the descent – a windproof top layer being the best defence.

One pass per day will probably be enough for most people, allowing time for a leisurely ascent with numerous pauses to absorb the changing panorama, eat things, and then go off for a wander at the summit before freewheeling down the other side. But as any member of the infamous *L'Ordre des Cols Durs* will tell you, it's feasible (if fit) to tackle several passes in one day. I read recently of one OCD member who set off from Andermatt before dawn, and during the following 18 hours pedalled over the Furka, Grimsel, Susten, Gotthard, Nufenen and Furka (again) – a total of some 235 kilometres and 6,400 metres of climbing!

Alpine Rough-stuff

For intrepid cyclists only, the ancient high-level tracks can act as useful links between valleys which otherwise could only be joined by biking long detours. These tracks are usually intended for walkers, are very rough going and often involve carrying the bike in places. It would be foolish to try one of these crossings without a large scale map, adequate clothing and food and a tent if there is a possibility of being out overnight.

Examples are: the difficult Gemmi Pass (2,314 metres) with its outstanding views which links Kandersteg and Leukerbad and provides a rare crossing right through the centre of the Bernese Alps; the Col du Sanetsch (2,243 metres) 10 kilometres south of Gstaad, links Gsteig with Sion, across the western end of the Bernese Alps; and the track from Grindelwald (east of Interlaken) by Grosse Scheidegg (1,962 metres) into the Rosenlauital valley which can be used to create a round-trip of this spectacular corner of Alps. There are many, many, more of these rough passes, a large number of them catalogued in the pass directories of OCD; for further information, enthusiasts should join that organisation (address on page 302).

Swiss Pass Guide

Pass (height in metres)	Location	Comments
Albula (2,315)	Tiefencastel – La Punt	narrow and quiet, great views and beautiful scenery. Open: June – Oct.
Bernina (2,323)	Pontresina – Tirano	narrow, winding and very picturesque, Chünetta viewpoint just south of Pontresina gives famous views of Pic Bernina and glacier. Open: all year.
Brünig (1,007)	Meiringen – Sarnen	has a rock overhang claimed to be the biggest over a European main road. Open: all year.
Champex (1,465)	Martigny – Orsières	a strenuous detour which can be used to avoid the north part of the busy St Bernard. Open: all year.
Croix (1,732)	Les Diablerets – Villars	narrow, picturesque. Open: June-Oct.

Flüela (2,383)	Davos – Susch	quite picturesque, with a desolate summit area. Open: June-Oct, Dec-May.
Forclaz (1,526)	Martigny – Chamonix	narrow in parts, picturesque. Open: all year.
Furka (2,431)	Andermatt – Gletsch	heavy traffic but one of the most picturesque passes with many hairpins and views of the Rhône glacier. Open: mid June – mid Oct.
Givrine (1,232)	Nyon-Les Rousses	pleasant views, wooded, Open: end Apr-Oct.
Great St Bernard (2,469)	Martigny – Aosta (Italy)	used since Celtic times but spoilt now by heavy traffic except for sections of old road over summit and on south side. Open: mid June – mid Oct.
Grimsel (2,165)	Gletsch – Innertkirchen	heavy traffic but picturesque with good views from the top and many hairpins. Open: mid June – mid Oct.
Jaun (1,509)	Bulle – Spiez	narrow and very attractive with light traffic. Open: all year.
Julier (2,284)	Tiefencastel – Silvaplana	used by the Romans, with beautiful scenery and views over the Upper Engadine. Open: all year.
Klausen (1,948)	Glarus – Altdorf	narrow, excellent scenery. Open: mid June – mid Oct.
Lenzerheide (1,549)	Chur – Tiefencastel	picturesque. Open: all year.
Lukmanier (1,916)	Disentis – Biasca	narrow, picturesque on south, gorges on north. Open: May – end Oct.

Maloja (1,815)	Silvaplana – Chiavenna (Italy)	wooded, very attractive with good views. Open: all year.
Marchairuz (1,447)	Le Brassus – Bière (Jura)	narrow, fine view of Lac de Joux. Open: end Apr – Oct.
Mosses (1,445)	Aigle – Saanen	picturesque. Open: all year.
Nufenen (2,478)	Ulrichen – Airolo	highest pass fully in Switzerland with magnificent mountain scenery and summit views. Open: mid June – end Sept.
Oberalp (2,044)	Andermatt – Disentis	quite heavy traffic, but wild and picturesque, with hairpins. Open: June – mid Oct.
Ofen (2,149)	Zernez – Santa Maria	picturesque, passes through national park. Open: all year.
Pillon (1,546)	Aigle – Gstaad	narrow, picturesque. Open: all year.
San Bernardino (2,065)	Chur – Bellinzona	except for 15 km of scenic hairpins over the summit, the old road shares its approach valleys with a new motorway. Open: June – mid Oct.
Simplon (2,005)	Brig – Domodossola (Italy)	quite heavy traffic, good views from the top. Open: all year.
Splügen(2,113)	Splügen – Chiavenna (Italy)	moderate traffic, narrow and picturesque. Open: May – mid Oct.
St. Gotthard (2,108)	Andermatt – Airolo	hardly worth the effort though sections of old road relieve the tedium, very heavy traffic. Open: May – mid Oct.
Susten (2,259)	Innertkirchen – Wassen	heavy traffic, but scenic, with many hairpins on west. Open: mid June – Oct.

| Umbrail (2,501) | Santa Maria – Bormio (Italy) | higher than the Nufenen but shared with Italy, heavy traffic, hairpinned. Open: June – mid Oct. |

Note: the 'opening' and 'closing' dates of passes can vary by as much as a month on the higher, lesser-used passes and by about 20 days on the major routes. Cyclists are banned from using the tunnels under the St Gotthard, Great St Bernard and San Bernardino passes.

Tour of the Swiss Alps

Definitely not for the faint of heart or leg, this mountain tour takes in eight major passes, with an optional detour of Italy's Stelvio national park which pushes the pass total up to fourteen. To loosen the legs the tour starts with a mild ride along the shore of Lake Geneva and a short foray into the Vaudois Alps; from then on the lakes, hairpins, glaciers, waterfalls and majestic peaks are regular companions as the route wends its way through the Bernese Oberland, Grisons and Engadine in a journey from virtually one end of the country to the other. There are many possibilities for shortening the route by using trains and options for adding to its length by making rides up side valleys. Using Switzerland's exciting rough-stuff passes would add yet another dimension. The start/finish towns are both on major European rail lines.

SWISS ALPS TOUR

Terrain: mountainous
Distance: 730 km
Start/Finish: Lausanne/Chur
Scenery: **
Interest: *
Maps: Michelin 1:200,000 nos 21, 23, 24

---

km	LAUSANNE
25	Montreux
15	Aigle
4	Ollon
9	Villars
	Col de la Croix
17	Les Diablerets
	Col du Pillon
21	Gstaad
3	Saanen
14	Zweisimmen
41	Thun
5	Oberhofen
3	Gunten

(alternative high-level route via Sigriswill and Beatenberg to Interlaken)

15	Interlaken
8	Gündlischwand
4	Lauterbrunnen
6	Stechelberg
10	Gündlischwand
12	Grindelwald
20	Interlaken
16	Brienz
17	Meiringen
6	Innertkirchen

(short cut via Susten Pass rejoins route at Wassen)

	Grimsel Pass
31	Gletsch
	Furka Pass
32	Andermatt

(short cut via Oberalp Pass to Chur and Landquart, which avoids Klausen Pass loop)

| 11 | Wassen |

26	Altdorf		Flüela Pass
	Klausen Pass	34	Zernez
64	Glarus		

(optional detour through Appenzell district, N via Schänis, Kaltbrunn, Wattwil, Krummenau, Chräzeren Pass, Appenzell, Altstätten, Oberriet, Gams, rejoins route at Sargans: 140 km)

(detour into Italian Alps via Ofen Pass, Sluderno, Spondigna, Stélvio Pass, Bormio, Foscagno Pass, D'Eira Pass, Livigno, Livigno Pass, Bernina Pass, Pontresina, [St Moritz], to rejoin route at La Punt-Chamues-Ch.: 200 km)

7	Mollis	20	La Punt-Chamues-Ch.
26	Walenstadt		Albula Pass
14	Sargans	40	Tiefencastel
7	Bad Ragaz		Lenzerheide Pass
6	Landquart	28	Chur
32	Klosters	31	Arosa
11	Davos	31	CHUR

Basic Information

Getting There

Air: Zurich, Geneva and Basle are one and a half hours from London, and Berne is two and a quarter hours.

Rail: The Clapham Junction of Europe, Switzerland is the focus of rail links to most corners of the continent. London to Lucerne (changing at Basle) for example, takes just under 18 hours.

Road: Calais to Lausanne by main road is about 700 kilometres.

Information Sources

Swiss National Tourist Office (SNTO): Swiss Centre, 1 New Coventry Street, London W1V 8EE (tel: 01-734-1921). Free information includes events calendar and useful maps. They also sell several publications, including maps (eg Swiss Ordnance Survey) and touring guides.

Local tourist bureaux: all resorts and large towns have tourist offices, variously titled according to area as: *Office de Tourisme* (French), *Verkehrsverein or Verkehrsbüro* (German), *Ente Turistico* (Italian). These can often be found at railway stations too, and are notable for the good quality maps they offer. Most can supply information of local walking trails.

Schweizerischer Radfahrer-und Motorfahrer-Bund, Schaffhausenstrasse 272, 8023 Zurich (tel: 469220.21). Affiliated to AIT and catering primarily for German speaking Swiss, and for cyclists.

Touring Club Suisse: Section Cyclotourisme, 9 rue Pierre-Fatio, 1200 – Geneva (tel: 366000). Affiliated to the AIT and the organisers of cycle-tours in various parts of the country, TCS has created several

'Cycling Centres' from which bikes can be hired and ridden out along signed cycle routes ranging in length from 15 to 80 kilometres. CTC members can join TCS *brevets* such as the annual 200 kilometre ride from Brunnen (souvenir badge presented to all who complete the distance in under 16 hours). TCS are unique in that they offer their members a special service should they be injured in an accident, covering the cost of airlifting the cyclist to hospital and paying for the transport of the bike home. The same service also applies to breakdowns, illness or theft.

Union Cycliste Suisse: 4 rue du Vieux-Collège, 1121 Geneva 3 (tel: 215206). Catering mainly for the French-speaking racing fraternity of Switzerland, but also the organisers of *randonnées*. UCS publish a small booklet, 'Randonnées à Vélo en Suisse Romande' which includes routes (with pass profiles) of several 'permanent' *randonnées* which can be ridden individually, and of *brevets*, ridden on a specific day with other cyclists.

Accommodation

Camping: With only about 450 camp sites throughout the country, some areas like the Jura and Grisons are sparsely served while in others like the Rhône Valley, Ticino and around Lucerne there seems to be a site every few kilometres. Facilities are generally very good, with most sites having food available and many with swimming facilities. Reductions in fees are sometimes available for holders of AIT cards.

Detailed camping guides can be bought from the SNTO and local tourist offices; the SNTO also publish a free list of sites.

'Wild' camping is permitted (ask at nearest farm, cafe, restaurant etc) so long as it occurs on uncultivated land – and since nearly half of Switzerland is in this state the scope is considerable. Lower, flatter land is invariably cultivated so the better opportunities exist at higher levels. Since it can get cold and windy, even in summer, you do need a tent if sleeping rough.

Youth Hostels: There are about a hundred youth hostels in Switzerland, and though they do tend to cluster in certain areas, on the whole it is possible to use them exclusively for a bike tour. There are plenty in the Bernese Alps, Grisons, and Pennine Alps, and in Mittelland. Ticino has few. Advance booking directly with the hostel is usually necessary during February, July and August, and during all national holidays. Priority is given to those under twenty-five, though older people will not be turned away provided there is space. In some Swiss hostels you sleep eight or ten abreast, along a kind of shelf, which can create interesting 'knock-on' effects if one of your neighbours is overly mobile.

Bed and Breakfast: Between the close contact of hostels and expense of hotels is the friendliness of staying overnight in a private home. Rooms are usually advertised by a sign in front of the house: *Zimmer/Chambres.*

Hotels: The Swiss have a reputation for running some of the best (and most expensive) hotels in the world, and with so much of the country devoted to tourism it's hardly surprising that hotels can be found virtually everywhere. The SNTO provides an annually revised list of some 2,700 hotels which belong to the Swiss Hotel Association. They have a grading from one star (simple) to five star (luxury).

Weather

For such a small country, Switzerland has a dramatic range of climatic conditions, and factors like altitude, exposure to sun and local winds all play a part in deciding whether you will be riding in shorts or 'longs'.

Summer weather is best described as warmish and variable. The warmest two months are July and August; if you look at the figures for the top of the St Gotthard pass you will see how much cooler it is likely to be when riding over the high passes. The least cloudy month is July.

Rainfall figures for Lucerne – one of the country's dampest towns – show the city is nearly three times as wet as London during July (the wettest month of the year), though rainfall in Switzerland does tend to deluge then depart fairly promptly, rather than hang around in a half-hearted fashion for days on end. In the southern parts of the Alps the climate becomes more Mediterranean, with Valais, Ticino and the Engadine being warmer and drier than elsewhere.

In winter and spring a vicious north-easterly, known as the *bise,* sometimes springs up, powering straight down from the polar ice cap and scourging the valleys. Warmer, and generally disliked by the Swiss, who claim it causes depression, another wind, the *föhn,* periodically heaves over the southern Alps from Italy, shedding torrents of water before compressing down into valleys like the upper Rhine, Reuss and upper Aare then bowling along at gale force getting hotter and drier as it moves north.

There are right and wrong ways of dealing with an unexpected *föhn,* and it is best to think twice before cycling into the teeth of one: pedalling south from Zug to Schwyz one August, we had been whiling away the kilometres by moaning at the thick grey clouds which seemed to be slowly sinking into the valleys and blotting out all view and light. By Brunnen a premature dusk had darkened the afternoon, a breeze stiffened, a few spots of rain fell, but we rode on, imagining it would blow over.

What we did not know then, is that the Reuss valley, into which we were pedalling, is one of the giant funnels into which the *föhn* plunges having careered over the Alpine ramparts around St. Gotthard. In the space of a couple of kilometres the wind accelerated, the clouds shrugged themselves free of their heavy burden, and we were riding in a maelstrom of lashing rain and howling wind. The suddenness was unnerving, and our first thought was to shelter till it passed over. Under a bridge in the gathering gloom, sharing chocolate with a Swiss and Irish hitch-hiker, we watched while the downpour increased its intensity and the spray from raindrops exploded on the tarmac in front of us.

As it grew dark, it became obvious the storm wasn't going to let up. Only 14 kilometres up the road was Bürglen youth hostel, close enough, so it seemed, to make a dash. No other traffic was on the road as we rode out and followed the eastern shore of Urner See, as it twisted and turned beneath the steep flank of Rotstock. Capes flying wildly about our shoulders, bodies hunched over the handlebars, eyes slit against the hammering rain we trod the pedals down that avenue of water, the bikes sheering this way and that as they caught blasts of wind deflected off the woodland and rocks.

My front light was useless, its puny beam beaten out of existence by rods of water; the only way I could keep on the road was by riding along the dotted white line in the centre. Ahead I could just make out the red light of Doug's bike, bobbing like a beacon in the dark, beckoning me on towards the sanctuary of Altdorf. When that light went away, and the thunder started to crash, things for a moment seemed desperate. Even the white line got harder to see, despite the flashes of lightning. With nothing to look at and no one to speak to, time and space lost their dimensions and with each shot of lightning and crack from the clouds I caught another euphoric charge; awe turned to exhilaration. I remember whooping and screaming at the gale as wildly as the wind which snatched the sounds away.

Whether that was the dreaded föhn or not, I'll never know, but I do know that as we biked south the rain never stopped till in Ticino we were driven from the bikes for a couple of days. Statistics show that in Altdorf the *föhn* is only meant to blow for two days a month in July and August, peaking at 6 days a month during March, April and May and slightly less in October and November. So its reputation is rather greater than its regularity.

A daily weather report can be obtained by dialling 162 on the telephone. Reports are also posted in main railway stations and important post offices.

Other considerations: The summer tourist season stretches all the way from May through till September, with July and August being very busy and early August the peak when many roads are disgustingly congested. Most passes are open between mid June and mid October, and the winter sports season lasts from December to April. The slopes are at their most colourful from May to July, when a sprinkling of wild flowers – among them narcissi, campanula and balsam – dots the hillsides. Rivers like the Rhine and Aare look their best, in full spate, during the summer, and the permanent snowline is about 3,000 metres. June is an interesting month for bike touring, before the bulk of the tourists arrives, while the snows are still impressive and the flowers fresh – though there is a risk of some of the higher passes still being blocked. September is about as warm as June, and all the passes should be open.

Average Daily Maximum Temperatures (Centigrade)

	alt. in metres	J	F	M	A	M	J	J	A	S	O	N	D
Geneva	405	4	5	10	15	19	23	25	24	20	14	8	4
Santis	2,500	-7	-7	-4	-2	3	6	8	8	6	1	-3	-6

Hiking

The Swiss claim to have nearly 50,000 kilometres of marked hiking trails, and the country is undoubtedly one of the best for walking trips.

Cycling Information

Cycle Shops

Cycling is enjoying a real comeback in Switzerland and this is reflected in the number of bike shops. Nearly all are concentrated in the towns of Mittelland; once you get into the Alps and Jura they are few and far between. In any case, it is prudent to make sure your bike is in tip-top condition before venturing into these mountains as they are simply not the place to discover your tyres are thin or brake blocks worn away! Racing is popular, so many of the shops have a good stock of lightweight components. Metric tyres and rims are the standard, so spare 27-inch equipment is not available.

Cycle Hire

If you are happy sticking to the valleys, the three-speed bikes available at some 630 Swiss railway stations are sufficient. There are over a thousand such stations that hire bikes throughout the country, with charges scaled so that the rate per hour drops the longer you hire the machine. There are reductions for holders of valid railway tickets. All stations of the Federal Swiss Railways accept reservations for bikes, and advance reservation is recommended. The bike can be left at any railway station and no charge is made for its return to the place of hire. Some privately owned railway companies also hire out bikes.

Transporting your Bicycle

Wholly electrified and very punctual, Switzerland's rail network is enviably efficient with lines not only covering the populous centre part of the country, but poking deep into the Alps and Jura themselves; any of these are spectacular feats of engineering. Most internal trains (but not Intercity) will convey bikes. For transport as accompanied luggage you should register the bike at least 30 minutes before the train leaves and there is a flat charge payable regardless of distance. The bike is usually loaded by station staff. For transport as unaccompanied luggage the charges are higher (about treble the accompanied charge) but still a flat rate regardless of distance. Bikes can be garaged as 'left luggage' at railway stations, for a daily charge. It is also possible to take a bicycle on the yellow coaches run by the Swiss Post Office (PTT) provided they have space. These operate in areas trains cannot reach, with services over the major passes. Tickets should be bought in the post office of departure as well in advance as possible.

The official Swiss summer and winter timetables, containing full details of services and fares of railways, postal coaches and lake boats, can be bought from the SNTO or any Swiss railway station. A wide selection of cheap deals are offered – details from SNTO.

Roads

Surfaces are generally very good, even on the small back roads, but they tend to deteriorate near the tops of the higher, lesser used passes where winter ice damage has not been repaired. Some mountain roads have gravel surfaces. Signs at the bottom of a pass indicate whether it is clear or blocked by snow, and information concerning road conditions, traffic and which passes are open, can be obtained by dialling 163 on the telephone.

Traffic on main roads, particularly through routes to other countries, is heavy during summer, though with nearly a thousand kilometres of motorway, there are now some quite lengthy sections of ridable old road. In places there are cycle tracks beside busy roads, and these should be used where they occur. Signposting is excellent.

A couple of hazards peculiar to Switzerland are the tunnels, where you should ride with both front and rear lights on, and the yellow post coaches which have priority over all other vehicles. On alpine roads this means they use as much of the tarmac as they like so be prepared when you hear their distinctive three-tone horns – the first three notes from the overture to 'William Tell'!

Organised Cycling Holidays

The SNTO publish a booklet containing details of group and accompanied cycling holidays, which normally include the use of the cycle and sometimes accommodation too.

Maps

For General Planning

Michelin No. 427, Schweiz, Scale 1:400,000. Inexpensive with rough attempt at hill-shading and scenic roads in green.

Reise-und Verkehrsverlag, Switzerland/Tirol, Scale 1:400,000. Good height shading, with special attention to detailing sections of road which have hairpins. The more feasible rough-stuff routes are shown (though not in anything like enough detail to follow on the ground), youth hostels and some camp sites are also marked.

Orell Fussli, Suisse, Scale 1:350,000. Good height shading but slightly less road and track detail than the RV. Some camp sites shown.

For Cycling

Michelin Nos 21, 23, 24, 26, Scale 1:200,000. Good, inexpensive series perfectly adequate for road biking, with scenic roads in green but at time of going to press only nos 23 and 24 have height shading. Insufficient detail for safe passage of rough-stuff routes.

Carte Nationale de la Suisse, Scale 1:100,000. Three sheets (Nos 102, 103 and 104) cover the central valley of Switzerland, beautifully presented and great for cycling, with tracks, contours, all roads and height shading.

For Rough-stuff and Hiking

Landeskarte der Schweiz, Scale 1:50,000. Very detailed series covering the entire country and invaluable for off-road biking and walking. Contours throughout, and all tracks marked.

AUSTRIA

Shaped like a frying pan – albeit a fairly bent and mis-shapen one – Austria sits at the little-populated eastern end of the great Alpine chain, partly enveloped by Czechoslovakia and Hungary. Except for her long Tyrolean 'handle', which nudges Switzerland and is sandwiched between southern Germany and northern Italy, the bulk of Austria is off the main European through-routes, a factor that has left parts of the country pleasantly free of tourism.

Comparisons with neighbouring Switzerland are tempting, for both countries are dominated by the Alps (all but 20% of Austria is a continuous range of mountains), though Austria is roughly twice the size of her neighbour, but with only the same total population – so people are quite thinly spread. With over a quarter of Austrians living in the city of Vienna, that leaves a lot of empty countryside, though as a rule the roads of the Austrian mountains are more frequent than those of the Swiss Alps.

Visually, Austria shares much of Switzerland's natural splendour but lacks the same financial prosperity. It's fair to say that the Austrian

Alps do not have the same variety and scale as Switzerland's mountains, being generally lower and wider. Nevertheless, the backdrop made famous by 'The Sound of Music' is real enough, and Austria does have the full gamut of Alpine splendour, from gorges to thundering waterfalls, glaciers to stark peaks. Sombre forests of conifer cloaking the lower slopes to about 2,000 metres exaggerate the odd vivid green patches of pasture, often terraced or clinging perilously to impossibly steep slopes. Sighing trees, pine resin on the air, carpets of tiny bright flowers and weathered timber barns solitarily baking in the sun are there for the slow traveller.

For cycling, Austria is most suited to the lover of grand scenery, good food and steep roads. Only in the distant east do the gradients lessen where the main attraction is the cultural centre of Vienna and the broad Danube valley. Cyclists (and motorists) have for long passed through Tyrol, mainly because it is conveniently close to surrounding Alpine attractions, but few people wander further east to enjoy the possibilities offered by the broad expanse of the Tauern Mountains. Throughout Austria's mountains, riding can be made more varied by making use of the thousands of rough tracks. The *Austrian Pass Directory* compiled by the O.C.D. is useful for gathering information on the higher passes (see Appendices for address).

Once the centre of an absolutely vast empire, Austria has for several centuries been a cultural catalyst, renowned for its architecture and producing some of Europe's most acclaimed composers, among them, Haydn, Mozart, Schubert, Bruckner and the Strauss Family. Food too is something of a national speciality, wholesome rather than delicate though like the French, the Austrians know to how to enjoy it. Dumpling soups, Wiener Schnitzel (veal dipped in egg and breadcrumbs and fried), goulash, hundreds of varieties of sausage, wines, beers are all favourites. Restaurants – where you can order tongue-twisters like *Leberknödlsuppe* (meat broth with dumplings), *Gumpoldskirchner* (Viennese white wine) and *Guglhup* (sponge cake) are identified with a 'G' if they are nationally recognised as fulfilling certain basic standards. Food can also be eaten in a *Gastätte*, tea and coffee in a café.

Austrian picnics can be memorable affairs, especially if you can afford to go wild on ingredients – picture two bicycles leaning against one of those country shops which always seem to stock a little of everything. Inside, two hungry riders, due to leave for the UK in a few hours, with a couple of handfuls of soon-to-be-unusable *schillings* burning holes in their pockets. It was a purchase finessed to the final *groschen;* a transaction which left us financial destitutes but calorific millionaires. Outside the village we found the perfect site (never difficult in Austria) on a south-facing slope of close-cropped grass which was gently cooking in the midday sun. There, on a clean green tablecloth overlooking the valley, a pannier disgorged itself of paté, garlic sausage, heavy brown bread, tight red tomatoes, three different cheeses, cucumber, a litre of fresh chilled milk and plums. An hour later we had reached that stage of blissful contentment so benign that an insect tickling your nose stays there because you simply can't be bothered to move it on.

Traditionals, the Austrians love folk-lore, they tend to conservatism, are courteous (hand-shaking is *in*) and are often jolly. The official language is German, though English is widely understood, especially in the Tyrol and Vorarlberg. The currency is the *Schilling* (AS) divided into 100 *Groschen*. Nearly all Austrians are Roman Catholic, and the country is a neutral federal republic.

Ride Guide

Vorarlberg and Tyrol

Jutting westwards from the main body of Austria, the long thin 'peninsula' that comprises Vorarlberg and Tyrol is the country's main tourist area. Some 150 kilometres long, and narrowing to as little as 32 kilometres in one place, it's an area of few roads so a tour of the region is given much more scope if parts of the surrounding countries are included. If you are biking the Italian Dolomites, Swiss Engadine or castles of Bavaria, then the Tyrol fits well into an itinerary.

Like the Swiss Alps, Tyrol is for the mountain-minded biker, and many of the quietest, most scenic roads are those which lead up tributary valleys, these rides tending to be of the there-and-back variety. There are precious few through-routes in the area, and those that do exist often have heavy traffic – at one point in the Tyrol, all east-west travellers are forced down into a single valley: the Inn. There are several challenging mountain passes to pedal up (see Austrian Pass Guide).

At the tip of the Tyrolean peninsula, the province of Vorarlberg looks more to Switzerland than it does to Austria, and has a different geography from its commanding neighbours. It's generally lower, with valleys dropping down to the shores of Lake Constance, and in the west a gentler aspect of farms, meadows and wooded hills. The attractive forests of Bregenzerwald are a popular holiday area. Compared to Tyrol, western Vorarlberg has a good scattering of towns and villages, and of minor roads. The deeply glaciated valleys of the Montafon and its tributary the Brand, are especially scenic parts to explore.

Beyond Bludenz the mountains start, and in two great parallel chains the ranges march relentlessly eastward. Along the southern border of Tyrol stride the mightily glaciated peaks of the Silvretta Mountains, Otztal Alps, Stubai Alps and Zillertal Alps, while along the

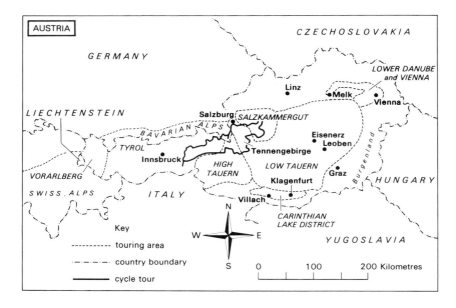

northern border with Bavaria are the lower but more rugged limestone ranges of the Lechtaler Alps, Karwendelgebirge and Kitzbühel Alps. The grander southern mountains are similar in scale and appearance to the Swiss and French Alps, with glaciers, small lakes and waterfalls, and can be approached by spectacular rides up valleys like the Pitzal and Otztal. Wildspitz (3,774 metres) is top peak round here and is Austria's second highest mountain. The northern limestone ranges are more heavily wooded, with their pale rock eroded into contorted peaks and deep gorges.

Throughout the Tyrol – a region long-favoured by outdoor-minded tourists who for decades have come here to walk, climb and enjoy the flora – there is a rustic charm which is best appreciated by occasionally leaving the bike and taking to the many hiking trails. The flat-bottomed valleys have carpets of green pastures dotted with farm buildings used to store hay for the bitter winter season when the cattle are brought down from the higher grounds. The villages are attractive and many of the houses, with low-pitched roofs and balconies, have delightful decorated exteriors. When the snow comes, the Tyrol transforms itself into one of Europe's premier skiing areas, centreing on resorts like Kitzbühel and St Anton. Tyrol's capital is Innsbruck, set against mountains at the crossroads of the main route from Italy to southern Germany and from Switzerland to Austria.

High and Low Tauern Mountains

These two mountain ranges are a natural extension of Tyrol's Zillertal Alps, and form the backbone of a number of adjacent hill ranges which occupy much of remaining Austria; to simplify matters I'll include with the High and Low Tauern all the massifs which stretch over as far as Vienna and Graz. Like the Tyrol, the roads of this area are invariably steep, while those that are more level tend to carry the main traffic flows through important valleys. Generally however, the Tauern receive less attention than the more trendy Tyrol, and there are more roads to choose from.

The Tauern and their surrounding slopes are also known for their gorges and caves; the province of Salzburg has the largest number of caves in central Europe – about 1,500 of them, the largest and most interesting being Eisriesenwelt in the Tennengebirge range, south of Salzburg city. Perhaps the grandest of gorges is the Lichtensteinklamm at St Johann im Pongau (south of Tennengebirge).

The High Tauern includes some of the most spectacular scenery in the Alps, culminating in the mighty Gross Glockner (3,797 metres), the highest of Austrian mountains. There's a heady ride up a curling road to a viewpoint specially constructed to provide a panorama over this peak and its attendant Pasterze Glacier. Fine stands of Austrian fir, spruce and larch clothe the lower slopes of these mountains, and at their western end the dramatic Krimml Falls plunge nearly 400 metres into the Salzach valley.

The Low Tauern is a relatively unspoilt area of mountains (mostly between 1,500 and 2,500 metres), rushing streams, forest, meadows and castles. Being sandwiched between the attractive cycling areas of Salzkammergut and the Carinthian Lake District, this central part of Austria offers variety in both scenery and hardness of cycling.

On the northern side of the Low Tauern, north of the Liezen-Leoben road, there is some fine cycling along tortuous roads and near Eisenerz is Leopoldsteiner See, its sparkling waters set beneath surrounding peaks; just south-east of here is Erzberg mountain, eaten away by iron-ore workings. Riding west you can follow the impressive Gesäuse gorges on the River Enns.

The southern slopes of the Low Tauern yield a variety of surprises: north from Klagenfurt are many castles (for example Hochosterwitz near St Veit), Gurk has a fine cathedral and Friesach is a medieval walled town. Between historic Graz and Bruck-an-der-Mur are the enormous Lurgrotte Caves, Rabenstein Castle (south of Frohnleiten) and Bärenschützklamm gorge (south of Pernegg). South of Graz the upland becomes softer and the climate more amenable, the vegetation richer and roads more numerous.

East of Leoben the slopes become milder, though there are still occasional opportunities for mountain cycling, for example around Semmering. Ultimately the Tauern peter out into the Danube plain; it's actually possible to cycle off the ends of the Alps straight into the suburbs of Venice.

Lower Danube and Vienna

To haters of hills it will come as a pleasant surprise that there is at least one part of Austria that provides reasonably level cycling. Centred on the one-time capital of the Holy Roman Empire, Vienna (Schubert, Strauss, romantic architecture, opera, theatre, festivals, beer cellars and so on), rides can be taken out along the flat Danube valley to delightful old Krems and thence upstream along pretty roads on the river bank through the Wachau district to Melk with its fabulous 18th-century abbey overlooking the river. Castles and vineyards add colour.

Hilly, but with enough variety for several excursions, are the roads among the beech trees of the famous Vienna Woods (Wienerwald). The wine gardens *(Heuringen)* of villages around here, like Grinzing, Neustift and Sievering (on the north-west side of the city) are popular on fine summer evenings. In a south-easterly direction, across flattish countryside, is the vast expanse of Neusiedler See, its southern shore in Hungary, and its environs a sanctuary for birds and water-sportsmen.

Burgenland, the province stretching southwards from this great lake, is an area of undulating corn-fields and woods, which get hillier as you cycle south, rich in castles and little visited by tourists.

Salzkammergut

An area long-associated with the extraction of salt, this is Austria's northern Lake District. It covers an area about 50 kilometres by 60 kilometres, and has enough roads and interest to provide a week of slow cycling, and it is also conveniently situated for combining with a ride through neighbouring Berchtesgaden and for exploring the city of Salzburg. Needless to say, the most scenic routes along the lakesides have long since been turned into tourist highways, so biking there means sharing the roads with other traffic. The smaller, southern lakes are quieter and just as beautiful as the northern ones, of which Wolfgang See is the most popular. Some of the best views are to be enjoyed from high-level paths which run along the valley sides; the classic lakeland view is that from the Schafberg (1,783 metres) just east of St Gilgen. In some places ferries can be used to escape from the worst of the traffic; for example on the road from Salzburg to Bad Ischl you can cross Wolfgang See to pretty St Wolfgang, then ride along the quieter northern shore. Similarly, rather than miss some of the scenery simply to avoid the traffic, consider riding early or late in the day along the corniche section of road beside Traunsee (Austria's deepest lake).

One of the most scenic of Salzkammergut's lakes is Hallstätter See; by Obertraun are the vast caverns of Dachstein, and above the village the peaks of Hoher Dachstein (2,995 metres) which is the most easterly mountain in the Alps to be snowy all the year round.

On the edge of Salzkammergut, and a dawdler's paradise, is the convivial city of Salzburg. The approach over the River Salzach into Judengasse, with its elaborate wrought-iron signs, then the baroque beauty of the cathedral, the enchanting squares and fountains, all lead the feet up towards the overpowering bulk of Hohensalzburg. From a high tower of this awesome fortress I can remember trying to spy our bikes parked far below, then watching the sun drawing back its dying rays from the patchwork of roof-tops and picking out the crenellations of the distant Berchtesgaden Alps. An American, whose guide book we'd been sharing for much of the day and who had been repeatedly stunned by its contents rather than by the city it was describing, flipped a page to exclaim: "Hey, you guys, hear this – it says here that there's a 'magnificent view of the town and mountains' from this tower", at which point he turned and set off for the next target without so much as a glance over the parapet!

Carinthian Lake District

Austria's southern Lake District claims to have 200 lakes in the sliver of Carinthia which lies along the Yugoslav border. Some are no more than a few metres across, others, like Wörther See (16 kilometres long) are much larger. It's an area renowned for its pleasantly warm and dry climate, especially around the 'basin' of Klagenfurt. It is also scenic, with wooded slopes climbing away from the reed-fringed lakes, many castles, and interesting old towns. In places the surrounding mountains reach 2,000 metres. The Carinthian Lake District has lots of small quiet roads good for cycling, though most involve a bit of climbing – it's the sort of area worthy of cycling through, rather than of forming the basis of a whole tour.

Austrian Rough-stuff

Austria is a virtually unlimited source of off-road riding – some easy and undemanding, some very challenging and arduous. Very often rough tracks can be used to link valleys or to avoid main roads; the 1:50,000 maps show the possibilities. Popular off-road cycling routes in Tyrol include the grand but straightforward Hochalpensattel (1,791 metres) from Scharnitz (north of Innsbruck) to Hinteriss and Vorderiss via the valleys of Karwendeltal, Johannestal and Risstal; near the summit is the

Karwendelhaus hut. In the same area is the 1,649-metre Plumsersattel, rough and steep in parts, from the Risstal valley to Gernalm and thence by track to Pertisau (north-west of Jenbach). The easy but attractive Kundler Klamm path (south-west of Wörgl in north Tyrol) follows the gorge from Mühlthal to Kundl. There's nothing special about these three routes; they're merely examples of Austria's off-road potential.

Austrian Pass Guide

Pass (height in metres)	Location	Comments
Alpsteig (1,099)	Krieglach – Birkfeld (NE of Bruck)	scenic, wooded.
Arlberg (1,793)	Bludenz – Landeck (W. Tyrol)	Austria's main E-W highway so very busy indeed; avoid if possible. Occasionally closed Jan – Apr.
Bielerhöhe (Silvretta) (2,036)	Bludenz – Landeck (W. Tyrol)	longer, scenic alternative to Arlberg with hairpins on west and great views. Open: mid June – mid Oct.
Brenner (1,370)	Innsbruck – Bolzano (Italy)	parallel motorway takes most motor traffic on this busiest of Alpine routes, scenically nothing special. Occasionally closed Nov – Apr.
Fern (1,210)	Reutte – Imst (N. Tyrol)	quite attractive but heavy traffic. Occasionally closed Nov – Apr.
Flexen (1,773)	Arlberg – Lech (N. Tyrol)	joins the Arlberg Pass road, good views and scenery, tunnels. Occasionally closed Nov – Apr.
Furka Joch (1,769)	Rankwel – Au (near Feldkirch, W. Tyrol)	narrow and picturesque.
Gaberl (1,551)	Judenburg – Köflach (W of Graz)	scenic.
Gerlos (1,507)	Mayrhofen – Mittersill (SW of Kitzbühel)	the road to the Krimml waterfalls, very picturesque and bendy, gentle; occasionally closed Nov – Apr.

Grossglockner (2,505)	Bruck – Lienz (High Tauern)	one of the classic Alpine passes now with very heavy traffic, fine scenery, hairpins and scenic excursion ride to Franz-Josephs-Höhe. Austria's highest pass. Open: mid May – end Oct.
Hahntennjoch (1,903)	Elmen – Imst (Lechtaler Alps)	narrow and picturesque.
Hengst (1,010)	Windischgarsten – Altenmarkt (NE of Liezen)	narrow and wooded.
Hochtannberg (1,679)	Schoppernau – Warth (W. Tyrol)	modernised road passing nature reserve, medium traffic. Open: May – end Oct.
Holzleitnersattel (1,126)	Nassereith – Telfs (W of Innsbruck)	easy, quite scenic, with good views from the western side.
Iselsberg (1,208)	Winklern – Lienz	busy but quite picturesque, with views from top.
Katschberg (1,641)	St Michael – Spittal	parallel motorway takes much of the traffic, but pass nothing special. Occasionally closed Nov – Apr.
Kreuzberg (1,077)	Greifenburg – Hermagor (SW of Spittal)	quite scenic, view of Weissensee.
Lahnsattel (1,006)	Mariazell – Mürzzuschlag	quiet and fairly pleasant
Loibl (1,368)	Klagenfurt – Kranj (Yugoslavia)	heavy traffic, with 17,000-metre summit tunnel well lit and safe for cycling. Open: mid May – mid Nov.
Nassfeld (1,530)	Hermagor – Pontebba (Italy)	narrow, winding and scenic with detour to panoramic viewpoint at Nassfeldhöhe. Open: March – end Nov.
Packsattel (1,169)	Köflach – Wolfsberg (SW of Graz)	very winding, not too busy, with views from top.

Plöcken (1,360)	Kötschach – Paluzza (Italy)	heavy traffic on largely re-constructed road. Open: May – Nov.
Präbichl (1,232)	Eisenerz – Leoben	busy, perhaps Austria's steepest pass, view from top.
Radstadter-Tauern (1,739)	Radstadt – Mauterndorf (Low Tauern)	heavy tourist traffic but good scenery. Occasionally closed Nov – Apr.
Reschen-Scheideck (1,504)	Landeck – Merano (Italy)	heavy traffic, used by motorists as an alternative to the Brenner, quite scenic. Occasionally closed Nov – Apr.
Rottenmanner (Tauern) (1,265)	Trieben – Judenburg (Low Tauern)	pleasant and not too busy.
Seeberg (1,253)	Mariazell – Bruck	scenic with good views.
Seeburg-Sattel (1,218)	Volkermarkt – Kranj (Yugoslavia)	lots of hairpins and view south from the top. Open: Apr – Oct.
Seefelder Sattel (1,185)	Mittenwald – Innsbruck	below average.
Sölker (1,790)	Stein – Schöder (Low Tauern)	narrow, quiet and scenic, with hairpins on south.
Thurn (1,274)	Kitzbühel – Mittersill	easy, with fairly heavy traffic but scenic. Occasionally closed Nov – Apr.
Timmelsjoch (2,497)	Sölden – St Leonhard (Italy)	hairpins and tunnels, fabulous views of mountains and glaciers. Open: mid June – Oct.
Turracherhöhe (1,763)	Predlitz – Reichenau (N of Villach)	one of Austria's steepest passes, no hairpins, medium traffic, scenic. Sometimes closed end Oct – Apr.
Wurzen (1,073)	Villach – Podkoren (Yugoslavia)	narrow, wooded, fairly quiet, one of the easier passes over the Karawanken range. Open: May – Nov.

Tour of Central Austria

Lots of hills to climb in this tour which explores some of the higher and more diverse parts of Austria. The route starts from one of the country's most delightful cities (good rail and air links), picking a mildly exerting course through the lake district of Salzkammergut before moving through the Tennengebirge to look at the mountains of the High Tauern and Tyrol. The tour finishes with a crossing of the Berchtesgaden Alps. The roads are on the whole quieter than those of the Swiss Alps, and there are all kinds of variations that can be made to this route by anyone with enough sense of adventure to use Austria's wealth of rough-stuff tracks. The route could be adapted for use of Innsbruck as a start/finish point.

CENTRAL AUSTRIA TOUR

Terrain: mountainous
Distance: 640 km
Start/Finish: Salzburg/Salzburg
Scenery: **
Interest: *
Maps: Mair Die General Karte, 1:200,000 nos 4 & 7

---

km	SALZBURG
5	Glasenbach (SE of Salzburg)
(14	Wiestal-Stausee)
2	Hinterebenau
8	Vordersee (N of Hintersee)
2	Anger
8	Fuschl
8	St Gilgen

(Attersee & Traunsee loop can be omitted by taking more direct route SE to Bad Ischl)

10	Au
13	Steinbach am Attersee
15	Neukirchen
6	Viechtau
8	Ebensee

17	Bad Ischl
9	Rettenbach
10	Altaussee
8	Grundlsee
6	Bad Aussee
12	Obertraun
4	Halstatt
15	Gosau
	Gschütt Pass
24	Annaberg
14	Neidernfritz-St. Martin
4	Eben
	Wagrain Pass
18	Wagrain
8	St. Johann im Pongau

(detour S to Lichtenstein-klamm)

8	Schwarzach
25	Dorf Dienten
	Filzensattel Pass
20	Saalfelden
19	Bruck
6	Kaprun

(detour S up Kaprunertal)

27	Mittersill
32	Krimml
	Krimml Pass
48	Mayrhofen

(detour up Tuxertal)

5	Hippach

(alternative high-level route to W, via Schwendberg & Zellberg. to rejoin route at Ried)

9	Aschau
9	Fügen
6	Bruck am Ziller
7	Brixlegg
8	Kundl
9	Thierbach
4	Mühlthal
12	Hopfgarten
14	Kirchberg
4	Gundhabing

(alternative route via Reith,
to rejoin route at Oberndorf)

3	Kitzbühel	5	Strub
6	Oberndorf	6	Lofer
1	Wiesenschwang	3	St. Martin b. Lofer
3	St. Johann in Tirol	7	Weissbach
10	Rosenegg (NW of Fieberbrunn)		Hirschbichl Pass
8	St. Ulrich	31	Königsee
7	Waidring	5	Berchtesgaden
		9	Markt-Schellenberg
		5	Grödig
		10	SALZBURG

Basic Information

Getting There

Air: international airlines serve Innsbruck, Graz, Vienna, Klagenfurt, Linz and Salzburg; flying time from London is about two hours.

Rail: good connections with other continental countries, journey time from London to Vienna being about 23 hours.

Road: Calais to Innsbruck by main road is 1,030 kilometres.

Information Sources

Austrian National Tourist Office (ANTO) 30 St George Street, London W1R 9FA (tel: 01-629-0461). General planning map, regional information, camp site list etc.

Local tourist bureaux: local tourist information can be obtained from *Verkehrsvereine* found in most towns, villages and resorts – often located at the railway station, or from the *Kurkommissionen* (spa administrations). In addition there are provincial tourist boards based at provincial capitals (addresses in ANTO booklet) whose knowledge of local affairs tends to be more up-to-date than that of the ANTO. By writing direct to the *Verkehrsverein* of a town or village, you can often acquire a detailed list of all the local accommodation possibilities and prices.

Oesterreichischer Fahrradverband, Hasnerstrasse 10, A-1160 Vienna, the organisation for non-competitive cyclists.

Oesterreichischer Radsportverband, Prinz-Eugen-Strasse 12, A-1040 Vienna (tel: 657339). The controlling body for national amateur and professional cycle-racing.

Accommodation

Camping: in Vorarlberg and Tyrol, Salzkammergut and the Carinthian Lake District, there are plenty of sites; elsewhere they are rather thinly spread. The sites at the western end of the country tend to fill up during the season, particularly with Germans heading south for their summer holidays. Facilities and standards are good, and most sites are compact rather than sprawling, and are often in attractive locations. It is usually possible to obtain fee reductions on presentation of a valid AIT card. ANTO publish a list of about 400 sites, together with a useful map.

Strictly speaking it is necessary to obtain the land-owner's permission (or that of a local official) before camping 'wild', but this is often not feasible. There are vast tracts of uncultivated land (37% alone is forested) and it isn't difficult to find innocuous overnight pitches. Most farmers do not mind a tent on a field once it has been cropped.

Youth Hostels: There are about a hundred Austrian hostels listed in the IYHA handbook; the same number as in Switzerland, but covering twice the area. There is a noticeable concentration of hostels in the Salzkammergut, and the mountains south of the Danube are not too badly served. But elsewhere, hostels are sparse, so if your route is not to be governed by their location, hostels are best used in conjunction with other types of accommodation. Some places, like Vienna and Salzburg, have four or five hostels per town. Preference is given to hostellers over thirty.

Aside from those listed by the IYHA, there are many other kinds of hostel-type accommodation, ranging from mountain huts to ultra-simple inns; ANTO list about 600 of these.

Administrative offices of youth accommodation are:
Oesterreichischer Jugendherbergsverband, Schottenring 28, A-1010 Vienna (tel: 635353).
Oesterreichisches Jugendherbergswerk, Freyung 6/11, A-1010 Vienna (tel: 631833).
Oesterreichisches Jugendferienwerk (Young Austria), Alpenstrasse 08a, A-5020 Salzburg (tel: 257580).

Bed-and-Breakfast: often you will find private houses offering accommodation; looks for signs saying *Zimmer Frei, Privat Zimmer, Fremdenzimmer* and *Fremdenheime.* These are normally reasonable value.

Inns/Hotels: simple, and often very charming, are country inns, described as *Gasthof* or *Gasthaus,* where you can be expected to take the evening meal. The hotels are of a high standard, expensive and plentifully distributed. Those in Vienna and Salzburg cost much more than those in rural areas, though both these cites have special 'students hostels' available for as little as half the normal rate between July and the end of September; normally one has to be under 27 to use these (addresses from local tourist offices or ANTO).

Weather

Austria's weather is typically Alpine, with freezing snowy winters and clear warmish summers which tend to wetness. Temperatures are generally similar to Switzerland, Carinthia in the south being the warmest region. And, like Switzerland, summer rains can be heavy, though they normally disperse fairly quickly (Innsbruck for example has about twice as much rain in July as does London). The wettest months are June, July and August; the driest part of Austria being the narrow strip of lowland on the eastern border.

Prevailing winds tend to be broken up by the mountains, though when it does blow, it is normally from the west (these winds bring heavy downpours to Salzkammergut). Vienna, further east, is one of the most windless places in Europe. The best time of day for viewing the mountains is the morning, before rising warm air brings clouds to the peaks. The notorious *föhn* wind periodically strikes Innsbruck, seldom in mid-summer, but about six days each month in March, April and May.

With the roads ranging from low valley to high pass you'll find the temperature and wind varying according to altitude and aspect to the sun. The permanent snow-line is about 2,500-metres.

Other Considerations: the same apply for Austria as for Switzerland; July and August are the most crowded months (with Tyrol roads especially busy), and most passes are open from mid-June to mid-October. The 'wild-flower season' is from May to July, both May/June and September/mid-October being pleasant compromises between best weather and least crowds.

Average Daily Maximum Temperatures (Centigrade)

	alt. in metres	J	F	M	A	M	J	J	A	S	O	N	D
Klagenfurt	498	-1	3	9	15	19	23	25	24	20	13	6	1
Zell am See	754	-2	0	7	13	18	21	22	22	19	12	5	0

Hiking

Austrians, and the Germans (who traditionally holiday here), are Europe's most avid walkers, and the mountains of Tyrol and Tauern are criss-crossed with hiking trails, often waymarked.

Cycling Information

Cycle Shops

Rarely found except in the valley of the Danube, around Vienna and in the Carinthian Lake District about the towns of Klagenfurt and Villach; in the mountains you have to be mechanically self-reliant. Sports shops often have a cycle department.

Cycle Hire

Possible at many tourist centres (advertised as *Fahrradverleih*), some of the better organised tourist offices publishing lists of hire-firm addresses. The Lake District of Salzkammergut and the lower hinterland to the north (the Innviertel and Mühlviertel districts about Linz) have quite a few hire centres, and being less strenuous than most parts of Austria, this would make a good area for some casual riding. Popular cities like Salzburg also have hire bikes.

Between 1 April and 2 November it is possible to hire bicycles from a selection of Austrian railway stations (about 70 in all). Most of these stations are in the province of Lower Austria (that's the top right-hand one around the Danube and Vienna), with just a few hire stations in the mountain areas. You pay by the day, but are entitled to a 50% reduction if you produce a rail ticket to that station. The bike can be returned to any station; a passport or identity card is required. The leaflet *"Fahrrad am Bahnhof"* (from ANTO) lists the stations and their phone numbers (so that you can reserve your bike).

Transporting your Bicycle

All the best touring areas can be reached by train, connections from Munich covering most of the country. Bikes can be taken as accompanied luggage on trains and a modest flat charge is payable, regardless of distance. Sent as unaccompanied luggage the charge is double and if the bike travels on a separate train it may arrive three days later. For an extra charge the bike can be insured for an unaccompanied journey. At the 'left luggage' departments of railway stations bikes can be garaged for a small daily charge. (Salzburg and Vienna stations are especially civilised, with showers available for passengers – worth remembering after a fortnight's exertions in the Tyrol!).

It is not possible to carry bikes on buses, cable-cars (or ski-lifts!).

Roads

Generally well-surfaced, though not up to Swiss standards; there are still numerous country roads with grit topping and on the higher passes frost can break up the tarmac. Barriers and warning lights indicate whether a pass is open or blocked by snow and the same information can be obtained by phoning 72.21.01 extension 7.

Traffic can be heavy, especially at weekends, during late July and August, and over German public holidays. (Austria has relatively few roads for its area, and has the third highest number of cars per kilometre among European countries). There are cycle-paths occasionally and these should be used. Watch out for the trams in Vienna!

Maps

For General Planning

Michelin No. 426, Austria, Scale 1:400,000. Inexpensive, with hill shading and scenic roads in green.

RV (Reise-und Verkehrsverlag), Austria, Scale 1:450,000. This map includes a large chunk of south-east Germany, and has good shading which gives a clear idea of terrain. Rough locations of mountain refuges, youth hostels and camp sites shown, as well as some rough tracks.

For Cycling

Mair, Die General Karte series, Scale 1:200,000. Compact, accurate and covering the country in eight sheets, these are the best general cycling maps of Austria. Scenic roads are shown in green, and gradient arrows indicate where you might be pushing the bike. They show many rough tracks and have good height-shading but do not distinguish between unsurfaced and surfaced small roads. The reverse side of these maps carries tourist information (in German) and town plans.

Freytag and Berndt, Wanderkarten series, Scale 1:100,000. A large scale series of 52 sheets, very detailed, contoured with height shading, way-marked paths, tracks and all roads shown. Good for detailed exploring (and rough-stuff too).

For Rough-stuff and Hiking

Kompass Wanderkarte series, Scale 1:500,000. Exceedingly detailed and recommended for all serious rough-stuff and hiking, with good height-shading, tourist features, way-marked paths, tracks and all roads shown. Covers the whole of Austria.

ITALY

Set slap in the centre of that most famous of inland seas, there can be nowhere more Mediterranean than Italy. It has all the ingredients: a relaxed life style, months of sun, its contrasts of poverty and luxurious hotels, chaos and calm; its diversity of scenery and plethora of historic remains. Its thinkers and do'ers have from Romanesque to Renaissance and beyond, sent out waves of influence across Europe, that have moulded our music, architecture, art, sculpture and science. Now the empire has shrunk, but the core is still there, a boiled-down concentration of all those great ages.

Italy is a bit bigger than Norway and not that different in shape; long and thin, lunging out from the ice of the Alps in the north towards the sand of the Sahara in the south. You are seldom more than a day or two's ride from the sea. The best scenery tends to be found in hillier areas; lowland Italy is either interminably dull, mosquito-ridden and flat-as-a-pancake with heavily-farmed plains like those of Foggia and the Po Valley, or is an unsightly strip of hotels, and roads along much of the Adriatic and Tyrrhenian seaboards. Many beaches are privately owned, while the public ones are crowded and grubby; seaside Italy is more geared to the sedentary hotel-tourist than the passing traveller wanting a swim. Some parts of the coast including Genoa, the mouth of the Tiber, the Bay of Naples and the big Adriatic cities are badly polluted.

Inland Italy, Calabria, Sicily and Sardinia are far less touched by this destructive century; touring some of these parts by bike definitely comes under the 'adventure' heading. The Dolomite roads are among the most impressive in the Alps, and you can find thousand-metre passes the entire length of the Apennines from Genoa to Reggio in Calabria; on Sicily and Sardinia too. Much of this mountainous country is raw, with unspoilt forest, rock and scrub, remote villages and empty rough roads. Easier-going cycling can be found between the 'art cities' of the centre.

Italy is neither the richest nor most politically placid of European states; governments seem no more durable than a bicycle-tyre ridden over a bed of thorns – strikes and demonstrations are frequent, and the people are not averse to actually hurting each other. The north is noticeably more affluent than the south, which has become steadily more desolate as people have moved away to find work.

Perhaps it's the tough terrain and search for better things that has made the Italians such avid bike-racers. They host the first and last major events of the European racing calendar: the Milan to San Remo, and Tour of Lombardy, not to mention the prestigious three-week Giro d'Italia and scores of local races up and down the country. Italy too is where the two greatest bike-racing rivals of all time – Fausto Coppi and Gino Bartali – duelled across dusty plains. Aspiring young professionals from all over the world come to Italy to learn their craft.

Yet despite this being one of the rare European countries in which bike racing can actually be called a 'national sport', the Italians show little enthusiasm for touring by bike. The closest they get to recreational cycling is on Sundays when fathers and sons don brightly-coloured jerseys and pedal out to the country on stripped-down racing machines. Lone cycle-tourists can be the subject of intense curiosity and much generosity.

The perpetual good weather and emphatic landscape have rubbed-off on the Latin temperament and most Italians manage to live up to their reputation for being gaily vivacious and keen to talk. The hoots and shouts you get from passing vehicles are not gestures of aggression but the equivalent of the British shy glance. The evening *passeggiata*, when whole communities head for the high street in their best clothes, promenading, gossiping and courting as the light fades, is a national institution. The men are invariably chauvinistic, some aggressively so, towards women tourists.

English is not that widely spoken, though German and French are sometimes understood. Italian is spoken throughout, except for the northern enclaves of Alto Adige (German) and Val d'Aosta (French). Ninety-five per cent of the population are Catholic, and head, shoulders, arms and legs should be covered before entering a church.

Cafés stay open all day, always a welcome haven from the heat; some serve snacks as well as drink (note that the prices posted are normally those charged for standing, and if you sit at a table, you pay more). The least expensive, and often most fun restaurants are *Trattorie*, while *Tavola Calda* or *Rosticceria* indicates a casual, sometimes self-service eating house. *Pizzeria* are good for carbohydrate and often 'take-aways'. Fresh fruit and vegetables for picnics are usually easy to find, eggs and milk less so. The unit of currency is the *lira*.

Ride Guide

The Dolomites

Sitting in the lee of the higher Alps due north, the sunny Dolomites have a Mediterranean rather than Central-European flavour and are one of the most spectacular parts of Europe's great mountain chain. They look different to the rest of the Alps, with pale limestone spires and walls leaping vertically (or nearly) from the green meadows and forests of the valleys to form a fierce skyline of jagged teeth and pinnacles. The individual massifs of the Dolomites are relatively compact, leaving many deep valleys and gorges for roads to find a way through; generally the passes are shorter than those in the Alps. The scope for biking is excellent and there are several adjacent areas that would fit in with a Dolomite tour; the Swiss Alps, Italian Lakes, High Tauern and especially the Austrian Tyrol are close by. In fact the Dolomites were once a part of the Austrian Tyrol, but were included in Italy following the First World War. To this day many of the street signs are in German *and* Italian.

The main massifs are those of Látemar and Catinaccio (either side of the Costalunga Pass, just east of Bolzano), the Cima della Vezzana and Pale di San Martino (east of San Martino di Castrozza), Sasso Lunga and the Gruppo di Sella (north of Canazei), La Tofane and Sorapiss (around Cortina d'Ampezzo) and the mightiest of them all, the 3,343-metre Marmolada massif (to the south-east of Canazei). On the north-east edge of the Dolomites is one of the most scenic massifs: the Tre Cima di Lavaredo, a new road into the heart of these peaks providing a very fine, if hard, detour ride.

A well-known ride among veteran cycle-tourists of the Dolomites is the 'Hundred Hairpin' circuit around the already-mentioned Sella group of mountains, taking in the Campolongo, Pordoi, Sella and Gardena passes. The 54 kilometres can be cycled in a day, and of course all

luggage can be left behind since you finish where you start; Corvara makes a good base. (Apparently a cyclist once managed to ride four laps in ten hours!)

Between the various massifs, roads trace a tortuous route, always climbing or descending, passing picturesque villages and the odd castle or lake. In spring the meadows are carpeted in wild flowers such as edelweiss, anemones, gentians and campanula. Tourist traffic concentrates on the scenic 'Dolomite Road' which runs from Bolzano via the Costalunga Pass to Canazei and thence to Cortina d'Ampezzo (a winter sport resort and the main tourist centre for the Dolomites). The main north-south routeway which comes over the Brenner Pass through Bolzano and Trento is also a major traffic artery. Bolzano (which has good rail links with the UK) is a handy starting point for a tour.

Italian Lakes

Every country seems to boast a 'Lake District' of some description, but Italy can claim the largest and possibly the most romantic. Since the days when Pliny the Younger (and Elder) had villas on their shores, the evocative tranquility of these long, thin lakes has been a focus of attention for poets, writers – and tourists.

The lakes occupy deep valleys originally scoured out by glaciers moving south from the Alps, and today strings of colourful villages, lush gardens, spacious villas and resorts scatter the shores, more often than not to a background of steep green hillsides or mountains. The winters here are mild, the summers hot, so one of the region's more unusual features is the widespread culture of sub-tropical plants. Spring-time colours are vivid: yellow forsythia, red and pink camellia, ornamental pink and white double cherry, palms and olives.

The only irritation for the cyclist is the numerous main roads which are forced to use the lake-sides as they make their way from Switzerland and Austria to the north Italian plain. So biking here means picking out the least-used shores of the lakes, making use of the many ferries to swap shores, and cycling over the hills between lakes using the small, steep roads. For this reason, a tour of the Italian Lakes can involve a lot of hill-climbing. The busiest roads are on the east side of Lake Orta, west side of Maggiore (probably the most attractive of the lakes), the N2 across Lugano, the east side of Como, east side of Iseo and the west side of Garda (reputedly the sunniest lake).

The Lakes fit in well with a tour of the Swiss Alps, while to the south there are a number of ancient cities boasting cathedrals, museums, fine art and palaces. These include Como, Milan, Bergamo, Brescia and Verona (one of the finest). Tottering on the edge of the Adriatic, some way to the east, is Venice, its peeling palaces and shadowy alleys a haunting relic of a once great empire (bikes are not allowed in the city and the least offensive approach is via Lido di Jésolo and thence by pedestrian ferry).

Between the fringes of the Alps and the start of the Apennines, is the vast Po Valley: hot and flat with plains of wheat and rice, mosquitos, and rows of poplars; it's an uninspiring bike ride. When I pedalled across the northern part of this valley I had imagined in my mind's eye that the

Po river itself would be spanned by the kind of architectural delight that can be found on the Loire. That the Po could be smelled before being seen was an omen. No soaring arches of hewn stone here, but a rusting Bailey bridge sagging across a slow-moving slurry of what looked like oxtail soup. A man lay on a bank of gravel, sunbathing.

Sprinkled across this great valley are a few interesting towns: Pavia, Cremona (home of violin-maker Stradivari), Mantova, Ravenna and lovely Bologna, birthplace of wireless-wizard Marconi and an antiquarian treasure-chest with palaces, Gothic churches, imposing towers and an historic appreciation of food. After the Po this was – quite literally – a breath of fresh air, and the city was pulsing with night-life as we rolled wearily up the main street. Diners on the arcades looked up from their dishes *alla Bolognese* to shout greetings as we passed by. Music and laughter billowed invitingly from doorways and children chased after us. I wondered if Bologna's welcome for the traveller arriving out of the night had changed since the Roman legions headed for Milan or Rome tramped tiredly over the same worn stone slabs now guiding our tyres.

Central Italy

This is the cultural heartland of Italy; a land which bore such masters as Michelangelo, Botticelli, Dante, Leonardo da Vinci, and Petrarch, and which is the site for some of Italy's most lovely towns and cities. It is also known for its scenic diversity and variety of terrain (from easy gently rolling roads to quite fierce climbing) so there is something for most cyclists.

Tuscany, Umbria and part of Latium fill the space between Florence and Rome, bounded by the coast on one side and the Apennines on the other. Hills and broad valleys, lakes, forests and vineyards are explored by a web of quiet roads and serve as a pleasant interlude between the scattering of historical gems. The two 'art cities' of Florence and Siena are within a day's ride of each other, and Pisa is day or two over towards the sea.

Southwards there is a succession of delightful towns, usually on defensive hill-top sites with superb views and an old-world ambience. Included here are such jewels as San Gimignano, Arezzo, Cortona, Gúbbio, Perugia, Assisi, Spoleto, Orvieto and Viterbo. The volcanic lakes of Bolsena (especially attractive) and Bracciano, make interesting additions to an itinerary, as does Trasimeno, the largest lake. North-west of Civitavecchia is the famous Etruscan burial ground at Tarquinia. The marble of Rome's ancient monuments is currently being turned to powder by car exhaust, but there's still a lot left and the city can easily absorb several days exploration – though it's a mad place to ride a bike.

The Apennines themselves are a very fine (if strenuous) cycling area, with scenic roads snaking over high passes and probing remote upland regions. In the north, the mountains reach 2,000 metres. The stark white limestone peaks of the Apuan Alps have been sliced up like cheese cut by wire, as the famous Carrara marble has been wrested from the bedrock.

Further to the south-east is the pocket republic of San Marino, the smallest and oldest republic in the world and founded by a Dalmatian stone-cutter called Marino. Its medieval walls perch high on a rocky bluff, a refreshingly cool viewpoint on summer evenings. I didn't find the coast south from Rimini at all attractive until I reached the spur of the Gargano peninsula in the distant south, and this northern portion of Italy's west coast is not much better either. Both have continuous and ugly tourist developments, with beaches which are often private. Both Florence and Rome make good starting or finishing points for a tour of central Italy. Alternatively, an interesting approach (which avoids the Po valley) is to ride in along the Italian Riviera from Genoa. Although it's very touristy, this rocky, indented coast is fun to ride by.

Abruzzi

If you can summon the energy, the cooler windy heights of the Abruzzi can be a contrasting antidote to the baking plains. Many incredibly twisty roads wriggle their way through this mountain region, offering fine views and an escape from the more congested lowland highways. It's an area of great draughty plateaux, of narrow ridges and deep gorges, and of wild forests. In the Abruzzi National Park (one of only four in Italy), wolves, eagles, bears and chamois survive among the maple and beech forests. North of the Park is the Gran Sasso massif, rising to the highest point (2,912 metres) in the Apennines. The Abruzzi are about two days gentle cycling from Rome, though they are rather closer to the Adriatic coast than to the Tyrrhenian.

South Italy

The most interesting tour of Italy's 'ankle' and 'foot' would be to mainly follow the coast, with occasional excursions inland. Or a tour could be tied in with Sicily, and parts of it would fit with an itinerary destined for Greece (via Brindisi or Bari).

Naples has rail and air connections with the UK and is the southern capital of Italy – a city whose many interesting features are all too often degraded by noise and dirt. Herculaneum, Pompeii and Vesuvius (well worth the walk if you've never looked inside a volcano) are all within an hour or so's biking of the city, and ferries run out to Capri and Ischia. South of Naples, the rocky Sorrento peninsula is one of the few scenic highlights on Italy's west coast, and provided you pedal it early in the morning, or out of season, the impressive corniche road is – despite the hotels – a pretty ride. Not much further south from here, on the other side of the sandy Gulf of Salerno, is the temple site of Paestum, one of the finest in Italy.

Beyond Paestum the coastline gets more interesting, running into the rocky Calabrian riviera. Inland Calabria is spectacularly wild, and at its most dramatic in the Sila Massif, a high plateau of granite reaching 1,929 metres above forests of oak and several lakes. This is a little-visited area, and biking the small, often unsurfaced, mountain roads is a thrill for the lovers of wilderness. The Col d'Ascione, south of Lake Arvo, carries the road up to a lofty 1,384 metres, and at the tip of Italy's toe, the views fro the roads over the Aspromonte heights are far-ranging.

The heel of Italy is a dry, limestone plateau whose most unusual feature is the peculiar domed dry-stone *trulli*, mainly found between Monopoli and Martina Franca (largest concentration at Alberobello). Just north-west of here are the caves of Castellana. Lecce is a fine old baroque town.

Moving further north, the spur of Italy juts out into the Adriatic; the limestone peninsula of Gargano is the only genuinely scenic piece of cycling on the entire east coast. In the centre of the peninsula high dense forests clothe the slopes, crossed by several good roads, while another route follows the dramatic lip of the peninsula, where sheer white cliffs plummet to a deep blue sea.

Sicily

Sardinia and Sicily are about the same size and are the two biggest islands in the Mediterranean. Yet with a population four times that of its neighbour, Sicily has a more 'lived-in' character. Since the earliest times the rocky triangle, that looks as if it's being kicked by the toe of mainland Italy, has been a focus of Mediterranean history, and many relics remain from as far back as the 8th century when the island was part of Magna Graecia (Greater Greece).

The attractions for a cycle-tour include the very great number of antiquities and their attendant museums, the varied coastline and wild interior. Furthermore, it is one of the few scenic highlights of the Mediterranean which can be cycled on relatively easy roads (though there are more than enough opportunities for pass-storming).

The interior of the island is rugged, and in summer, very hot. Numerous small roads wind their way through valleys of citrus fruit and almond trees, vineyards clinging to the slopes. The northern part has the biggest mountains (Etna, still 'live', is over 3,000 metres) and roads clamber to dramatic heights. Several passes over 1,000 metres cross the Nebrodi range. Biking the interior can sometimes mean riding rough surfaces and the villages are often poor and desolate with little or no accommodation, a contrast to the more affluent coast with its beaches, colourful fishing villages and many towns. While summer can be stiflingly hot – particularly when the *scirocco* is blowing – spring brings a kaleidoscope of flowering shrubs and plants.

Traffic has been drawn away from some of the main roads by a few hundred kilometres of motorway; the big towns are a chaos of cars. Normal access is via Palermo (plane from the UK and ferry links with Sardinia) or across the Strait of Messina. The island also has ferry links with North Africa.

Sardinia

Scenically Sardinia – 'home' of the sardine – is rather the poor neighbour to Corsica, just 12 kilometres to the north. The Italian island is bigger, and in high summer has a more burnt aspect, its scrubby hills and mountains split by stony valleys. But while it does not have cliffs and mountains of Corsica's scale, it does have an exciting network of mountain roads and excellent beaches. The weather can be absolutely scorching and strong winds periodically scour the island. For riders wanting a range of different cycling terrain and interest, Corsica and Sardinia complement each other and can be conveniently linked by ferry to form a longer tour. Sicily would have to be added as well if the historical dimension is to be included.

Sardinia's interest lies mainly in its natural rather than man-made splendours – the most absorbing architectural items being the many ancient stone towers known as *nuraghi* and the old and decaying churches. The most dramatic cycling is to be found in the east; the coastal road winding its way north from Cagliari via Arbatax and Dorgali threads a precarious route past gorges and awesome cliff scenery. Inland, similarly contorted roads snake through the central mountains, the highest and most dramatic being the Gennargentu range (1,834 metres at Punta la Marmora) whose lower slopes are clothed in cork oaks and chestnut. There are several lakes too.

Unless you stick to the flatter, less interesting western coast, cycling on Sardinia involves a lot of hill-climbing, though generally the gradients are not as steep as those on Corsica. Distances between villages can be substantial, especially in the mountains, so be sure to keep topped up with water and food. On the developed parts of the coast, the story is rather different, and local entrepreneurs have seen to it that restaurants and hotels are replacing shepherds' huts.

Rough-Stuff Routes in Italy

The Italian Alps have several exciting rough-stuff routes; details found in the pass guides of the O.C.D. (see appendices for address).

Italian Pass Guide (Dolomites and Alps)

Pass (height in metres)	Location	Comments
Aprica (1,172)	Edolo - Tresenda (E of Sondrio)	nothing special. Open: usually all year.
Campo Carlo Magno (1,682)	Dimaro - Tione di Trento (SW of Bolzano)	picturesque and easy. Occasionally closed.
Campolongo (1,875)	Corvara - Arabba	easier ridden from north to south. Open: Apr - Nov.
Cimabanche (1,529)	Dobbacio - Cortina d'Ampezzo	easier alternative to the Tre Croci. Open: Apr - Nov.
Costalunga (Karer)	Bolzano - Vigo	picturesque smallish road with pretty lake, tunnels and steeper gradients on W side. Open: May - Nov.
Croce Dominii (1,892)	Breno - Cóllio (S of Edolo)	narrow and picturesque, steep. Open: May - Nov.
Del Zovo (1,496)	Comélico - Auronzo di Cadore	narrow, picturesque, rough surface. Occasionally closed.
Duran (1,601)	Villa - Agordo	narrow, quiet and picturesque. Occasionally closed.
Falzárego (2,105)	Cortina d'Ampezzo - Cernadoi	many hairpins, easier ridden from W, rugged untamed scenery with views of Marmolada and glacier. Open: June - Nov.
Fedáia (2,057)	Canazei - Rocca Piétore (N of Marmolada)	narrow, excellent scenery. Open: May - Nov.
Forcola di Livigno (2,315)	Livigno - La Motta (Switzerland)	picturesque. Open: May - Nov.
Foscagno (2,291)	Livigno - Bormio	narrow and picturesque. Open: May - Nov.
Fugazze (1,161)	Rovereto - Vicenza	picturesque to north, hairpins. Occasionally closed.
Gardena (2,121)	Selva - Corvara	quite easy, very good scenery, excellent views. Open: May - Nov.

Gavia (2,621)	Bormio - Ponte di Legno	one of the favourite cycling passes, steep, unsurfaced, beautiful scenery and views, summit refuse. Open: June - Oct.
Giau (2,233)	Cortina d'Ampezzo - Selva di Cadore	a fine pass, narrow on the south side, picturesque. Open: June - Oct.
Lavardêt (1,542)	S. Stéfano di Cadore - Comeglians (E of Auronzo di Cadore)	rough surface, narrow, picturesque. Open: June - Nov.
Mauria (1,295)	Pieve di Cadore - Ampezzo	fairly easy, quite scenic. Occasionally closed.
Mendola (1,363)	Bolzano - Fondo	wooded, good views from top. Occasionally closed.
Monte Croce di Comélico (Kreuzberg) (1,636)	S.Candido - S.Stéfano (N of Auronzo di Cadore)	lovely scenery, quiet and fairly easy. Occasionally closed.
Monte Giovo (Jaufen) (2,099)	Vipiteno - Merano	steep and picturesque, hairpins. Open: May - Oct.
Nigra (1,688)	Bolzano - Vigo	one of the approaches to the Costalunga, steep and rough in places. Open: May - Nov.
Pellegrino (1,918)	Moena - Agordo (S of Marmolada)	picturesque, quiet and fairly easy. Open: June - Oct.
Pénnes (Penser Joch) (2,215)	Vipiteno - Bolzano	picturesque, fairly easy. Open: June - Oct.
Platzwiesen (1,993)	Monguelfo - Carbonin (N of Cortina d'Ampezzo)	picturesque and steep, rough surface in places. Open: June - Oct.
Pordoi (2,239)	Arabba - Canazei	highest road in Dolomites, narrow, picturesque, many hairpins, fine views of Marmolada and Sella Massif. Open: Sella Massif. Open: June - Oct.

Presolana (1,297)	Edolo - Clusone	narrow, picturesque. Occasionally closed.
Rolle (1,970)	Predazzo - S. Martino di Castrozza (SW of Marmolada)	busy, fairly easy, beautiful scenery. Open: Jun - Oct.
San Angelo (1,756)	Carbonin - Tre Croci Pass	beautiful scenery, Lake Misurina to S. Open: Jun - Oct.
Sella (2,240)	Plan Canazei	very picturesque, fine views over Dolomites, harder approach from S. Open: Jun - Nov.
Sella Campigotto (1,790)	Lozzo di Cadore - Ampezzo	alternative to busier Mauria, rough surface, picturesque, narrow. Open: Jun - Oct.
Sestriere (2,035)	Cesana Torinese - Turin	picturesque. Occasionally closed.
Staulanza (2,157)	Selva di Cadore - Longarone	quiet, picturesque. Open: Jun - Nov.
Stelvio (2,758)	Trafoi - Bormio	an old cycling favourite; one of highest in Europe; 3rd highest in Alps; 48 numbered hairpins on E side; splendid views; Fausto Coppi memorial on summit, heavy traffic; side-road from summit climbs to 3,008 metres. Open: early Jun - mid Oct.
Tonale (1,883)	Ponte Legno - Dimaro (W of Bolzano)	busy, fairly easy, picturesque. Open: May - Nov.
Tre Croci (1,805)	Cortina d'Ampezzo - Auronzo di Cadore	picturesque, fairly easy, good views. Open: May - Nov.
Valles (2,033)	Falcade - Panevéggio (S of Marmolada)	picturesque, narrow, quiet, fairly easy. Open: May - Nov.
Valparolo (2,192)	La Villa - Falzárego Pass	narrow, picturesque. Open: May - Nov.

Vivione (1,828)	Edolo - Schilpário	narrow, picturesque, on road to Presolana Pass. Open: May - Nov.

Note that 'opening' and 'closing' dates on passes can vary by as much as a month; it has been known for the 2,000-metre passes to be temporarily blocked early in September. As the snows recede through June, it is also the case that 'closed' notices can be up when the pass is perfectly negotiable by bike.

Tour of Central Italy

The accent of this tour is history and art, set against the gracefully rolling landscapes of Latium, Umbria and Tuscany; the route makes no attempt to include the more dramatic scenery of the neighbouring Apuan Alps, high Apennines or Abruzzi national park, all of which could easily be incorporated if the time and spirit were available. The ride starts relatively leisurely, linking the three great volcanic lakes, then picks up a sinuous trail between some of Italy's best preserved medieval towns, many of them perched imposingly on hill-tops, with a fabric that has changed little over the centuries. The roads used in this tour are not always the most adventurous; touring central Italy is always a toss-up between riding quiet but hilly roads or flatter, more busy ones. The suggested route here is something of a compromise and a glance at the maps will reveal the many alternatives guaranteed to add excitement and muscle. Pisa, Florence and San Marino could all conveniently be added to the northern section of the tour if desired. Rome is not the best place to start or finish a tour, simply because its environs are unpleasant cycling – it is however the most accessible. The tour could be adapted for a more tranquil start and finish by using Pisa or Florence (both on rail links to the UK, and some flights).

CENTRAL ITALY TOUR

Terrain: hilly
Distance: 800 km (excluding detours)
Start/Finish: Rome/Rome
Scenery: *
Interest: **
Maps: Touring Club Italiano 1:200,000 nos 13, 15, 16, 17

km	
	ROME (Leonardo da Vinci airport)
58	Bracciano
31	Ronciglione
21	Viterbo
17	Montefiascone

(detour round W side of lake: 38 km)

15	Bolsena
22	Orvieto
42	Città della Pieve
7	Chiusi
12	Chianciano Terme
9	Montepulciano

(alternative route NW on smaller roads via Monte Olivéto Maggiore, to Siena: 70 km)

22	S. Quírico D'Orcia
16	Buonconvento
28	Siena
23	Colle di Val D'Elsa
13	S. Gimignano

(detour NE to Florence & rejoin route at Arezzo)

11	Poggibonsi
53	Montevarchi
33	Arezzo

29	Cortona		28	Terni
45	Umbértide		35	Civita Castellana
30	Gúbbio			
40	Perúgia			*(detour to Rome)*
17	Assisi		13	Nepi
15	Cannara		25	Anguillara Sabázia
10	Bevagna		50	ROME (Leonardo da Vinci
7	Montefalco			airport)
24	Spoleto			

*(detour SE to explore Gran Sasso and
Abruzzi national park)*

Basic Information

Getting There

Air: Italy's international airports are Alghero, Bari, Bologna, Brindisi, Cagliari, Genoa, Milan, Naples, Palermo, Pisa, Rimini, Rome, Turin, Venice and Trieste. Flight time from London to Rome is $2\frac{1}{4}$ hours.

Rail: from the UK a through-route via Calais goes to Milan (change for Bologna, Florence, Rome, Pisa, Genoa), Verona and Venice. London to Milan takes 22 hours; to Naples, 30 hours.

Road: Milan is 1,060 kilometres from Boulogne by main road.

Ferry: Italy has excellent ferry connections with most other parts of the Mediterranean, including Sardinia, Sicily, Corsica, Yugoslavia, Greece, North Africa, Spain and Malta.

Information Sources

Italian State Tourist Office (ENIT): 201 Regent Street, London W1R 8AY (tel: 01-766-397). Helpful information handbook and interesting 'Art in Italy' booklet.

Local tourist bureaux: There are offices of the *Ente Provinciale per il Turismo* (EPT) in main towns throughout the country, and in addition there are about 400 local offices in smaller places and resorts.

Federazione Ciclistica Italiana, Via Leopoldo Franchetti 2, 00100 Rome. (tel: 36857255). The federation of Italian cycle-racing clubs with a mammoth membership of a hundred thousand.

Touring Club Italiano, Corso Italia 10, 20122 Milan. A general touring club affiliated to the AIT.

Unione Velocipedistica Italiana, Palazzo delle Federazioni, Viale Tiziano 70, Rome 00100. A national cycle-racing body.

Accommodation

Camping: sites congregate along the coast, and get very crowded during the summer; the better ones have good facilities, with grass and trees for shade, but some can be spartan, open to the sun, and sandy. Detailed lists are available from the Touring Club Italiano (Corso Italia 10, 20122 Milan) and from the Federcampeggio (Casella Postale 23, 50041 Calenzano) whose guide is in English and notes those sites giving discounts to AIT members and holders of International Camping Carnets (the same list is available free from ENIT). Local tourist bureaux can also supply lists for their neighbourhood.

When biking Italy's more remote inland regions, wild camping can be the only option. Permission should be asked before using land which is farmed.

Youth Hostels: unless you are confining yourself to the Po Valley and Italian Lakes, to the north Apennines or to the country immediately south of Naples, there are not enough hostels on which to base a bike tour: less than 60 for the whole country. The average number of beds is about 80, with a couple of 400-bed mega-hostels at Florence and Milan.

Student Hostels: available to students on holiday in Italy and costing about the same as the youth hostels. Apply to 'Casa dello Studente' of towns with universities, or write for the *Guide for Foreign Students* (Italian Ministry of Education, Viale Trastevere, Rome).

Mountain Huts: the Club Alpino Italiano has huts in mountain regions which do not cost much more than camp sites and can be used if you are planning some hiking. Information from CAI, Via Ugo Foscolo 3, Milan.

Farmhouses: a national organisation coordinates the renting of farmhouses and cottages. May be worth considering for fixed-centre touring. Details from Agriturist, Corso V. Emanuele 101, Rome.

Hotels/Pensions: usually friendly and good value, there are three classes of *Pensione,* all of them more basic than the 4th class hotel *(Locande* and *Aloggi* are also inexpensive). Hotels come in 5 classes, from Deluxe to 4th and prices have by law to be fixed with the provincial tourist board. A rate card should be attached to the back of each door, and check that this includes the supplementary charges (which can increase a bill by a third). Hotels and pensions outside towns are generally better and cheaper than urban addresses, and overall those in the north are better quality than those in the south of the country. The official and annually revised list is the *Annuario Alberghi,* available for reference at good travel agents and ENIT.

Weather

With the north of the country influenced by the Alps, and the south affected by the Sahara, it's not surprising that Italy's climate changes over its length.

In the Alps and northern Apennines the summers are very warm and winters snowy and freezing (though not as severe as Switzerland). South-facing slopes are markedly warmer. As you move south, temperatures increase (southern Italy is about 4°C warmer than the north) and most of peninsula Italy has hot dry summers with lots of sunshine, even in winter. In the mountains, temperatures are affected by altitude.

Rain is fairly heavy in the Alps and north Apennines (Bolzano in July and August is nearly as moist as the English Pennines) and is spread evenly throughout the year. The flat northern plain (Po Valley) has a spring and autumn maximum of rain, which can arrive in sudden thunderstorms, whereas peninsula Italy is very dry during the summer with rain becoming increasingly rare as you move south. Throughout the country, the east coast is dryer than the west.

Spring can bring *bora*-type winds (see Yugoslavia) to Venice and the western Italian Alps, and in summer the hot, dry, dusty *scirocco* from North Africa can blast northern Sicily. The prevailing wind between mid-May and mid-October tends to be northerly, getting stronger through the day and weakening by night.

Other Considerations: the sea is warm enough for comfortable bathing from June to early October. If you plan to spend time exploring the big cities, bear in mind that July and August can make the streets unbearably hot and smelly. Italian holidays are the first three weeks in August, when beaches are at their most crowded and when traffic in places like the Dolomites (where roads are limited) can make cycling difficult. June is a good month for cycling.

Average Daily Maximum Temperatures (Centigrade)

	alt. in metres	J	F	M	A	M	J	J	A	S	O	N	D
Bolzano	271	5	9	14	19	23	26	28	27	24	19	11	6
Cosenza	256	11	13	15	18	23	29	32	32	28	22	17	13

Cycling Information

Cycle Shops

Big cities like Bologna, Milan, Turin, Genoa, Florence, Rome and Naples are well-supplied with shops which can handle repairs and sell spares – though they are invariably oriented towards racing cyclists; replacement touring equipment can be hard to find. Shops are sometimes hidden away in obscure locations and the easiest way of finding them is often to ask a passing local cyclist. In Sardinia, Sicily and the southern mainland, spares and shops are rare.

Transporting Your Bicycle

Bikes can be carried as accompanied luggage on Italian trains (except on *Rapido* or *Autorail*), and should be taken to the *'Bagagli Portenze'* office, normally found at one end of the station, at least half-an-hour before departure. Station staff will load and unload the bike. Charges for carriage are sometimes disproportionately high; over a short journey the bike can cost four times the passenger fare. The procedure is the same for sending an unaccompanied bike. Major rail stations have left-luggage offices which hold bikes.

Queues at ticket offices can be long and a shade unruly and trains tend to be crowded, so it pays to arrive early and grab a seat. The national network is thorough and quite efficient, with the fastest routes along the coast and more limited slower services inland, on Sardinia and Sicily. Italy is well-connected with Europe's long-distance TEE network.

Some buses will carry bikes.

Roads

Surfaces on the busy *strade statali* (the main 'state' roads) are normally good tarmac; these are sometimes paralleled by an *autostrada* (motorway) in which case traffic will be reduced but the surface may have been allowed to deteriorate. The best roads for cycling – the narrow local byways – are generally surfaced, though in mountain districts (especially the south) they may be loose grit. Cobbles still exist in many towns and some, like Milan, have the added hazard of tramlines. Nearly all roads are well-graded, with few severely steep stretches.

Of far greater concern is Italian traffic; the roads are the second most crowded in Europe. Italian drivers have a lively disregard, not only for each other but for road-signs, pedestrians and cyclists too. In towns this means a car might reverse out of a side-road into your path, Fiats race round at breakneck speed and the air continually zips with the sound of motor-bikes and scooters. The smog and vehicular maelstrom of places like Rome, Milan and Turin make them unhealthy cities for bikes.

Italy has an exceptional number of bypasses; even small villages can have a special road skirting their perimeter for use by through-traffic. On a bike it's nearly always worth ignoring these bypasses and heading for the 'Centro', as the route through the centre of the town or village will invariably be shorter and more interesting. Sign-posting is not good, with road numbers often omitted; good maps are important unless you enjoy detours.

Maps

For General Planning

Michelin No. 988, Switzerland and Italy, Scale 1:1,000,000. Very limited number of minor roads shown, no indication of heights. Scenic roads in green.

Reise-und Verkehrsverlag (RV), Italy, Scale 1:800,000. Clear shading gives good indication of terrain. Some minor roads marked and comprehensive tourist information. Covers Switzerland too.

Kümmerly & Frey, Italy, Scale 1:500,000. Good detail for a map of this scale, with scenic roads, helpful height shading and tourist information.

For Cycling

Touring Club Italiano series, Scale 1:200,000. The standard cycling map for touring Italy, in 15 (rather too large) sheets. Scenic roads, gradients, hill shading, limited tourist information and useful indication of unsurfaced roads.

For Rough-stuff and Hiking

Freytag & Berndt, Wander Atlas Dolomiten, Scale 1:75,000 . Detailed guide to the Dolomite region, with contours. Information on mountaineering and hiking, and mountain refuges. Fairly expensive.

Kompass Wanderkarten series, scale 1:50,000. Very detailed, with height shading, tourist features, waymarked paths, tracks; covering the Italian Dolomites and Italian Lakes and Alps.

YUGOSLAVIA

Like Greece, Yugoslavia rejoices in a largely rugged and wild interior, a beautiful coastline, hot summery weather and a powerful history which brings colour and interest to many of its towns and villages. Cycling ranges in grade from easy seaside dawdles to arduous mountain riding.

Scenically, it's a country of immense variety, with verdant pastures, sun-scorched plateaux and yawning gorges, vast forests and rolling plains. But Yugoslavia's most acclaimed scenic feature is its 2,092-kilometre coastline and adjacent archipelago of over 700 islands (60 are inhabited); hugging the shore as close as they do makes them more acccessible than most island groups. About three-quarters of the country is mountain or plateau, and about a third is under forest.

Predictably, the motor-tourists stick to the commercialised honeypots along the coast; you don't have to pedal far off the beaten track (and that means literally taking to the *un*-beaten tracks) to find wilderness areas unsullied by the twentieth century. Yugoslavia is about the same size as the United Kingdom yet has less than half the population – which leaves a lot of empty countryside.

The great natural beauty of this Mediterranean land is not always matched by the urge for conservation in which other richer countries can afford to indulge. I remember looking forward for several miles to a village described in the guide-book as being 'remarkably colourful' and indeed its rustic buildings and long, high-powered boats nudging the current beneath the graceful spans of a medieval bridge were an enchanting sight. But someone had thrown a lavatory in the lilies. While on first viewing this didn't exactly enhance the scene, the juxtaposition of curving white porcelain against flowering monocotyledons and weathered limestone did, if you stared at it long enough, take on a pleasing surreal quality! And while eco-travellers may blanch at such *laissez-faire* ethics of refuse disposal, I've no doubt that the person who did it would be equally appalled by the more insidious pollution of industrial Europe.

There have been many invaders, all leaving some degree of influence. Yugoslavia was an outpost of the Roman Empire till the fifth century when the Slavs arrived from Poland (Yugoslavia means 'land of the southern Slavs'). Other visitors included the Byzantines, Bulgarians, Turks, Venetians, Hungarians and Austrians. Today Yugoslavia is a non-aligned, unorthodox communist regime surrounded by 7 different countries, and embraces under her banner of a 'Federal Socialist Republic' a total of 6 socialist republics, which include 5 different nationalities of people. Add to that 4 languages, 2 alphabets and 3 religions and you have quite some melting pot! Yugoslavs are passionate about their freedom and voluble on the subject of politics; the many war memorials across the land often stand out as being not only moving reminders but sculptures of high artistic merit.

Serbo-Croat is the main language, not too difficult to handle with the aid of a good phrase-book, and closely allied to the two other Yugoslav tongues, Slovenian and Macedonian. English is the first foreign language taught at schools and many young people are quite fluent, or at least eager to demonstrate their knowledge. German and Italian are also widely understood. A line north from Dubrovnik to the Hungarian border separates those who use the Roman alphabet to the west, and those to the east who use the Cyrillic alphabet (in a version very similar to the Russian one but with some additional characters; in coastal areas Roman equivalents are normally given). Nearly half the population are Orthodox, the rest being mainly Roman Catholics or Moslems (you may not be allowed in some mosques; shoes should always be removed before entering).

Cuisine varies according to region; grilled meat, salami, Turkish coffee, beer and *sljivovica* (plum brandy) are all regular fare. Away from the coast, food can be less plentiful, with some country shops having very limited supplies. My recollections of arriving ravenous at remote village stores to find not much more than sardines and balls of string on the shelves are vivid. (At the time of writing, certain items such as coffee, cooking oil and washing powder are rationed.) Most big villages have a bar or café *(Kavarna* or *Kafana)*, open all day and evening, where you can rest in the shade with delicious cool beers, soft drinks and sometimes food. The national currency is the *dinar* (divided into 100 *paras)*, and inflation in Yugoslavia is romping away at about 30%.

A couple of points to note are that the Yugoslavs are unusually sensitive about photography, so think twice before pulling out a camera near the border or by military installations (there are sometimes obvious signs bearing a camera with a red line through it). There also seem to be an awful lot of snakes; I've never had anything but friendly encounters but how do you extract one from the spokes of a bicycle wheel?

Ride Guide

Alpine Yugoslavia

Yugoslavia has but a modest share of the Alps: a couple of smallish mountain ranges which seldom top 2,500 metres but which have many scenic merits and can be toured along with the adjacent mountains of southern Austria, the Italian Dolomites or, say, with the Istrian peninsula. The snowy peaks, cropped green pastures and chalet-style houses have more in common with Austria than with the rest of Yugoslavia – which isn't surprising since the area spent a thousand years under Austrian rule. Cycling here is exerting, because the most interesting roads climb to 500 to 1,000 metres. There are something like 7,000 kilometres of hiking trails in these mountains.

The two ranges are separated by the 'Ljubljana Gap' – the main routeway which runs down from the north-west bringing road, rail and the River Sava. To the west of the Gap are the Julian Alps, whose pale limestone buttresses focus around Triglav, at 2,863 metres Yugoslavia's highest mountain. North of this peak, from the village of Mojstrana, a delightful tributary valley climbs past the Pericnik waterfall to Aljazev Dom, from where routes lead up to the summit of Triglav (a serious mountain walk). There are very fine rides to be had south of Triglav, past the touristy lake at Bled, with its castle and views, to the larger, quieter and higher Bohinjska lake in the upper reaches of the Sava Bohinjska valley (waterfall, seven lakes and hiking in the Triglav national park). Not far south of here a parallel road runs through the lovely Baca valley, a secluded partisan lair during the Second World War. To the west of Triglav is the superb Vrsic Pass (1,612 metres), which is strenuous but very scenic. Close to the pass, and running along the mountain crest, is the Italian-Yugoslav border, the other side of which are the Dolomites.

YUGOSLAVIA

Key
--------- touring area
-.-.-.-. country boundary
——————— cycle tour

0   50   100 150 Kilometres

Southwards, the Julian Alps are milder and there is the renowned (among spelaeologists) cave district. The most famous caverns are those at Postojna (on the Trieste-Ljubljana road) whose 12 miles of halls and tunnels are reputed to be the most striking in Europe. There are other, less commercial caves, and a celebrated 'disappearing lake' also in this area. Eventually the Julian Alps merge into the rolling hills, vineyards and ubiquitous 'karst' landscape. ('Karst' is the name given to the distinctive landscape created when limestone is eroded of its covering layer, leaving porous rock through which surface water will seep. Disappearing lakes, rivers which suddenly dive underground, vast caverns, strange depressions, coastal fjords and inlets are all typical features).

On the eastern side of the 'Ljubljana Gap' are the smaller Kamnik Alps (really a part of the long thin Karawanken range which forms Austria's southern border). Cycling possibilities are limited here; the classic route into the heart of the mountains starts from the town of Kamnik, and passes through Stahovica, Gornji Grad, Radmirje, Luce, Solcava and thence up the valley of Logarska Dolina to the face of the two highest mountains: Grintovec (2,588 metres) and Ojstrica. East from this range, the Alps have a final fling in the form of the Pohorje hills, before rolling down to Yugoslavia's best wine-producing area.

South of the Pohorje, and between the cities of Maribor and Zagreb, is the rolling and pleasant district of Zagorje, with castles and old churches, picture-book villages and a rustic atmosphere. Tito's childhood home (and museum) is at Kumrovec.

Istrian Peninsula

For a mild, not too exerting tour, the triangular peninsula hanging off the top of the Adriatic coast is a possibility. It's popular with package-holiday operators, so the roads get crowded, while the more attractive towns are highly developed. It is very accessible, with main rail stations and airports at Trieste, Pula and Rijeka.

The coast road around Istria is not too difficult for cycling, and the main centres of interest are Piran, Portoroz, Porec, Rovinj, Pula, Rabac and Labin. The sinuous inlets of Lim, Rasa and Pula would look more at home in Scandinavia than in the Mediterranean.

Inland there are many small quiet roads, and the interior is relatively untouched. There are castles around every corner and many other traces of Istria's many conquerors, from Romans, to Austrians to Italians. It is generally less mountainous that the rest of Dalmatia, being mainly a *karst* plain with not many rivers but lots of caves.

In winter, Istria is frequently scoured by the dreaded *bora*, though in summer this same wind can be something of a relief from the heat – unless you are cycling into it!

Dalmatian Coast

One of the longest continually attractive coasts in Europe, the Dalmatian shore has a natural splendour made fragile by four decades of increasingly intense tourism. A bike tour here can be an unforgettable experience, but only if care is taken over choice of route and choice of season. Between the wars, travel along this coast was difficult; now there is the Adriatic Highway (or *Magistrala*), a well-surfaced road running for 601 kilometres between Rijeka and Dubrovnik. During July and August, traffic on this one-and-only coast-road is very heavy. The solution is either to tour out of season or to 'island-hop' down the coast, making full use of the several large offshore islands to cut out sections of the Highway.

Air links to the Dalmatian coast are good, with airports at Pula, Rijeka, Zadar, Split and Dubrovnik. There are no railways running along the coast, although there are links inland from Zadar, Sibenik, Split and Ploce. There are also ferry links between the Dalmatian coast and Italy (Pula, Zadar, Losinj, Primosten, Split, and Dubrovnik all have services to various Italian ports from Venice down to Bari); Split, and Dubrovnik also have services with Greece and Turkey. With all these options, the variations of linear and circular cycle-tours, with or without the islands and inland mountains, are many. To get a bit of everything, try pedalling the entire coast from Rijeka to Dubrovnik, returning north by ferry (30 hours).

The whole of the coast, much of the inland mountains and the islands, are dominated by *karst* scenery. It's a rocky coastline, much indented, with clean white limestone dropping to surprisingly clear water, usually seen against a backdrop of mountain-sides or distant islands. Fishing fleets add colour to the many small ports and *vaterpolo* is a big sport, usually played in specially constructed sea-water pools, at night under floodlights. I once watched a hard-fought match between a team from Rijeka and one from Hercegnovi, the whistles, cheers, hoots and general pandemoniac uproar being no less restrained than an English football match or Italian bike race.

Historically, the Dalmatian coast − once a haven for some of the fiercest pirates in the Mediterranean − looks seaward towards Italy rather than inland to the rest of Yugoslavia; right behind the thin coastal strip is a steep mountain range, crossed by few easy passes. The most extreme example of this is the 150-kilometre long Velebit range which rushes up to 1,700 metres right from the water's edge. If you ride up to the crest (and you need to be strong of leg and heart to do this) you will be just a handful of kilometres from the Adriatic, yet rivers you can look down into will be flowing hundreds of kilometres in the opposite direction, to the Black Sea. The incredibly steep hair-pinned descent down this slope to the small town of Karlobag is a major test of rider and brakes.

The most interesting towns along the coast, and the most crowded too, are Zadar, Sibenik, Trogir, Split and Dubrovnik (the pearl of the entire coast, completely walled and barred to all wheeled traffic except bicycles and wheel-barrows). As a ride, the Adriatic Highway is not especially strenuous, and there are no major passes to cross, though the heat can be intense during high summer. The ever-changing views from the saddle are excellent. Hotels, inns and camp-sites are found at frequent intervals.

Of the islands, Losinj, Brac, Hvar and Korcula offer the most to cyclists, though the best parts can often only be reached by taking to rough tracks. There are many other, smaller islands worth a visit; Mljet, Vis and Lastovo deserve mention. Rab has one of Yugoslavia's most delightful Venetian towns; neighbouring Cres and Krk are large and flat. In general the islands are low, sometimes covered in dark green vegetation, with the odd red-roofed cluster of a village by the shore. Others are completely barren and waterless. Finding shade can sometimes be a problem. The main towns of these islands tend to get jammed with tourists during high summer, whereas outlying villages, which are harder to reach for less mobile holiday-makers, can remain delightfully tranquil. On Brac for example, Bol and Supertar can be thronged, yet nearby Postire can be quiet.

Inland from the Adriatic Highway there are many possibilities for mountain excursions, though protracted bike touring of this wild and often desolate region is the territory of the adventurous, self-sufficient cyclist. Camp sites and hotels are few and far between (though it's easy to find impromptu pitches for a sleeping bag or tent); the heat can be severe, water hard to find, there are often large distances between places with shops and the roads are invariably climbing or falling.

Notable inland high-spots (from north to south) include the beautiful necklace of Plitvice Lakes (on the Zagreb – Zadar road), the caves and canyons of the Paklenica national park (in the Velebit mountains inland from Zadar) and the most photographed bridge in Yugoslavia, at Mostar. Many of the inland towns have an enchanting Oriental influence, with domes and slim minarets, narrow alleys and cobbled streets. Sarajevo, flash-point of the First World War, has mosques and *souks*, Travnik to the north-west was once the residence of the Turkish *vizirs* (governors) and pretty Jajce also looks east, with mosques and old fortifications.

Montenegro

This touring area bases itself loosely on the socialist republic of the same name and provides an exciting opportunity for an adventure-tour which takes in a remarkable section of coast and some wild mountain country. There are airports at Dubrovnik, Tivat and Titograd, and a spectacular new railway linking Bar with Belgrade. Ferries run between Bar and Dubrovnik, and both ports have services to Italy and Greece.

The few main roads in the area have reasonable tarmac surfaces, but elsewhere you would be riding on rough gravel where the bumpiness is compensated by absence of traffic. It's fairly strenuous, with most roads falling and rising continuously. The Adriatic Highway south of Dubrovnik is not as scenic (except for Bokor Kotorska), and quite a bit hillier than the northern section of the Highway.

Apart from Dubrovnik, the main interest on the Montenegrin coast is Boka Kotorska – the fabulous Gulf of Kotor. It is an extraordinary sight, and rivals the best of Norwegian fjords for sheer drama. From the still waters of its long inlets, steep mountain walls leap to a craggy skyline quite dwarfing the many picturesque water-side villages of which Perast, with its mariners' dwellings and pretty offshore islets, is the most charming. The inner Gulf is the most spectacular part, and you can cycle right round it on a flat tarmac road.

The earthquake of 1979 savaged the Gulf area mercilessly; cycling here a couple of years after the disaster I recall one village not far from Hercegnovi where the road simply disappeared into the sea, and we carried our bikes along a makeshift path, over walls and through back gardens until the tarmac re-emerged from the water. A clump of trees stood up to their waists in the Mediterranean. Grand old houses leaned, many had no roof, some had walls missing and most had gaping cracks. Windows stared eyeless across a silent bay. Reconstruction was going on at a vigorous pace.

Near the dilapidated, fascinating old walled town of Kotor, the 'Serpentine Road' winds its way up the flank of the mighty Lovcen, the biggest mountain hereabouts. I'd put this among my top ten most breathtaking rides in Europe, for as the tarmac hairpins curl higher and higher an astonishing view unfolds until you can look over the entire Gulf and much of the adjacent coast. The 20-kilometre uphill ride climbs to 926 metres, passing through thick woods full of noisy bird chatter before emerging onto clear rocky slopes, with Kotor a tiny toy-town beneath your wheels. After wending its way across a plateau of peaceful, almost Alpine, pastures the road crosses another pass to Cetinje.

Other places on the Montenegrin coast worth a pause are attractive Cavtat, dignified Hercegnovi and walled Budva, though much of this coast has been taken over by glossy tourist developments. Many of the resorts are used by Yugoslavs, where nut-brown old men with saggy stomachs, and not a lot to do, roll in the sand or go into conspiratorial huddles on the sea wall. There are plenty of chances for bathing.

Inland Montenegro is a complete contrast to the coast, with bare limestone mountains, rocky hillsides, shady gorges and forests. Making a living from such a desolate landscape is not easy, and fields where farmers grow maize occupy small hollows in the *karst*, giving the impression of lots of little green pockets strewn across pale lumpy terrain. Montenegro has a proud and warlike history of resistance to invaders; forts and memorials abound.

Mountain roads lead to pretty backwaters like Rijeka Crnojevića;

decaying, historic Cetinje; Mount Lovcen, and further inland to the beautiful Durmitor range (and national park); the Sutjeska national park, and the gorges of the Tara and valley of the Drina, down which it is possible to make raft trips (hire from Foca). Further inland, the towns of Peć, Novi Pazar, Pristina and Prizren all have a Turkish flavour, while the valleys of the Morava and Ibar have many well-preserved medieval Serb-Orthodox churches and monasteries. The most exciting route out of Montenegro towards Greece is via the tough Tresnjevik Pass (1,570 metres) and Cakor Pass (1,849 metres), to Peć.

Yugoslavia's Highest Road

Between Andrijevica and Peć, crossing the mountains near Albania's northern border from Montenegro towards Greece, is the infamous Cakor Pass, rising to 1,849 metres.

A Tour of Yugoslavia's Mountains and Coast

An exciting, in places arduous, tour of great scenic variety, though the ferries, airports and railway stations along the route offer several start and finish points, and many opportunities for cutting the itinerary down if the beaches and ice-cream prove more alluring than the pedalling! The first part of the tour crosses some of Yugoslavia's rugged interior, passing the Plitvice Lakes and crossing the steep Velebit Mountains to reach the coast. Beyond the grand Paklenica national park you turn seaward and begin a ride past some of Yugoslavia's most outstanding Adriatic towns and islands. There are multiple options for island-hopping if the traffic on the *Magistrala* is too heavy or if the Robinson Crusoe instinct in you yearns for more isolated parts to explore.

YUGOSLAVIA TOUR
Terrain: hilly/mountainous
Distance: 700 km)
Start/Finish: Zagreb/Dubrovnik
Scenery: **
Interest: *
Maps: Freytag & Berndt Yugoslavia 1:600,000
Mair, Die General Karte,
Dalmatinische Küste I, II, III.

Km	ZAGREB
30	Jastrebarsko
24	Karlovac
50	Slunj
20	Rakovica
13	Plitvice
15	Babin Potok
25	Lesće
35	Gospić
40	Karlobag

(optional ferry to Pag, then south-east down peninsula for quieter route to Posedarje)

46	Starigrad Paklenica
25	Posedarje
26	Zadar

(trains back to Zagreb; various ferries)

73	Sibenik

(trains back to Zagreb; various ferries)

61	*Trogir*		Vela Luka
22	*Split*	7	Blato
		40	Korcula

(trains back to Zagreb; various ferries; *ferry to mainland*
there are many permutations of route Orebic
here, with opportunities to ride on the
islands of Solta, Brac, Hvar and *(cycle to Trpanj for ferry to Ploce then*
Korcula, cutting out sections of the *train to Zagreb)*
Magistrala; the option given below is 84 Slano
just one of many) 42 DUBROVNIK

ferry to Hvar *(planes to Zagreb and most*
    Hvar (explore western end of *international destinations; 30-hour*
    island) *ferry north to Rijeka then 180-km ride*
ferry to Korcula *to Zagreb)*

Basic Information

Getting There

Air: Yugoslavia's international airports are: Belgrade, Dubrovnik, Ljubljana, Pula, Rijeka, Split, Tivat (near Kotor), Zadar and Zagreb. Flight time from London to Belgrade is $3\frac{3}{4}$ hours.

    Rail: Limited connections with the rest of Europe, journey time (on the Tauern Express) from London to Zagreb is 30 hours.

    Road: Rijeka is 1,450 kilometres from Calais by main road.

    Ferry: Yugoslavia has excellent ferry connections with Italy, from Venice in the north to Bari in the south, with northern Greece and with Turkey.

Information Sources

Yugoslav National Tourist Office (YNTO): 143 Regent Street, London W1R 8AE (tel: 01-734-5243). Useful regional guides, hotel and camping lists.

    Local Tourist Bureaux: there are major offices in nine main cities and local offices in nearly all resorts and important towns. If you want information on a particular area, write to the 'Turisticki biro' of the nearest large town.

    Auto-Moto Savez Jugoslavie (AMSJ): Ruzveltova 18, 11001 Belgrade (tel: 401699). Really a motoring organisation but can provide information on road conditions to members of AIT. Offices in major towns.

    Yugoslavian Cycling Federation: Terazije 35/1, 11000 Belgrade (tel: 335189/334616). The adminstrative body for national cycle racing.

Accommodation

Camping: Camp-sites are fairly thickly-spread in the Yugoslav Alps, along the Dalmatian coast and among the more popular islands; elsewhere they are few and far between. Most sites offer reasonable facilities and some are prepared to give out-of-season discounts. The free list from YNTO gives details (including prices) of about 200 sites.

Officially, wild-camping is very much frowned upon, and it is not uncommon to come across a distinctive sign bearing a tent with a red line through it; it's best not to push your luck and I have met people who have been moved on by the police. Inland, however, there is little choice because the distances between places with accommodation are often further than one day's cycling. You certainly make yourself more obvious if you put up a tent.

Youth hostels: there are only 31 in the whole country, and most are located along the coast. They are neither in the best positions nor frequent enough to be used exclusively for a bike tour but would be useful if supplemented with other low-cost accommodation. Some have space for tents, none have self-cooking facilities, and priority is given to hostellers under twenty-seven.

Private Accommodation: some local tourist offices carry address lists of approved private homes which offer rooms – less expensive than hotels and often more pleasant. The prices, facilities and addresses of officially-approved private homes can be found in YNTO's annually revised list. As you're riding along you may sometimes spot a sign *sobe* (meaning 'rooms') and especially in out-of-the-way places these can be good value for money.

Inns/Pensions: there are three grades of pension – all less expensive than hotels.

Hotels: there are five classes of hotel, from 'L' (Luxury), 'A' (first class) to 'D' (economy), or if you prefer, 'dire'. Away from the coast, your daily route and cycling distance will be governed by the location of the next convenient hotel – they are not found away from the tourist trail. Standards are generally good though staff tend to lack the personal touch. In July and August especially, it's virtually impossible to find an un-booked hotel room, so if you intend to rely on this type of accommodation, prior reservation is vital.

Weather

The Yugoslav Alps have similar weather to the rest of the southern Alps, the best touring season being between June and September. Interior Yugoslavia has enormous seasonal variations, with scorching summers and severe winters. The narrow band of coastal land, hemmed in between the sea and the mountains has a typical Mediterranean climate, with hot dry summers and lots of sunshine. Winters are mild. You can tour here as early as May and as late as October.

Throughout the country, July and August are the hottest months, with temperatures reaching the 30s. The southern part of the coast is about 4°C warmer than the rest of the country during July.

Inland, rainfall peaks during the summer months, with Belgrade having about as much rain as London, the high mountains have much more, and the Dinaric Alps and peaks of Montenegro have similar rainfalls to the UK's well-known 'wet Wales'.

Yugoslavia's own unique wind is the *bora*, a north-easterly which is at its worst during the winter when it can hurtle over the mountain ridges with tremendous force; it once flung a goods train off the now-defunct Split to Sinj line. It's similar to the famous French *mistral*, and in Trieste blows for an average of 39 days each year. Locals claim that clouds over Mount Ucka (on the Istrian peninsula), over the island of Losinj, or on the Velebit range, are signs of an impending onslaught. Needless to say, biking into the teeth of the *bora* is a particularly fruitless exercise, so think twice before taking a winter tour of northern Dalmatia.

Other Considerations: outside the months of July, August and September, accommodation may be as little as half the summer-season price. July and August are the most crowded months in resorts and along the Adriatic Highway. The sea is comfortably warm for bathing from June through till early October. May and June see the rich profusion of wild flowers at their best. Overall, June is a very hard month to beat for a cycle tour.

Average Daily Maximum Temperatures (Centigrade)

	alt. in metres	J	F	M	A	M	J	J	A	S	O	N	D
Ljubljana	299	2	5	10	15	20	24	26	26	22	15	8	4
Split	125	10	11	14	18	23	27	30	30	26	20	15	12

Cycling Information

Cycle Shops

Although they do exist in the bigger, flatter, inland cities like Ljubljana. Zagreb and Belgrade, proper bike shops are as rare as saunas in the Sahara. Most of the bikes sold in Yugoslavia come from Eastern Europe, so spares for, say, UK or French-made machines are nearly impossible to find. So you have to be mechanically self-sufficient. Locally made models like the Unis 'Sprint' and Rog 'Elite Sport' appear to be low quality.

Transporting Your Bicycle

The Yugoslav rail network is not very extensive and neither are its trains known for their speed or promptness. There are no routes along the coast, and most of the inland lines are slow because of the steep gradients. With the exception of the main central line via Zagreb, Belgrade and Skopje, which is quite fast and dull, most Yugoslav train journeys take in superb scenery. The new and remarkable link from Bar to Belgrade uses 234 bridges and 254 tunnels. Bikes can be transported by rail, usually on the same train as the passenger. If sent as unaccompanied luggage, you pay for the bike according to the distance.

Independent bus companies cover areas between rail lines and some of these companies will carry bikes.

Roads

Surfaces and traffic on Yugoslav roads have got one thing in common: they are either there, or they are not. Yugoslavia has one of the lowest traffic densities in Europe (level with Norway), yet because nearly all motorists stick to the relatively few main routes, one finds columns of cars and coaches on for example the Adriatic Highway and the E94/E5 *autoput* (in July and August anyway), yet hardly any traffic at all on the secondary (often unsurfaced) roads. I've cycled along some seemingly quite important mountain roads and not seen other vehicles for three hours at a time. Yugoslavia has about the same density of roads as Austria i.e. not very many.

The major roads which link big towns and cities have acceptable tarmac, while back roads are often loose stone and dirt. Since much of the dramatic cycling is on these back roads, adventurous riders have to be prepared for slow-going and rough treatment on the tyres. Even the tarmac can be erratic, and freewheeling down long hills at top speed can be a dicey business. Great heat ripples or waves can appear in the surface, not to mention unannounced potholes. Cobbles are prevalent in some parts and there are tram-lines to watch for in the cities. In mountain regions you can find yourself plunging into quite long, unlit tunnels.

Yugoslav drivers deserve special mention. It's not that they intend to kill or maim but more that they are unaware of concepts like brake failure or the rights of other road users. In Yugoslavia, when I hear a vehicle approaching I just accept that my presence on the highway will have little effect on the consciousness of the driver and prepare myself for the inevitable shower of dust and gravel as he passes too close. Trucks with their engines turned off to conserve fuel bounce and thunder down mountain passes spewing gravel and rubber smoke in a hair-raising contest between gravity and nerves. At the other extreme, there is the super-casual attitude of the driver I saw hunched over his steering wheel reading a newspaper as his gigantic truck-trailer combination ground at walking pace up one of those 20-kilometre passes.

The infamous *autoput* I've already mentioned, which runs from Zagreb, through Belgrade, Nis and Skopje, should be avoided at all costs. Not only is it illegal to cycle parts of it but the chances of emerging unscathed are small as Germans hurtle past on their non-stop route to Greece, and long-distance coaches and heavy goods vehicles race each other down this mad macadam highway to the sun.

Lest I make all this sound too nightmarish, let me conclude by pointing out that if you cycle out of season, or if you have the patience to ride rough surfaces, you'll find Yugoslav roads some of the quietest and most fun in Europe.

Maps

For General Planning

Geographia Pocket Map Series, Yugoslavia, Scale 1:1,000,000. Very compact, with good height shading which gives clear indication of where the hills are to be found, and helpful road grading showing those likely to be unsurfaced. Scenic roads marked.

Kümmerly & Frey, Yugoslavia – Hungary, Scale 1:1,000,000. Similar to the Geographia, with height shading, road grading and scenic roads, but more bulky.

For Cycling

Freytag & Berndt, Yugoslavia, Scale 1:600,000. Although this would normally be too small a scale to recommend for detailed cycling, with the exception of those noted below, there are no readily available large scale touring maps of inland Yugoslavia. Every Yugoslav road that can be comfortably cycled (and a lot that cannot) is marked on this map, together with clear height shading.

Mair, Die General Karte, Dalmatinische Küste I, II and III, Scale 1:200,000. Absolutely invaluable for a coastal tour, very detailed, with tourist information, scenic roads, spot heights and shading, covering the entire coast from Trieste to Albania.

APPENDICES

1. Useful Organisations

Alliance Internationale de Tourisme, 2 Quai Eustave-Ador, Geneva, Switzerland. By obtaining their membership card (free from AIT-affiliated organisations such as the CTC) you can request information from the many other AIT-affiliated organisations.

Association of Cycle and Lightweight Campers, 11 Grosvenor Place, London SW1 0EY; tel: (01)828.1012. Quarterly bulletin sometimes includes useful information on tents and stoves etc.

Audax United Kingdom, 188 Runcorn Road, Warrington, Cheshire WA4 6SY; tel: (092 574) 248. The UK offshoot of a French organisation, encouraging cyclists to undertake long-distance rides *(randonnées)*, with trips to foreign events now on the AUK calendar.

British Cycling Federation, 16 Upper Woburn Place, London WC1H 0QE; tel: (01) 387 9320. The national association of UK cycle-racing clubs, with an information service for members.

Cyclists' Touring Club, Cotterell House, 69 Meadrow, Godalming, Surrey GU7 3HS; tel: (04868) 7217. *The* organisation for cycle-tourists, with insurance facilities, a mail-order department which stocks some foreign maps, a touring information service with comprehensive fact sheets on foreign cycling and technical matters, a group holiday programme and bi-monthly magazine *Cycletouring*. The CTC also issue camping carnets.

English Schools Cycling Association (ESCA), 6 Malmerswell Road, High Wycombe, Buckinghamshire HP13 6PD; tel: (0494) 446857. Dedicated to instruction of children, with facilities for issuing awards in the fields of racing and touring.

Globetrotters' Club, BCM/Roving, London WC1V 6XX. A worldwide travel information exchange, with a bi-monthly magazine *Globe*.

L'Ordre des Cols Dur, 39 Delahays Road, Hale, Altrincham, Cheshire WA15 8DT. tel: (061) 980.5033. Essential for riders keen on riding in mountains, with many *Pass Guides* available detailing conditions and points of interest on European cols, and a regular newssheet/magazine, *Cycloclimbing*.

Rough-stuff Fellowship, 4 Archray Avenue, Callander, Perthshire FK17 8JZ. tel: (0877) 30104. For the off-road rider, with a bi-monthly journal (which sometimes features European rough-stuff) and a library of routes.

The Tandem Club, 25 Hendred Way, Abingdon, Oxfordshire OX14 2AN. Offers a tandem spares and advice service and publishes a bi-monthly journal.

The Tricycle Association, 37 York Close, Market Bosworth, Nuneaton, Warwickshire. A racing, touring and social organisation for trike riders, with a quarterly gazette.

Youth Hostels Association (England and Wales), National Office, Trevelyan House, 8 St Stephen's Hill, St Albans, Hertfordshire AL1 2DY; tel: (0727) 55215. Can supply membership necessary for hostelling abroad.

Scottish Youth Hostels Association, National Office, 7 Glebe Crescent, Stirling FK8 2JA; tel: (0786) 2821. Can supply membership necessary for hostelling abroad.

International Youth Hostel Federation, Midland Bank Chambers, Howardsgate, Welwyn Garden City, Hertfordshire. Publishers of the *International Youth Hostel Handbook*.

2. Reading On

Maintenance Manuals

The Penguin Bicycle Handbook by Rob van der Plas; Penguin Books Ltd, 1983. Illustrated technical paperback covering everything from 'Gearing Theory' to custom-built cycles to maintenance.

Richard's Bicycle Book by Richard Ballantine; Pan Books, 1975 (latest edition 1983). Almost the classic manual, again a finely illustrated paperback with detailed sections on setting up a bike and maintenance, bountiful tips and an entertaining style.

General Cycling Books

Adventure Cycling in Europe, by John Rakowski; Rodale Press, 1981. A detailed guide written by an experienced American cyclist, covering 27 countries, including Eastern Europe.

Bike Touring; The Sierra Club Guide to Outings on Two Wheels, by Raymond Bridge; Sierra Club Books, 1979. Hefty American paperback dealing comprehensively with setting up and riding a touring bike, and choosing equipment.

Cycle touring in Britain and the rest of Europe, by Peter Knottley, 1975. The first third of the book deals with touring bikes, equipment and hints, the remainder being a guide to 27 countries, among them being those of Eastern Europe.

The Great Bike Race, by Geoffrey Nicholson, Magnum Books, 1977. A vivid and excellently written account of the 1976 Tour de France, essential reading for anyone planning to follow a part of the Tour by bike.

My Nineteenth Tour de France, by J.B. Wadley, J.B. Wadley (Publications) Ltd, 1974. Written by that most revered of British bike journalists 'Jock' Wadley, it tells the story of how he followed the course of the 1973 Tour de France by bicycle. It is a lovely pot-pourri of racing reminiscences and Anglo-French insight.

The Penguin Book of the Bicycle, by Roderick Watson and Martin Gray, Penguin Books 1978. A very complete look at the bicycle in history, sport and recreation; in cities and at war, plus sections on maintenance and safety.

Tour de France, by Robin Magowan; Stanley Paul, 1979. An exciting account of the 75th anniversary Tour de France, penned by an American seeing the great race for his first time.

Wheels of Choice, by Tim Hughes; Cyclographic Publications, 1980. An inspirational picture-book with 95 first-class photographs, many of them taken on the continent. If you want to know what bike touring feels like, buy this.

Touring Guides

Atlas des Cols des Alpes, Altigraph, B.P.1, Bouchemaine, 49000 Angers, France. Selective guide (in French) to the major Alpine passes, with clear cross-sections illustrating changes of gradient. A similar guide to the Pyrenees is available from the same company.

Catalogue des Cols de France, Robert Chauvot, 29 Avenue des

Marronniers, 69270 Fontaines-sur-Saone, Comprehensive guide (in French) to all the road passes in France, and many rough-stuff passes too, with comments indicating conditions of each route.

Alpenpässe, edited by ADAC Verlag, Munich, 1981. The most detailed guide to Alpine passes published, covering a total of 618, with gradients, heights, tourist facilities, opening dates and so on – all in German. Available by mail order from: ADAC Verlag, Postfach 700126, Am Westpark 8, 8000 München 70 (tel: 089-76.76-0).

Michelin 'Green' Guides, Michelin Tyre Co Ltd. Conveniently shaped for slipping into panniers, these slim tourist guides cover all the main attractions, with copious illustrations. At the time of going to press, English-language titles include Austria, Germany, Italy, Portugal, Spain, Switzerland, Brittany, Châteaux of the Loire, Dordogne, French Riviera, Normandy, Provence and Paris.

OCD Pass Guides see 'Useful Organisations'.

Books to Make you Brave

Daisy Daisy, by Christian Miller; Routledge and Kegan Paul, 1980. Beautifully written adventure story cum travelogue about the 56-year old author's journey across America on a folding aluminium bike; she made the 4,200-mile ride with not one puncture.

Fat Man on a Bicycle, by Tom Vernon; Michael Joseph, 1981. A gastronomic odyssey described with great humour and freshness as 19-stone Vernon pedals gently across France.

Full Tilt, by Dervla Murphy; John Murray, 1965. Stirring tale of a lone woman's journey from Ireland to India by bicycle, written with perception and sympathy.

Round the World on a Wheel, by John Foster Fraser; Chatto and Windus, 1982. First published in 1899, the book describes an epic 19,000-mile bike journey which involved its three heroes in a succession of bizarre and frightening incidents.

Three Men on the Bummel, by Jerome K. Jerome; Penguin Books, 1983 (first published 1900). The classic story of George, Harris and J. making an intrepid bicycle ride through the Black Forest at the turn of the century.

Cycling Magazines

All the magazines listed below carry some features and information on cycle-touring, though the CTC's *Cycletouring* is the only one devoted exclusively to touring. *Cycling* (mainly racing) usually has a brimming small ads section useful for buying second-hand bikes and equipment, as does *Cycletouring*. All except *Cycletouring* and *Bicycling* should be available from UK newsagents.

Bicycle, 89-91 Bayham Street, London NW1. tel: (01) 482.2040. Monthly.

Bicycle Times, 26 Commercial Buildings, Dunston, Gateshead NE11 9AA. tel: (0632) 608113. Monthly.

Bicycling, 33 E. Minor Street, Emmuns, PA 18049, USA tel: (215) 967-5171. Monthly from March to August; bi-monthly September to February.

Cycletouring, Cyclists' Touring Club, Cotterell House, 69 Meadrow, Godalming, Surrey GU7 3HS. tel: (04868) 7217. Bi-monthly.

Cycling, Surrey House, 1 Throwley Way, Sutton, Surrey SM1 4QQ. tel: (01) 643.8040. Weekly.

Cycling World, Andrew House, 2A Granville Road, Sidcup, Kent DA14 4BN. Monthly.

Cyclist Monthly, Surrey House, 1 Throwley Way, Sutton, Surrey SM1 4QQ. tel: (01) 643.8040.

Cycling Annual

International Cycling Guide, The Tantivy Press, Magdalen House, 136-148 Tooley Street, London SE1 2TT. Tel: (01)407.7566. Bulky paperback published each year and covering all aspects of cycling. Includes articles from European countries and directories of foreign cycle-touring holidays, continental bike shops and information on foreign cycling magazines and organisations.

3. Map Suppliers

Bauermeister Booksellers, 19 George IV Bridge, Edinburgh EH1 1EH. Tel: (031) 225.7236.

Blackwells, Broad Street, Oxford. Tel: (0865) 249111. Foreign maps and a good stock of travel books too.

Heffer's Map Shop, 3 Green Street/Sidney Street, Cambridge. Tel: (0223) 350701.

The Map Shop, A.T. Atkinson & Partner, 4 Court Street, Upton-upon-Severn, Worcestershire WR8 0JA (06846) 3146.

McCarta Ltd, 122 King's Cross Road, London WC1X 9DS. Tel: (01) 278.8278. An excellent range of large-scale maps suitable for cycling. Mail order too.

Stanfords International Map Centre, 12-14 Long Acre, Covent Garden, London WC2E 9LP. Tel: (01) 836.1321. Probably has more maps on its shelves than any other shop in the country, with large-scale editions for all European countries and an excellent range of travel books too. Mail order also.

W.H. Willshaw Ltd, 16 John Dalton Street, Manchester M2 6HS. Tel: (061) 834.0257.

4. Equipment Check Lists

You need not take *everything* on these check lists – the chances are that, as well as reminding you of the things you ought to take, the lists include things suitable for a different type of person on a different type of tour. For example gloves and a scarf are for cool-weather biking only. And not everyone needs a skirt. So be selective!

Clothes
windproof/waterproof jacket or
    training top
pullover
shirts/T shirts
cycling trousers
'evening' skirt or trousers
shorts
underclothes
socks
shoes for cycling
light 'evening' shoes or sandals
handkerchiefs
hat
gloves/mitts
scarf
swimming costume

Miscellaneous
tin opener/corkscrew
matches
watch
maps
guide books
biro/pencil
notebook
other hobby equipment
sunglasses
needle and cotton
compass
small rucksack
elastic luggage straps
camera, lens and film
towel
toiletries
spare spectacles or contact lenses
money belt/pouch
soap powder
plastic bags/stuff sacs
bicycle lock
youth hostel handbook/camp site or

hotel lists
bicycle pump

Documents/Money
passport
credit cards
cheque book and cheque card
travel cheques
cash (foreign, and home)
friends/relations addresses for mailing
    postcards
membership cards
Form E111
medical insurance policy documents
personal medical information (blood
    group, allergies, diabetic etc)

Bike Tools
allen keys to fit bike
spoke key
screwdriver, assorted spanners to fit
    bike
tyre levers
file
pliers
chain-link extractor
freewheel removal tool
crank removal tool

Spares
spokes
nuts/bolts
thin wire
inner tube
front and rear axle
long brake cable
long gear cable
a few chain links
cotter pins (if cottered chain set)
lamp batteries
lamp bulbs
puncture repair kit

First Aid
crepe bandage (5cm wide)
net dressing retainer *(Netalast)*
zinc oxide strapping plaster (2.5cm x 3m)
triangular bandage
4 *Melolin* dressings (5cm x 5cm)
assorted size *Elastoplast* dressings
antiseptic cream
cotton wool
sun screening lotion *(Uvistat, Lipsyl)*
insect repellent
stiff-backed razor blade
clean needle
scissors
safety pins
water-purifying tablets

any personal drugs
drugs for: pain killing, diarrhoea, constipation, indigestion (see your doctor for appropriate types)

Camping/Cooking
sleeping bag
sheet sleeping bag
sleeping mat/groundsheet
tent
stove and fuel
pots
mug
knife, fork and spoon
water bottles
pot cleaner

Gear Ratios

Through quaint tradition, the gear ratios of bicycles are expressed in inches in the US and UK. To work out your gear ratio, you multiply the number of teeth on the chainring by the diameter of the wheel, then divide the result by the number of teeth on the rear sprocket. Or you use the chart below. In each box, the upper figure refers to bikes with 27-inch wheels and the lower figure to those with 26-inch wheels.

(For tables please see overleaf)

number of teeth on chainwheel

					Number of teeth on rear sprocket						
	12	13	14	15	16	17	18	19	20	21	22
26	58.5	54	50.1	46.8	43.9	41.3	39	36.9	35.1	33.4	31.9
	56.3	52	48.3	45.1	45.3	39.8	37.6	35.6	33.8	32.2	30.7
28	63	58.2	54	50.4	47.3	44.5	42	39.8	37.8	36	34.4
	60.7	56	52	48.5	45.5	42.8	40.4	38.3	36.4	34.7	33.1
30	67.5	62.3	57.9	54	50.6	47.6	45	42.6	40.5	38.6	36.8
	65	60	55.7	52	48.78	45.9	43.3	41.1	39	37.1	35.5
32	72	66.5	61.7	57.6	54	50.8	48	45.5	43.2	41.1	39.3
	69.3	64	59.4	55.5	52	48.9	46.2	43.8	41.6	39.6	37.8
34	76.5	70.6	65.6	61.2	57.4	54	51	48.3	45.9	43.7	41.7
	73.7	68	63.1	58.9	55.3	52	49.1	46.5	44.2	42.1	40.2
36	81	74.8	69.4	64.8	60.8	57.2	54	51.2	48.6	46.3	44.2
	78	72	66.9	62.4	58.5	55.1	52	49.3	46.8	44.6	42.5
38	85.5	78.9	73.3	68.4	64.1	60.4	57	54	51.3	48.9	46.6
	82.3	76	70.6	65.9	61.8	58.1	54.9	52	49.4	47	44.9
40	90	83.1	77.1	72	67.5	63.5	60	56.8	54	51.4	49.1
	86.7	80	74.3	69.3	65	61.2	57.8	54.7	52	49.5	47.3
42	94.5	87.2	81	75.6	70.9	66.7	63	59.7	56.7	54	51.5
	91	84	78	72.8	68.3	64.2	60.7	57.5	54.6	52	49.6
44	99	91.4	84.9	79.2	74.3	69.9	66	62.5	59.4	56.6	54
	95.3	88	81.7	76.3	71.5	67.3	63.6	60.2	57.2	54.5	52
45	101.3	93.5	86.8	81	75.9	71.5	67.5	63.9	60.8	57.9	55.2
	97.5	90	83.6	78	73.1	68.8	65	61.6	58.5	55.7	53.2
46	103.5	95.5	88.7	82.8	77.6	73.1	69	65.4	62.1	59.1	56.5
	99.7	92	85.4	79.7	74.8	70.4	66.4	62.9	59.8	57	54.4
47	105.8	97.6	90.6	84.6	79.3	74.6	70.5	66.8	63.5	60.4	57.7
	101.8	94	87.3	81.5	76.4	71.9	67.9	64.3	61.1	58.2	55.5
48	108	99.7	92.6	86.4	81	76.2	72	68.2	64.8	61.7	58.9
	104	96	89.1	83.2	78	73.4	69.3	65.7	62.4	59.4	56.7
49	110.3	101.8	94.5	88.2	82.7	77.8	73.5	69.6	66.2	63	60.1
	106.2	98	91	84.9	79.6	74.9	70.8	67.1	63.7	60.7	57.9
50	112.5	103.8	96.4	90	84.4	79.4	75	71.1	67.5	64.3	61.4
	108.3	100	92.9	86.7	81.3	76.5	72.2	68.4	65	61.9	59.1
51	114.8	105.9	98.4	91.8	86.1	81	76.5	72.5	68.9	65.6	62.6
	110.5	102	94.7	88.4	82.9	78	73.7	69.8	66.3	63.1	60.3
52	117	108	100.3	93.6	87.8	82.6	78	73.9	70.2	66.9	63.8
	112.7	104	96.6	90.1	84.5	79.5	75.1	71.2	67.6	64.4	61.5
53	119.3	110.1	102.2	95.4	89.4	84.2	79.5	75.3	71.6	68.1	65
	114.8	106	98.4	91.9	86.1	81.1	76.6	72.6	68.9	65.6	62.6
54	121.5	112.2	104.1	97.2	91.1	85.8	81	76.7	72.9	69.4	66.3
	117	108	100.3	93.6	87.8	82.6	78	73.9	70.2	66.9	63.8

23	24	25	26	27	28	29	30	31	32	33	34	
30.5	29.3	28.1	27	26	25.1	24.2	23.4	22.6	21.9	21.3	20.6	26
29.4	28.2	27	26	25	24.1	23.3	22.6	21.8	21.1	20.5	19.9	
32.9	31.5	30.2	29.1	28	27	26.1	25.2	24.4	23.6	22.9	22.2	28
31.7	30.3	29.1	28	27	26	25.1	24.3	23.5	22.8	22.1	21.4	
35.2	33.8	32.4	31.2	30	28.9	27.9	27	26.1	25.3	24.5	23.8	30
33.9	32.5	31.2	30	28.9	27.9	26.9	26	25.2	24.4	23.6	22.9	
37.6	36	34.6	33.2	32	30.9	29.8	28.8	27.9	27.0	26.2	25.4	32
36.2	34.7	33.3	32	30.8	29.7	28.7	27.7	26.8	26.0	25.2	24.5	
39.9	38.3	36.7	35.3	34	32.8	31.7	30.6	29.6	28.7	27.8	27.0	34
38.4	36.8	35.4	34	32.7	31.6	30.5	29.5	28.5	27.6	26.8	26.0	
42.3	40.5	38.9	37.4	36	34.7	33.5	32.4	31.4	30.4	29.5	28.6	36
40.7	39	37.4	36	34.7	33.4	32.3	31.2	30.2	29.3	28.4	27.5	
44.6	42.8	41	39.5	38	36.6	35.4	34.2	33.1	32.1	31.1	30.2	38
43	41.2	39.5	38	36.6	35.3	34.1	32.9	31.9	30.9	29.9	29.1	
47	45	43.2	41.5	40	38.6	37.2	36	34.8	33.8	32.7	31.8	40
45.2	43.3	41.6	40	38.5	37.1	35.9	34.7	33.5	32.5	31.5	30.6	
49.3	47.3	45.4	43.6	42	40.5	39.1	37.8	36.6	35.4	34.4	33.4	42
47.5	45.5	43.7	42	40.4	39	37.7	36.4	35.2	34.1	33.1	32.1	
51.7	49.5	47.5	45.7	44	42.4	41	39.6	38.3	37.1	36.0	34.9	44
49.7	47.7	45.8	44	42.4	40.9	39.4	38.1	36.9	35.8	34.7	33.6	
52.8	50.6	48.6	46.7	45	43.4	41.9	40.5	39.2	38.0	36.8	35.7	45
50.9	48.8	46.8	45	43.3	41.8	40.3	39	37.7	36.6	35.5	34.4	
54	51.8	49.7	47.8	46	44.4	42.8	41.4	40.1	38.8	37.6	36.5	46
52	49.8	47.8	46	44.3	42.7	41.2	39.9	38.6	37.4	36.2	35.2	
55.2	52.9	50.8	48.8	47	45.3	43.8	42.3	40.9	39.7	38.5	37.3	47
53.1	50.9	48.9	47	45.3	43.6	42.1	40.7	39.4	38.2	37.0	35.9	
56.3	54	51.8	49.8	48	46.3	44.7	43.2	41.8	40.5	39.3	38.1	48
54.3	52	49.9	48	46.2	44.6	43	41.6	40.3	39.0	37.8	36.7	
57.5	55.1	52.9	50.9	49	47.3	45.6	44.1	42.7	41.3	40.1	38.9	49
55.4	53.1	51	49	47.2	45.5	43.9	42.5	41.1	39.8	38.6	37.5	
58.7	56.3	54	51.9	50	48.2	46.6	45	43.5	42.2	40.9	39.7	50
56.5	54.2	52	50	48.1	46.4	44.8	43.3	41.9	40.6	39.4	38.2	
59.9	57.4	55.1	53	51	49.2	47.5	45.9	44.4	43.0	41.7	40.5	51
57.7	55.3	53	51	49.1	47.4	45.7	44.2	42.8	41.4	40.2	39.0	
61	58.5	56.2	54	52	50.1	48.4	46.8	45.3	43.9	42.5	41.3	52
58.8	56.3	54.1	52	50.1	48.3	46.6	45.1	43.6	42.3	41.0	39.8	
62.2	59.6	57.2	55	53	51.1	49.3	47.7	46.2	44.7	43.4	42.1	53
59.9	57.4	55.1	53	51	49.2	47.5	45.9	44.5	43.1	41.8	40.5	
63.4	60.8	58.3	56.1	54	52.1	50.3	48.6	47	45.6	44.2	42.9	54
61	58.5	56.2	54	52	50.1	48.4	46.8	45.3	43.9	42.5	41.3	

6. UK Embassies and Consulates

Austria Reisnerstrasse 40, 1030 Vienna (tel: 73.15.75). Consulates at Innsbruck and Vienna.

Belgium 28 rue Joseph II, 1040 Brussels (tel: 219.11.65). Consulates at Antwerp, Brussels, Ghent, Liège and Ostend.

Denmark Kastelsvej 36-40, Copenhagen 0 (tel: 26.46.00). Consulates at Aalborg, Aarhus, Esbjerg and Odense.

Finland Uudenmaankatu 16-20, 00120 Helsinki 12 (tel: 647.922). Consulates at Kotka, Oulu, Pori, Tampere, Turku and Vaasa.

France 35 Rue du Faubourg St Honoré, Paris 8 (tel: 266.91.42). Consulates at Bordeaux, Lille, Lyon, Marseille, Strasbourg, Le Havre, Biarritz Boulogne, Calais, Cherbourg, Dunkirk, Epernay, Metz, Nantes and Perpignan.

West Germany Friedrich-Ebert Allee 77, 5300 Bonn (tel: 23.40.61). Consulates in Bremen, Dusseldorf, Frankfurt am Main, Hamburg, Hanover, Munich, Stuttgart and West Berlin.

Greece 1 Ploutarchou Street, Athens 139 (tel: 7362.11). Consulate in Thessalonika.

Italy Via XX Settembre 80a, Rome (tel: 475.5441). Consulates at Cagliari, Florence, Genoa, Messina, Milan, Naples, Palermo, Trieste, Turin and Venice.

Luxembourg 28 Boulevard Royal, Luxembourg (tel: 29864).

The Netherlands Lange Voorhout 10, The Hague (tel: 64 58 00). Consulates at Amsterdam and Rotterdam.

Norway Thomas Heftyesgate 8, Oslo (tel: 56 38 90). Consulate in Bergen.

Portugal Rua Santo Domingos à Lapa 35-39, Lisbon (tel: 66 11 91). Consulates at Figueira da Foz, Oporto, Portimão and Vila Real de Sao Antónia.

Spain Calle Fernando el santo 16, Madrid 4 (tel: 419.02.00). Consulates in Algeciras, Alicante, Almeria, Barcelona, Bilbao, Cadiz, Ceuta, Jerez de la Frontera, Gijon, Granada, Ibiza, Las Palmas, Malaga, Palma de Mallorca, San Sebastian, Santa Cruz de Tenerife, Seville, Tarragona, Valencia and Vigo.

Sweden Skarpögatan 6, 115 27 Stockholm (tel: 67 01 40). Consulates in Gothenburg and Malmö.

Switzerland Thunstrasse 50, 3005 Berne (tel: 44 50 21). Consulates at Basle, Geneva, Montreux, Lugano and Zurich.

Yugoslavia Generala Zdanova 46, 11000 Belgrade (tel: 645.055). Consulates at Split and Zagreb.

7. Velo Vocab

Bike Parts

English	Dutch	French	German	Italian	Spanish
ball bearings	kogellager	roulement à billes	Kugellager	cuscinetto a sfere	cojinete de bolas
battery	accu	batterie	Batterie	batteria	batería
bell	bel				
bolt	bout	boulon	Bolzen	bollone	perno
brake	rem	frein	Bremse	freno	freno
bulb	lampje	ampoule	Birne	lampadina	foquito
carrier	bagagedrager	porte-bagage	Gepäckträger	portabagagli	parilla
chain	ketting	chaîne	Rollenkette	catena	cadena
chainwheel	kettingwiel	plateau de pédaler	Kettenrad	ingranaggio	estrella
cog	naaf	moyeu	Nabe	pignone	engranajes
cotter pin	spie	clavette	Kurbelkeil	chiavetta	chaveta hendida
crank	crank	manivelle	Trekkurbel	pedivella	palanca
derailleur	derailleur	dérailleur	Kettenschaltung	cambio	cambio de marchas
dynamo	dynamo	dynamo	Lichtmaschine	dinamo	dínamo
fork	voorvork	fourche	Vordergabel	forcella	horquilla
frame	frame	cadre	Rahmen	telaio	cuadro
freewheel	freewheel	roue libre	Freilauf	ruota libera	rueda libre
front light	voorlicht	feu avant	Vorlicht	faro anteriore	luz anterior
front wheel	voorwiel	roue avant	Vorderrad	ruota anteriore	rueda anterior
grease	vet	lubricant	Schmierstoff	grasso	grasa
handlebars	stuur	guidon	Lenker	manubrio	guia
hub	wielnaaf	moyeu	Radnabe	mozzo	cubo da rueda
inner tube	binnenband	chambre à air	Luftschlauch	camera d'aria	camara de aire
lock	slot	anti-vol	Schloss	lucchetto	seguro o cerrojo
nut	(schroef) moer	écrou	Mutter	dado	tuerca
oil	olie	huile	Oel	olio	aceite
pedal	pedaal	pédale	Pedal	pedale	pedal
pump	pomp	pompe	Pumpe	pompa	inflador
rear light	achterlicht	feu arrière	Rücklicht	faro posteriore	luz trasera
rear wheel	achterwiel	roue arrière	Hinterrad	ruota posteriore	rueda trasera
reflector	reflector	réflecteur	Rückstrahler	riflettore	reflector
rim	velg	jante	Felge	cerchione	aro
saddle	zadel	selle	Sattel	sella	silla
spoke	spaak	rayon	Speiche	raggio	rayo de rueda
tyre	buitenband	pneu	Reifen	neumatico	neumático
valve	ventiel	valve	Schlauchventil	valvola	válvula
wheel	wiel	roue	Rad	ruota	rueda

Tools and Bits

spanner	moersleutel	clef	Schlüssel	chiave inglese	llave inglesa
screwdriver	schroevedraaier	tournevis	Schraubenzieher	cacciavite	destornillador
pair of pliers	buigtang	pinces	Zange	pinza	alicates
soft wire	buigzaam draad	fil mou	Weichdraht	filo metallico dolce	alambre flexible
jubilee clip	slangenklem	collier	Schlauchklemme	fascetta stringitubo	abrazadera 'jubilee'

The Desperate Request

Can you...	Kunt U...	Pouvez-vous...	Können Sie...	Può...	Puede usted...
repair my	mijn fiets	réparer ma	meìn Fahrrad	riparare la mia	reparar mi
bicycle?	repareren?	vélo?	reparieren?	bicicletta?	bicicleta?
How soon?	tot wanneer?	quand sera-t-elle prête?	Bis wann?	fina a quando?	cuándo estará reparado?
How much will it cost?	hoeveel zal de reparatie kosten?	combien la réparation coûtera-t-elle?	Was wird die Reparatur kosten?	quanto costerà la riparazione?	cuánto costará la reparación?

8. Conversion Formulae

To convert

Feet to Metres	Multiply by 0.3048	1000 feet = 300 metres
Metres to Feet	Multiply by 3.281	1000 metres = 3300 feet
Miles to Kilometres	Multiply by 1.609	10 miles = 16 km
Kilometres to Miles	Multiply by 0.6214	10 km = 6 miles
Fahrenheit to Centigrade	Subtract 32 & multiply by 0.56	see below
Centigrade to Fahrenheit	Multiply by 0.56 & add 32	see below
Pints to Litres	Multiply by 0.5682	2 pints = 1.1 litres
Litres to Pints	Multiply by 1.76	1 litre = 1¾ pints
Pounds to Kilograms	Multiply by 0.4536	10 lbs = 4.5 kg
Kilograms to Pounds	Multiply by 2.205	10 kg = 22 lbs

Conversion Chart for Temperature

Centigrade	-5	0	5	10	15	20	25	30	35
Fahrenheit	23	32	41	50	59	68	77	86	95

Conversion Chart for Gradient

Continental	5%	7%	9%	11%	13%	15%	17%	19%	21%	23%	25%
British	1:20	1:14	1:11	1:9	1:8	1:7	1:6	1:5	1:5	1:4	1:4

9. Opening Hours

Full details of each country's shop, post office and bank hours can be found in the literature of the national tourist boards; the times noted below are generalisations, being the hours that whatever the country, you can be sure to find the establishment open that you want to use.

Shops

Monday to Friday 9 – 12, 2 – 5, except for Greece, southern Italy, Portugal, Spain and Yugoslavia, where shops tend to open from 8 am to 8 pm with a 3-4 hour siesta in the middle of the day. In the Netherlands shops close on Mondays, in France some are closed on Mondays and in Luxembourg and Switzerland shops are closed on Monday afternoons. All shops are open between 9 and 12 on Saturdays.

Post Offices

Monday to Friday 9 – 12, 2 – 4, with the same exceptions as described above. Closed on Saturdays.

Banks

Monday to Friday 10 – 12; Saturday closed.

10. National Holidays

New Year's Day	Epiphany (Jan)
Shrove Monday	Shrove Tuesday
Maundy Thursday	Good Friday
Easter Monday	May Day
Ascension (May)	Whit Monday (May or June)
Corpus Christi (May or June)	Midsummer Day (June)
15 August (Assumption)	1 November (All Saints)
2 November (All Souls)	11 November (Armistice)
8 December (Conception)	24 December (Christmas)
25 December (Christmas)	26 December (Christmas)
Additional Holidays	

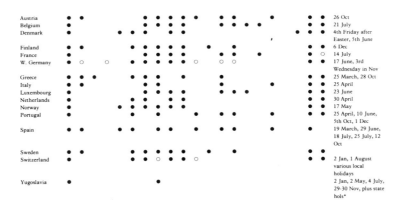

Austria — 26 Oct
Belgium — 21 July
Denmark — 4th Friday after Easter, 5th June
Finland — 6 Dec
France — 14 July
W. Germany — 17 June, 3rd Wednesday in Nov
Greece — 25 March, 28 Oct
Italy — 25 April
Luxembourg — 23 June
Netherlands — 30 April
Norway — 17 May
Portugal — 25 April, 10 June, 5th Oct, 1 Dec
Spain — 19 March, 29 June, 18 July, 25 July, 12 Oct
Sweden
Switzerland — 2 Jan, 1 August various local holidays
Yugoslavia — 2 Jan, 2 May, 4 July, 29-30 Nov, plus state hols*

*Yugoslavia's Republican national holidays are as follows:
7 July: Serbia; 13 July: Montenegro; 22 July, 1 November: Slovenia; 27 July: Croatia, Bosnia, Herzegovina; 2 August, 11 October: Macedonia.

On the dates marked on the chart, expect to find all shops and offices closed and note that in some places, for example Scandinavia, shops start to close at one o'clock on the day preceding the national holiday. Things are made more confusing by some countries, like Finland, moving their national holidays to the nearest Saturday, and by the Mediterranean countries who give themselves extra local holidays. Both the Spanish and the Italians close shops on local feast days staged in honour of the town's patron saint, and to cap it all Greece's Easter is later than the Roman one; their Whit Monday falling some 50 days beyond Easter Sunday.

11. UK Passports

You need an up-to-date passport for visiting the continent; in theory there are some borders that can be crossed by using other forms of identification (such as a driving licence) but since this depends on the goodwill of the border officials, it is safer to carry the 'real thing'. There are various types, among them a British Visitors Passport (available over the counter if you are in a hurry). Application forms for full passports can be obtained from main post offices; applications should be made at least 4 weeks before you plan to travel. Take great care not to lose it.

12. Poste Restante

Useful if you want to pick up mail once touring, or if you want to get in touch with another traveller, is the *poste restante* facility operated by all European post offices. When sending a latter, write on the envelope in clear bold letters:

LIONEL SPROCKET (ie. your name)
POSTE RESTANTE
MAIN POST OFFICE
ORLEANS
FRANCE.

On receipt, the post office will usually hold the letter for a maximum of 30 days. When you call in you will be expected to show your passport to prove identity, and to pay a small charge for the service. When sending letters, never write 'Lionel Sprocket *Esquire*' on the envelope, because the French clerk will be programmed to hand the correspondence to nobody but Mr Esquire. The sender's name should be on the back of the envelope.

13. Commercial Bike Holidays

This listing includes both the all-in package holiday and the do-it-yourself deal whereby you are supplied with a map and route only. Note that the Cyclists' Touring Club has a full programme of foreign tours each year, organised by its members on a non-profit basis.

Anglo-Dutch Sports Ltd, 30a Foxgrove Road, Beckenham, Kent BR3 2BD, UK. (tel: 01-650.2347). Netherlands.

ANWB, 220 Wassenaarseweg, 2596 EC The Hague, The Netherlands (tel: 070-264426). Netherlands, Austria, Switzerland, Germany, France.

Bike Events, 66 Walcot Street, Bath, Avon, UK (tel: 0225-65786). France.

Biking Expedition Inc., Hall Avenue (PO Box 547), Henniker, New

Hampshire 03242, USA (tel: 603-428.7500). France.

Country Cycling Tours, 167, West 83rd Street, New York, NY 10024, USA (tel: 212-874.5151). France.

Dansk Cykelferie/Dantourist A/S, Hulgade 21, DK-5700 Svendborg, Denmark (tel: (09) 21 07 41). Denmark.

EACH Cycling Holidays, Holly Tree Farm, Yoxford, Suffolk IP17 3JP, UK (tel: 072877 - 246). Netherlands, France, Denmark.

Ekenäs City Tourist Agency, Skillnadsgatan 16, 10600 Ekenäs, Finland (tel: (9) 11 14 600). Finland.

VVV Friesland-Leeuwarden, Stationsplein 1, 8911 AC Leeuwarden, Netherlands (tel: 05100-32224). Netherlands.

Gerhard's Bicycle Odysseys, 4949 S.W. Macadam Avenue, Portland, Oregon 97201, USA (tel: 503-223.2402). Germany, France, Austria.

Grenå Tourist Bureau, Markedsgade, Postboks 33, DK-8500 Grenå, Denmark (tel: 06-32 12 02). Denmark.

Nederlands Jeugdherberge Centrale, Prof. Tulpplein 4, 1018 GX Amsterdam, Netherlands (tel: 020-264433). Belgium, Netherlands.

Porvoo Rural Commune/Tourist Information Office, Rihkamakatu 3, SF-06100 Porvoo 10, Finland (tel: (9) 15 146 133/238). Finland.

Provinciale VVV Gelderland, Apeldoornseweg 53, 6814 BJ, Netherlands (tel: 085-513713). Netherlands.

Provinciale VVV Overijssel, De Werf'l, 7607 HH Almelo, Netherlands (tel: 05490-18765), Netherlands.

Sierra Club, 530 Bush Street, San Francisco, California 94108, USA (tel: 415-981.8634). Denmark, France.

Streek VVV Hart van Brabant, Spoorlann 416a, 5038 CG Tilburg, Netherlands (tel: 013-436131). Netherlands.

Susi Madron's Cycling Holidays Ltd, 11 Normal Road, Platt Fields, Manchester M14 5LF, UK (tel: 061-224.2139). France.

Svenska Turistföreningen, Box 7615, 103 94 Stockholm, Sweden (tel: 08-22 72 00). Sweden.

VVV Texel, PO Box 3, 1790 AA Den Burg/Texel, Netherlands (tel: 02220-2844). Netherlands.

Verkehrsbüro, Lanzerheide-Valbella 7078, Switzerland (tel: 081-341588/89), Switzerland.

Welcome Swiss Tours, Avenue Benjamin-Constant 7, 1003 Lausanne, Switzerland (tel: 021-20682). Switzerland.

YHA Travel, 14 Southampton Street, London WC2E 7HY UK (tel: 01-836-8541). Luxembourg, Netherlands, France.

14. Bike Hire Abroad

An alternative to taking your own bike abroad – and an option for those who do not own their own machine – is to hire a bicycle. Availabilities are noted in the 'country chapters' of this book. Bikes for hire are normally heavy, with single speeds (three if you are lucky) and only the most basic equipment. Check the brakes work and that the tyres are sound, before setting off. You normally have to show some kind of identification (eg passport) and leave a deposit (a credit card is sometimes sufficient). Rental charges are calculated by the hour, day and week, with reduced rates for longer periods.

15. Rules of the Road

Regulations concerning cyclists are roughly the same throughout the countries covered in this book; where there are special conditions concerning use of designated cycle-paths, these are mentioned in the appropriate country chapters of this book. It is a safe assumption that if your bicycle conforms to all the mechanical and safety standards required by British Law, then it will be legally acceptable throughout Europe. A few specific memory-joggers are noted below:

1. Ride on the right.

2. Traffic coming from the right has priority unless signs indicate to the contrary. Various road signs indicate priority and loss of priority; make sure you know them well!

3. A road sign with a picture of a cycle in the centre of a white circle with a red border indicates that cycling is prohibited.

4. A round blue sign with a white bicycle in the centre means that the adjacent cycle-path must compulsorily be used; cyclists may not use the roadway under any circumstances.

5. Cyclists may ride side-by-side so long as they do not in any way impede traffic, and so long as the road is safe. Germany is an exception though.

6. Motorways are strictly forbidden to cyclists.

7. Cyclists may not use designated footpaths.

8. When you wish to change direction, make clear your intention well in advance by signalling with right or left arm.

9. Vehicles approaching a roundabout have priority over those already circulating, unless otherwise signposted. Note that this is the opposite of the UK regulation. Keep to the outside to make your exit easier. An exception is Sweden where, as in Britain, vehicles *in* the roundabout have priority.

10. Note that different countries use different colours for their road signs, so that in Switzerland a motorway is indicated by green signs and trunk roads in blue – the opposite of the British convention ... so don't be fooled!

11. Never rely on receiving right of way at a junction. In small villages and on back roads the locals may assume it is their right of way regardless of oncoming foreign cyclists.

INDEX